Congressional
Anecdotes

Praise for *Congressional Anecdotes*

"If you love Congress, you'll love *Congressional Anecdotes*. If you hate Congress, you'll love *Congressional Anecdotes*. Buy this book, you can't go wrong."   Congresswoman Pat Schroeder

"Entertaining. . . .Full of wit, wisdom."   *Milwaukee Journal*

"Boller recounts comic, tragic, and rousing incidents. . . .This entertaining book provides a fascinating. . .informal history of the nation's lawmaking body."   *Tampa Tribune*

"[Boller's] fourth such volume of political anecdotes. . .is as engaging as the others. . . .This book shows the human and humorous side of Congress. . . .A must read for political junkies and raconteurs."
                    Library Journal

"Some of [Boller's] items are serious, many humorous, and almost all are interesting. This will be a very useful book for the multitude of Congress watchers in the Capitol and throughout the nation."
                    Congressional Affairs Press

1. Daniel Webster	8. Henry Clay
2. Adam Clayton Powell, Jr.	9. Sam Nunn
3. Joseph McCarthy	10. Ted Kennedy
4. Sam Rayburn	11. Sam Ervin
5. William Fulbright	12. Lyndon B. Johnson
6. Hubert Humphrey	13. Everett Dirksen
7. Robert Taft	14. John C. Calhoun

Jacket illustration by Victor Juhász.

Congressional
Anecdotes

PAUL F. BOLLER, JR.

★ ▰ ★

OXFORD UNIVERSITY PRESS
New York   Oxford

for Joe and Eleanor

Oxford University Press

Oxford   New York   Toronto
Delhi   Bombay   Calcutta   Madras   Karachi
Kuala Lumpur   Singapore   Hong Kong   Tokyo
Nairobi   Dar es Salaam   Cape Town
Melbourne   Auckland

and associated companies in
Berlin   Ibadan

First published in 1991 by Oxford University Press, Inc.,
200 Madison Avenue, New York, New York 10016

First issued as an Oxford University Press paperback, 1992

Oxford is a registered trademark of Oxford University Press

Library of Congress Cataloging-in-Publication Data
Boller, Paul F., Jr.
Congressional anecdotes / Paul Boller.
p.   cm.   Includes bibliographical references and index.
ISBN 0–19–506092–X
ISBN 0–19–507706–7 (PBK.)
1. Legislators—United States—Anecdotes.
2. United States. Congress—History—Anecdotes.
3. United States—Politics and government—Anecdotes. I. Title.
E183.B7 1991
328.73—dc20   90–49603

2 4 6 8 10 9 7 5 3 1

Printed in the United States of America

Preface

Poll-takers like to rate the Presidents, but they don't bother much with the nation's lawmakers. Here, as elsewhere, the President has an "awesome advantage" over members of Congress, as Richard and Lynne Cheney pointed out in their study of Congressional leaders, *Kings of the Hill*, published in 1983. "He was one and they were many. He had merely to decide and act, while they had a multitude of viewpoints on what should be done."[1] Only forty men (from George Washington to George Bush) have served as President since the adoption of the Constitution, but over 11,000 men and women (mostly men) have served in the House and Senate between 1789 and 1989. The vast majority have inevitably disappeared into obscurity.

How do Congressmen achieve fame? Some become well known because, like James K. Polk and Harry Truman, they go on to become President. Others become famous for championing great causes: emancipation (Thaddeus Stevens), the fight against privilege (Robert M. La Follette), social justice (Hubert Humphrey). Others are remembered because their names were attached to important measures: the Pendleton Civil Service Act, the Morrill Land Grant Act, the Wagner Labor Relations Act. Still others became known for important speeches they made in Congress: Daniel Webster's second reply to Robert Hayne, Charles Sumner's "Crime Against Kansas," Margaret Chase Smith's "Declaration of Conscience" against McCarthyism. Parliamentary skill—Henry Clay's, Thomas B. Reed's, Sam Rayburn's—also forms the basis for some Congressional reputations. And on occasion, eccentricity—John Randolph's—and sheer demagoguery—Joseph R. McCarthy's—confer a kind of immortality.

Sometimes, though, Congressional renown comes as a fluke. Ohio's

Republican Senator John Sherman has gone down in history as the author of the 1890 Anti-Trust Act, even though about all he did was to agree to introduce it into the Senate. "I doubt very much whether he read it," his colleague, George F. Hoar of Massachusetts, said. "If he did, I do not think he ever understood it."[2] David Wilmot, a Pennsylvania Democrat, is another member of Congress whose name turns up in every American textbook today, because of a proviso, only sixty-nine words long, which he introduced into the House of Representatives in August 1846. Wilmot served only six undistinguished years in Congress; he didn't write the proviso entirely by himself; and though the House adopted it, the Senate didn't, and it never became law. But the so-called Wilmot Proviso kept Congress in a state of agitation for months because it raised the question of slavery in the Federal territories at a time when the lawmakers were trying to evade the issue.

In his memoirs, published in 1920, Missouri's Champ Clark, Speaker of the House while Woodrow Wilson was in the White House, took a high view of his Congressional calling. "A man must learn to be a Representative or Senator," he wrote, "just as he must learn to be a farmer, carpenter, blacksmith, merchant, engineer, lawyer, doctor, preacher, teacher or anything else. . . . The best plan for a constituency to pursue is to select a man of good sense, good habits, and perfect integrity, young enough to learn, and re-elect him so long as he retains his faculties and is faithful to his trust. Such a man grows into power and high position as surely as the sparks fly upward."[3]

But fame is fickle. Some Congressmen achieve prominence in their own day and then fade from the national memory soon after they pass from the scene. In the early 1930s, James E. Watson, Republican Senator from Indiana, was dictating his memoirs one day to a man in his thirties who had studied at Harvard and Oxford, and he happened to mention the name of Thomas B. Reed. "Senator," interrupted the young man, "who was Thomas B. Reed? I never heard of him before." Watson almost fell out of his chair; as Speaker of the House, Reed had been one of America's best-known political leaders during the last part of the 19th century. Turning to some friends in his office, Watson sighed: "What's the use?"[4]

American historians of course remember Speaker Reed; and Senator Watson, too, for that matter. For most Americans, however, Congressional history is largely *terra incognita*. But the American people have their Congressional remembrances all the same; Henry Clay's name still rings a bell in the popular imagination, and so does that of Daniel Webster. There is general agreement among people interested in the nation's past that men like Clay and Webster (and John C. Calhoun, too) played crucial roles in shaping the events of their day and that they far overshadowed many of the Presidents at crucial junctures in American history. Historians and biographers turn time and again to Senators like Clay, Webster, and Calhoun, and to Representatives like John Quincy Adams (who did better in Congress than in the President's House), Thaddeus Stevens, and Sam Rayburn. They are not much interested in Presidents like Franklin Pierce, Chester A. Arthur, and Warren G. Harding.

Clay and Webster of course appear frequently in the pages that follow; and Speaker Reed and Senator Watson make their appearances too. But so do Samuel "Sunset" Cox and "Private" John Allen, able and engaging members of Congress, once well known, but now largely forgotten, except by specialists in American history. And even obscurer figures turn up from time to time in this book whenever I think they help to illuminate the history of America's national legislature.

The present book is not exactly a history of Congress, but there is plenty of history in it. The Greek word, *historia,* from which the word, history, comes, means inquiry, and I have singled out special topics—campaign activities, Congressional debates, oratory, humor, behavior on and off Capitol Hill, and relations between Congress and the President—for exploration in the pages that follow. But *historia* has also come to mean narrative, and to enliven my inquiries I have recounted many incidents, dramatic and comic, which I think reveal a great deal about the history of Congress, procedural and substantive, from 1789 to 1989. And in the course of my inquiries I have much to say about the Great, the Near Great, and the Not So Great who peopled the House and the Senate during the first two hundred years of the young republic's existence. My best sources have been the remembrances and ruminations of members of Congress themselves about things past, but I have also found much of interest in newspapers, magazines, and in the *Congressional Record* itself. There is much more to the Congressional story than appears here, of course, but there is, I think, a great deal here.

Clio, history's fair-haired Muse, is notoriously picky and choosey. The past may be implacable, but history is what historians say it is; and historians are a disputatious lot, rarely agreeing on anything for long. My own predilections have necessarily shaped my choice of people and events to write about, as well as the way I have written about them. One assumption, though, I trust my readers will share with me: the belief that Congressional history is endlessly fascinating. And perhaps another: that Congress, by and large and on the whole and in the main and despite all its shortcomings, has done fairly well by the American people through all the years of storm and stress since 1789.

Today, as so often in the past, Congress is under heavy attack. While I was writing this book, the *New Republic* featured an article, "Capitol Hell," in one of its issues, and *Business Week* had a lead story: "Congress: It Doesn't Work. Let's Fix It." And about the same time opinion polls revealed that a sizable number of Americans thought that (1) half or more of the law-makers were corrupt and that (2) it was time to limit the number of terms a person could serve in Congress. I think they are wrong on both counts. I also think that California Democrat Vic Fazio, a member of the House Committee on Standards of Official Conduct, put it all best in an interview with the *New York Times*'s Robin Toner in May 1990. "I realize there are people who stay here too long," Fazio told Toner, "and I realize there are people who don't get to stay here as long as they should. I realize there are some people who shouldn't ever have gotten here. But the genius of this system is that you have a mix of all these people—the good, the bad, the ugly. It's a mirror of the country."[5]

Texas Christian University   Paul F. Boller, Jr.
Fort Worth

Contents

Congressional
Anecdotes

I

★ ★ ★ ★ ★ ★ ★ ★

At the Creation
1789–91

★ ✠ ★

Why does Congress appear first in the U.S. Constitution? Was it the "original intent" of the Constitution-makers to assign primacy in the American system to the legislative branch of government? Apparently so. The men who drew up the Constitution had a profound fear of executive tyranny. During debates in the Constitutional Convention in 1787, Pierce Butler warned against an American Catiline; George Mason expressed concern about the development of monarchy in the new nation; and Edmund Randolph was so bothered by the dangers of "unity in the Executive magistracy" that he thought it would be safer to have three executives than one. Benjamin Franklin was worried too. "I am apprehensive . . . that the Government of these States, may in future times, end in a Monarchy . . . ," he told the Convention. "The executive will always be increasing here, as elsewhere, till it end in Monarchy."[1]

But executive tyranny wasn't the Constitution-framers' only concern. Franklin's Pennsylvania colleague James Wilson thought the legislature might get out of hand too. "Is there no danger of a Legislative despotism?" he asked at one point. "Theory and practice both proclaim it."[2] The men who drafted the Constitution were fearful of despotism in any form, and they ended by devising a complicated (and frequently frustrating) system of checks and balances which they hoped would trick public officials into behaving themselves. Still, it was abuse of power by the Chief Executive that worried them the most, and perhaps that is why they put Congress first in the frame of government they constructed in Philadelphia during the summer of 1787. The Executive came second, and then the Judiciary.

Congress appeared first on the scene, too, when the "Founding Fathers," as Warren G. Harding called them, launched the new government they had devised in the spring of 1789. March 4 was the date agreed upon for opening the first Congress, but there weren't enough Congressmen in town by then to form a quorum. On March 30, the House of Representatives had enough members present to begin organizing itself; and on April 6 the Senate was able to hold its first meeting. George Washington arrived in New York, the temporary capital of the young republic, on April 23; and on April 30, his inauguration as first President, carefully planned by Congressional committees, took place. The third branch of government came finally into existence in September, when Congress passed a Judiciary Act providing for a system of Federal courts, and when, soon after, the Senate approved Washington's appointment of John Jay as first Chief Justice of the Supreme Court. By that time both houses had adopted rules and formed committees for conducting business and were beginning to concentrate on substantive issues.

Before getting down to serious business Congress had to dispose of a triviality: what titles to use in addressing the President and Vice President. A Senate committee recommended calling the Chief Executive "His Mightiness the President of the United States of America and Protector of Their Liberties," but the House of Representatives balked at such pretentious nonsense. When Vice President John Adams delivered a long, solemn lecture on the "efficacy of pageantry" in government and suggested, "His Highness, or if you will, His Mighty Benign Highness," as an appropriate appellation for America's Chief Executive, some members of Congress exploded in laughter. Pennsylvania Senator William Maclay thought the word "Highness" belonged "to some huge Patagonian"; Senator Ralph Izard coined a title, "His Rotundity," for the Vice President himself; and Speaker of the House Frederick Muhlenberg told Washington that the title "High Mightiness" would come to seem ridiculous if later Chief Magistrates were physically smaller than the tall and imposing first President.[3]

In the end, the House, led by Virginia's James Madison, decided that a plain and simple title, "the President of the United States," was sufficient for all purposes. Elegant titles, explained Madison, "are not very reconciliable with the nature of our Government or the genius of the people." The "more simple, the more republican we are in our manners," he added, "the more rational dignity we shall acquire."[4] The Senate was finally persuaded. In a resolution on the subject, the Upper Chamber (so-called because it met on the second floor of New York's Federal Hall) expressed a preference for "titles of respectability," but announced that, "desirous of preserving harmony with the House of Representatives," it would, in addressing the Chief Executive, "act in conformity with the practice of the House," and say, *"to the President of the United States,* without addition of title."[5] But some members of the first Congress insisted on calling Washington his "Excellency," despite the official rejection of grandiose titles for America's President.

The first Congress was prodigiously busy. It met for three sessions, put in 519 days of work, discussed 269 bills, and enacted 118 statutes, many of them of crucial importance for getting the young American republic off to a good start. By March 1791, when the two houses finally adjourned, they had done a remarkable job: organized executive departments (State, Treasury, War); formulated a Bill of Rights, in the form of ten amendments to the Constitution, for submission to the states for ratification; enacted a tariff and levied an excise tax for raising revenue; adopted Secretary of the Treasury Alexander Hamilton's arrangements for funding the nation's domestic and foreign debt and for taking over the Revolutionary debts of the thirteen states; established the Bank of the United States for handling the government's accounts; and agreed to locate the national capital (after a temporary sojourn in Philadelphia) on the banks of the Potomac River.

But the sailing was by no means smooth. "In every step," reflected Representative James Madison, who played a major role in the work of the first Congress, "the difficulties arising from novelties are severely experienced. . . . Scarcely a day passes without some striking evidence of the delays and perplexities springing merely from the want of precedent."[6] The two houses frequently quarreled, the President collided with the Senate when he presented a treaty to the upper house, and within both Senate and House there were clashes of personalities as well as deep-seated sectional and economic cleavages. By the end of Washington's second term, two energetic political parties—the Federalists (pro-business and pro-British) and the Republicans (pro-agriculture and pro-French)—had sprung into existence and taken to endless wrangling in Congress and outside over domestic and foreign policies. The Republicans, who thought the Federalists "monocrats," looked to Secretary of State Thomas Jefferson to save their country from monarchy. The Federalists called the Republicans "mobocrats," and hoped Secretary of the Treasury Alexander Hamilton would protect them from mob role.

James Madison, a leading light in the first four Congresses, sympathized with the Republicans, but he was also close to the Washington administration. He was, in fact, the first presidential ghostwriter. In 1789 he helped prepare Washington's Inaugural Address and then, after drafting the lower house's reply to Washington's address, helped Washington prepare his reply to the lower house's address. But while advising the first President on speeches, he was also taking the lead in the work of the first Congress. During the five-month session of the first Congress that commenced in

April 1789 he took the floor 124 times, far more than any other Congressman, and played a major role in framing legislation to establish an effective government under the new Constitution. Madison, Fisher Ames of Massachusetts told a friend, "is a man of sense, reading, address and integrity. . . . His language is very pure, perspicuous and to the point. . . . He is our first man."[7]

Madison persuaded Washington to propose amendments to the Constitution to protect liberty without endangering "an United and effective government," and then saw to it that the House of Representatives endorsed Washington's recommendations in its formal response to the President.[8] This was more than mere velleity on Madison's part; he went on to take the initiative in formulating a group of amendments that became a Bill of Rights for the new nation. He carefully studied the 200 amendments proposed by various state conventions that had ratified the Constitution, boiled them down to nineteen, and introduced them into the lower house on June 8, 1789. In the end, Congress approved eleven of them and the states accepted ten. But the first ten amendments comprising the Bill of Rights reflected Madison's views. They do not offer government protection for individual rights; they simply take it for granted that Americans possess these rights as human beings and flatly forbid any governmental interference with them. Twentieth-century philosophers, historians, and political scientists dismiss the idea of natural rights as unscientific nonsense; but it is important to remember that the Bill of Rights—and the Constitution itself, as well as the Declaration of Independence—was based squarely on the eighteenth century's natural-rights philosophy.

Madison didn't get everything he wanted in the Bill of Rights. He favored a provision that "no person religiously scrupulous of bearing arms shall be compelled to render military service in person," which was not adopted. He also wanted safeguards for individual liberty "against the states," and proposed a clause (not adopted): "No State shall violate the equal rights of conscience, or the freedom of the press, or the trial by jury in criminal cases." Madison's concern for religious freedom and church-state separation, moreover, was so keen that he even opposed supporting chaplains by tax money. "The establishment of the chaplainship to Congress," he declared, "is a palpable violation of equal rights, as well as of Constitutional principle." If Congressmen wanted chaplains, why shouldn't they pay for them out of their own pockets? "How small a contribution from each member of Congress would suffice for the purpose!" he exclaimed. "How just would it be in its principle! How noble in its exemplary sacrifice to the genius of the Constitution and the divine right of conscience." He felt the same way about chaplains in the armed forces.[9]

After having played a leading part in formulating legislation that enabled the new Federal Government to become a viable organization,

Madison became increasingly convinced that Treasury Secretary Hamilton's funding and banking measures favored the big financial interests at the expense of farmers, planters, mechanics, and small manufacturers, and he gradually distanced himself from the Washington administration and in time became the leader of the opposition in the House. He kept on good terms with the President, however, and provided him with suggestions for his Farewell Address.

About the time Congress finally adjourned its first session, the Earl of Dartmouth asked an American visiting London how many members there were in America's first Congress. "Fifty-two," the American told him. "Why, that is the number of cards in a pack," said his Lordship brightly. "How many *knaves* are there?" "Not one," snapped the American. "Please remember that *knaves* are *court-cards.*" Most Americans expected their system of government to attract purer public servants than those of the Old World monarchies.[10]

The nation's lawmakers turned out to be quite human, of course, all too human. In the years to come there were to be plenty of brilliant, hard-working, high-minded, conscientious, concerned, and dedicated members of both houses. But during the next two hundred years Congress was to have plenty of mediocrities as well: petty, mean-spirited, shallow, lazy, narrow-minded, and bigoted. But from the beginning the lawmakers themselves were acutely aware of their shortcomings. Pennsylvania's William Maclay filled his notes on the first Congress with cracks at his colleagues; but he was only the first of many Congressmen who groused about the deficiencies of the people with whom they worked. Self-criticism became an essential part of the new law-making branch of government.

☆ ☆ ☆

Cool It

The House was given great powers: to originate revenue measures, impeach Federal officers, elect the President if none of the candidates received a majority of votes cast in the Electoral College. But the Founding Fathers gave the Senate the power to amend or reject legislation coming from the House and to initiate its own legislation. Alexander Hamilton said the Senate was created to "correct the prejudices, check the intemperate passions, and regulate the fluctuations" of the House. Thomas Jefferson, however, doubted the wisdom of so aristocratic a body, chosen by the states rather than by the people. At breakfast with George Washington, according to an old tale, he protested the creation of the Senate as a check on the House. "Why did you pour that coffee into your saucer?" asked Washington. "To cool it," said Jefferson. "Even so," said Washington, "we pour legislation into the Senatorial saucer to cool it." Years later, however,

Missouri's Champ Clark, Speaker of the House when Woodrow Wilson was President, insisted that "the hot Senate" needed cooling off as frequently as the House did.[11]

Smudging

William Maclay, the democratic-minded Senator from Pennsylvania who kept a diary of proceedings in the First Congress, took an almost immediate dislike to Vice President John Adams who sat in a chair at one end of the Senate hall to preside over the meetings. Maclay thought Adams had monarchical tendencies and brought the elegant ways of Old World courts to the young republic's national law-making body. "I have really often looked at him with surprise mingled with contempt when he is in the chair, and no business is before the Senate," wrote Maclay. "Instead of that sedate, easy air which I would have him possess, he will look on one side, then on the other, then down on the knees of his breeches, then dimple his visage with the most silly kind of half smile which I cannot well express in English. The Scotch-Irish have a word that fits it exactly—*smudging*. God forgive me for the vile thought, but I cannot help thinking of a monkey just put into breeches, when I see him betray such evident marks of self-conceit."[12]

Perks

Virginia's Benjamin Harrison, a signer of the Declaration of Independence and an ancestor of two Presidents (William Henry Harrison and Benjamin Harrison), was a member of the first Congress and fond of the good things of this life. One day he joined a friend after a long session in the House and headed for a nearby tavern. When the two lawmakers called for brandy and wanted to charge it to Congress, the tavern-keeper told them that liquor wasn't included in the supplies furnished Congressmen. "What is it, then, that I see New England members [of Congress] come here and drink?" Harrison asked indignantly. "Molasses and water," the tavern-keeper told him, "which they have charged to stationery." "Very well," cried Harrison, "give me brandy and water, and charge it as fuel!"[13]

Levees and Dinners

President Washington held receptions ("levees") and dinners by way of official entertainment, but the fiercely anti-monarchical Senator Maclay was afraid that "from these small beginnings we shall follow on, nor cease, until we have reached the summit of court etiquette, and all the frivolities, fopperies and expense practiced in European governments." He did turn up at the President's house on occasion, but always with misgivings. A typical journal entry: "Went to the levee, made my bows, walked about, turned about and came out." He regarded the levees as smacking of British royalty and deplored the fact that republicans like himself felt obliged to support them for fear that if they didn't they would be accused of lacking respect for Washington. "He is but a man," Maclay insisted, "but a really good one, and we can have nothing to fear from him, but much from the precedents which he may establish."

While serving in the first Congress, Maclay was invited six times to the President's dinners. Of one of them he wrote: "It was a great dinner—all in the taste of high life. I considered it as a part of my duty as a Senator to submit to it, and am glad it is over. The President is a cold, formal man, but I must declare that he treated me with great attention . . . yet he knows how rigid a Republican I am. I cannot think that he considers it worth while to soften me. It is not worth his while. I am not an object if he should gain me, and I trust he cannot do it by an improper means." Of another Presidential dinner he wrote that it was "a dinner of dignity. All the Senators were present, and the Vice-President. I looked around the company to find the happiest faces. Wisdom, forgive me if I wrong thee, but I thought folly and happiness most nearly allied. The President seemed to bear in his countenance a settled aspect of melancholy. No cheering ray of convivial sunshine broke through the cloudy gloom of seriousness."[14]

Whiskey Tax

In December 1790, Secretary of the Treasury Alexander Hamilton asked Congress to vote for an excise tax on whiskey, and his proposal touched off a cry of rage among backwoods farmers in Pennsylvania and elsewhere for whom whiskey was an easy product to manufacture, transport, sell, use for barter, and imbibe.

Hamilton's proposal provoked opposition in Congress as well as in the backwoods. While Congress was debating the measure, Hamilton airily remarked that if the farmers didn't like the tax they should stop drinking and that in any case Americans tippled too much for their own good. When the College of Physicians in Philadelphia heartily endorsed Hamilton's advice, Georgia Congressman James Jackson angrily told his colleagues that the farmers in his district "have been long in the habit of getting drunk . . . in defiance of a dozen collages [sic] or all the excise duties which Congress might be weak or vicious enough to impose." He also warned that the good doctors might next ask Congress to pass a law "interdicting the use of catsup because some ignorant persons had been poisoned by eating mushrooms," and he gloomily predicted: "I plainly perceive that the time will come when a shirt shall not be washed without an excise." But Massachusetts' Samuel Livermore told the House he thought the people would approve the excise—"they will consider it as drinking down the national debt." In the end Congress voted for the whiskey tax to help pay for Hamilton's funding schemes.[15]

The Speaker and the Reporter

Newspapers didn't give Congress much coverage at first. Only two or three papers devoted much space to Congressional proceedings and only one newspaper sent a reporter to cover debates in the House on a regular basis. The House let the reporter keep a little table in the rear of the chamber; but his reports were so critical of Treasury Secretary Alexander Hamilton that when Theodore Sedgwick, a staunch Federalist, became Speaker, he ordered the doorkeeper to remove the table and keep the reporter out of the House chamber.

The newsman refused to be silenced. When he arrived at the House one day to find his table in the corridor, he simply picked it up, slipped up the stairway, and put it down in the back gallery where the Speaker couldn't see him. Sedgwick was amazed to see the reporter's stories about House debates continue to appear in the newspapers, angrily looked into the matter, discovered the hideaway, and barred the reporter from the gallery too. After that the reporter had to depend on friendly Congressmen for information. He did all right with his contacts. In 1800, when the presidential election ended in a tie between Thomas Jefferson and Aaron Burr, the House met behind closed doors to resolve the contest. It took a week and thirty-six ballots before the states finally picked Jefferson. But the reporter managed somehow to get full reports for his paper on how the states voted each day. Sedgwick was never able to discover the source of the "leaks" and felt doubly frustrated when Jefferson was elected President.[16]

Senatorial Mystery

At first the Senate, unlike the House, sat with closed doors. Then, it opened its proceedings to the public, as the House was doing, and after that confined its secret sessions to executive nominations and treaties. To the uninitiated these secret sessions had an air of mystery about them, even though they were usually tame affairs.

One day a man who had just become a member of the House happened to be on the floor of the Senate when an executive session was ordered. The galleries were cleared, he was asked to leave, and the doors were closed; and as he returned to the House he couldn't help wondering what important business the Senate was going to discuss in secrecy. A few years later he was elected to the Senate, and he looked forward with some eagerness to the first executive session he would be attending. Finally the big day arrived: one of the older Senators moved one afternoon that the Senate go into executive session, people filed out of the galleries, the doors were closed, and the Senators were at last alone. Then came the great moment: the venerable old Senator moved that the Senate confirm the appointment of some man to a postoffice somewhere in the country. "Without objection," announced the Vice President, "it is so ordered." Then came a motion to adjourn and the mysterious executive session was over.[17]

II

★　★　★　★　★　★　★　★

Congress-Bashing

★ ⚑ ★

The American people are hard on their Presidents, particularly the competent ones, but even harder on their Congressmen. Congress-bashing is
almost as old as the Federal Government itself: even members of the House
and Senate go in for it. The first Congress had scarcely assembled in 1789
when Pennsylvania Senator William Maclay began mumbling and grumbling about the foolishness of his colleagues; two hundred years later
Congressman William Ford of Michigan acknowledged ruefully that a
person had "a constitutional right, when elected to Congress, to be a damn
fool and act like one."[1]

Satirists have had a field day with the nation's legislature. "Suppose you
were an idiot," wrote Mark Twain during the Gilded Age. "And suppose
you were a member of Congress. But I repeat myself."[2] H. L. Mencken was
equally harsh in the 1920s. The House of Representatives, he declared,
"consists of nearly 500 men. Of them perhaps forty are of such dignity that
it may be said of them that they cannot be bought. . . . Of the forty
perhaps a dozen have genuine intelligence. What of the rest? They are
absolutely indistinguishable, gathered in plenary session, from a convention of garage keepers." Mencken thought somewhat better of the Senate,
at least for a time, but then decided that the adoption of direct elections
(17th Amendment) had resulted in filling the Upper Chamber mostly with
mountebanks and "boob bumpers."[3] There was, of course, a pronounced
anti-democratic strain in HLM's strictures, as there is in much Congress-
baiting.

For Will Rogers, a kindlier and gentler observer, the legislative branch of
government was "a never-ending source of amusement, amazement and
discouragement." Congress, he once reported, "has promised the country

that it will adjourn next Tuesday. Let's hope we can depend on it. If they do, it will be the first promise they have kept this session." Elsewhere he wrote: "When Congress makes a law, it's a joke; and when Congress makes a joke, it's a law." Still elsewhere: "You know, Congressmen are the nicest fellows in the world to meet. I sometimes really wonder if they realize all the harm they do." Still, Rogers loved Capitol Hill. "I never lack material for my humor column," he once said gratefully, "when Congress is in session."[4]

Sometimes the sniping turns nasty. In 1942, popular writer Rex Stout published a book about Congressional incompetents, *The Illustrious Dunderheads,* filled with scorn and contempt; and about the same time the widely syndicated newspaper columnist Raymond Clapper let loose an angry blast at the law-makers.[5] "As a force in our Government Congress is sliding downhill," announced Clapper. "Congress has remained a collection of two-bit politicians who could serve well enough in simpler days. But the ignorance and provincialism of Congress render it incapable of meeting the needs of modern government. . . . People don't give a damn what the average Senator or Congressman says. The reason they don't care is that they know what you hear in Congress is 99 per cent tripe, ignorance and demagoguery and not to be relied on. . . ."[6] Clapper's assault led historian Charles A. Beard to come to Congress's defense. "As a more than casual student of the *Congressional Record,*" he wrote in the *American Mercury* in September 1942, "I venture the opinion: It is possible to pick out of the *Record* for the past ten years addresses . . . which, for breadth of knowledge, technical skill, analytical acumen, close reasoning, and dignified presentation, compare favorably with similar utterances made in the preceding century by the so-called great orators."[7]

Despite his defense of the lawmakers, Charles Beard (and other friendly critics) admitted that Congress needed reforming. And in Congress itself there was a movement in the 1940s to renovate the institution in the interest of speed and efficiency. "If Congress goes down," warned California Congressman Jerry Vorhees, one of the reformers, "so does the American government."[8] Florida Senator Charles O. Andrews was struck by the anachronisms on Capitol Hill. "You know," he said, "in the Senate we still keep the old snuffbox right up there where it's been for more than 80 years, though nobody ever dips into it. If you've noticed, too, there's a little silver box on each desk, and what do you think is in that? Burnt sand that we're supposed to use when we sign our names in ink! Well, our legislative system is about as anachronistic in some ways as that snuff-box and sandboxes."[9] In 1946 Congress came up with the Legislative Reform Act designed to streamline its committee system and improve its ways of transacting business.

But Congressional reforms after World War II hardly stilled the criticism. One morning Republican Senator Homer Capehart of Indiana hailed a taxi in front of the Mayflower Hotel in Washington and agreed to share his ride with a charming woman who was in a hurry. As the taxi started on its way, the driver turned on the radio and the passengers heard a newscaster quoting something the Indiana Senator had said on the Senate floor the day before. "Those Senators make me tired," fumed the woman, turning to Capehart. "They don't know what they are talking about and yet they are always shooting their mouths off. We would be better off without them!" Capehart nodded vaguely and said nothing; he had heard it all before.[10]

There have, of course, been plenty of windbags in Congress through the years; and there have been deadbeats, hypocrites, bigots, womanizers, drunks, and slobs too. And there have always been some Congressmen on the take, especially during ages of greed, like the 1870s, 1920s, and 1980s. In the Gilded Age, Collis P. Huntington, director of the Central Pacific Railroad, sent scores of agents to Washington to push his interests on Capitol Hill, and, for convenience's sake, grouped Congressmen into three categories: "clean" (so sympathetic to his interests that they didn't need to be bought); "commercial" (open to purchase); "communist" (couldn't be bought).[11] During the Roaring Twenties, H. L. Mencken charged that if the "right pressure" were applied, Congressmen "would cheerfully be in favor of polygamy, astrology or cannibalism."[12] And in the 1980s the widely publicized "ethics scandals" involving prominent Congressmen touched off a round of snide jokes about corruption in Congress. "Public regard for Congress, never high," reported *Newsweek,* "has degenerated into late-night talk-show jokes." Comedian Jay Leno, for one, announced that a toy company was "making action figures modeled after the U.S. Senate, and they're pretty realistic—each Senator is sold separately."[13] The fact that corruption in the executive branch of government during the 1980s—as during the Gilded Age and the Roaring Twenties—far exceeded anything turning up in Congress seems to have escaped critics in the 1980s as it did in the 1870s and 1920s. No matter who they are—Grant, Harding, Reagan—Presidents always come off better with the public than Congressmen do when scandals came to light in the Federal Government.

Missouri's Champ Clark, Speaker of the House during Woodrow Wilson's Presidency, deeply resented the unremittent assault on Congress. "The Congress of the United States is the greatest legislative body in all history, and I take pride in that fact," he wrote in his memoirs in 1920. "Yet every evil-disposed person in the land can find some slander to utter about the American Congress. If the House takes time enough to discuss an important measure, these slanderers savagely assail it for being too slow. If the House puts in overtime and hurries a bill through, these same malignants fiercely denounce it for sending half-baked measures to the Senate." No right-thinking person, Clark acknowledged, objected to fair, honest, and intelligent criticism; but, he added, "abuse, ridicule, and slander are very different things from criticism and do immense damage, because they have a tendency to bring the whole system of representative government into disrepute, thereby sapping its very foundation."[14]

Emmanuel Celler, a Congressman from New York for more than forty years, thought the American people expected too much of their lawmakers. The ideal Congressman, he once said, had to possess "the wisdom of Solomon, the perspicacity of a bill collector, the curiosity of a cat, cunning of a fox, thick skin of an elephant, eagerness of a beaver, amiability of a lap dog, kindness of a loving wife, diplomacy of a wayward husband, and the good humor of an idiot."[15] Even so, he would probably be a target for mudslingers.

Massachusetts Congressman Silvio O. Conte shared Celler's chagrin. He thought it was difficult—well-nigh impossible, in fact—for a member of Congress to keep on the right side of the voters. In a talk to a convention of restaurant owners in Berkshire County, Conte explained how frustrated a Congressman could become while trying to please his constituents with his behavior in Washington. He cited his own experience. Whenever he returned to his district to hold office hours, he said, there were complaints that he was spending too much time there and ought to be working down in Washington; but when he didn't make it back to his home district for several weeks, people complained: "Who's that guy think he is? We only see him during elections." Shortly after being sworn into office, Conte recalled, he returned home in his old car and people were upset because it looked like something the farmers used for hauling trash; but later on, when he bought a new car, they said the lobbyists had gotten to him. The first time he came home wearing an old suit from his Massachusetts Senate days, people said: "Look at him! Just an old bum!" But when he bought a new suit, they cried: "For crying out loud, he's gone 'high hat' with that Ivy League suit of his." One Sunday, he said, he missed church because he got tied up talking to some of his constituents, and some people said that being down in Washington had made an atheist of him; but several weeks later, when he was again back home and did get to attend church, people said: "Why that pious fraud! He's just trying to dig up votes!" To top it off, he said, when he returned to his office Sunday night he found an angry letter from one of his constituents awaiting him; the man complained that Conte spent too much time up in the district making personal appearances and holding office hours and not enough time in Washington.[16]

Long before Conte voiced his complaints, Speaker of the House Nicholas Longworth decided that Congress-bashing went with the territory and that there wasn't much anybody could do about it. "I have been a member of the House of Representatives twenty years," he told an interviewer in 1925. "During the whole of that time we have been attacked, denounced, despised, hunted, harried, blamed, looked down upon, excoriated, and flayed. I refuse to take it personally. I have looked into history. I find that we did not start being unpopular when I became a Congressman. We were unpopular before that time. We were unpopular when Lincoln was a Congressman. We were unpopular even when John Quincy Adams was a Congressman. We have always been unpopular. From the beginning of the Republic it has been the duty of every free-born voter to look down on us, and the duty of every free-born humorist to make jokes at us. Always there is something—and, in fact, almost always there is almost everything—wrong with us. We simply can not be right."[17]

Longworth came to believe that no matter what Congress did, it was fated to be unpopular with the public. "Supppose we pass a lot of laws," he said. "Do we get praised? Certainly not. We then get denounced by everybody for being a 'Meddlesome Congress' and for being a 'Busybody Congress.' Is it not so? But suppose we take warning from that experience. Suppose that in our succeeding session we pass only a few laws. Are we any better off? Certainly not. Then everybody, instead of denouncing us for being a 'Meddlesome Congress' or a 'Busybody Congress,' denounces us for being an 'Incompetent Congress' and a 'Do-Nothing Congress.' We have no escape—absolutely none. Suppose, for instance, that we follow the President. Suppose we obey him. Suppose we heed his vetoes. What do we get called? We get called a 'flock of sheep.' We get called 'echoes of the master's voice,' a 'machine.' Suppose, then, we turn around and get very brave, and defy the President and override his vetoes. What, then, do we get called? We get called 'factionists.' We get called 'disloyalists.' We get called 'disrupters of the party.' We get called 'demagogs.' We have no chance—just absolutely no chance. The only way for a Congressman to be happy is to realize that he has no chance."[18]

Why do Presidents have an easier time of it with the public than Congressmen? Because members of Congress speak largely for localities, Longworth pointed out, while the President, elected by the whole country, speaks for the nation as a whole. "When Congress is making up its mind," he noted, "it is making up five hundred and thirty-one minds. [The President] can make it up privately and silently. We have to make our minds up publicly and audibly." The upshot: "We have no chance—we most particularly and especially have no chance against a President. That is, we have no chance—absolutely none—against him for 'popularity.' It is unavoidable. It is inevitable. It cannot be otherwise."[19] Forty years later, during the Watergate crisis, President Nixon's popularity dropped to 30 percent, according to the Harris poll, but public admiration for Congress went down even farther: to 21 percent.[20] Longworth would not have been surprised.

In a book about Congress published in 1965, Texas Congressman Jim

Wright (who was to become Speaker of the House in 1987) lamented the fact that the word "Congressman" evoked unpleasant images in the minds of so many Americans. "If an archaeologist of the twenty-fifth century were to dig up a time capsule containing a cache of twentieth-century political cartoons and editorials," he wrote, "he easily might come to the conclusion that this country was governed by a collection of ignoble brigands, fat and venal, stupid and demagogic, ruthless and immoral."[21]

There is fun, to be sure, in all this Congress-bashing, but there is also irony. As dictatorial regimes began collapsing in Eastern Europe during the fall and winter of 1989 and people there began looking to United States as a kind of model for free government, Congressman Mickey Edwards of Oklahoma found it disturbing that so many Americans continued to hold their national law-making body in such low esteem. "Irresponsible Congress-bashing," he observed, "would come as a shock to, say Eastern Europeans, who hunger for freedom, for Congress symbolizes that freedom. They admire this institution of freely elected representatives, which possesses real power to determine the national agenda and to exercise a crucial check on executive authority."[22]

Congressman Edwards was right, of course, but there was a further irony—a kind of Hegelian irony—in all this Congress-bashing. The average American's orneriness—his ingrained habit of grousing about government while accepting its benefits—may well be an important factor in helping keep the country free.

☆ ☆ ☆

Disgrace

Two newly elected members of the House got to talking, according to an old tale, and the first asked: "How did you ever come to run for Congress, anyhow?" "Well, sir," said the second, "I did it to bring disgrace on an uncle of mine up in New York. You see, he treated me very badly when I was a boy, and I took a fearful vow that I would humiliate him, and I have done it." "What business is your uncle engaged in?" "He's making shoes in Auburn penitentiary."[23]

Wondering

In 1861, when Oregon Senator James W. Nesmith returned home for his first vacation, one of his constituents asked him what he thought of the Senate. "The first month I was there," Nesmith told him, "I wondered how I ever broke in. And ever since I have been wondering how the rest of them broke in!" Years later Senators Harry Truman and Robert Dole were reported to have made the same kind of remark.[24]

Costs Money

In the years right after the Civil War there was so much corruption in both the executive and the legislative branches of government that Mark Twain, in collaboration with Charles Dudley Warner, wrote a satirical novel about the period which he called *The Gilded Age* (1873) and thus gave the period its name. "A Congressional appropriation costs money," says one of the characters in the novel (the president of the Columbus River Slackwater Navigation Company). "Just reflect, for instance. A majority of the House committee, say $10,000 apiece—$40,000; a majority of the Senate committee, the same each—say $40,000; a little extra to one or two chairmen of one or two such committees, say $10,000 each—$20,000; and there's $100,000 of the money gone, to begin with. Then, seven male lobbyists, at $3,000 each—$21,000; one female lobbyist, $10,000; a high moral Congressman or Senator here and there—the high moral ones cost more, because they give tone to a measure—say ten of these at $3,000 each, is $30,000; then a lot of small-fry country members who won't vote for anything whatever without pay—say twenty at $500 apiece, is $10,000; a lot of dinners to a lot of jimcracks for Congressmen's wives and children—these go a long way— you can't spend too much money in that line—well, these things cost in a lump sum, say $10,000—along there somewhere. . . ."[25]

All That Way

Maine Congressman Thomas B. Reed, Speaker of the House in the 1890s, once wrote a fanciful tale satirizing Senatorial conceit, but he could tease about the House as well as about the Senate. Once he called on the family of a Congressman who was ill, and when he inquired about the man's condition his wife said he was out of his head much of the time and didn't know what he was talking about. "He ought to come up to the House," murmured Reed. "They are all that way up there."[26]

Not Guilty

There was a story in the 1890s about the Senator who dozed off during a roll call and, when the clerk called his name, woke up suddenly and cried: "Not guilty!" He was probably the same Senator who sometimes absent-mindedly addressed the Chair as "Your Honor."[27]

Robbers in the House

A Congressman's wife, according to an old tale, shook her sleeping husband vigorously. "Wake up, John," she cried. "There are robbers in the house." "Nonsense, my dear," said the Congressman drowsily. "In the Senate, yes, but in the House, never!" The same story was told of President Cleveland, who quarreled with the Senate but got along fairly well with the House of Representatives.[28]

Don't Do Nothin'

A Congressman was campaigning in one of the back counties of his district, and he came upon a woman sitting on the roadside watching her husband split rails up on a hill. He greeted the woman, and she asked what he was doing in that neck of the woods and then tried to guess what his occupation was. She quickly ruled out preaching, for, she said, "preachers don't pack their bottles in their outside pockets." At this, the Congressman took out his bottle and offered her a drink. After taking one, the woman again asked: "What do you do for a living?" "I'm a member of Congress," he said proudly. The woman gave a long, low whistle. "Bill," she called up to her husband, "he don't do nothin' for a livin'; he's a member of Congress." The husband came at once down the hill, and, as the Congressman later told it, "there were three less drinks in the bottle as I rode on."[29]

In and Out

In 1893, when Massachusetts Congressman William Everett returned to Boston for a visit after entering the House, a friend asked him how he liked Congress. "Oh, it is the funniest place I ever saw," said Everett, who was struck by the difficulty of getting bills passed. "In the House they have got things fixed so that you can't get anything in, and in the Senate they have arranged things so that you can't get anything out."[30]

Prayer

Unitarian minister Edward Everett Hale became chaplain of the Senate in 1903, and after he had opened sessions with a prayer for a few weeks someone asked him: "Do you pray for the Senators, Dr. Hale?" "No," he smiled. "I look at the Senators and pray for the country." This story has become generic; it has been told ever since in a variety of ways with different characters peopling the story.[31]

Strange

Years ago, the story goes, when North Carolina Senator Robert Strange was in his last illness, he called for his son and told him: "I've decided what I want on my tombstone: 'Here lies an Honest Congressman,'" "And then your name?" said the son. "No," said Strange with a twinkle in his eye, "that won't be necessary. People who read it will say, 'That's Strange'!"[32]

Not a Congressman

There were many jokes about Congress in the 1920s. One of the most popular was the story about the man visiting Washington who found, on arriving at his destination, that he did not have enough money to pay his cab fare. "That's all right," the driver is supposed to have said, after looking him over, "you can pay me next time. I'll trust you. I can see you are not a Congressman."[33]

Circles

Another old joke: "Why did they provide the Capitol with a rotunda?" "So that the statesmen will find it easier to run around in circles."[34]

Best Show

On a trip home from Washington, Colorado Congressman J. Edgar Chenoweth met an elderly woman who had spent several weeks in Washington not long before, visiting relatives and taking in the sights. When Chenoweth asked how she had liked Washington and whether she had seen any of the shows while there, she said: "No, I never went to any shows. I just went to Congress and that was the best show I ever saw!"[35]

Influence

There's a story about the aging Senator who was asked what medicine he was taking to keep himself so happy, energetic, and interested in his work. "Don't need medicine," he said. "I'm under the influence of money."[36]

Different Story

There used to be a popular story on the Hill about the lobbyist who drove an elegant Rolls-Royce to the home of a Senator and announced: "Senator, my organization wants you to have this." The Senator was outraged; he said he was shocked to think that any organization had the impression he would accept anything that could be interpreted as a bribe in order to influence his vote on some upcoming legislation. The lobbyist backed off at once, apologized, and exclaimed: "You are absolutely right, Senator. It would be deplorable if such an interpretation could be made. And it could. But now, sir, what would you think if I were to tell you that we would like to *sell* you this car for fifty dollars?" "Well," said the Senator at once, "that's a different story. In that case, you can put me down for two!"[37]

Don't Give a Darn

In the old days, when a Senator came to town, business virtually stopped as people gathered to meet him. Expecting to stir up a little excitement, Republican Senator Fred Hale of Maine dropped one day into a store in a little Maine town and started talking to the proprietor. But almost immediately someone came in the store to buy a couple of yards of calico and the proprietor at once left Senator Hale in order to wait on the customer. When he finished the transaction, Hale started talking to him again, but someone else came in wanting a pound of butter; and after that there were more customers and a dozen or so more interruptions. Increasingly irked by the way he was being relegated to the background, Hale finally told the storekeeper: "You don't seem to like me." Replied the old grocer: "I don't like you; I don't dislike you; I don't give a darn about you."[38]

How to Be a Congressman

It wasn't easy, being a lawmaker, in America. In 1940 Alabama's Luther Patrick submitted a satirical set of "Rules for a Congressman" to the House, which summed up the inordinate demands the American people make on their representatives in Congress:

1. Entertain with a smile constituents, their wives, their sons, sons' wives, etc. Go with them to the White House; show good reason why you are unable to personally have them meet the President; take daughters to meet midshipmen at Annapolis.
2. Explain what bill is up for debate; points for discussion; how it will be passed; how you will vote and why.
3. Attend to balcony and point out Speaker Bankhead, leaders Rayburn and Martin, Ham Fish, Dewey Short, that man Martin Dies, and name each lady member of Congress.
4. Respond to worthy causes; make after-dinner speeches, before-dinner speeches; learn to eat anything, anywhere, any night—work all day, dictate all night, and be fresh as a rain-washed daisy for next day's duties.
5. Be a cultured gentleman, a teller of ribald stories, a profound philosopher, preserve a story of "Confucius say" gags, be a ladies' man, a man's man, a he-man, a diplomat, a Democrat with a Republican slant, a Republican with a Democratic viewpoint, an admirer of the Roosevelt way, a hater of the New Deal, a new dealer, an older dealer, and a quick dealer.

6. Learn how to attend six to eight major functions, rushing home and back during each term on one round-trip travel.
7. Have the dope on hot spots in town, with choice telephone numbers for the gay boys from back home, and help to contact all local moral organizations and uplift societies in Washington.
8. Learn to be expert guide. Keep car in tip-top shape.
9. Know names and dates related to all points of interest, and be able to explain and supply information regarding public buildings and statuary about Washington.
10. Be an authority on history, travel, psychology, philosophy, education, economics, civics, finance, export trade, government printing, international relations, neckties, and fishing tackle.[39]

Congress-Bashing Through the Years

In July 1942, Illinois' Everett Dirksen took note of the bitter attacks on Congress in the months following Pearl Harbor and reminded his colleagues that Congress-bashing in times of crisis was a good, old American custom. To prove his point he read his colleagues a long list of assaults on the lawmakers appearing in newspapers and magazines through the years. Among them:

1837: "A more weak, bigoted, persecuting, and intolerant set of instruments of malice and every hateful passion, were never assembled in a legislative capacity in any age or any land."

1857: "How can we expect integrity or uprightness in our legislatures or in Congress when the barroom and bullies furnish the candidates?"

1873: "We are not certain that it is not possible to make the situation worse and Congress would probably speedily reach that result if that were possible."

1893: "Does the Senate understand that at the present writing it is the most thoroughly despised body of public men in the world?"

1908: "If God had made Congress, he would not boast of it."

1942: "It is true that for collective brains, guts, vision, and leadership, the Seventy-seventh [Congress] would stand pretty close to the bottom in any ranking of the seventy-seven Congresses that have assembled biennially since 1789."[40]

Only One Way

In 1947, when Katharine St. George, New York Republican, arrived in Washington after being elected to the House for the first time, she was filled with pride about her new position. But soon after entering the House she got to talking with a young woman who had come to town to visit her own Congressman and had asked a taxi driver how one should address a Congressman. "There is only one way to address a Congressman," the cabbie told her. "Louse!" Sighed St. George after hearing the tale: "I can assure you that since that time I have been very careful about proclaiming the fact that I was a Member of Congress."[41]

Letting Relatives Know

One day an old fellow was driving his cart, pulled by a jackass, through the best part of town, and the jackass dropped dead in front of the home of the leading citizen. The old fellow unhitched the cart and took it away but left the jackass in front of the house. When the owner came home and saw the jackass he called his Congressman in Washington about it and the latter angrily told him to bury the animal and stop bothering him about it. "That's all right, Congressman," said the irate citizen. "I'll be glad to bury the jackass." "Well," said the Congressman, still annoyed, "Why in heck did you call me up about it?" "Congressman," said the constituent, "I intended to bury the jackass. But before I did, I wanted to let his relatives know he was dead."[42]

Enjoy Reading

After a woman read a copy of the *Congressional Record* containing a bunch of memorial addresses that are traditionally made after the death of a colleague, she wrote to her Congressman: "Please send me more *Records* containing speeches on behalf of some of you dead Congressmen. I enjoy reading them so much."[43]

Escaped

Once a Senator was entertaining an elderly woman who was a constituent of his, and when he was called away on some urgent business, he asked his page to take her to the Senate gallery, identify the Senators for her, and explain what was going on. But the lad had been a page for only a short time and didn't really know much more about the Senate than the woman did. The Senate was busy that day; bells were continually ringing for quorum calls as well as for roll calls. Puzzled, the woman finally asked: "Why do these bells ring so constantly and so stridently?" "I'm not quite sure," said the boy, after thinking about it for a moment, "but I think maybe one of them has escaped."[44]

Foursquare

There are many jokes about how hard it is to pin a Congressman down on the issues, especially when he is running for re-election. When an angry constituent demanded by telegram to know whether his Congressman was for or against Universal Military Training, the Congressman is said to have wired back: "I certainly am." Another tale has a reporter asking a Senator running for re-election what he thinks about the military-industrial complex and the latter answering: "I think I'm undecided—but I'm not sure." "Senator," cried the reporter, "I want to congratulate you on the straightforward manner in which you dodged my question!"

One of Illinois Congressman Sidney Yates' favorite stories was about the Congressman who made straddling the issues practically an art form. Asked for his views on inflation, he declared, "I am totally against inflation." "Well," said the reporter, "I guess you are for *de*flation." "No," said the Congressman, "I'm against that too." "Well," said the reporter, "what are you for?" The candidate thought for a moment and then announced: "I guess I'm foursquare for *flation!*"[45]

Windy

One day comedian Bob Hope met Senator Alben Barkley at the Capitol for a trip together to crown a queen at the Apple Blossom Festival in Virginia. As the two stepped outside the Capitol for a picture, Hope remarked: "Windy out here." Returned Barkley, "You ought to see it inside."[46]

Senate Expert

Once a liberal Republican Senator proposed appropriating $600,000,000 to cope with the nation's sewage problem and, knowing that President Nixon opposed the measure, he gave a carefully prepared speech on the subject in which he discussed household affluents and sanitary tunnels in some detail. When he finished, New Hampshire's curmudgeonly old Norris Cotton went up to him, assured him of his esteem and affection, and then said: "I never realized until now what you were an expert on, but now I know." "What's that, Norris?" asked the Senator. Said Cotton: "Shit." The Senator looked at him for a moment and then exclaimed: "Norris, can you think of anything more important to be an expert on in the United States Senate than that?"[47]

Dumb or Lazy

North Carolina Congressman Robert Doughton liked to tell a story which he thought Congressmen who poll their constituents to find out how to vote ought to heed. When he first went to the House, Doughton said, he wrote letters to constituents whose views he respected, asking them how they thought he ought to vote on crucial issues. But he quickly abandoned the practice after receiving a letter from an Ashe County farmer. "Doughton, I've got my spring plowing to do," the farmer wrote, "and I can't spend my time telling you how to vote. We elected you to Congress at a big salary to study these questions and vote on them in the way you think best for us. If you're too dumb or too lazy to do that, come home and we'll send somebody else to Congress in your place."[48]

Nothing Lower

One day Iowa Congressman Guy Gillette's maid noticed his picture in the paper with a caption suggesting he might be nominated for the Upper Chamber. "Is a Senator higher than a Congressman?" she asked. "Yes," answered Gillette, "they are so considered because a Senator represents an entire state and a Representative represents a District of a state." "Well," said the maid, "is there anything lower than a Congressman?" With a mournful look, Gillette told her that most Americans thought "there was indeed nothing lower than a Congressman!"[49]

First Time

Once Senator Warren R. Austin (R) of Vermont invited Senator William W. Barbour (R) of New Jersey to visit a farm in Virginia where he was planning to graft some apple trees. Barbour was a large man and his part of the operation was easy: carrying around a small cracker box with the spirit lamp and paraffin. Whenever Austin finished cutting and inserting the scions, Barbour solemnly marched up to the spot and gently touched the cut surfaces with hot paraffin. Observing the two men at work, a neighbor finally exclaimed: "This is the first time I have ever actually seen one Senator grafting and another Senator covering it up!"[50]

The Retort Courteous

Some lawmakers lashed back when they received letters from the voters blasting them. Ohio Congressman Wayne Hays had a standard reply to nasty letters from his constituents: "Dear Sir: Today I received a letter from some crackpot who signed your name to it. I thought you ought to know about this before it went further." Wisconsin Senator Alexander Wiley's response to poison-pen letter-writers was different. "Sir," he sometimes wrote, "my stenographer, being a lady, cannot type what I think of you. I, being a gentleman, cannot think it. You being neither, will understand what I mean."

Ohio Senator Stephen M. Young became famous for his tart replies to venomous letters. Sometimes he returned them with a note saying, "Some jackass is using your name." Once, a man wrote saying Young was a "stupid fool" for favoring gun control, and added, "I am sure you could walk upright under a snake's tail with your hat on and have plenty of head room." The man also gave his telephone number and said: "I would welcome the opportunity to have intercourse with you," Young's response: "Sir: I am in receipt of your most insulting letter. I note your offer in the final paragraph, 'I welcome the opportunity to have intercourse with you.' No indeed. You go ahead and have intercourse with yourself." To a lawyer who accused him of underestimating the danger of Communism, he wrote: "Don't give me any more of this unsolicited advice. I know it costs nothing, but that is exactly what it is worth." To a woman who had been sending a series of vituperative letters, he finally wrote: "Dear Madam: You should know that some idiot in your town is sending me a series of crazed letters—and signing your name." His shortest answer was reserved for an Oklahoma editor who asked him to take back everything he had said in criticism of ultra-right-wingers: "Sir: No."

One Congressman received a highly critical letter from an old woman in his hometown who, upset by the way he had voted on a bill, not only excoriated him for his vote but also told him: "Congressman, even if you were St. Peter, I would not vote for you." The Congressman wrote back to explain the reasons for his vote and then added: "I note your statement that even if I were St. Peter, you wouldn't vote for me. Allow me to point out, Madam, that if I were St. Peter, you couldn't vote for me. You wouldn't be in my district."[51]

Qualified

Arizona Senator Paul Fannin had a shaggy-dog story he enjoyed telling. In a Texas courtroom, according to the story, an attorney challenged a witness on the ground that the latter didn't understand the obligation of an oath. "Do you know what will happen," the judge asked the witness, "if you don't tell the truth?" "If I tell one lie," replied the witness, "I'll go to the State legislature. If I tell two, I'll go to Congress." The judge held him qualified.[52]

Didn't Want to Go That High

Congressman Bill Stuckey, a Georgia Democrat, received a call one day from a constituent in Macon who said her garbage hadn't been picked up. Somewhat miffed, Stuckey asked her why she hadn't looked up the number of the Department of Sanitation in her phone book and called the Director to complain. "Well, Congressman," she said, "quite frankly, I didn't want to go up that high!"[53]

First Congressman

Florida's Claude Pepper, Senator for many years and then a member of the House, liked to tell the story about the Congressman and the bishop who arrived in heaven at the same time and how the Congressman was given a lavish suite of rooms while the bishop was assigned a small, barren room with no view. When the bishop disappointedly asked about it, St. Peter said he knew how he felt, but that "we have thousands of bishops up here; this is the first Congressman we ever got!"[54]

Applause

In 1976 Nancy Dickerson published a book about her many years as a reporter in Washington and decided to include some boosting as well as bashing when discussing Congress. "As I look back over the years," she wrote, "I think of how despondent I was during the McCarthy era. Then I recall one of my most vivid memories: Senator John Stennis standing tall in the early morning hours to condemn McCarthy for dragging the Senate into 'the slush and slime of the gutter.' And when my own despair was at its nadir during the Nixon disgrace, I was heartened by the men and women called 'ordinary' representatives—the members of the House Judiciary Committee—who showed they were most extraordinary as they carried out their duties with dignity. When we feared most for the future of America, these men and women restored our faith. While I have known about the drunks, the phonies and the brown envelopes stuffed with money, I have also seen the greatness of some of the people who came to the capital. . . . I have no illusions about the men and women who come here. I have seen their warts, their flaws, their human failings. Even so, I have profound respect for them. They have shown us that they can make the system work. . . . Despite the national cynicism, I have been in Washington too long to do less than applaud their arrival. Surely in Paradise they will be a rung above those who only criticize or, even worse, do nothing out of despair or disinterest."[55]

III

★   ★   ★   ★   ★   ★   ★   ★

Manners
and Morals

★ ◪ ★

In their salad days both House and Senate developed elaborate rules and regulations for carrying on the public business in an orderly fashion. But the emergence of political parties in the 1790s and the development of acute sectional animosities in the 1820s introduced tensions into Congressional proceedings that tested the lawmakers' ability to behave with dignity and decorum. The democratization of American politics during the Age of Jackson also militated against the lofty behavior that the Founding Fathers, when they wrote the Constitution, apparently expected to prevail in Congress.

The House, it seems, was always more prone to unruly behavior than the Senate. As early as 1809, Massachusetts Congressman Josiah Quincy was deploring the unseemly squabbling and crude behavior he encountered there. A few years later, during the War of 1812 (i.e. War of 1812–15), when British forces were approaching Washington and someone suggested that Congress march out as a body to meet them, Henry Clay, Speaker of the House, laughingly declared that he "should be sorry to lead such a *disorderly* body into battle."[1] And after the war, the appearance in Congress of homespun and plain-spoken politicians who mocked the aristocratic airs of their more sedate colleagues shocked respectable people and produced lamentations about the decline of America's legislative branch of government.

Behavior in both House and Senate became increasingly indecorous in the 1830s and 1840s. William ("Sausage") Sawyer, a former blacksmith from the Ohio backwoods, liked to stand by the Speaker's chair during debates noisily munching sausages and cornbread and using his pants for a napkin and his jack-knife for a toothpick.[2] Alabama's Felix Grundy Mc-Connell was raucous both on and off the floor of the House. Once he interrupted the celebrated Norwegian violinist, Ole Bull, in the midst of a dazzling performance at a Washington concert with the words: "None of your high-falutin, but give us *Hail, Columbia,* and bear hard on the treble!" On another occasion, Mac, as he was called, turned up at a party with a comely French shop-girl on each arm and tried to introduce one of them to President James Polk. "Mr. Polk," he cried, "allow me the honor of introducing to you my beautiful young friend Mamselle—Mamselle—Mamselle—*parley vous Français*—whose name I have forgotten!"[3]

Visiting Washington in January 1832, Alexis de Tocqueville was dismayed by what he saw of the House of Representatives. "The eye frequently does not discover a man of celebrity within its walls," he observed. "Its members are almost all obscure individuals, whose names present no associations to the mind; they are mostly village lawyers, men in trade, or even persons belonging to the Lower Classes of society. In a country in which education is very general, it is said that the representatives of the people do not always know how to write correctly."[4]

Tocqueville had a higher opinion of the Senate. The upper house, he reported, contained "eloquent advocates, distinguished generals, wise magistrates, and statesmen of note, whose language would at all times do honor to the most remarkable parliamentary debates of Europe."[5] But the young French aristocrat's observations, appearing in *Democracy in America* (1835), his celebrated study of American culture during the Age of Jackson, irritated Missouri Senator Thomas Hart Benton no end. Not only did Benton insist that members of both houses were "of the same order and class"; he also pointed out that most Senators had served first in the House. "The Senate is a smaller body," he wrote, "and therefore may be more decorous; it is composed of older men, and therefore should be graver; its members have usually served in the highest branches of the State governments, and in the House of Representatives, and therefore should be more experienced; its terms of service are longer, and therefore give more time for talent to mature, and for the measures to be carried which confer fame. Finally, the Senate is in great part composed of the pick of the House, and therefore gains double—by brilliant accession to itself and abstraction from the other."[6]

Benton himself didn't always preserve the decorum he attributed to Senators; sometimes he got into heated debates with his colleagues that came close to blows. Once, Henry Clay reminded the Senate that Benton, a good Jacksonian Democrat, had been Andrew Jackson's bitter foe a few years before and had once warned that if the hot-headed Old Hickory ever became President, Congress would have to protect itself with pistols and dirks. Benton exploded in wrath at Clay's assertion; he hotly denied having ever said anything of the kind and accused the Whig leader of having uttered "an atrocious calumny." It was now Clay's turn to blow up. "What!" he cried in a fury. "Can you look me in the face, sir, and say that you never used that language?" "I look and repeat that it is an atrocious calumny," glared Benton, "and I will pin it to him who repeats it here." In a rage, Clay yelled back: "Then I declare it before the Senate that you said to me the very words!" "False! false! false!" shouted Benton; and the Senator who was presiding called frantically for order as the two men headed angrily for each other. But their colleagues managed to separate them and they finally calmed down. "I apologize to the Senate," announced Benton, "for the manner in which I have spoken—but," he added, "not to the Senator from Kentucky." Clay promptly chimed in: "To the Senate I also offer an apology—to the Senator from Missouri, none!" But a half hour later, observed a reporter, the two men shook hands "as lawyers often do after abusing each other in court."[7]

The Clay-Benton quarrel centered on politics: Whigs vs. Democrats. Far more serious were the disputes between Northern and Southern Congressmen over the expansion of slavery into the Federal territories. During the 1850s the sectional strife generated by the slavery issue became so acute that Congress gradually turned into a kind of armed camp, with members from both sections carrying concealed weapons—pistols, bowie knives, derringers—when attending debates. The only Congressmen not carrying a knife and a revolver, observed one Senator, were those who carried two revolvers.[8] One day a Congressman who was riffling through his papers accidentally discharged his pistol and the ball went crashing through the desk in front of him. "In an instant," recalled Indiana's William S. Holman, "there were thirty or forty pistols in the air, and the scene looked more like a Texas bar-room, than the Congress of the United States."[9]

The 1850s were, to be sure, unusual, for the country was headed inexorably, it seems, in retrospect, toward a war between the sections. But even after the Civil War peace and propriety never seemed to reign long on Capitol Hill. "Some of the scenes would remind an Irishman of the good old days of Donnybrook Fair," recalled Edmund Alton, a former Senate page, writing in 1886. "I have seen members roll up their sleeves. I have seen two disputants rush down the aisles, from either side of the Hall, into the area of freedom, shaking their fists at each other in so vigorous a manner as to induce younger House pages to run over to the Senate and, waving their hands to their friends, breathlessly exclaim: 'Come on, boys, quick! there's going to be a fight!'—an invitation which would instantly deplete the Chamber of every House and Senate page, and cause a tumultuous stampede to the Hall. I have seen two such members facing each other like gladiators, both vociferating and violently gesticulating, when one has referred to the other as 'the *member* from New York.' This violation of parliamentary courtesy was treated as an insult. 'Say *gentleman!*'—'Well, then, *gentleman!*' retorted the other, and the sarcastic emphasis he put upon the word was even more irritating than his first offense. One wild Congressman, in a memorable scene, ten years ago, so lost his wits, that he jumped upon his desk in the very eloquence of his wrath!"[10]

After the Civil War, sloppiness as well as stridency offended some observers. Visiting Washington while Grant was President, Mark Twain was more impressed by the slovenly behavior of Congressmen than by their contentiousness. In *The Gilded Age,* his 1873 satire, he gave an amusing picture of the House after viewing things from the gallery a few times. "Below," he wrote, "a few Senators lounged upon the sofas set apart for visitors, and talked with idle Congressmen. A dreary member was speaking; the presiding officer was nodding; here and there little knots of members stood in the aisles, whispering together; all about the House others sat in all the various attitudes that express weariness; some, tilted back, had one or more legs disposed upon their desks; some sharpened pencils indolently; some scribbled aimlessly; some yawned and stretched; a great many lay upon their breasts upon the desks, sound asleep and gently snoring. The flooding gaslight from the fancifully wrought roof poured down upon the tranquil scene. Hardly a sound disturbed the stillness, save the monotonous eloquence of the gentleman who occupied the floor. Now and then a warrior of the opposition broke down under the pressure, gave it up and went home."[11]

Some presiding officers cracked down on the slovenry. When Maine's Thomas B. Reed became Speaker of the House in 1889, he decided to enforce minor as well as major rules during debates. He banished smoking; he also bannned shirtsleeves, insisting that members keep their coats on during proceedings. One day a Congressman wearing low shoes and white socks leaned back and put his feet on the desk, and Reed promptly sent a page over with an urgent message: "The Czar commands you to haul down those flags of truce." One warm summer day, during a long debate on the tariff, a Congressman from Massachusetts took off his coat during a meeting of the Committee of the Whole, when Reed was absent, and finished his speech in shirtsleeves. When Reed heard what had happened he was outraged; and the next day he remained in his chair long beyond his usual lunch hour. When a Congressman asked him about it, he said: "Well, I'm afraid if I leave the chair some graceless scamp may get up and take off his trousers. It's hotter today than it was yesterday." A few years later, when he left New York's James S. Sherman in the chair while he was on some business, the New Yorker got into a parliamentary quarrel with an Indiana Congressman and the next thing he knew the other members began taking sides, yelling, shouting, shaking their fists, and milling about, and the place was in an uproar. Suddenly the doors opened and in walked Speaker Reed. "The effect of his appearance was electrical," recalled one onlooker. "It was like a big country school. In the teacher's absence the pupils had thrown all discipline to the winds. With the teacher's return all was quiet." Speaker Reed proceeded to give a little lecture on the rules of the House.[12]

Like Reed, Missouri's Champ Clark managed to keep things under control most of the time during his Speakership early in the twentieth century. "It goes without saying that Members of Congress should deport themselves properly," he declared, "and they do as a rule; but an election to Congress does not in any way, or to any degree, reduce the human quality in men. They bring with them their passions, prejudices, tempers, likes, dislikes, and their ideas as to behavior. Consequently there are ugly scenes, quarrels, and alas! sometimes, but infrequently in these latter days, fights on the floor of the House." Clark minimized the strife by cutting off debaters when they became too vehement, and he was proud of his peace-keeping achievements. He was convinced, too, that when he was there the House was a much better behaved place than the supposedly dignified and decorous Senate.[13]

In the twentieth century Congressional behavior was probably an improvement over what it had been through most of the nineteenth century. At any rate members of the House and Senate no longer went to Capitol Hill bearing arms; nor did they attack each other during debates with knives, canes, and fire-tongs, as in the good old days. But fistfights continued to be common; so common, in fact, that in February 1927, James A. Gallivan, a Massachusetts Democrat, submitted the following resolution to the House:

"Whereas the physical exercise of hostile encounter by means of human fists is becoming of daily occurrence in the House of Representatives; and

"Whereas such encounters are being conducted in an irregular manner, with small regard to race, weight, reach, height, or classification of Members to insure equality and fair fighting; and

"Whereas most of the principal communities of the United States have boxing boards or commissions, whose duty it is to regulate the sport and insure fair play: Therefore be it

"*Resolved*, That a committee be appointed by the Speaker of the House, who shall be chairman ex officio, to be known as the Boxing Board of the House of Representatives, to have full authority in the arranging of bouts between Members according to weight, corporeal and mental, age, and experience; and be it further

"*Resolved*, That said board shall arrange to hold the bouts in Statuary Hall, under the paternal eyes of the fathers of the Republic, and under no circumstances shall said board authorize bouts either in the House of Representatives or before committees of the House unless contestants sign written agreements, approved by the chairman, to abstain from hair pulling, profanity, and tobacco chewing, and the use of wrist watches or flasks; and be it further

"*Resolved,* That the Honorable William D. Upshaw, of Georgia, is appointed permanent referee of all bouts held under the jurisdiction of said board, his salary and expenses to be paid out of the contingent fund of the House."[14] Gallivan's resolution was referred to the Committee on Rules, excited mirth for a time, and then died.

Fistfights on Capitol Hill naturally produced a great deal of criticism in the press, but some observers were more upset by the lawmakers' off-duty shenanigans than by their behavior on the House and Senate floors. Congressional misbehavior, at least in public, was more common in the early years of the American republic than in the 1980s, and there were lamentations in the public prints from time to time about what was going on in Washington: boozing, gambling, womanizing. In November 1837, the *Baltimore Transcript* published an indignant editorial about the scandalous activities of members of Congress while sojourning in the nation's capital and called on the press generally to "speak out in exposition of their immoralities."[15]

One paper which did speak out at this time was the *Philadelphia Public Ledger*. Whenever Congress met for its annual sessions, according to the *Ledger*, "Washington swarms with Faro banks, gamesters and courtezans, and the quantity of wine and spirits consumed in the course of a long session, by public officers, would exceed belief." The editor of the *Ledger* knew the Washington scene well and he was thoroughly aroused. "We have often said," he wrote, "that members of Congress behaved at Washington, openly and in broad day-light, as they would not dare to behave at home, even in secret. We have seen intoxication the most shameless, on the very floor of the Representatives Hall; we have seen from the boxes below, Senators and Representatives in the third row of a theatre, in company of those with whom they could not be seen at home, with any hope of going to Congress again. We have heard from authentic sources, for we never saw it, that members of Congress very openly attended gaming houses, and played with notorious blacklegs. We have seen abandoned women enter some of the committee rooms, from windows on the east front of the capitol, and have immediately seen high officers of the House, leave their seats, and enter these rooms. In short, if the sovereign people of the United States could observe for one week the private deportment of members of Congress, at Washington, they would think that some very rigorous measures were necessary to enforce some regard to *appearances*, if not to principles."[16]

The *Ledger*'s was by no means the last—or even first—word on the subject. Through the years lamentations about Congressional behavior on and off Capitol Hill have been a regular part of America's political discourse. And reporters in the late twentieth century, as in the early nineteenth, disagreed among themselves as to their responsibility to "speak out," as the *Ledger* advised, on Congressional immoralities.

One night in the 1970s Washington reporter Rudy Maxa received a call from a man in North Carolina who was eager to tell him all about a woman in his hometown who was having an affair with a Congressman. "She goes to Washington every weekend and has been [doing so] for the last six weeks," said the man, and he went on to give Maxa the woman's name, address, and telephone number. "Is this woman on the Congressman's staff?" Maxa asked. "No," said the caller. "Is she—would you have any way of knowing?—traveling to Washington at the taxpayer's expense?" Maxa wanted to know. "No," said the caller, "I don't think so." Maxa then told the caller that he didn't think the information would be of any interest to the *Washington Post* because it sounded like a "routine affair," with no illegality involved. "But this Congressman is *married!*" protested the caller and slammed down the receiver.

A few days later, when Maxa repeated the conversation over lunch with conservative columnist John Loftin, the latter exclaimed: "Oh, I think I'm beginning to understand. A Congressman cheats on his wife with one of his employees and that's a story. A Congressman simply cheats on his wife and that's not a story. In other words, a politician who violates the D.C. code or some Congressional regulation and you'll happily write about it. But a politician who simply *violates one of God's Ten Commandments* and you just shrug it off!"

Maxa acknowledged the problem. Some reporters, he knew, hated to invade a politician's privacy, especially when it seemed likely that his personal behavior had no bearing on his performance as a public official. Other reporters, he admitted, held that the press shouldn't wait until a politician's drinking habits or philandering had a direct effect on his work before reporting his excesses, because his private behavior was probably an indication of both his character and the outlook he might bring toward certain kinds of legislation. They had a point, of course, but was it not possible that prurience, not public-spiritedness, motivated much of the delving into the lawmakers' off-duty activities?[17]

☆ ☆ ☆

The Spitting Lyon

On January 30, 1798, when the plain-spoken Vermont Jeffersonian Republican Matthew Lyon voiced objections to presenting President John Adams with a formal reply to his annual message to Congress, Roger Griswold, stalwart Federalist from Connecticut, began making fun of Lyon for having shown cowardice during the American Revolution. Lyon took as much of this as he could (which wasn't much), and then walked over to Griswold and spit contemptuously in his face. A resolution to expel the "spitting Lyon" for disorderly behavior failed of passage, but Griswold soon got even. On the morning of February 15, right after the chaplain's prayer, he walked over to where Lyon was sitting and started beating him over the head with a large yellow hickory cane. Lyon managed to struggle to his feet, grab some firetongs, and start hitting back; and, as the two rolled around on the floor, some of their colleagues grabbed their legs and tried to pull them apart. "What!" cried the House Speaker Jonathan Dayton indignantly, "take hold of a man by the legs! That is no way to take hold of him!" But it worked; and after the two had been subdued the other Congressmen spent the rest of the day keeping them from renewing the struggle on the House floor and in the lobby. The following day the House adopted a resolution requiring the combatants to promise the Speaker that "they will not commit any act of violence upon each other" from that day forward, and the two men solemnly took the pledge. People in the gallery were disappointed at the dénouement. "There is nothing to do in Congress today—," they grumbled, "there's no fighting going on."[18]

Randolph of Roanoke: Tertium Quid

In the young republic's earliest years, Virginia's John Randolph was perhaps the most striking figure to appear in the House and then in the Senate. He called himself "Randolph of Roanoke" to distinguish himself from a distant cousin by the same name with whom he had a fierce quarrel. Tall, slender, beardless (a childhood illness left him impotent), he rode to the Capitol just before sessions commenced, turned his horse over to the groom, and then, with riding whip in hand and small cap on his head, walked to his seat in the House, put down his cap and whip, and began slowly removing his gloves. After a while, if the debate caught his interest, he fixed his large, round, piercing eyes on the Speaker, and in a shrill voice called for recognition, and, once he gained the floor, launched into a discourse, usually lengthy, often brilliant, and frequently filled with biting wit, that held even his adversaries' absorbed attention. "Tims, more toast-and-water!" he instructed one of his servants periodically, for watered toast helped settle his unruly stomach; but reporters, insisting he was occasionally drunk, turned the request into, "Tims, more porter!"[19]

Randolph's associates found him at times frustratingly unpredictable. Once an acquaintance told him, "I passed by your house this morning, Mr. Randolph," only to be told, "I hope that you will always continue to do so." On another occasion a man who had a good chat with him at a dinner party saw him walking to the Capitol the following day and rushed over and cried: "Good morning, Mr. Randolph, how do you do, Sir!" "Good morning, Sir," said Randolph, without stopping or looking up. "You walk very fast, Sir," protested the man. "I have had great difficulty in overtaking you." "I'll increase the difficulty, Sir," returned Randolph, and quickened his pace.[20]

"I am an aristocrat," Randolph once announced. "I love justice and hate equality" He began his political life as a Jeffersonian Republican and served as a kind of floor manager for President Jefferson for a time. But he eventually broke with Jefferson, charging compromises with principle, and began calling him "St. Thomas of Cantingbury." He thought Jefferson's successors—James Madison and James Monroe—equally false to the principles of pure republicanism; and, as for John Quincy Adams, Monroe's successor, he regarded his activistic view of government with abhorrence, and showered him with abuse during his four years in the Executive Mansion. Once he met an Adamsite on a narrow sidewalk in Washington, and the latter stopped in the middle of the walk and announced belligerently: "I never step out of my way for puppies!" "I always do," said Randolph calmly as he stepped aside. "Pass on."[21]

Randolph was fiercely independent. He came in time to call himself a *tertium quid*, a third something or other, unaffiliated with either of the two major parties, with only a handful of sympathizers in Congress. (*Niles' Register,* which printed the names of Republicans in italics and the names of Federalists in Roman letters, printed Randolph's name half in italics and half in Roman.)[22] Randolph was essentially a states' righter ("When I think of my country, I mean the Commonwealth of Virginia") who became disillusioned with Jefferson when the latter approved the Louisiana Purchase in 1803 and favored purchasing Florida from Spain in 1806.[23] He also vehemently opposed the War of 1812–15. A hero to some twentieth-century conservatives (Russell Kirk, for one), he was, unlike them, hostile to military establishments, opposed to war as society's most powerful centralizing force, and without much liking for the business ethic (*richesse n'oblige pas*) that was coming to replace the aristocratic ethic (*noblesse oblige*) in the nation's rapidly developing economy.

Toward the end of his life, Randolph seems to have become crack-brained, tearing up papers in sudden rages, "dressing and undressing himself" on the House floor, and spouting interminable speeches which were increasingly incoherent and unendurable. In his heyday, though, for all his quirks and crochets, he was the most quotable man on Capitol Hill. He was buried facing the west, it was said, so he could keep an eye on Henry Clay, whose nationalistic views he detested.[24]

Clay Always Wins

"Isn't it a pity that your husband gambles so much?" a prim and proper New England woman once remarked to Clay's wife. "Oh, I don't know," said Mrs. Clay carelessly. "He always wins."[25]

Slambanging into War (1812)

On June 1, 1812, President James Madison sent a message to Congress discussing the nation's grievances against Britain and summing up the situation: "On the side of Great Britain a state of war against the United States, and on the side of the United States a state of peace toward Great Britain." Whether the United States should continue to put up with British aggression or choose forcible resistance, was, he said, "a solemn question which the Constitution wisely confides to the legislative branch of government."

But the legislative branch had trouble responding. During the House debate on Madison's message, opponents of war with Britain were in a minority, but held the floor for long hours, day and night, in order to stave off a declaration of war. One day an elderly New England Federalist launched into a discourse on peace that went on so long that most of his colleagues eventually dozed off. "The Speaker of the House and most of the members, making a bare quorum, were asleep," according to one account, "and there was nothing to disturb the solemn silence but the Dominie-like drawling of the member on the floor,—didactic, monotonous, and slow; the clerk's head bent low down upon the journal; when, lo! sudden noises, rattling, dashing, bounding down the aisles, awoke and astonished the Speaker's chair and the clerk's desk; spittoons were bounding and leaping in the air, and, falling, reverberating their sounds like thunders among the crags of the Alps. 'Order! order! order!' was the vociferous cry; but, in the midst of the slap-banging of the no longer drowsy night, the humdrum debater who had the floor took his seat from fright, and a belligerent Democrat snatched the pause to move the 'previous question,' which was seconded, and the declaration of war against Great Britain was thus got at. . . ." The spittoons seem to have helped the hawks. The House voted for war, 79 to 49, on June 4, and the Senate followed suit, 19-13, on June 17. Madison signed the war declaration on June 18.[26]

High-toned Duel: Clay vs. Randolph

In 1824, when Henry Clay threw his support in the House to John Quincy Adams in the disputed election of that year and then became Adams' Secretary of State, there was much talk of a "corrupt bargain" between the two, which, though unfair, caused Clay considerable embarrassment. Virginia Congressman John Randolph was particularly sarcastic about the alliance between Clay and Adams. In a speech in the House on March 30, 1826, he talked contemptuously about the "alliance, offensive and defensive," between "old Massachusetts and Kentucky; between the frost of January and young, blithe, buxom and blooming May," and then compared Adams and Clay to two unsavory characters in Henry Fielding's popular novel *Tom Jones:* "the coalition of Blifil and Black George . . . , the combination unheard of till then of the Puritan with the blackleg." Adams didn't mind being called a Puritan, but Clay resented the epithet, blackleg, which meant crooked gambler, and at once challenged Randolph to a duel.

The two men met on the afternoon of April 8 on the Virginia bank of the Potomac River, attended by two seconds and a surgeon, with Senator Thomas Hart Benton of Missouri present "as a mutual friend." At the first exchange Randolph's bullet struck a stump behind Clay, and Clay's knocked up some dirt on the ground behind Randolph. Benton then intervened to stop the fight, but the two men both insisted on another shot. This time Clay again missed his mark, merely piercing the flamboyant white dressing gown Randolph was wearing, while Randolph deliberately fired his shot in the air and announced: "I do not fire at you, Mr. Clay." Then he walked over to Clay, pointed to the bullet hole in his dressing gown, and said: "You owe me a new coat, Mr. Clay." "I am glad the debt is not greater," returned Clay. The two men then shook hands and the quarrel was over.

The Clay-Randolph encounter was, Benton said later, "about the last high-toned duel" he ever witnessed. The night before the duel, he later learned, Randolph had told a friend: "I have determined to receive without returning Clay's fire; nothing shall induce me to harm a hair of his head. I will not make his wife a widow, or his children orphans. Their tears would be shed over his grave, but when the sod of Virginia rests on my bosom there is not in this wide world one individual to pay his tribute upon me."[27]

Duel Process of Law

Dueling wasn't common in America until about the time of the war for Independence, when European officers (particularly French) brought it here; and after that it was a fairly widely accepted method of settling disputes among gentlemen, especially in the South, until the Civil War. Southern and Western Congressmen were in the habit of carrying dueling pistols with them and spending a great deal of time practicing in preparation for the day when they might have to prove their manhood on the "field of honor."

Dozens of Congressmen fought duels in antebellum America, even though in most states there were laws against dueling. In 1808 Clay took on Humphrey Marshall, when both were members of the Kentucky legislature, but fortunately neither was seriously wounded. Clay's duel with Randolph in 1838 also ended bloodlessly. But in a duel Thomas Hart Benton fought in St. Louis in 1817, the future Senator, to his regret, succeeded in killing a promising young lawyer Charles Lucas who had challenged him for calling him a "puppy."

What touched off challenges? Insults, slanders, and aspersions on one's honor and integrity were the usual causes of "honorable altercations," but sometimes inadvertently bumping into someone could produce a challenge. In March 1854, during a debate on the Kansas-Nebraska bill, New York's Francis B. Cutting charged that Kentucky's John C. Breckinridge had indulged in "one of the most violent, inflammatory, and personal assaults" ever made in the House, and added that the Kentuckian had "skulked" in the position he took on the bill. "Skulked!" hissed Breckinridge. "I ask the gentleman to withdraw that word!" "I withdraw nothing!" cried Cutting. "I have uttered what I have said in answer to one of the most violent and most personal attacks that has ever been witnessed on this floor!" "Then," said Breckinridge, "when the gentleman says I skulked he says what is false!" At this point Congressmen from the South began gathering around Breckinridge, and the Speaker pounded his gavel and pronounced the offensive remark out of order. "Mr. Chairman," said Cutting quietly, "I do not intend upon this floor to answer the remark which the gentleman from Kentucky has thought proper to employ. It belongs to a different region. It is not here that I will desecrate my lips with undertaking to retort in that manner." He was referring to the "field of honor," of course, and a duel seemed inevitable. But some of the friends of the two men intervened and the quarrel was finally settled "under the code of honor," without recourse to weapons.

Northern Congressmen generally rejected the *code duello*. But Ohio's Benjamin Wade, an excellent shot, refused to be intimidated. "I am here in a double capacity," he announced, when he entered the Senate in 1851. "I represent the State of Ohio, and I represent Ben Wade. As a Senator I am opposed to dueling. As Ben Wade, I recognize the code." When it looked as if Georgia's Robert A. Toombs, resentful of something Wade had said in the Senate, might send him a challenge, Wade proposed squirrel rifles at twenty paces, "with a white paper the size of a dollar pinned over the heart of each contestant." This didn't seem quite right for an "affair of honor" and the challenge never came. And in April 1860, when John F. Potter of Wisconsin chose bowie-knives after a quarrel in the House with Virginia's Roger A. Pryor, there was a big discussion about bowie-knives as dueling weapons.

"The great question of the hour," wrote House clerk John Forney in *The Press,* discussing the Potter-Pryor quarrel on April 15, 1860, "is whether the bowie-knife is any more 'vulgar,' unchristian, or savage than the pistol, the double-barrelled gun, the small-sword, or the rapier. The friends of Potter are multiplying dates and strengthening themselves by going back to the code of honor in the days of chivalry, and coming down to the present era. They allege that the battle-axe was the favorite weapon in the tournaments of old, and was used by the bravest and most polished knights of the Middle Ages. They contend that the small-sword exercise continues to be used in France, and the broad-sword in Germany; and that the preliminaries of these contests are duly and carefully arranged. They argue, further, that the bowie-knife, being a Southern production, has been for long years regarded as an improvement upon all; that it is used by many Southern gentlemen; and that, to this day, the Arkansas 'toothpick' is regarded as an important part of the Southern code of honor."

Forney himself took a dim view of dueling, whatever the weapon. "The whole code, as it is upheld in the South," he declared, "is a barbarous practice, and I have not been able to draw the distinction between that humanity which sends a human soul, unanointed and unshrived, into eternity by a bullet, and that other system which destroys life with 'an ordinary bowie-knife.'" Fortunately the Potter-Pryor quarrel was settled without a duel. And Virginia Whig Henry Wise's efforts to bait Democratic James E. Polk into challenging him when the latter was Speaker of the House also came to naught. Polk was "a Southron," but kept calm and avoided a duel.

Sad to say, not all Congressional disputes ended peacefully. In February 1838 came a duel between Kentucky Congressman William J. Graves and Maine Congressman Jonathan Cilley that ended in the death of the latter. The Graves-Cilley duel was unusual in that it involved a dueling rule which held that refusal to accept a challenge borne by the challenger's second constituted an insult to the second, who, in turn, was obliged to issue a challenge himself. The quarrel began when Cilley made some critical remarks about Colonel James Watson Webb, a New York newspaper publisher, in a House debate, leading Webb to send Cilley a challenge through his second, Congressman Graves. Cilley refused to accept Webb's challenge on the ground that under the Constitution he was not responsible outside of Congress for anything he said in the House. Graves admitted Cilley was legally correct in the stand he took, but felt required, under dueling rules, to challenge Cilley himself, and Cilley similarly felt that he had to accept the challenge. In the confrontation which followed, Cilley was mortally wounded during the third exchange of shots. This was a duel fought solely on a point of honor, for the contestants hardly knew each other. Just before being killed, in fact, Cilley said he entertained "the highest respect and most kind feeling" for his adversary.

Cilley's death produced much adverse comment about dueling in both the press and in Congress. Senator Benton, still remorseful about his duel with Lucas, came to favor severe penalties for Congressmen engaging in duels, including removal from office. Lamented Benton: "The frequency, the wantonness, the barbarity, the cold-blooded cruelty, and the demoniac levity with which homicides are committed with us, have become the opprobrium of our country." With the collapse of the plantation aristocracy during the Civil War, dueling gradually became a thing of the past.[28]

Tobacco-Tinctured

In the days of yore Congressmen chewed as well as dueled. Charles Dickens called Washington the "headquarters of tobacco-tinctured saliva," but the habit of chewing and expectorating among American males was ubiquitous during the Age of Jackson: in theaters, restaurants, hospitals, and courts of law throughout the land, as well as in the Senate and the House. "It was symbolic," according to historian Joseph C. Robert, "that America early in the nineteenth century turned from snuff and knee breeches to the quid and long trousers, both once the habit of ordinary laborers. Chewing had its strongest hold on the people in the Jackson era, when the common man reigned supreme. While pipe and snuff customs had filtered down from the leaders of fashion to the common folk, tobacco chewing was a practice which, by some democratic capillary attraction, seeped from the common man upwards into the higher ranks of society. The people now had the ballot, and every statesman must needs be politician enough to identify himself with the masses. The log-cabin-and-hard-cider campaign put William Henry Harrison in office; Daniel Webster apologized publicly for not having been born in a log cabin."

Visitors from abroad were struck—and repelled—by the tobacco habit. In 1828, Mrs. Basil Hall, wife of a British naval officer, reported that "the gallery of the House of Representatives was an inch thick with dirt; the floor where the members sat was actually flooded with their horrible spitting." Frances Trollope, another English visitor in the early 1830s, was similarly disgusted. Of the House of Representatives she wrote: "It was . . . really mortifying to see this splendid hall, fitted up in so stately and sumptuous a manner, filled with men sitting with their hats on, and nearly all spitting to an excess that decency forbids me to describe." She found the Senate more decorous but the expectoration just as lively. Harriet Martineau, another Britisher, visited Washington in January 1835 and she was just as repelled as Mrs. Trollope. "If the floors of boarding-houses, and the decks of steamboats, and the carpets of the Capitol, do not sicken the Americans into a reform, if the warnings of physicians are of no avail, what remains to be said? I dismiss the nauseous subject." Foreigners thought the spittoon should replace the bald eagle as America's national emblem.

Charles Dickens, who spent three months here in 1842, wanted to dismiss the subject in his book about the United States, but simply couldn't; it was too overwhelming. "The Senate is a dignified and decorous body, and its proceedings are conducted with much gravity and order," he granted. "Both Houses are handsomely carpeted"; but, he added, with evident revulsion, "the state to which these carpets are reduced by the universal disregard of the spittoon with which every honorable member is accommodated, and the extraordinary improvements on the pattern which are squirted and dabbled upon it in every direction, do not admit of being described. I will merely observe, that I strongly recommend all strangers not to look at the floor; and if they happen to drop anything, not to pick it up with an ungloved hand on any account. . . . It is somewhat remarkable, too, at first, to say the least, to see so many honorable members with swelled faces; and it is scarcely less remarkable to discover that this appearance is caused by the quantity of tobacco they contrive to stow within the hollow of the cheek. It is strange enough, too, to see an honorable gentleman leaning back on his tilted chair, with his legs on the desk before him, shaping a convenient 'plug' with his penknife, and when it is quite ready for use, shooting the old one from his mouth as from a pop-gun, and clapping the new one in its place."

But it wasn't only foreign observers who were put off by the vogue for the quid in America. In October 1837 the Washington correspondent of the *Baltimore Transcript* was so disgusted by the condition of the House chamber when Congress adjourned that he could think of no more appropriate term than "modern Goths" for members of Congress. "I went on the floor afterwards," he wrote, "and I wish you could only see the state of the whole hall—a hog pen is actually a drawing room, compared with its abominable condition. The beautiful straw colored matting, which at the beginning of the session was so much admired for its neatness and coolness, is now in such a plight, that not all the soap and scrubbing-brushes in christendom would make it fit for a peasant's hut. Its whole extent is covered with a disgusting compound of tobacco juice, wafers and sand, making it so slippery as to endanger the necks of those walking hastily on it. In fact, I have observed for the last two weeks, that the boys in attendance, whenever going down the main aisle in a hurry, would always secure their footing by sliding over the unstable surface! The marble bases of the columns, too, once of a Parian whiteness, are now streaked with the same brown liquid; while in the interstices of their sculptured work, are lodged sundry enormous *quids,* thrown there by these legislative Goths! It is utter desecration!"[29]

Game Adjourned

Before the Civil War Congress passed strict laws prohibiting gambling in the nation's capital, but they were a dead letter. The northern side of Pennsylvania Avenue, between the Indian Queen Hotel and the Capitol gate, was lined with faro banks, and was frequented by Congressmen, as well as other citizens, particularly during the long week-end adjournments from Thursday afternoon until Monday morning.

One Thursday afternoon, North Carolina Senator Montford Stokes sat down to play a game of brag with Montjoy Bailey, the Senate's Sergeant-at-Arms, and the two continued their game, with time out for snacks and naps, Thursday night, all day Friday, Friday night, all day Saturday, Saturday night, all day Sunday, and Sunday night. On Monday morning they were still going full blast, when, suddenly, at 10:00 a.m., Bailey proposed an adjournment, pointing out that his duties as Sergeant-at-Arms required his presence in the Senate Chamber. Senator Stokes protested vehemently against stopping the game at that point, but Bailey persisted and got up to go. As he left, Stokes complained bitterly that had he known Bailey was going to break up the game so soon, he wouldn't have sat down to play with him in the first place.[30]

Webster and the National Debt

Whenever Massachusetts Senator Daniel Webster had a visitor, the first thing he did was to open the sideboard, take down an old decanter, and pour out a glass of brandy. If the visitor drank it, he was doubly welcome. But if he refused, Webster was less cordial. A friend once said that Webster (in Shakespeare's words) was always "calling spirits from the vast deep."

Like many of his contemporaries, Webster often imbibed too freely at the dinner table. At one dinner he was in such bad shape by the time he came to speak that a friend sat just behind him to help out. As Webster stood wavering after the introduction, the friend whispered, "Tariff." Webster came alive. "The tariff, gentlemen," he exclaimed, "is a subject requiring the profound attention of the statesmen. American industry, gentlemen, must be—" Then he began nodding. "National debt," prompted his friend. "And, gentlemen," Webster perked up, "there's the national debt—it should be paid [loud cheers, which roused Webster]; yes, gentlemen, it should be paid [more cheers], and I'll be hanged if it sha'n't be—[taking out his pocket-book]—I'll pay it myself. How much is it?" As the audience, familiar with Webster's impecuniousness, roared with laughter, the "god-like Daniel" sank back into his chair and was soon sound asleep.[31]

Steadying Webster

One evening Albany's leading citizens honored Webster by arranging a big dinner for him which included thirteen courses, thirteen different kinds of wine, and, to top it off, generous portions of the famous "Regency rum." When the dinner was over, a colorful parade, assembled by *Albany Knicker-*

bocker editor Hugh J. Hastings, a devout Webster fan, marched to the residence where Webster was dining and demanded a speech. When Webster went out and, somewhat unsteadily, began speaking, Hastings took a position right next to him and whenever Webster made a gesture to emphasize a point he was making and started falling, Hastings caught hold of him and prevented him from toppling off the porch. Afterward Webster grasped his hand and exclaimed: "Young man, you prevented me from disgracing myself. I thank you and will never forget you." Webster was one of the few men who could speak effectively even when full of booze, and his speech received much acclaim. Many a young lawyer, in fact, concluded that Webster did his best work while "under the influence" and purposely drank to excess in the hope of becoming a second Webster.[32]

Webster Still Lives

When Webster was on his deathbed, he overheard the doctor tell an attendant: "Give him a spoonful of brandy in fifteen minutes, another in half an hour, and another in three-quarters of an hour, if he still lives." The attendant followed his instructions faithfully, but when it came time for the third spoonful Webster looked so far gone that the attendant asked the doctor whether to bother with the third dose. At this point Webster, who had been watching the clock, raised his head a little and said faintly, "I still live." The attendant then gave him the brandy, and he soon sank into a deep sleep from which he never awakened.[33]

Roll Call and Round-up in the House

In the old days to be absent from a roll-call vote in the House was to risk formal censure and the imposition of a fine. Occasionally the House simply refused to adjourn until the House clerk had brought in all the absentees and the Speaker had queried them about their delinquency.

Late one night in 1848, with doors locked, the House clerk began bringing members who had been absent for a vote to the well of the House so the Speaker could question them about their neglect of duties. "You have been absent from this House without its leave and contrary to its order," he told the offenders. "If you have any excuse to offer, you will now be heard." A Maryland Congressman said he was paid *per diem*, not *per noctem* (members then received *per diem* salaries), for his services in the House; he was promptly fined. A Georgian said he had gone to the home of a friend whose child was "sick unto death"; he was excused. A Virginian explained that one Congressman was holding forth at length when "the usual hour for refreshment had passed," and that he had "preferred the arguments of the stomach to the arguments of the gentleman, so I went home." But he, too, was fined. A Tennessean did no better. "I left the Hall at ten o'clock," he told the Speaker, "and, in accordance with the custom of all orderly men, went to bed." He also received a fine. "I sat in this House for ten hours," said a Tennessean, "and was tired, hungry, and sleepy. I believed it would be a night of speech-making and not of business, and, as I have generally been an attentive listener to speeches, I concluded I had done my share of that part of legislative duty, and, therefore, at ten o'clock I paired off with a friend." The Speaker fined him.

Some of the absentees managed to outwit the Speaker and the clerk. Though the doors were locked, they succeeded in getting into the House chamber while the absentees were being rounded up. An Alabama Congressman sneaked in through a window behind tne Speaker's chair; another absentee risked his life by sliding down one of the marble pillars from the gallery and was in his seat when the Speaker began questioning absentees. Neither was fined, for the clerk hadn't arrested them and they were in their seats during the round-up and second roll call. One observer questioned the wisdom of spending so much time and energy tracking down and punishing Congressmen who missed late-night sessions. Describing the scene in the House at dawn, he wrote: "Daylight looks upon faces pale with watching and sleepless eyes that scarce take note of its approach. What have the public interests gained? Nothing."[34]

Altered Man

In 1848 Illinois Congressman Abraham Lincoln saw one of his colleagues with a prostitute on his arm. "He went home with her," Lincoln noted, "and if I were to guess, I would say, he went away a somewhat altered man—most likely in his pockets, and in some other particular. The fellow looked conscious of his guilt."[35]

Longest Speech: Douglas'

One day during debates on the Kansas-Nebraska bill in 1854, New York Senator William T. Seward tapped Illinois' Stephen A. Douglas on the shoulder, whispered that he had some bourbon in his office which was twenty years old, and said he wanted to get Douglas' opinion about it. Douglas politely declined; he said he planned to speak in a few minutes and wanted his brain unclouded by liquor. He went on to give an impassioned speech and then sank down in his chair exhausted, apparently unaware of all the congratulations showered on him. At this point, Seward seized his arm and took him off to his office. "Here's the bourbon, Douglas," he said enthusiastically; "try some; it's sixty years old." "Seward," said Douglas thoughtfully, "I have made today the longest speech ever delivered; history has no parallel for it." "How is that?" asked Seward puzzledly. "Don't you recollect," said Douglas, "that a moment before I obtained the floor you invited me to partake of some bourbon twenty years old, and, now, immediately after closing my remarks, you extend to me some of the same liquor, with the assertion that it is sixty years old!—a forty years' speech was never delivered before!" Seward smiled and acknowledged the "corn."[36]

Sam Houston's Hearts

Texas Senator Sam Houston had a hobby: carving soft pine sticks into toys for children and heart-shaped souvenirs for the ladies. When he attended church he took his big ivory-handled clasp knife with him and did his whittling during long sermons, leaving a pile of shavings by the pew for the sexton to clean up afterwards. And during Senate debates he frequently worked on blocks of wood about the size of the hand supplied him by the Senate cabinetmaker. Sometimes, when he completed a heart, he summoned a page and, pointing to a "fair spectator" in the gallery, instructed him: "Give this to that lady up there, with General 'Sam' Houston's compliments." The souvenirs were highly prized. Some women attended Senate proceedings mainly in the hope of receiving one of Houston's famous hearts.[37]

The Caning of Senator Sumner

In May 1856, Massachusetts' Charles Sumner delivered a passionate anti-slavery speech in the Senate during the course of which he made critical remarks about several pro-slavery Senators, including Andrew F. Butler of South Carolina. Butler, he said, "has chosen a mistress to whom he had made his vows, and who, though ugly to others, is always lovely to him; though polluted in the sight of the world, is chaste in his sight. I mean the harlot Slavery." Two days later the son of one of Butler's cousins, Congressman Preston S. Brooks, walked into the Senate Chamber where Sumner sat writing at his desk and exclaimed: "Mr. Sumner, I have read your speech twice over carefully. It is a libel on South Carolina, and on Mr. Butler, who is a relative of mine." Then he beat Sumner into insensibility with a stout gutta-percha cane. After Sumner was taken home, to begin his long convalescence, the Senate Republicans had an emergency meeting and decided that Henry Wilson, Sumner's colleague from Massachusetts, would call the attention of the upper house to the incident the following day.

"Mr. President, the seat of my colleague is vacant today," exclaimed Wilson in his speech the next morning. "That seat is vacant today for the first time during five years of public service. Yesterday, after a touching tribute of respect to the memory of a deceased member of the House of Representatives, the Senate adjourned. My colleague remained in his seat, busily engaged in his public duties. While thus engaged, with pen in hand, and in a position which rendered him utterly incapable of protecting or defending himself, Mr. Preston S. Brooks, a member of the House of Representatives, approached his desk unobserved, and abruptly addressed him. Before he had time to utter a single word in reply, he received a stunning blow on the head from a cane in the hands of Mr. Brooks, which made him blind and almost unconscious. Endeavoring, however, to protect himself, in rising from his chair his desk was overthrown; and while in that condition he was beaten upon the head by repeated blows until he sank upon the floor of the Senate exhausted, unconscious, and covered with his own blood. He was taken from this chamber to the anteroom, his wounds were dressed, and then by friends he was carried to his house and placed upon his bed. He is unable to be with us today to perform the duties that belong to him as a member of this body." Wilson went on to express his horror at Brooks' attack. "Sir," he said, "to assail a member of the Senate . . . 'for words spoken in debate,' is a grave offense not only against the rights of the senator but the constitutional privileges of this house; but, sir, to come into this chamber and assault a member in his seat until he falls exhausted and senseless on this floor, is an offense requiring the prompt and decisive action of the Senate." When he finished, New York's William T. Seward proposed an inquiry, but the Senate committee appointed to investigate the incident concluded that Brooks' assault, though a breach of the privileges of the Senate, was punishable only by the House of which he was a member.

The Brooks caning shocked the nation. Northern newspapers, even those hostile to Sumner, denounced Brooks' behavior in the strongest terms; and meetings were held and resolutions passed in just about every Northern city to condemn the South Carolina Congressman. In the South, a few people called Brooks' action "unjustifiable, unmanly, ill-timed, ill-advised, cowardly, dastardly," but most Southerners hailed the South Carolinian as a hero. Wherever he went he received lavish praise and sometimes gold-headed canes, inscribed with the words, "Hit him again!" "A *Good Deed,*" approved the *Richmond Whig.* "The only regret we feel is, that Mr. Brooks did not employ a horsewhip or a cowhide upon his slanderous back, instead of a cane." A House investigating committee recommended Brooks' expulsion, and a majority of the members of the House (but not the required two-thirds) voted to expel him. Brooks defended himself in a speech in the House and then resigned, but he was promptly re-elected to his seat by his constituents.

In another speech in the Senate, Henry Wilson denounced the "brutal, murderous, and cowardly assault," and was at once challenged to a duel by

Brooks. But Wilson contemptuously refused the challenge; dueling, he said, was "the lingering relic of a barbarous civilization, which the law of the country has branded a crime." In the House, Anson Burlingame of Massachusetts also condemned Brooks, who, he said, "stole into the Senate, that place which had hitherto been held sacred against violence, and smote [Sumner] as Cain smote his brother." "That is false!" cried one South Carolina Congressman. "What!" shot back Burlingame, "strike a man when he is pinioned—when he cannot respond to a blow! Call you that chivalry! In what code of honor did you get your authority for that?" Brooks at once challenged Burlingame to a duel. Burlingame accepted the challenge, but picked the Canadian side of Niagra Falls as the meeting place. Brooks then called it off; it wouldn't be safe, he said, for him to travel through the North to get to Canada.

Sumner's recovery from the caning was slow and painful; it took more than three years for him to regain his health. Not until December 1859 did he return to the Senate to resume his struggle against slavery. By then Brooks was gone; he died seven months after his assault on Sumner.[38]

Scalp

Late one night in February 1858, when the House was debating the admission of Kansas to the Union, South Carolina's hot-tempered Laurence M. Keitt called Pennsylvania's Galusha Grow "a black Republican puppy," and Grow shouted: "No slave driver shall crack his whip over me!" Then, as the two men lunged at each other, their friends joined in and soon there was a free-for-all on the House floor, with Congressmen kicking, beating, punching, and wrestling each other. The Speaker of the House and the Sergeant-at-Arms tried in vain to stop the fighting, but suddenly, when one Congressman grabbed another by the hair, pulled his wig off, and cried, "Hooray, boys, I've got his scalp!" everyone started laughing and the fighting quickly petered out. But such laughter was rare. Sectional hatreds steadily intensified during the 1850s, and a kind of cold war—with Congressmen shaking fists at each other, shouting insults, and flourishing knives and pistols—came to prevail in both houses of Congress.[39]

The "Washington Tragedy": Sickles and Key

Daniel E. Sickles was a competent Congressman (D, New York, 1857–61), but that was not why he became well known. His fame came from the fact that on February 27, 1859, he shot and killed Philip Barton Key, the handsome son of *The Star-Spangled Banner*'s Francis Scott Key, for having an affair with his attractive young wife Theresa. Sickles was a philanderer himself, but his astonishment when he learned about his wife's infidelity exploded into fury.

Ambitious politically, Sickles was too caught up in Congressional matters to spend much time with Theresa. When it came to social life, he entrusted her to the keeping of his good friend Barton Key, whom he had persuaded President Buchanan to appoint as United States Attorney for the District of Columbia. Barton, a widower, was willing to oblige; he took Theresa to teas, parties, and theater performances, which Sickles was unable to attend, and also went horseback riding with her for long hours. Rumors surfaced about the two, but Sickles brushed them aside.

Then one day came an anonymous letter giving Sickles details about a house which Key had rented on 15th Street, near Lafayette Square, for secret meetings with the Congressman's wife. When Sickles looked into the matter and discovered that the allegations were true, he was by turns filled with rage and plunged into grief. Finally he summoned his wife, made her write out a lengthy confession of her sins, and then armed himself and went out to confront Key in a park near his house. "Key, you scoundrel!" he yelled. "You have disgraced my house—you must die!" "Don't shoot— don't shoot!" pleaded Key, as Sickles began firing, but he was soon mortally wounded. "Yes, I've killed him!" Sickles told his wife when he got back to the house. He then surrendered himself to the authorities and entered the seedy District jail to await trial. "Don't you have a better room?" he asked the jailer who took him to his cell. "No," said the jailer. "This is the best place you members of Congress have afforded us."

The "Washington Tragedy," as it was called, made headlines every- where. And when Sickles went on trial for murder, flocks of reporters and pencil-sketch artists descended on Washington to cover the proceedings. Defense lawyers argued that Sickles was temporarily insane when he shot Key and that he was justified by the "unwritten law" in killing "the defiler of his marriage bed." The prosecution, for some reason, did not make use of evidence it uncovered about some of Sickles' own infidelities. In the end, the jury acquitted Sickles; and in the end Sickles forgave his wife. Though respectable people regarded her as beyond the pale, Sickles, in an unusual action for those days, took her back as his wife and they lived together again until her death a few years later. By that time he had won new fame as a Union General who lost his leg at the Battle of Gettysburg.[40]

Thad Stevens' Wonders

Thaddeus Stevens was a compulsive gambler. On one occasion he was said to have lost two thousand dollars at a single session at euchre but returned the next night for more. On another occasion he played into the small hours of the morning, and toward dawn a teamster delivering a load of hay broke in on the game. "What shall I do with this?" he asked. Stevens looked up and cried: "Put it all on the ace of spades!"

Once James G. Blaine was walking home long after midnight and ran into Stevens coming out of a high-toned gambling house on Pennsylvania Avenue. Just as he greeted Stevens a black preacher came up and asked for a contribution toward building a new church for his people. Stevens, who had been winning, took a roll of bills out of his pocket, peeled off the one on the outside and handed it to the preacher. To the latter's surprise it was one hundred dollars. Thinking Stevens had made a mistake (he had, in fact, mistaken the bill in the dark), the preacher offered to return it. But "Old Thad," as he was called, waved him away and observed solemnly: "God moves in a mysterious way His wonders to perform."[41]

The Page and the Prayer

In December 1872, on his first day as a page, Edmund Alton placed the gavel on the Vice President's desk, as instructed, and then bowed his head as the Senate chaplain delivered a short prayer. To his astonishment, the prayer was hardly finished when nearly all the Senators began clapping their hands noisily, and, amid the din, an old man in the gallery, echoing his own thoughts, exclaimed: "Well, I'll be hanged ef I saw anything pertikerlerly fine about that prayer!" But the boy quickly realized the Senators weren't applauding the prayer; they were summoning the pages. As the other pages leaped into action to carry out the instructions of the lawmakers, Alton wasn't quite sure what to do. At last one Senator looked over at him and clapped, and he started walking over to him, but another page raced ahead of him and beat him to it. "I tried about a dozen times to answer calls," the page wrote later, "but was beaten by the other boys." Presently Senator Roscoe Conkling beckoned him with the forefinger of his right hand and Alton started in his direction. Conkling was standing behind his desk holding a letter, and a number of boys rushed over and put up their hands and fought with each other to grab the letter first. But Conkling ignored them, and when Alton came up, he reached over their heads and gave him the letter with instructions as to what he should do with it. "After that episode," said Alton later, "I felt all right."[42]

Cox's Gift

One morning Congressman Samuel ("Sunset") Cox of Ohio opened his mail and found a large envelope containing stocks and bonds in a railroad corporation which was pressing for some legislation in Congress at the time. He at once handed the securities to John O'Connor, his private secretary, and instructed him to put them in another envelope and send them back to the president of the road. "Mr. Cox," said O'Connor thoughtfully, "pardon me for suggesting that the better plan in this matter would be for me to go to New York and deliver the shares in person and take a receipt for the same. It would not be wise to send them back through the mail," he added, "for in the event of future trouble with this corporation, say, a Congressional investigation or anything of that kind, the company would say that it had given you the stock in it and there would be nothing for you to show that you had not accepted it." Cox at once realized his secretary was right, so he sent him to New York with the shares and obtained a receipt for them the following day. Not long after, there was a Congressional investigation of that particular railroad, as O'Connor had expected, and the receipt saved Congressman Cox considerable embarrassment.[43]

Fun with Peffer

"What is your amusement?" a reporter asked Kansas' humorless William A. Peffer, known for his long, wavy beard, soon after he joined the Senate in 1891. "Well," said Peffer proudly, "I don't attend theatres, nor baseball, nor dog fights, nor cock fights, nor horse races; I don't play cards. I don't play billiards." Then, taking "as much of his fuscous mahogany beard as he could" in his hand, according to the reporter, he added thoughtfully: "I get the most real fun in playing with the children in the street."[44]

A Round with Conkling

New York's Roscoe Conkling was good at both boxing and wrestling. When he first went to Washington as a Senator, he installed a gymnasium in his house, worked out there regularly, and was proud of his muscular development. One day Wisconsin Senator "Matt" Carpenter had dinner with him and when they had finished their post-prandial cigars Conkling showed off his gym, performed a few calisthenics for him, and then asked whether he was up to a little boxing. Carpenter gamely doffed his coat, put on gloves, and began striking and parrying with the athletic New Yorker. In short order, though, Conkling gave him a thorough drubbing; and Carpenter laughingly cried uncle and took off his gloves.

Carpenter wasn't as amused as he pretended to be. Secretly, in fact, he yearned for revenge. A few weeks later he had occasion to meet a professional boxer named Jem Mace and at once got a brilliant idea: take Mace with him the next time he visited Conkling, pass him off as one of his constituents, and maneuver the New Yorker into a round with the man. His plan worked beautifully. Conkling showed Carpenter and Mace his gym after some small talk and then asked Carpenter if he wanted to try another round. Carpenter said he had had enough but added that perhaps Mace would like to box. Conkling gladly assented, cocky about his prowess, and the rest was inevitable: Mace mopped the floor with the New Yorker, from one end of the room to the other, while Carpenter stood by with a big smile on his face. When Carpenter and his boxing friend left, they found that their host was "less exuberant in his adieus than in his welcome."[45]

Breath

Senator Reed Smoot, Republican of Utah, used to tell the story of a pompous Senator who was overimpressed with his own importance. One day he was in a Washington hotel, being shaved by an old black barber who had seen many Senators come and go through the years. "Uncle," said the Senator, "you must have had among your customers many of my distinguished predecessors in the Senate." "Yes, sar," answered the barber. "I'se knowed most all of dem; by de way, Senator, you remind me of Dan'l Webster." The Senator beamed. "Is it my brow or my speeches?" he purred. "No, boss," said the barber, "it's your breath."[46]

Saw Cannon

One night Representative Joseph W. Fordney of Michigan sat in on a poker game with Illinois' Joseph G. Cannon and lost. The next day a friend met him and said, "Uncle Joe is back in town. Have you seen him?" "Yes, I saw him last night," said Fordney ruefully. "I saw him with three aces against my three kings."[47]

Senator Williams, Shatisfied

Once Mississippi's John Sharp Williams and another Congressman entered the House chamber, slightly pickled, walked down the aisle to their seats on the Democratic side, arms around each other, weaving back and forth and holding each other up. When they reached their seats, they sat for a little while as if listening intently to a Congressman who was making a long, dull speech to which almost nobody was paying any attention. At some point the Congressman mentioned some event in history that occurred on the ninth day of June, 1786, and at this, Williams and his colleague perked up, and the latter asked permission to interrupt. "Certainly," said the Congressman, "I shall be very happy to be interrupted by the distinguished gentleman." So Williams' spifflicated colleague solemnly asked: "What date did the gen'leman fixsh?" "The ninth day of June, 1786," replied the speaker. Williams' colleague then sat down, went into a huddle with Williams, and a moment later Williams got up and asked the privilege of interrupting, which he readily received. "I want to shay to the gen'leman," said he, "that the date ish entirely shatishfact'ry." Then he and his colleague put their arms around each other and weaved their way back up the aisle to the cloakroom.[48]

Senator Williams' Original Thoughts

One day, after Mississippi Congressman John Sharp Williams had made a particularly bitter speech against the Irish, while the Versailles Treaty was under consideration, Indiana's James E. Watson walked with him from the Capitol over to the Senate Office Building. As they were going along, Watson remonstrated with him for drinking so much and asked him why he did not take a couple of good "snorts," and quit, the way most drinkers do. Williams stopped him. "Jim," he said, "I don't allow men to talk to me about my personal habits, because they are my own business and nobody else has a right to interfere. But you and I have been friends for so long a time, and then you are such a damned good-natured fool anyhow, that I will answer you." He went on to explain. "One time I made up my mind that I would never take another drink, that I would quit forever. I abstained absolutely for six months, and I tell you the honest truth, Jim, when I say that in that whole six months I never had an original thought."[49]

Boies Penrose's Apology

When Pennsylvania Senator Boies Penrose was riding the train from Washington to Philadelphia one day, a little drunker than usual, he bumped into a fellow passenger, who, like him, was feeling no pain, and they got into a fight. Penrose admitted he was intoxicated, but said that since he wasn't a common drunk he was entitled to the right of way. The other man then threatened to punch him in the nose and Penrose called the conductor. "I hate drunken men," he told the conductor. "Please have this man thrown off the train. I've had a few drinks myself but I don't mind that. This man's a nuisance." So the conductor had the train stopped and shoved the man off.

The following day the angry ejectee notified the railroad he was suing it for an enormous sum. The railroad appealed to Penrose. Penrose at once telephoned his apologies to the man, took him to dinner, and presented him with two cases of champagne and a barrel of Pennsylvania's best whiskey. When a newsman covering the story declared that it was "a gracious and magnanimous gesture," Penrose waved him off. "Didn't cost me a cent," he said. "A distiller sent the whiskey and a wine agent contributed the champagne. All I did was telephone. Apologize to the fellow? Of course I did. In politics it's a fine thing to apologize to an individual. But never apologize to a mob. The first is gracious; the second is cowardly.[50]

No Apollo

One fine afternoon, during a yachting party, Pennsylvania Senator Boies Penrose suddenly emerged from his cabin, quite drunk and stark naked, and approached the yacht's rail for a dive. There was a scream from one of the women aboard. Turning around and seeing her holding her hands in front of her eyes, he exclaimed: "Madame, I grant that mine is not the form of Apollo, but it is too late for either of us to do anything about that. But if I present what to you are strange and unfamiliar phenomena, it is you who should be ashamed, not I." And he leaped into the water.[51]

Penrose and the Kansas Dry

Pennsylvania's Boies Penrose despised hypocrisy. He had nothing but contempt for the Congressman from Kansas who was a "fanatical dry" in public, but who went up to him one afternoon, took him aside, and in a whisper asked if Penrose could get him a bottle of whiskey. "What is it you want?" bellowed Penrose. "Speak up, speak up. Stop hissing in my ear!" "Shh!" breathed the embarrassed Kansan. "I have some constituents coming and if you can recommend a reliable bootlegger—" "Oh," roared Penrose, so loudly that people around them looked up, "Oh, a bootlegger! What do you want, Scotch or rye? I'll send you a couple of bottles. But I don't know any bootleggers. They're all rats. If you drys would stop supporting them—" But the embarrassed Congressman had fled. That night Penrose arranged for a group of drunks to gather in front of the Congressman's house to sing, "What's the matter with—? He's all right!" He also sent a messenger to the man's home the next morning carrying a package, which, after he made clear to everyone around for whom it was intended, he dropped with a loud crash on the lobby's tile floor.[52]

Checking the Record

The Eighteenth (Prohibition) Amendment, added to the Constitution in 1919, didn't prevent conviviality on Capitol Hill. During the 1920s there were numerous parties in the Capitol at night which featured corn whiskey. Many Congressmen had their own bootleggers; one of them, who became known in the headlines as "the man in the green hat," was arrested while delivering his wares in the House Office Building. Pennsylvania Senator Boies Penrose despised Congressmen who "talked dry but lived wet," but he wasn't the only one. Massachusetts Congressman James A. Gallivan shared his views. A strong wet, Gallivan kept a well-stocked bar in his office, together with a record of how his colleagues voted on the Prohibition issue. Whenever a Congressman dropped by for a drink, Gallivan first checked his record; if he had voted dry, he left Gallivan's office dry.[53]

Senator Watson's Prince Albert

On May 9, 1929, the day the Senate passed a bill over the leadership of Indiana's James E. Watson, the Majority Leader appeared in the Senate chamber wearing a black suit known as a "Prince Albert." When a colleague asked why, he sighed: "Well, I believe in being properly dressed, and when I go to a funeral, I dress for it."[54]

Brother "Z"

Democratic Congressman Marion Zioncheck from the state of Washington, who swept into office on Franklin Roosevelt's coattails in 1932, was one of Capitol Hill's biggest boozers. He seems to have set new records in guzzling; he swallowed anything with ethanol in it, but liked absinthe the best. His favorite pastime was driving his big white Cadillac around the nation's capital, filled with girl friends, singing, yelling, tippling, and shouting smart remarks at people on the street. Once he drove up on the sidewalk in front of a fancy Washington hotel, and when the police helped him out of the car, beer cans and bottles came tumbling crazily out with him. Another time he and a bunch of young women stopped to take a shower at an open fire hydrant. Sometimes, too, Brother "Z," as he was called, would stop his car, take off his pants, and jump into one of the city's fountains.

One day, when Brother "Z" was deep in his cups, he tried to help an attractive young woman, obviously a beginning driver, who was maneuvering her car in front of the Capitol. For a half hour or so he stood there, wobbling a bit, but giving authoritative instructions about turning right and turning left, as she jerked her car back and forth in the parking space. Finally the car lurched out and Zioncheck announced triumphantly: "Okay, my dear, you're on your own now." "Are you crazy?" screamed the woman. "I was trying to *park* this car!"[55]

The Kingfish

Huey Long, "the Kingfish," was elected to the Senate when he was thirty-seven and took the oath in January 1932. His fellow Louisianan Edwin Broussard was supposed to escort him to the front when he took his oath, but Long purposely quarreled with him so he could break precedent and have a Senator from another state—Arkansas' Joseph Robinson—escort him instead and that way attract more attention. He then violated another Senate tradition by carrying a lighted cigar as he marched up the aisle with Robinson and parking it on the clerk's desk while taking the oath. Afterward, when he was presented to William E. Borah, he embraced him heartily, to Borah's astonishment; then he prodded James E. Watson in the ribs and went on to treat everyone boisterously, galloping about the Senate chamber, it was said, "like a colt turned out to pasture." When Robert R. Reynolds, proud of his ability to impress people, hurried over to Long, stuck out his hand, and announced grandly, "I'm Senator Reynolds of North Carolina," the Kingfish barely looked up. "I knew you when you ran an ice-skating rink in New Orleans," he said shortly, and turned away.

Long said he came to the Senate "with only one project in mind," which was to "do something to spread the wealth of the land among all the people." He resigned from committees to which he was assigned and demanded more important posts. His main objective, he announced, was to secure heavy taxes on wealth. The conservative *Chicago Tribune* ran a cartoon showing Long wearing a Russian costume, carrying a red flag, and holding up posters reading, "Soak the Rich" and "Confiscate Property." The *Tribune*'s caption: "Patriotism *versus* Communism—the Real issue in Washington." But Long was no bolshevik; though a demagogue, he was also an old-fashioned American populist who inveighed against the unequal distribution of wealth in America in one Senate speech after another.[56]

Senator Long Ain't Even Close

Soon after entering the Senate Huey Long got into an informal contest with Illinois Democrat J. Hamilton Lewis for honors as the Senate's best-dressed man. Long's attire tended toward the gaudy, while Hamilton favored a subdued ensemble when appearing on the Senate floor. One day, though, to everyone's surprise, Long showed up in the Senate chamber modestly attired: in a dark gray suit with a conservative pattern, with a wing collar and bow tie, and a plain white handkerchief in his outer breast pocket. Armed for battle, as it were, he strode onto the floor, looked about, and called out noisily: "Where is the estimable Senator from Illinois?" At that moment Lewis walked into the room, wearing a sportsy, double-breasted brown suit and featuring a bright necktie and a colored handkerchief. Stunned by the switch, Long walked over, circled his rival for a moment, and then threw up his hands, rolled his eyes in mock despair, and exclaimed: "Lord, I ain't even close! I give up."[57]

In Flagrante Delicto

One day Huey Long went into the Senate dining room and, seeing Alben Barkley having lunch with an attractive young woman who was not his wife, walked over, ogling, smirking, and wriggling his eyebrows to indicate that he thought he had caught the Kentucky Senator *in flagrante delicto*. Barkley let him go on for a while and then got up, bowed, and said: "Senator Long, meet Laura Louise, my daughter." "Oh!" murmured Long.[58]

Good Things

In the early thirties, when pennies could still buy something, New York Congressman Sol Bloom used to walk up the steps of the Capitol every morning quietly strewing pennies, nickels, and dimes along the way. When Congressional doorkeeper William ("Fishbait") Miller asked about it one day, Bloom said: "Shhh. Let the little children find them when they come to see the Capitol. In this Depression, someone has to show them that good things can happen."[59]

Joe Martin's Derby

In the summer of 1939, when the King and Queen of England visited Washington to cement the informal British-American alliance on the eve of World War II, Massachusetts Congressman Joe Martin was on the committee to welcome them at the Capitol; and, like everyone else, he was expected to don morning coat, striped trousers, and silk topper for the occasion. But the day before the visitation Texas' Sam Rayburn told Martin he didn't have a topper and wasn't going to get one. "I'm just going to wear a derby," he said. Martin did have a topper, but since Rayburn didn't have one, he decided that out of collegiality he would copy Rayburn and wear a derby too. When he got to the Capitol the next morning, however, he found Rayburn wearing a high silk hat after all, which someone had lent him. Martin toyed with the idea of dashing back to his apartment to grab his own topper, but then decided against it, and appeared at the reception for the royal couple wearing his derby.

Martin's derby was big news. Newspapers made much of the fact that at the reception for King George VI and Queen Elizabeth everyone wore toppers except Martin, and there was considerable criticism, especially among the wives of the other Congressmen. But in Massachusetts' 14th District, Martin's, he became a hero. Letters poured into his office praising his plucky performance. "Good for you, Joe," said one letter. "Glad someone down there has the gumption to stand up to the King of England and not feel he has to crawl into a high hat." "Thank God," came another letter, "we've got one independent man in Congress!"[60]

Hardly the Moment

When the Democratic convention met in Chicago in 1944, Virginia's Senator Harry F. Byrd occupied Room 621A in the Stevens Hotel and received many visitors. But an attractive young woman who was visiting the convention had Room 621, in the opposite wing, and many of the Democratic leaders coming to see Byrd mistook her room for the Byrd suite. She was amused at first and then got tired of explaining that Senator Byrd was staying in Room 621A, not Room 621. Finally she decided to have a little fun. She put on her most enticing negligee and waited. Soon came a knock on the door. She opened it, and as the caller got a look at her, his eyes popped. "I would like to speak to Senator Byrd," he stuttered. "We-ll," she breathed. "This is hardly the moment, is it? Some other time, perhaps?" "Of course! Of course!" said the man hastily. "Please do not think of disturbing him. I understand how things are." He left posthaste.[61]

Gentlewomen in the House

The first women to become members of Congress were something of a curiosity to most of their male colleagues. In the 1920s Speaker Nicholas Longworth called them "gentlewomen" and encouraged chivalric behavior toward them in the House chamber. There was much applause (and sometimes flowers) when they took the oath of office, and the men in the House sometimes made kind remarks about the fair sex in speeches and on occasion ostentatiously deferred to them in debates. Once, when Mary T. Norton, New Jersey Democrat, challenged the views of a Republican House member, he exclaimed: "We can, dear lady, reason with you only with our hearts, not our minds!" And when Ruth Owen made a telling point one day during an exchange with New York's Fiorello LaGuardia, the latter responded: "If it were not for the irresistible appeal made by the charming Representative from the State of Florida, I would object; but under the circumstances, I cannot." There was a great deal of this kind of gentle teasing in the 1920s and 1930s. Edith Nourse Rogers once asked if a male colleague would yield and he said facetiously: "Not now. It's not very often that we men are in a position where we can make the ladies sit down and keep quiet!"

For years the committee assignments given Congresswomen were usually minor ones. But now and then their male associates went out of their way to make them feel important. On one occasion some New York Congressmen purposely withdrew an amendment to a tax bill so that the "gentlewoman from New Jersey," Mrs. Norton, could have the privilege of introducing it. And on another occasion House leaders permitted Alice Robertson, "the lady from Oklahoma," to preside over the chamber. It was during a roll call, however, and the Oklahoman held the gavel in her hand for only a minute or two, and no one got to address her as "Miss Speaker."

Even Franklin Roosevelt at times overlooked the women in Congress. Toward the end of 1938, when the 75th Congress adjourned, the White

House invited all the Congressional Democrats to a three-day gathering at the Jefferson Island Club in Maryland for fun and talk. But it turned out that the Maryland club excluded women, and that meant dropping the six Democratic Congresswomen, most of them good New Dealers, from the guest list. The women decided to grin and bear it. "We all will have a chance to give [the President] our views another time in less crowded circumstances," said one of them, "when we won't have to compete for his attention with all those males."

As the years passed, the "gentlewomen" came increasingly to resent being patronized. Ohio Republican Frances Bolton, for one, became upset if anyone used the word, Congresswoman, when addressing her. "I'm a Congressman," she insisted. "A poet is not a poetess and an author is not an authoress. It's degrading to call her that." New Jersey's Mary Norton bristled when a Congressman condescendingly called her "the lady" during a debate. "I am not *the lady*," she said indignantly. "I am a member of Congress, elected by the Thirteenth New Jersey District." But such forthrightness irked some of her male colleagues. "Will the gentleman yield?" she asked during another debate. "No, not now," said Texas Democrat Thomas L. Blanton testily. "I yielded to the lady once, and she was not quite courteous, and I learned not to yield to her." At this point Ohio Democrat Martin L. Sweeney gallantly intervened. "My observation," he declared, "is that the women of this body behave like perfect gentlemen, while some of the men behave like a lot of old women!" To some people this seemed like praising with faint damns.

In January 1947, Congressman Charles L. Gifford, Massachusetts Republican, summed up the old-fashioned Longworth view of the matter. In a speech at the opening of the 80th Congress, Gifford confessed his "anxieties about the present Congress" and his eagerness to find out what "abilities and opinions" the new members would bring to the work of the House. Then he turned his attention to the women and essayed the light touch. "As I look over to my left I see the face of a new lady Member," he said. "I wish that all other lady Members were present. May I say to her, one of the great worries I have in Congress itself is lest we have too many of you. Although I say this in a somewhat jocular way, still I am a little serious about it."

Gifford went on to praise the "lady Members," but also to point out the problems they posed in the House. "The lady Members we have today are extremely satisfactory to us. But they, like all women, can talk to us with their eyes and their lips, and when they present to us an apple it is most difficult to refuse. Even old Adam could not resist. Women have a language all their own. I do not like to particularize but I should. I see the gentlewoman from Ohio [Mrs. Bolton] is present. I read or listen carefully to everything she says on the floor. She is a truly marvelous woman; such a command of language as she possesses. She is a world traveler. . . . She convinces us that she knows what she is talking about. Because I admire her so much I could hardly resist, I fear, supporting any measure that she would propose, especially if she looked at me as such a woman can. The gentlewoman from Maine [Margaret Chase Smith], who is almost always sitting over there at my left, never seems to have a vacant chair beside her that I could take and get acquainted with her. Why? She is so able and popular. These ladies are so attractive. They are dangerous in that they may influence us too much. Suppose we had fifty of them. Seemingly, I note flirtations enough now, but what would there be with fifty of them?" Gifford concluded by assuring the "lady members" that they already had many times the influence they would have if equal-rights legislation were adopted. But if they asked him to support such legislation—well, he sighed, "I suppose I would."[62]

Tom Connally's Two Extensions

Men talk as much as women do, of course, but in the good old days jokes about wordy women were extremely popular. One day Texas Senator Tom Connally had to preside at a committee meeting at which a woman with a reputation for garrulity wanted to state her views, and the other members of the committee were plunged into despair. But Connally reassured them; he wouldn't let the woman speak longer than fifteen minutes, he promised, and at the same time he would keep her in good humor. The other Senators were skeptical; they said she was short-tempered, when crossed, as well as long-winded. But Connally performed nicely. When the meeting opened, he let the woman take the floor; but when she had spoken only five minutes he interrupted and said her time was up. The woman protested angrily, as he had expected, and he then gallantly gave her a five-minute extension. But after five minutes he stopped her again, and when she again protested, he graciously bestowed another five minutes. The third time, when the five minutes was up, she had finished her remarks, and left the committee room extremely pleased that she had wangled two extensions out of Connally. As she left, Connally looked triumphantly at his colleagues as if to say, "I won my bet!"[63]

Do's and Don'ts

In 1945, when Adam Clayton Powell, Jr., Baptist minister in Harlem, walked into his House office for the first time, he found a memo on his desk containing a list of "Do's and Don'ts for Negro Congressmen." One of the first on the list: "Don't eat in the House Dining Room."

Two years later, when Republican Congressman Kenneth Keating, also from New York, first entered the House, he was outraged to learn that Powell was unable to get seated in either the House or the Senate dining rooms and he decided to do something about it. He picked the Senate dining room, where the Vice President ate when he lunched on Capitol Hill, as his target, persuaded a liberal Senator he knew to invite him to lunch there, and then asked Powell and his wife, Hazel Scott (the jazz pianist and singer), to be his guests.

When Keating and the Powells walked into the Senate dining room, the black headwaiter, Paul Johnson, who had been working there since 1908, almost collapsed. "Congressman," he told Keating, "you know that no colored folks are allowed to eat here. You're going to get me in a lot of trouble." Keating assured the headwaiter he would take full responsibility for the guests, and he took the Powells over to the table where his Senate friend was sitting. Keating's action paved the way for ending the color barrier in the Senate dining room.

Powell himself broke the segregation rule in the House dining room after he had gained some influence in Congress. He also became the first black man to use the Congressional shower and to have a haircut in the Congressional barbershop. He fought racial prejudice among the Capitol police, too, and saw to it that black policemen received just as good assignments as the whites did. He also got black reporters admitted to the press gallery. And after he had been in Congress awhile he also began calling his colleagues by their first names. "Keep the faith, baby," he sometimes called out to Arkansas Senator John McClellan, or, "See you later, John," as McClellan cringed at the audacity.[64]

Powell's Bombs

Soon after entering the House, Adam Clayton Powell, Jr., had a chat with House Speaker Sam Rayburn. "Adam," said Rayburn, "everybody down here expects you to come with a bomb in both hands. Now don't do that, Adam. Oh, I know all about you and I know that you can't be quiet very long, but don't throw those bombs. Just see how things operate here. Take your time. Freshmen members of Congress are supposed not to be heard and not even to be seen too much. There are a lot of good men around here. Listen to what they have to say, drink it all in, get reelected a few more times, and then start moving. But for God's sake, Adam, don't throw those bombs!" "Mr. Speaker," laughed Powell, "I've got a bomb in each hand, and I'm going to throw them right away!" Rayburn exploded in laughter at this point and the two apparently got along well after this. In his memoirs, Powell, a Baptist minister, reported that he had many chats about religion with the House Speaker and finally talked him into joining the church.[65]

Powell's Annapolis Appointee

When Powell entered the House, he soon learned that each Congressman had the privilege of appointing five young men to the U.S. Naval Academy at Annapolis, Maryland, and he decided to make a black appointment. "Who is your outstanding Negro graduate this year?" he asked a Washington educator. "Wesley Brown," the educator told him. Powell at once phoned Brown, told him he wanted him to go to Annapolis, and persuaded him to accept the appointment. After Brown had been at Annapolis a few months, Powell wrote Secretary of the Navy James V. Forrestal, complaining that there were "forces at work at Annapolis Naval Academy that are about to put Wesley Brown out." The letter disturbed Forrestal so much that he went to Annapolis himself to investigate and then wrote Powell to assure him that Cadet Midshipman Brown was doing fine at the Academy. Powell was not surprised; he had "fabricated that letter," he later admitted, to make sure that "nothing would happen to Wesley Brown." Sometime later Powell ran into Forrestal at a cocktail party. "Adam," said Forrestal, "why did you lie to me?" "Jim," said Powell, "I had to lie in order to make sure that Wesley Brown would not be touched by anyone." And so Brown became the first black man to graduate from Annapolis; and he went on to have a successful career in the U.S. Navy.[66]

Preacher as President

In 1960, a few weeks before the Democratic convention met, Louisiana Congressman Hale Boggs presided informally over a get-together of Southern Democratic Congressmen to discuss possible presidential candidates. One Congressman mentioned Jack Kennedy. "No," said Boggs, "He's a Catholic." Another suggested Stuart Symington. "No," said Boggs. "He's too stiff. Can't project himself." Someone else brought up Hubert Humphrey. "No," said Boggs. "Talks too much." Then, for the fun of it Boggs said: "Well, now, what about Adam Clayton Powell?" At this, his colleagues sat in shocked silence. "You're right," said Boggs quickly. "The country's not ready for a Baptist preacher to be President!"[67]

Senator Humphrey's Choice

One night, soon after entering the Senate, Hubert H. Humphrey went to a party with his wife at a fancy place where he was lionized as the "bright, new liberal Senator." Humphrey enjoyed the attention and basked in the praise. But as they drove home afterward, his wife Muriel said, "Hubert, you have to make a choice. Now." Puzzled, Humphrey asked, "What do you mean?" "Well," said Mrs. Humphrey, "you can turn into a social butterfly, a Washington phony, or you can skip this sort of evening and become a good Senator. You have the choice." Humphrey became a good Senator.[68]

Senatorial Etiquette

"If some colleague refers to you as 'the distinguished Senator from Ohio,' consider yourself lucky," Kentucky Senator Alben W. Barkley once told Ohio's Stephen M. Young when Young was new to the Senate. "If this same colleague refers to you as the 'able and distinguished Senator from Ohio,' be on your guard, for the knife is getting sharper. If, however, your colleague refers to you as 'the able and distinguished Senator from Ohio and my good friend,' then duck fast because he's trying to see if the jugular vein is exposed. And, in case your colleague should refer to you as 'my very good friend, the able, distinguished and outstanding Senator from Ohio,' then run for your life!"[69]

Senator Smith Costs Less

When Congresswoman Margaret Chase Smith ran for the Senate in 1948 she was breaking new ground for women. Six women had preceded her in the Senate, but five had been appointed by their state governors to fill the unexpired terms of Senators who had died in office, and the sixth had won an "interim" election and served only two months until the next regular election took place. With her victory at the polls, Margaret Chase Smith became the first woman to win a six-year term in the Senate, the first woman to serve in both houses of Congress, and the first Republican woman to serve in the upper house. After taking her oath of office she found she couldn't use many of the facilities open to her male colleagues—the barbershop, swimming pool, gymnasium—but accepted the deprivation graciously. "I am proud," she said, "that I cost the American taxpayer less money than any of the other Senators."[70]

Mr. Smith Goes to Washington

Brigadier-General William C. Lewis, Jr., Air Force Reserve, was Senator Margaret Chase Smith's assistant and frequently accompanied her on trips. To his embarrassment some of the people they met called him "Mr. Smith." The first time a person did it, he ignored it; and even the second time he overlooked the mistake. But when the same person called him "Mr. Smith" for the third time, he usually placed his hand gently on the person's arm and with a nice smile said softly: "Please don't be so formal. Why don't you just call me Margaret?"[71]

Sabath and Cox

Adolph Sabath of Illinois, chairman of the Rules Committee from 1940 to 1952, once outfoxed the able tactician Eugene Cox of Georgia. Cox, the second ranking Democrat on the committee, wanted to vote on a resolution to change the committee's rules so that any committee member could call up bills for votes even if the chairman objected. Sabath, then in his eighties, begged Cox not to insist on the resolution. His voice breaking, he told Cox he had a weak heart and added: "Mr. Cox, this will kill me, if you pass this resolution. The humiliation! It will kill me!" Cox, leader of the Southern Democrats in the House, refused to yield. "I don't care," he said. "You have delayed this too long." At those words, Sabath abruptly lurched forward, pitched out of his chair, and fell sprawling onto the floor at Cox's feet, where he lay motionless. Cox leaped up in a panic. "My God!" he cried, "I've killed him!" Panic-stricken, he and the other Congressmen carried Sabath into the adjoining office, laid him out on a large leather couch, and then rushed off to get a doctor, leaving Ohio's Clarence Brown to stand watch. Brown, still puffing from the exertion of carrying Sabath into his office, stood watch over the prostrate chairman for a minute or two, and then to his surprise saw Sabath open one of his eyes and steal a look around the room. "Why you old rascal!" cried Brown. "There's nothing wrong with you." "Well," grinned Sabath, "Mr. Cox didn't get his resolution, did he?"[72]

Stephen Young's Disclosure

Members of Congress were not required to reveal their stock holdings, but shortly after entering the Senate in 1959 Ohio's Stephen M. Young decided to disclose his financial holdings in a letter to the secretary of the Senate. He listed all his property, including stocks, and, in addition, explained that he had disposed of his holdings in certain corporations because he thought they would hamper his work on some of the committees to which he was assigned. His decision to declare his assets turned out to be a good break for his wife. She was visiting in Key West, Florida, at the time, was down to her last $8, and asked the manager of the motel where she was staying if he would cash a check. He demanded identification, but when she told him who she was, he said: "That's all right. I just saw your husband's name on the front page of the *Miami Herald*. It says his net worth is $270,000. I think we can take your check."[73]

Senator Green's Appointment

Rhode Island Senator Theodore F. Green had the reputation of attending all the cocktail parties he could in Washington. At one Washington party a woman asked him: "Senator Green, how many cocktail parties have you been to this evening?" "This is my fourth," said Green, and pulled a little notebook out of his pocket and began leafing through it. "Are you checking to see where you're going next?" she asked curiously. "No," he replied. "I'm checking to see where I am now."[74]

Walter Rogers Dresses for the Occasion

Once Texas Congressman Walter E. Rogers (D, 1951–67) accepted an invitation to a fancy affair in Washington and then learned, to his chagrin, that the men were wearing tuxedos for the occasion. But his wife persuaded him to get out his tux, have it dry-cleaned, and promise to wear it. When the day arrived, however, the House held a late session in order to dispose of the annual defense appropriation bill, and as the hours passed Rogers realized he wasn't going to have time to go home and change. But his wife was equal to the occasion; she took the tux to the Capitol and saw to it that he left the floor and made a quick change in his office. When he reappeared in the House chamber in his tux to await the final vote, however, his colleagues started laughing and teasing him. "Gentlemen," he finally said, "when it comes time to vote on a forty-four-billion-dollar appropriation bill, I think we owe it to the taxpayers to dress for the occasion!"[75]

Undivided Attention

Alabama Senator John Sparkman (who was Adlai Stevenson's running mate in 1952) was liked and respected by all his colleagues, but as he got older he tended to doze off at unlikely moments. Once, when he was chairman of the Foreign Relations Committee, he was host at a luncheon for the Prime Minister of Botswana. When the guests finished eating, he got up, made a few brief remarks, and then presented the Prime Minister to the Senators gathered in the committee room. "I'm terribly happy to be here," the Prime Minister began, in his clipped British accent. "The last time I came to America, the attention of the entire nation was focused on Vietnam, and especially on Watergate. I'm afraid the problems of Africa were placed on the rearmost burner." Then, warming to his subject, he went on: "But now, things seem to be totally different. I'm happy to say the concerns of Africa appear to be getting the undivided attention of your government. . . ." At that point, Sparkman, who had been nodding throughout, fell into a deep sleep; his head dropped onto the shoulder of Botswana's Prime Minister and the latter had to push it away.[76]

Notorious

Once a Senator got a call around midnight from the manager of the Willard Hotel, where he was occupying a room. "Senator," said the manager, "you have a woman in that room with you and you are registered as a single occupant. I thought I should inform you, sir, that the house detective is quite disturbed." To this the Senator said: "I'll have you know that the young lady is my secretary and I don't appreciate being disturbed." With that he banged down the receiver. A few minutes later the manager rang the room again. "Senator," he murmured, "I apologize once more for disturbing you, but I think you ought to know that the woman in your room is really a most notorious prostitute known all down Pennsylvania Avenue as such. For the sake of your own career and reputation I tell you this." "Notorious!" cried the Senator. "Notorious, you say! Why, I had no idea! I'll discharge her in the morning!"[77]

Stubbing Toe in the Senate

The popular notion that the Senate was some kind of secret society in which members protected each other no matter what irked Prescott Bush, Connecticut Senator whose son George became President in 1989. Once Senator Bush was entertaining some of his constituents in the reception room of the Senate, and one of the women asked: "Is it true, Senator Bush, that the Senate is the most exclusive club in the world?" "Well, that could possibly be said," replied Bush solemnly. "We all call each other by our first names. We treat each other with scrupulous courtesy. We and our wives occasionally get together socially. But," he added vehemently, "if one of our members stubs his toe, WE EAT him!"[78]

Sober Spells

It was never a secret that at any given time a fair number of Congressmen had a drinking problem and that sometimes it affected their performance. An old Congressional riddle went this way: "What's the difference between a discussion and a fight?" The answer: "Six Bourbons." South Carolina's L. Mendel Rivers was a major target of Congressional wits. One Congressman would say: "I never knew Mendel Rivers drank until I saw him sober," and the other would respond: "Yeah, he has sober spells."[79]

No Class

Democratic Congressman F. Edward Hébert of Louisiana was so pleased when his rise to seniority led him to be assigned a nice new office with a small entryway that he proudly installed a little fountain in the latter. Some of his colleagues were envious, until they heard about the put-down by one of Hébert's constituents. The man had come up from New Orleans and been shown around the office by Hébert himself. "Well, it is all right," he said afterward, "but the man ain't go no class. He keeps a urinal right in his outer office."[80]

Green's Pet Bill

When Senate Majority Leader Lyndon Johnson arrived home one night after a late session, his wife who had just come in from a dance, exclaimed: "I don't see why you can't take some time off for fun, Lyndon. All the other Senators do. Why, Senator Green, who is so much older than you, was there and having a fine time. I danced with him twice." "Senator Green!" exploded LBJ in laughter. "It was passing his pet bill through the Senate that kept me at work so late tonight!"[81]

LBJ's Special Gift

After the Congressional elections of 1958, a large number of new Democrats entered the Senate and several of them were assigned to New Hampshire Republican Norris Cotton's Committee on Commerce, where Republican losses had been heavy. One day Cotton was meeting in a subcommittee with several of the newcomers and noticed they were all wearing large silver cuff links bearing the seal of the Senate. When he asked about them, one of the Senators explained that on a recent trip to Mexico Democratic Majority Leader Lyndon B. Johnson had procured a supply of cuff links there, had them inscribed with the Senate seal, and then presented a pair to each of the new Senators. Soon afterward, however, Cotton began noticing similar cuff links worn by a large number of other Senators, both Republicans and Democrats.

At length Cotton's turn came. One day, when he happened to be in the elevator with Johnson, the latter cried, "Norris, I have been looking for you. Come into my office for a minute." When they got to the office, LBJ opened a drawer in his desk, took out a small cardboard package, and announced dramatically: "Norris, when I was in Mexico recently, I had some cuff links made to give to a few personal friends in the Senate. I consider you one of my particular friends, and this is the first opportunity I have had to present them to you." Cotton expressed thanks and assured LBJ he would cherish them.

About three weeks later Cotton bumped into LBJ again in the Capitol and the latter grabbed him by the shoulder and cried, "Norris, I have been looking for you. Come into my office." Then he took Cotton into his office, opened a desk drawer, produced the cardboard package, and, using the same words he had used on the previous occasion, presented Cotton with a second pair of cuff links. The cuff links may have been special, Cotton concluded, but LBJ had distributed so many of them that he could no longer remember who had received them and who had not.[82]

Dirksen's Marigold

Illinois Senator Everett Dirksen loved flowers, particularly marigolds, and every spring he made a speech in the Senate proposing the marigold as America's national flower. "It is as sprightly as the daffodil," he exclaimed in one speech, "as colorful as the rose, as resolute as the zinnia, as delicate as the chrysanthemum, as aggressive as the petunia, as ubiquitous as the violet, and as stately as the snapdragon. It beguiles the senses and ennobles the spirit of man. . . . Since it is native to America and nowhere else in the world, and common to every state in the Union, I present the American marigold for designation as the national floral emblem of our country." He never succeeded in having his proposal adopted, but he always drew large crowds when he launched into his marigold speech.

While Dirksen crusaded to make the marigold our national flower, Maine Senator Margaret Chase Smith waged an equally aggressive campaign for the rose. When Dirksen died in 1969, the entire Senate, along with members of the House and many of the President's Cabinet heads, accompanied his body to see it laid to rest in his hometown of Pekin. Just before the graveside service began, Senator Smith approached the coffin and gently laid a marigold on it.[83]

Young, Too

In 1962, when Edward M. ("Ted") Kennedy was first elected to the Senate at the age of thirty, he paid a courtesy call on Georgia's venerable Richard Russell. "You were young, too, when you were elected to the Senate," Kennedy told him. "Yes, I was," said Russell, with an avuncular smile. "But by that time I had been governor of Georgia, and before that, Speaker of the Georgia House of Representatives for four years." Kennedy changed the subject.[84]

The American Family

In 1973, when beef prices were soaring, Chicago Congressman Frank Annunzio introduced an amendment in the House Banking and Currency Committee that froze the price of beef, and succeeded in getting it adopted. Afterwards, *Wall Street Journal* reporter Al Hunt interviewed him and asked for his comment on the amendment. "This is a victory for the American people," Annunzio told him contentedly. But overnight the beef lobby went into action and the next day the committee voted to reconsider Annunzio's amendment and rejected the freeze on beef prices. Reporter Hunt at once sought another interview with Annunzio and asked for his reaction to the vote to reconsider. "The American people got fucked," Annunzio said tartly. "I can't put that quote in," Hunt protested. "This is a family newspaper." "Then," said Annunzio, "tell 'em the American family got fucked!"[85]

IV

* * * * * * * *

Oratory

* 📖 *

Years ago—in the 1820s, to be more precise—a Senator who prided himself on his public speaking once asked Virginia Congressman John Randolph of Roanoke: "What have you to remark, sir, about my oratory?" "Nothing, sir," said Randolph in his abrupt way. "It is not remarkable."[1] He could have said the same of most speeches in the House and Senate, including many of his own lengthy and frequently helter-skelter outpourings. But sometimes Randolph himself was stunningly eloquent; and on occasion both he and some of his colleagues held their audiences, including visitors in the galleries, bewitched for hours on end.

Until the age of ghostwriters, media consultants, opinion pollsters, and TelePrompTers, the American people took speech-making seriously. They flocked to campaign rallies where celebrated speakers like Henry Clay, Daniel Webster, and William Jennings Bryan were scheduled to appear; they crowded the galleries of the House and the Senate when lawmakers noted for their eloquence announced they were going to hold forth at some appointed hour on a public issue of consequence; and they devoured books of oratory, like *The Columbian Orator* (many editions) containing masterpieces such as Webster's reply to Hayne, and saw to it that school children committed the best of them to memory.

Congressional orators responded to the vogue for elocution with verve and imagination. They worked hard to live up to public expectations. When Martin Van Buren left the Senate in 1828 and arranged to sell his household furniture at auction, some of the customers noticed that the carpet in front of the large looking-glass in his study was worn threadbare; it was where he had stood when rehearsing his Senate speeches.[2] Massachusetts Senator Charles Sumner was just as conscientious about his

70

speech-making. Before he delivered his famous blast against slavery, "The Crime Against Kansas," in May 1856, he carefully wrote out his remarks (they take up 112 pages in print), rehearsed the address aloud, memorized it, and then spent two days delivering it grandiloquently to a crowded Senate floor and jam-packed gallery. He never dreamed that his cracks at Mississippi Senator Andrew Butler, only a minor part of his oration, would provoke Preston Brooks, a relative of Butler's in the House, into attacking him with a cane.

Pennsylvania's Thaddeus Stevens, Sumner's anti-slavery co-worker, once minimized the importance of Congressional declamations. "I seldom listen to speeches," he said. "I always listen to bills, from which I can find out something, which I seldom ever can from speeches."[3] But Stevens himself spoke blazingly at times and moved his listeners to both anger and applause. And so did the other great Congressional orators: Clay, Webster, Benton, Calhoun, Douglas, Seward, Blaine, Reed, LaFollette, Borah. At crucial intervals, thoughtfully composed addresses in the House and Senate did make a difference in molding opinions, mustering votes, and in shaping legislation. From the beginning there was, to be sure, plenty of bombast in both houses; the word, bunk, soon appeared to describe Congressional word-mongering. But from the outset there was also plenty of splendid oratory: speeches carefully prepared, movingly delivered, and, when it seemed appropriate, delightfully hilarious as well.

In 1894, when the House was debating a bill for lowering the tariff sponsored by William L. Wilson, a Democrat from West Virginia and chairman of the Ways and Means Committee, there was opposition among some of the Democrats as well as from the Republicans, most of whom subscribed to their party's protectionist doctrine; the outlook for the bill was not good. Toward the end of the debate, Maine's Thomas Reed delivered a powerful attack on the bill, and then Wilson himself rose to defend his handiwork. He began quietly enough, but as he proceeded he became deeply moved by the free-trade gospel animating his views and ended with a passionate plea for passage of the bill. "This is not a battle over percentages, over this or that tariff schedule," he exclaimed. "It is a battle for human freedom. . . . This is a roll of honor. This is a roll of freedom, and in the name of honor and in the name of freedom, I summon every Democratic member of this House to subscribe his name to it!" Wilson's speech produced an uproar; and when he tried to take his seat three Congressmen—Virginia's Henry St. George Tucker, Nebraska's William Jennings Bryan, and Mississippi's John Sharp Williams—rushed over, lifted him onto their shoulders, and paraded him triumphantly out of the House. A little later, when the roll was called, at least twenty Democrats who had been critical of the bill voted in favor of it and the bill carried. "An hour ago," New York's John DeWitt Warner told Missouri's Champ Clark, "those men had no more idea of voting for that bill than flying." Never again, Clark said afterwards, would he doubt that speeches could change votes.[4]

Champ Clark thought the severest test of oratory was to elicit applause from a hostile audience. But Daniel Webster, an orator who faced audiences both friendly and hostile, tended to take a more romantic view of the art. "True eloquence does not consist in speech," he declared. "It cannot be brought from afar. Labor and learning may toil for it, but they will toil in vain. Words and phrases may be marshaled in every way, but they cannot compass it. It must exist in the man, in the subject, and in the occasion. Affected passion, intense expression, the pomp of declamation, all may aspire to it; they cannot reach it. It comes, if it comes at all, like the outbreaking of a fountain from the earth or the bursting forth of volcanic fires, with spontaneous original native force."[5]

In the twentieth century, "skyscraping orations," as Champ Clark called them, fell gradually into desuetude. To the modern sensibility the volcanic eloquence which Webster celebrated came to seem hyperventilated, grotesque, even funny. There was, to be sure, a great deal of affection in the 1950s and 1960s for Illinois Senator Everett Dirksen's old-fashioned outpourings; but this probably came less from nostalgia for the ancient ways of speaking than to their resemblance to film comedian W. C. Fields' take-offs on the old-time solemnities. The new rule—for there are always rules—was the staff-researched, group-prepared, ghost-written text delivered efficiently by a Congressman trained, perhaps, by public-speaking expert Dorothy Sarnoff in the niceties of speech dynamics.[6]

☆   ☆   ☆

Fisher Ames' Speech on Jay's Treaty

In 1796 the debate in Congress over Jay's Treaty produced one of the most famous addresses ever delivered by a Congressman: Fisher Ames' speech urging the House of Representatives to appropriate funds for implementing some of the provisions of the treaty with Britain. Joseph Priestley, British scientist who had heard Pitt, Burke, and Fox hold forth in the House of Commons, listened to Ames' speech in the House gallery and pronounced it "the most bewitching piece of parliamentary oratory" he had ever heard.[7]

Jay's Treaty represented President Washington's effort to preserve peace with Britain, which, at war with France, was interfering with America's rights on the high seas and unwilling to make any serious concessions to the young nation's sensibilities. The pro-administration Federalists in Congress acknowledged the treaty's shortcomings, but supported it as an alternative to war; the anti-administration Republicans dismissed it as a sellout to America's old enemy and castigated negotiator John Jay as a near-traitor. Despite Republican opposition, the Senate ratified the treaty by a close vote in June 1795, and in March 1796 Washington sent it to the House with a request for funds to activate the agreement. House Republicans balked at voting the money. First, they asked to see all the treaty papers, which Washington, asserting executive privilege, refused to give them; next, they sought to deny Washington the funds he needed to carry the treaty into effect. "All America," Secretary of State Thomas Jefferson wrote a friend, "is a tip-toe to see what the House of Representatives will decide on it."[8] Congressional Republicans, led by Virginia's James Madison, argued so persuasively against Jay's Treaty, as it came to be called, that the Federalists despaired of mustering enough votes to support the President. "Here, we dance upon the edge of the pit," Massachusetts Federalist Fisher Ames wailed; "it is but a little way to the bottom." Ames lamented that a recent illness had left him too feeble to take an active role in fighting for the appropriation.[9]

But it was to the frail and sickly Ames that the Federalists at length decided to turn for help. A member of Congress since 1789, the fifty-one-year-old conservative was known for his wit, erudition, and masterful way with words, as well as for his deep devotion to President Washington and the Federalist cause. "Is Ames sick . . . ?" queried New Hampshire's William Plumer. "I hope he will be able to attend and . . . make a display of that eloquence and intelligence so rare in this country."[10] Pressed hard by his Federalist confreres, Ames finally agreed to speak for the treaty. And on April 28, when word got out that he was about to address the House, Congressmen began hurrying to their seats in the House Chamber; and Vice President John Adams rushed over from the Senate to join Supreme Court Justice James Iredell and all the other people who had gathered in the galleries for the occasion, including (for the first time) several women, among them Adams' wife Abigail.

"Mr. Chairman," began Ames quietly, when the chamber was still, "I entertain the hope, perhaps a rash one, that my strength will hold me out to speak a few minutes."[11] These words electrified the audience; and soon, as he launched into a defense of the treaty, his colleagues and people in the galleries were listening with fascinated attention to his impassioned plea for peace with Britain. "It was a masterly display of the highest kind of eloquence," Jeremiah Mason recalled years later. "After the House had been . . . tired almost to death with discussions of the most talented men in the nation," said Mason, Ames "revived and excited the highest state of feeling, and was heard with the most profound interest."[12] Ames, said another observer, "addressed himself to every faculty of the mind. . . . Argument, remonstrance, entreaty, persuasion, terror, and warning fell now like music and now like the thunder of heaven from his lips. . . . He threw a spell over the senses, rendering them insensible to everything but himself."[13]

In his speech Ames reminded the House that the choice was "Treaty or war," and that the treaty wasn't all bad and that war with Britain would be far worse. The young republic needed peace, he insisted, to develop unity and strength, and if the House rejected funds for the treaty and thus embroiled the nation in war, "even I, slender and almost broken as my hold upon life is, may outlive the Government and the Constitution." Before he finished, Ames spoke an hour and a half, without notes, and even anti-treaty Republicans were deeply moved by his way of putting things. "Let us not hesitate, then, to agree to the appropriation . . . ," he cried, at the end. "Thus we shall save the faith of our nation, secure its peace, and diffuse the spirit of confidence and enterprise that will augment its prosperity."[14]

The response was overwhelming. "My God, how great he is . . . ," Justice Iredell breathed when Ames resumed his seat. "Bless my stars, I never heard anything so great since I was born!"[15] New Hampshire Congressman Jeremiah Smith told Ames afterward that his speech was so moving "that he ought to have died in the fifth act; that he will never have an occasion so glorious; having lost this, he will now be obliged to make his exit like other men."[16] Even Pennsylvania Republican Albert Gallatin, hostile to the treaty, acknowledged that Ames' was the "most brilliant and eloquent speech" delivered during the treaty debate.[17]

The day after Ames spoke the House voted, fifty-one to forty-eight, to appropriate funds for the treaty; and Ames, now feeling better physically as well as emotionally, told friends he saw "nothing but blue sky" for his country after that.[18] His speech became legendary; for years it was re-garded as one of the greatest speeches ever made in Congress.

Aaron Burr's Farewell Address

One of the most highly praised speeches delivered to the Senate during its early years was Aaron Burr's. Burr was not in good repute at the time; he had killed Alexander Hamilton in a duel a few months earlier, and both New York and New Jersey had issued indictments against him. But he had presided over the impeachment trial of Justice Samuel Chase with fairness and dignity, and his term as Thomas Jefferson's Vice President was now coming to an end. The Chase trial ended in acquittal on March 1, 1805, and on March 4 George Clinton was to replace Burr as Vice President. On March 2, around one o'clock, Burr rose from his chair and, to the surprise of the Senators, announced he had a sore throat and wanted to make some remarks before leaving early. "Every gentleman was silent," New York Senator Samuel Mitchill wrote later, "not a whisper was heard, and the deepest concern was manifested."

In his farewell speech, Burr reminisced informally about his years as presiding officer over the Senate. He admitted he had made some mistakes in his rulings; he also apologized for any offense his conduct in the chair may have given any of the Senators, and reminded them that he had "always tried to be fair and impartial." He went on to urge the Senate to continue observing the rules and decorum he had encouraged governing debates, even though "the ignorant look upon such matters as unnecessary and trivial." The Senate, he declared, was "a sanctuary, a citadel of law, of order and of liberty . . . and if the Constitution be destined ever to perish by the sacrilegious hands of the demagogue or the usurper, which God avert, its expiring agonies will be witnessed on this floor."

When Burr finished, he descended from the chair, walked to the door, and closed it behind him. "He did not speak to them, perhaps, longer than twenty minutes or half an hour," Senator Mitchill wrote his wife a little later, "but he did it with so much tenderness, knowledge and concern that it wrought upon the sympathy of the Senators in a very uncommon manner. . . . There was a solemn and silent weeping for perhaps five minutes." Mitchill himself was profoundly moved by Burr's performance. "For my own part," he said, "I never experienced anything of the kind so affecting me as this parting scene of the Vice President from the Senate in which he had served for six years as a Senator and four years as a presiding officer. My colleague, General Smith, stout and manly as he is, wept as profusely as I did. He laid his head upon his table and did not recover from his emotion for a quarter of an hour or more. And for myself, though it is more than three hours since Burr went away, I have scarcely recovered my habitual calmness. . . . He is a most uncommon man, and I regret more deeply than ever the sad series of events which have removed him from public usefulness and confidence. . . . Burr is one of the best presiding officers that ever presided over a deliberative assembly. Where he is going or how he is to get through with his difficulties I know not."

After Burr left the Senators adopted a unanimous resolution thanking him for "the impartiality and ability with which he has presided over their deliberations" and assuring him of their "entire approbation of his conduct in the discharge of the arduous and important duties assigned to him as President of the Senate." The *Washington Federalist* called Burr's farewell "the most dignified, sublime, and impressive that ever was uttered." It may have been Burr's finest hour.[19]

John Randolph on Oratory

In the early nineteenth century Virginia's John Randolph was one of the great Congressional orators. "His voice is loud and shrill, yet melodious," reported Anne Royall, the popular travel writer, "and his gestures pertinent and graceful; never at a loss, his language is flowing, refined and classical, his remarks brief and cutting." One day Massachusetts Congressman Josiah Quincy got into a conversation with him about oratory and finally asked him who was the finest orator he had ever heard. "The greatest orator I ever heard was a woman," Randolph told him. "She was a slave. She was a mother, and her rostrum was the auction-block." Then he got up and in moving words imitated the way the slave mother had appealed to the compassion of the bystanders for her anguish at having her children sold away from her; and he recalled the passionate indignation with which she finally denounced the slave traffickers. "*There* was eloquence!" Randolph exclaimed when he finished. "I have heard no man speak like that. It was overpowering!" Then he sat down and was silent for a moment; but suddenly, as if recalling that he was talking to an anti-slavery Northerner, he launched into a defense of the South's "peculiar institution."[20]

Bunk

During the debate over the Missouri Compromise, every Congressman felt obliged to put his two cents in so as to please his constituents, and the speeches became increasingly banal and boring as the controversy dragged on. Finally, on February 25, 1820, when Felix Walker, an obscure Congressman from a North Carolina district that included Buncombe County, got up to speak, members of the House refused to listen to him. Walker then reportedly explained that the voters in his district expected him to say something about Missouri and that he needed to "make a speech for Buncombe." The phrase, "speaking for Buncombe," at once became popular in Washington and eventually ended up as "bunkum" or just plain "bunk."[21]

Webster: "Expounder of the Constitution"

Daniel Webster had a majestic appearance: broad shoulders, stalwart frame, massive head, heavy eyebrows, and a wealth of black hair. "I have seen a man!" breathed soprano Jenny Lind, the "Swedish nightingale," after she first caught a glimpse of him. He was "a living lie," it was said, "because no man could be as great as he looked."[22] His swarthy complexion won him the nickname "Black Dan," but his New England admirers referred to him as "the godlike Daniel." He was also known as the "Defender of the Constitution" and, better still, as "the Great Expounder of the Constitution." As Representative, Senator, and lawyer handling cases before the Supreme Court, he emphasized the nationalizing tendencies of the great document of 1787.

Webster loved playing with words. When New York's Charles H. Ruggles asked him if he had seen the junction of the Missouri and the Mississippi, he cried: "There is no junction. The Missouri seizes the Mississippi, and carries it captive to New Orleans." On another occasion, when Ruggles was holding forth on the importance of the Mississippi as an indissoluble bond of national union and spoke of it as "the great fact of this country," Webster responded: "Sir, it may be a great fact; but let me tell you, the great chain of lakes is a very *broad hint!*" Talking to his friend John Trout one day, Webster said: "John, you are an amphibious animal." When Trout asked what he meant, Webster said gaily: "It means, John, an animal that lies equally well on land and on water!"[23]

But Webster did more than turn out neat phrases and amusing quips. He poured deep feeling into his speeches, whether in Congress or in the courtroom, especially when talking about the American Union. Two of his Senate speeches became legendary: his second response to Robert Hayne in 1830 and his speech supporting the Compromise of 1850. For the first (putting the Union above states' rights) he won admiration from Unionists; for the second (putting the Union above the anti-slavery cause), excoriation from abolitionists.

The Reverend William Pinkney, son of the Maryland diplomat of the same name, found Webster's oratory irresistible. "He was calm, collected, deliberate in the main," Pinkney recalled a few years after Webster's death; "and yet his great soul was sometimes roused, and his lion spirit stirred; and then there was the lightning flash in his eye, and the thunder tone on his tongue. At such times, there was an awful sublimity in his thoughts, and a bold, massive structure in his style, that were admirably adapted to the occasion. He bore down, like a roused lion, upon his antagonist, and desperate and well-timed were the blows of his stalwart arm. He was master of every passion, and his countenance glowed with the most varying expression. I was privileged to witness one of those noblest bursts of oratorical power. . . . Never shall I forget the withering scorn, the biting sarcasm, the deep affecting pathos and fearful sublimity, that alternately thrilled and delighted the rapt assembly."[24]

Webster's Reply to Hayne

In 1830 Daniel Webster achieved oratorical immortality. That was the year of the celebrated Webster-Hayne debate which dramatized the nation's steadily deepening sectional cleavage.

The debate began almost by accident. Late in December 1829 Connecticut's Samuel A. Foote introduced a resolution in the Senate restricting the sale of public lands, and when the Senate got around to discussing it in January 1830, Missouri's Thomas Hart Benton delivered an angry speech charging that Foote's proposal was an attempt to check the development of the West; he also castigated New England for hostility to emigration to the West and appealed to the South to support his part of the country. The following day South Carolina's Robert Y. Hayne, a disciple of John C. Calhoun and, next to Calhoun, the South's ablest debater, came to Benton's support, denounced New England, particularly Massachusetts, as vehemently as Benton had, and called for an alliance between the West and the South, not only on public-lands policy, but on the tariff as well. Daniel Webster, returning to the Senate from arguing a case before the Supreme Court, happened to hear Hayne's speech, and resolved at once to join the debate both to defend his own section and to uphold the nationalist view of the American Union. By this time everyone had forgotten about the Foote resolution and it was eventually dropped.

Some people wondered whether Webster was equal to the task; Hayne's address was shrewd, informed, and skillfully presented. But Webster was supremely confident, for in several cases he had argued before the Supreme Court he had carefully formulated his views on the issues involved. When the news spread that Webster was going to respond to Hayne all Washington was agog. "Almost everyone is thronging to the Capitol to hear Mr. Webster reply to Col. Hayne's attack on him and his party," reported Margaret Bayard Smith, Washington society leader. "A debate on any political principle would have had no such attraction. But personalities are irresistible. It is a kind of moral gladiatorship, in which characters are torn to pieces, and arrows, yes, poisoned arrows . . . are hurled by the combatants against each other. The Senate chamber, is the present arena and never were the amphitheatres of Rome more crowded by the highest ranks of both sexes than the Senate chamber is. Every seat, every inch of ground, even the steps, were *compactly* filled, and yet not space enough for the ladies—the senators were obliged to relinquish their chairs of State to the fair auditors who literally sat in the Senate. . . . Yesterday there were 300 ladies besides their attendant beaux on the floor of the Senate."[25]

Webster's first reply to Hayne—a defense of Massachusetts and of the Northeast in general—came on January 20 and was enormously effective. But Hayne's response to Webster was, if anything, even more impressive. Encouraged by John C. Calhoun, who, as Vice President, presided over the proceedings and from time to time sent notes to Hayne containing suggestions, Hayne made a bold defense of the nullification theory. "Hayne bore down in a strain of eloquence alternately grave, indignant and witty, upon the Senator from Massachusetts," observed a New York Congressman seated in the gallery, "the like of which I have never witnessed and which, as I thought, completely demolished him. Webster suffered. He seemed uneasy in his seat; sometimes he took notes—then audibly dissented, anon assented, and occasionally leaned back in his chair." But the New Yorker's misgivings—and those of Webster's friends—turned out to be needless. When Edward Everett called on Webster that evening he found him in good spirits. "Did you take notes of Mr. Hayne's speech?" he asked anxiously. "Yes," said Webster, showing him a piece of paper. "I have it all.

This is his speech." When Judge Joseph Story offered to help assemble material to answer Hayne's arguments, Webster politely declined. "Give yourself no uneasiness, Judge Story," he said. "I will grind him as fine as a punch of snuff."[26]

At noon on January 26, when Webster was ready to deliver his second reply to Hayne, the Senate chamber was, if anything, even more crowded than it was the last time he spoke. Alabama Congressman Dixon H. Lewis, a mountain of a man, rushed over to the Senate with the other Congressmen and got wedged in the mass of people behind Vice President Calhoun's chair, where he could neither see nor hear Webster. But by slow and strenuous efforts, pausing occasionally to take deep breaths, he managed to get to one of the painted-glass windows flanking the Vice President's chair on both sides. There he stopped, unable to make any more headway through the crowd, but, still determined to get a good view of Webster, he got out his knife, made a large hole in one of the panes of glass, and was able to peek at the great orator while he was replying to Hayne. Lewis was himself an ardent states-righter like Hayne, but he didn't want to miss out on what he knew was a big event.

In his second reply to Hayne, which took two days to deliver, Webster rejected Calhoun's "compact" theory of the Union out of hand. The government of the United States, he insisted, was an agent of the American people, not of the various state governments. "It is, sir," he cried, in a passage foreshadowing Abraham Lincoln, "the people's Constitution, the people's government, made for the people, made by the people, and answerable to the people." States-righters might talk of "Liberty first and Union afterwards," he exclaimed in his passionate peroration, but for most Americans it was "Liberty and Union, now and forever, one and inseparable!"[27]

When Webster finished, Vice President Calhoun rapped his gavel and called, "Order! Order!" But his gesture was gratuitous, for Webster's vast audience sat in silence for a moment or two, almost as if bewitched, when Webster was done, and then began to leave the Senate chamber quietly. "Mr. Webster," said a Southern Senator, as Webster took his seat, "I think you had better die now and rest your fame on that speech!" But Hayne at once interposed: "You ought not to die. A man who can make such speeches as that ought never to die."[28] When the two Senators met that night at a White House reception, they politely shook hands. "How are you this evening, Colonel Hayne?" murmured Webster. "None the better for you," sighed Hayne.[29]

The Old Man and Webster's Reply to Hayne

Webster was apparently surprised and moved when he heard about the response of Captain John Thomas, an elderly friend who had fought in the

Revolutionary War, to his encounter with Hayne. The old man, he learned, read Hayne's first speech when it appeared in the *Columbian Sentinel* and then devoured Webster's reply to it with delight. But when he read Hayne's second speech in the next issue of the *Sentinel,* he was plunged into gloom, for its reasoning seemed so cogent that he strongly doubted Webster could come up with a convincing reply. He threw the paper away, retired to his bedroom, and, though his family tried to cheer him up, remained inconsolable for the next few days. "It can't be answered, Henry," he is reported to have told his son. "It can't be answered."

In due course came the next issue of the *Sentinel,* containing Webster's second reply to Hayne, and Henry took it up to the old man at once. "Father, I have brought you the *Sentinel,*" he said, "I thought you might like to look at it." "No, Henry" sighed the old fellow. "I don't want to see it." "It contains the second speech of Mr. Webster, in reply to Colonel Hayne," pressed the son. "Oh, Henry!" cried the father, "it is of no use; it can't be answered; I don't want to see it." Henry finally left, joined the rest of the family below, and discussed ways of bringing the old soldier out of his depression. Suddenly they were startled to hear a tremendous shout from the father's bedroom; and, rushing upstairs, they found the old man sitting on the side of his bed, with the *Sentinel* in one hand and a candle in the other. "Bring me my boots, Henry!" crowed the father as they entered the room. "Bring me my boots!" He was so overjoyed by Webster's stirring reply to Hayne's second speech that he talked about it for days.[30]

The Triumvirate: Clay, Webster, Calhoun

In January 1840, William Mathews, author of books on American oratory, spent two weeks in Washington where he heard speeches by all the leading men in both houses of Congress. He regarded Webster's reply to Hayne as the greatest speech ever made in America, but he thought that Kentucky's Henry Clay was on the whole the greatest orator of them all, except perhaps for Patrick Henry. His first day in Washington he spent in the House where the debate became so heated that Congressmen shook fists at each other and gave invitations to "coffee and pistols," and the Speaker called for adjournment to keep things from getting out of hand.

Mathews next tried the Senate. He had no sooner entered the gallery when he heard a voice which he thought sounded like "the music of the spheres." It came, he wrote later, "from the lips of a tall, well-formed man, with a wide mouth, a flashing eye, and a countenance that revealed every change of thought within. It had a wonderful flexibility and compass, at one moment crashing upon the ear in thunder-peals, and the next falling in music as soft as that of 'summer winds a-wooing the flowers.' It rarely startled the hearer, however, with violent contrasts of pitch, and was equally distinct and clear when it rang out in trumpet tones, and when it sank to the lowest whisper. Every syllable, we had almost said, every letter, was perfectly audible, and as 'musical as is Apollo's lute.' There was not a word of rant, not one tone of vociferation; in the very climax of his passion he spoke deliberately, and his outpouring of denunciation was as slow and steady as the tread of Nemesis. He gesticulated all over. As he spoke, he stepped forward and backward with effect; and the nodding of his head, hung on a long neck,—his arms, hands, fingers, feet, and even his spectacles and blue handkerchief, aided him in debate. Who could it be? It took but a minute to answer the question. It was,—it *could* be no other than— Henry Clay. He had just begun an attack on another giant of the Senate; and the scene of intellectual fence that followed, during which they cut and thrust, lunged at each other and parried, some half-a-dozen times, is one of those that root themselves forever in the memory. Indeed, their very words have clung like burs to our recollection."

Clay was at this point taking on another master of speech: South Carolina's John C. Calhoun. Calhoun's oratory was quite different from Clay's. The great nullifier lacked Clay's ease, grace, and charm; his forte was power of analysis, intense earnestness, and depth of conviction. "Clay's words, when assailing an enemy," Mathews observed, "were usually courteous and polished, while Calhoun's were fierce, blunt, and rudely terrible." As for Daniel Webster, the third of the great Senatorial triumvirate, his strength, Mathews decided, lay in his grasp of facts and skill in arranging them. On small subjects—at public dinners or on parade day— Webster was dull as dishwater and floundered "like a whale in a frog-pond." On big subjects, however, he was a Titan; he was "like a mighty line-of-battle ship, which is not easily set in motion, but whose guns, when she is once fairly engaged, crush everything opposed to her."[31]

Sesquipedalian Speech-maker

When Virginia's pedantic William S. Archer entered the Senate, his preference for "dictionary words" soon became a source of amusement among his colleagues. His ideas flowed sluggishly, clothed as they were in "words of awful length and thundering sound," and most of the time people had difficulty following his line of thought. Daniel Webster heartily disliked grandiloquence and *sesquipedalia verba* in public speaking and was quite put off by Archer's pronouncements. "What sort of a fellow is this new Virginia Senator?" he asked South Carolina's Colonel Preston one day."Do you know him?" "Yes," replied Preston, "very well; and a very clever fellow he is. What do you think of him?" "Why," Webster replied impatiently, "I dined with him today, and think him a preposterous aggregation of heterogeneous paradoxes and perdurable peremptorences!"[32]

Clay's Pause

When speaking in public Henry Clay usually became completely absorbed in his theme. "I do not know how it is with others," he once said, "but on such occasions, I seem to be unconscious of the external world. Wholly engrossed by the subject before me, I lose all sense of personal identity, of time, or of surrounding objects." Clay's "thunder," it was said, was rarely "checked in mid volley" for lack of thought or words. But once, when addressing the Virginia legislature, he began to quote the famous lines of Sir Walter Scott, beginning "Breathes there a man," and then suddenly stopped, unable to recall the rest of the passage. Closing his eyes, he pressed his forehead with the palm of his hand, to aid his memory, and became silent. But the audience thought he had stopped because he was overcome by the power and intensity of his feelings and was deeply moved by the spectacle. In a few moments the lines came to his lips and he pronounced them: "Breathes there a man with soul so dead, Who never to himself hath said, This is my own, my native land!" A "profound sensation pervaded the assembly," at this point, it was said, and most of the people there were in tears.[33]

Shallowest Place

One of Mississippi Congressman Robert W. Roberts' constituents took him to task for taking so little part in House debates while other Congressmen made many speeches and attracted a lot of national attention. "Well, my friend," said Roberts, "I will tell you. When I was a young man I used to ride a good deal at night, and frequently got lost. Whenever I came to the bank of a stream, I put my ear to the ground, and ascertained where the water made the noise; at that place I always marched in—it was sure to be the shallowest place!"[34]

Old Man Eloquent: John Quincy Adams

John Quincy Adams was the only President to serve in Congress after leaving the Executive Mansion; he was also the only President, and only Congressman too, to give a series of lectures (at Harvard as a young man) and publish a book on the subject of eloquence, which he regarded as indispensable in a free society. But as Congressman from Massachusetts Adams didn't pay much attention to the principles he laid down in his *Lectures on Rhetoric and Oratory* (1810). Where the book opposed appealing to the emotions, Adams filled his speeches in the House with anger, sarcasm, indignation, outrage, and contempt. The speeches produced anger and indignation, too, but they also won grudging admiration, even from his bitterest enemies. He came finally to be known as "Old Man Eloquent."

In 1846 Adams suffered a paralytic stroke; and although he was finally able to return to the House, with his intellect undimmed, his body was frail and his voice reduced to a whisper. Occasionally when he heard things said that he didn't like, he forgot his infirmities and tried to rise; then he abandoned the attempt, but looked at the speaker in such a way that it was clear that the man speaking was lucky Adams couldn't reply. "In the galleries and in the House itself," observed one Congressman, "it came to be understood that the color of Adams' head was the index of his feelings, it often becoming as red as living coals of fire under the violent declamations of Southern men." Once, a Southern fire-eater was vehemently denouncing Northern anti-slavery men, and Adams' head began firing up with his usual indignation. Suddenly, a waggish Congressman told the speaker: "He says you are lying." The speaker stopped and cried angrily, "Who says I am lying?" "Adams!" cried several Congressmen. As the House broke up in laughter, Adams put his hand on his head and nodded, as if to say, "I do say he was lying!"[35]

Tom Corwin's Face

Ohio Congressman Thomas Corwin's oratory in the 1840s became something of a legend in Congressional history. His witty speech in the House on February 15, 1840, replying to General Isaac Crary's attack on William Henry Harrison, Whig candidate for President, was so devastating that a few days later John Quincy Adams referred to the latter in a speech as "the late General Crary of Michigan." Corwin's speech on February 11, 1847, denouncing the Mexican War as unjust and predicting a sectional conflict growing out of U.S. acquisition of Mexican territory was also famous; it won him both praise and condemnation. Corwin thought his propensity for humor in his speeches blighted his career; but his bold anti-war speech during the conflict with Mexico probably hurt him even more.

Years after Corwin's death in 1865, Champ Clark, Congressman from Missouri and Speaker of the House for a time, checked a collection of Corwin's speeches out of the Congressional library and turned eagerly to the speech ridiculing General Crary. To his surprise he found the speech a disappointment; while not exactly dull, it fell far short, in his opinion, of the high rank assigned it by tradition. Somewhat puzzled, he sought out Ohio's Charles H. Grosvenor, one of his older colleagues, and asked him whether he had ever read Corwin's speech on General Crary, and when Grosvenor replied in the affirmative Clark told him: "One of two things is true; either that report [of the speech] is not correct or Corwin is vastly overrated as a humorist." "Neither proposition is true," replied Grosvenor. "Tom Corwin was not overrated, but no report of his humorous speeches, however accurate, will sustain his reputation. His wonderful effect upon an audience depended more upon his marvelous facial expression than upon anything he said."

Grosvenor went on the tell Clark a story about Corwin to illustrate his point. Once, he said, Corwin got into a hot discussion with a preacher in Lebanon, Ohio, and after it ended, it was taken for granted that the preacher would "skin" Corwin from the pulpit the following Sunday. So when Sunday arrived, everyone, including Corwin, attended that particular church to hear the skinning. "Corwin took a seat in the amen corner, facing the audience," said Grosvenor. "The preacher did not know Corwin was in the audience, but he proceeded to excoriate him nevertheless. As the preacher spoke, Corwin, facing the audience, punctuated and illustrated the speech with all sorts of facial contortions and grimaces. Interrogation points, exclamation points, and all sorts of points and comments appeared on Tom's dark and mobile countenance. The audience began to smile, the smile grew into titters, and at some severe thrust made by the preacher, and some extraordinary facial grimace by Corwin, the audience burst into a roar of laughter. The preacher looked around, saw Corwin, and grew so angry that he quit speaking suddenly, and left the victory to Corwin."[36]

Corwin and the Quakers

Once, when Tom Corwin was at the height of his fame as an orator and humorist, he made a speech in a Pennsylvania town inhabited (though he did not know it) largely by Quakers. He began by telling one of his most fetching anecdotes, but there was nary a ripple of applause nor even a smile from the audience. He then tried another funny story, with no more success, and after that, somewhat nettled, poured out all the wit, humor, sarcasm, and irony he could muster for the next two hours. But the audience sat as grave as a tombstone throughout and he finally gave up in disgust. As he was leaving, an old fellow approached him and said, "Friend Thomas, at times thee almost made me laugh!" "And why the deuce didn't you laugh?" roared Corwin angrily as he strode away, realizing for the first time that he had been speaking to a crowd of Quakers.[37]

The Great Debate (1850)

The Mexican War (1846–48)—which the Mexicans called *la invasión norteamericana*—added vast new lands to the national domain but also produced an acute sectional crisis that threatened to tear the nation apart. After the war, when Congress took up the question of organizing the new territories acquired from Mexico in the peace treaty, there was a fierce battle between Northerners and Southerners over the status of slavery in those territories that took seven months of sharp and acrimonious debate to settle peacefully. During the debate over what came to be called the "Compromise of 1850," the nation's most celebrated lawmakers—Henry Clay, Daniel Webster, and John C. Calhoun—took the center of the stage for the last time.

Henry Clay took the lead in putting together a compromise offering something to both sections. For the North there was the admission of California into the Union as a free state, the establishment of the boundary between Texas, a slave state, and New Mexico, likely to be a free state, in the latter's favor, and the prohibition of the slave trade in the District of Columbia. For the South there was a provision letting the people of New Mexico and Utah decide whether they wanted slavery or not, the assumption by the Federal Government of Texas' public debt (held mainly by Southerners), and, above all, a new and stringent Fugitive Slave Law. "Mr. President," said Clay in a moving address appealing for sectional compromise, "never, on any former occasion have I arisen under feelings of such deep solicitude. I have witnessed many periods of great anxiety, of peril, and of danger even to the country; but I have never before arisen to address any assembly so opposed, so appalled, so anxious." He went on to discuss each of the proposals in some detail, called for a "great national scheme of compromise" to avoid the horrors of civil war, and begged both North and South "solemnly to pause—at the edge of the precipice before the fearful and disastrous leap is taken in the yawning abyss below, which will lead to certain and irretrievable destruction." When he finished, men and women crowded around him to offer congratulations and assure him of their moral support.

On March 4, South Carolina's John C. Calhoun, in his last illness, appeared on the Senate floor, looking like a ghost, to repond to Clay. He was too feeble to speak himself, so he entrusted his carefully prepared speech to Virginia Senator James M. Mason. As Mason read it to the Senate, Calhoun scanned the faces of his listeners to observe their reactions, and from time to time he made little gestures to underline the points being made. Clay's proposals, Calhoun declared, stacked the cards in favor of the free states, and without more concessions the South would be forced to "choose between abolition and secession." He went on to call for equal rights in all Federal territories and a halt to all anti-slavery agitiation in the North.

Three days after Calhoun's speech came Daniel Webster's famous Seventh of March speech supporting Clay's proposals. Like Clay, Webster took a solemn view of the occasion. "Mr. President," he said, "I wish to speak today, not as a Massachusetts man, not as a Northern man, but as an American. . . . I speak for the preservation of the Union. 'Hear me for my cause.'" His words "flowed as the Mississippi rolls from its fountains," according to one observer, as he took up Clay's recommendations, one by one, and tried to show that they were fair ways of dealing with the issues at stake. When he finished there was a tremendous burst of applause; but his endorsement of fugitive slave legislation produced a torrent of criticism in the North, as he had feared it would, and prominent people in his own state—Ralph Waldo Emerson, Henry Wadsworth Longfellow, and James Russell Lowell—scornfully dismissed him as an unprincipled opportunist.

On March 11, New York's William H. Seward made a long speech challenging Webster's position. Seward was no abolitionist; he was a Free Soiler who favored the gradual emancipation of the slaves with compensation to the slaveowners. But he was implacably opposed both to the extension of slavery into new areas and to fugitive slave measures binding the inhabitants of the free states. In his speech Seward pointed out that the Preamble to the Constitution singled out union, justice, defense, welfare, and liberty as the objectives of the Federal Government, and went on to say that it was these objectives, not slavery, that should prevail in all the new territories acquired by the United States. "But there is a higher law than the Constitution," he added, "which regulates our authority over the domain, and devotes it to the same noble purposes."

Seward's brief reference to a "higher law than the Constitution" was widely misunderstood. His Southern colleagues charged that he was denigrating the Constitution and virtually calling on people to take the law into their own hands, and some of them called for his expulsion from the Senate. But Seward was not advocating anarchy, or even civil disobedience; he was simply stating what he regarded as unexceptionable: that basic moral principles ("higher law") dictated the "same noble purposes" that the Constitution's Preamble enumerated. For some reason, Seward never adequately explained what he meant, and amid the torrent of criticism that followed his speech he won the reputation of being a radical, even though he was actually a moderate who was willing to let slavery alone in the states where it already existed.

In the end the Senate finally voted to accept a series of separate bills, one after another, which embodied the substance of Clay's original proposals, and the House of Representatives soon adopted them too. With the Compromise of 1850 a reality, Clay expressed the belief that the peace between the sections would be permament. Webster was similarly heartened. "I can now sleep at night," he told a friend. "We have gone through the most important crisis which has occurred since the foundation of our government, and whatever party may prevail hereafter, the Union stands firm." Northern Senators like William Seward and Southern Senators like Jefferson Davis opposed the compromise to the bitter end, but the majority of Congressmen and most Americans seem to have welcomed the settlement with relief. Throughout the country newspapers put out special editions headlining the news: "THE COUNTRY SAVED." But it was peace's last victory over freedom in the perennial clash of values that makes up history.[38]

Irons in the Fire

Once Senator Tom Corwin was cornered by a pompous colleague who insisted on reciting long passages from speeches he had given which he thought were well-nigh immortal. "Why," he said, "if I didn't have so many irons in the fire, I'd publish every one of my speeches for posterity." "Take my advice, Senator," said Corwin, edging away from the man, "and put your speeches where your irons are!"[39]

Jeff Davis' Farewell

The news that Mississippi's Jefferson Davis was going to announce his resignation from the Senate on January 21, 1861, produced great excitement in Washington. When Davis arrived at the Capitol that morning, the place was so jam-packed with people that he had a hard time threading his way through the crowd to the Senate floor. About noon he rose in his place, sought recognition, and, as the Senate chamber became still, began speaking in a low tone of voice. "I rise, Mr. President," he said, "for the purpose of announcing to the Senate that the State of Mississippi, by a solemn ordinance of her people, in convention assembled, has declared her separation from the United States. . . ." He paused, overcome with emotion, for a moment, and then proceeded, with increasing forcefulness, to remind his colleagues of his long-held belief in state sovereignty and the right of secession, as well as of his firm rejection of the belief that the phrase, "all men are created equal," in the Declaration of Independence, applied to blacks as well as whites. "I am sure I feel no hostility toward you, Senators from the North," he declared. "I am sure there is not one of you, whatever sharp discussion there may have been between us, to whom I cannot now say, in the presence of my God, I wish you well, and such, I am sure, is the feeling of the people whom I represent toward those whom you represent." He went on to express hope for peaceful relations between North and South but declared his section's determination to "vindicate the right as best we may." Then, after another long pause, he talked for a few minutes about his service in the Senate, recalled the collisions he had with colleagues who disagreed with him, and offered his "apology for any pain which, in the heat of discussion, I have inflicted." Then he came to the end. "Mr. President and Senators," he exclaimed, "having made the announcement which the occasion seemed to me to require, it only remains for me to bid you a final adieu."

When Davis finished and left the Senate chamber with four of his

Southern colleagues, there were tears in the eyes of some of the people on the Senate floor and in the gallery, but the Republicans sat for the most part unmoved by his words. One Southern Democrat was openly hostile: Andrew Johnson of Tennessee. The only Southerner not to leave the Senate on the eve of the Civil War, Johnson had harsh words for the Mississippi Senator, who, he pointed out, was a graduate of West Point. "When I consider his early associations," said Johnson in a Senate speech a couple of weeks after Davis' departure, "when I remember that he was nurtured by this government . . . I cannot understand how he can be willing to hail another banner. . . . It seems to me that if I could not unsheathe my sword in vindication of the flag of my country . . . I would return the sword to its scabbard. I would never sheathe it in the bosom of my mother! Never! Never!"[40]

Butler's Bloody Shirt

After the Civil War, Massachusetts' Benjamin F. Butler, former Union general, served several terms in the House and aligned himself with the Radical Republicans who looked on the South as a "conquered province" and called for drastic reconstruction of the former Confederate states before readmitting them to the Union. Butler even proposed redrawing the boundaries of the Southern states and giving each of the new territories a special name. Virginia would become the territory of Potomac; North Carolina, the territory of Cape Fear; South Carolina, Georgia, and Florida, lumped together, would become the territory of Jackson; Louisiana, the territory of Jefferson; Texas, the territory of Houston; and Arkansas, the territory of Lincoln.

When Southern whites organized the Ku Klux Klan in 1866 to resist Congressional reconstruction, Butler championed a "Ku Klux Klan" bill empowering the President to use the army to enforce the law in the South. In one speech on the situation in the South, he dramatically waved a bloodstained nightshirt, taken, he told the House, from the back of an Ohio-born white teacher in a Mississippi school for blacks, who had been kidnapped and brutally flogged by Klansmen. From this gesture came the phrase, "waving the bloody shirt," to refer to the way Republicans used the Civil War as an issue against the Democrats during political campaigns for the rest of the nineteenth century.[41]

Lamar's Eulogy of Sumner

On April 27, 1874, Mississippi's L. Q. C. Lamar, a former Confederate colonel, made a speech in the House that surprised his colleagues and attracted attention everywhere. The occasion was the death of Senator

Charles Sumner, the Massachusetts abolitionist and civil-rights advocate who for years was probably the most hated man in the South. Though Mississippi was still occupied by Federal troops under military reconstruction, Lamar took the opportunity to praise Sumner and seek reconciliation with the North. "Charles Sumner," he said, "was born with an instinctive love of freedom, and was educated from his earliest infancy to the belief that freedom is the natural and indefeasible right of every intelligent being having the outward form of man. In him, in fact, this creed seems to have been something more than a doctrine imbibed from teachers, or a result of education. To him it was a grand intuitive truth, inscribed in blazing letters upon the tablet of his inner consciousness, to deny which would have been for him to deny that he himself existed. And along with this all-controlling love of freedom he possessed a moral sensibility keenly intense and vivid, a conscientiousness which would never permit him to swerve by the breadth of a hair from what he pictured to himself as the path of duty. Thus were combined in him the characteristics which have in all ages given to religion her martyrs, and to patriotism her self-sacrificing heroes."

Lamar's speech produced a sensation throughout the country. Massachusetts Congressman George F. Hoar expressed astonishment at Lamar's boldness and said that probably no other man in the South could have spoken as he did without committing political suicide. Some observers believe the healing of the wounds of the Civil War dated from Lamar's eulogy of Charles Sumner on the Senate floor.

A day or two afterward Lamar went to a circus with Ohio Senator Allen G. Thurman. In the middle of one performance a woman lost her balance on the flying trapeze but managed to grasp another as she fell from a great height. "Lamar, that reminds me of you," said Thurman. "How so?" asked Lamar. "About your speech, you know," said Thurman. "You caught all right; but if you had missed, you'd have broken your neck."[42]

Might Have to Shoot

For a number of years one of Kentucky's Senators was a dreary pedant. He filled his speeches with dull financial details and boring statistics, droned on for hours, and became, it was said, "the terror of his colleagues and the nightmare of visitors in the galleries." His cry, "Mr. President," was the signal for a general exodus from both the Senate chamber and the galleries.

One day the Kentuckian, books and documents piled high around him, solemnly addressed the chair. As usual, the visitors in the gallery started heading for the exit; but this time Colonel Dick Wintersmith, an old friend of the Senator's, planted himself in front of the door, with a revolver in each hand, and sternly ordered the people to resume their seats and remain there quietly until the Senator finished his remarks. They returned to their seats at once, of course, and sat there, bemused, hour after hour as the Senator droned on. At length, as night fell, the Senator finished his speech and took his seat. The Colonel then put his pistols away and motioned for the visitors to leave. They did so with relief; but as the last man was leaving, he turned to the Colonel and said earnestly: "Mister, that was all right, no fault to find, but *if it was to do over again, you might [have to]* *shoot!*"[43]

Sledgehammer Orators

Edmund Alton was impressed by the variety of orators he heard while working as a page boy in the Senate during the 1870s. "Certain Senators," he recalled, "could not rise to address the Senate but it would be a signal to prepare for amusement. There was a galaxy of humorous speakers, beneath whose pleasantries, however, lay good common sense. There were, also, quaint talkers, who expressed their views in a peculiar style that charged the ear by its novelty; there were impassioned, eloquent Senators; there were keen, quick debaters; and there were oratorical logicians. Many of the Senators were masters of rhetoric, and when they spoke, their associates and the people in the galleries gave the closest attention. A few, belonging to a class known as 'sledge-hammer orators,' were not so fastidious about rhetoric and syntax; they rained down clinching blows of logic, but they sometimes damaged the English language as well as silenced their antagonists. One of them was making a very strong argument against certain propositions advanced by the Opposition; and he concluded each point with the words, 'Now, Mr. President, I ask, Can it be *did*? I repeat, Can it be *did*?' After pausing to give any other Senator a chance to say that it *could* 'be did,' he brought his fist down upon the desk, with a force that made the ink-well rattle, and added: 'No, Mr. President, it can *not* be did! It can *not* be did!!' And then he proceeded to show that something else proposed by the other side could not be did. Those remarks, as may be taken for granted, were revised by the official reporters before publication in the *Record.*"

The former page boy was struck by the "eccentricities of gesture" as well as of speech which he encountered in the Senate. Senator Timothy Howe (R, Wisc.), he noted, always threw one of his legs across the arm of a chair when beginning a speech, and kept it there until he finished. Senator Francis Kernan (D, New York) "had a habit of striking out with his hands exactly like the movements of a swimmer; that was the only gesture I ever saw him make." Senator Matthew Hale Carpenter (R, Wisc.) "usually spoke with his hands in his pockets." Senator James W. Nye (R, Nevada) "generally turned his back upon the Vice President and talked to the ladies in the gallery; from his attitude, a stranger might have been pardoned for assuming that the presiding officer of the Senate sat upon the roof." As for Senator Richard J. Oglesby (R, Ill.), he had "entirely original methods of emphasizing his remarks. I well remember one instance. He had the floor on a question of great national interest, and spoke with marked effect. During the speech he pushed aside the chairs near his desk, and as his eloquence increased he excitedly paced back and forth in the space thus cleared. With a grand flourish of words he concluded. The people in the galleries started an applause. I could hear it coming, like the rumbling of distant thunder. The Senator knew that he had scored a triumph, and, casting upon the other law-makers a compassionate smile, he sat down— upon the floor!"[44]

Columbian Orator

One day Michigan's Julius Caesar Burrows was holding forth eloquently in the House, and when he got to his peroration he spoke so movingly that people both on the House floor and in the galleries were practically in tears. But not Ohio's witty Samuel S. Cox. While Burrows was speaking, Cox motioned for a page boy to come over and then sent him out to get a book from the Congressional library. The book which the boy brought back was *The Columbian Orator,* a collection of famous speeches which Cox had read as a boy. Cox riffled through the book until he found what he wanted; and when Burrows finished speaking, he rose and read to the House, word for word, the peroration which the eloquent Michigander had just given. From that day on Burrows was known as the "Columbian Orator."[45]

Mark Twain's Speech

One evening Chauncey Depew, Republican Senator from New York who was famed for his wit and oratory, was scheduled to speak at a banquet on the same program with Mark Twain, who spoke first, for about twenty minutes, and received a big ovation, as usual, when he finished. Then it was Depew's turn. "Mr. Toastmaster and Ladies and Gentlemen," said Depew as he arose, "before this dinner, Mark Twain and I made an agreement to trade speeches. He has just delivered my speech, and I thank you for the pleasant manner in which you have received it. I regret to say that I have lost the notes of his speech and cannot remember anything he has to say." Then he sat down amid much laughter. The following day a man who had been at the banquet ran into Twain. "Mr. Clemens," he said, "I consider you were much imposed upon last night. I have always heard that Mr. Depew is a clever man, but really, that speech of his you made last night struck me as being the most infernal rot!"[46]

Last Speaker

Kentucky's J. Proctor Knott was one of Congress' wittiest orators. In his younger days he made a satirical speech in the House in which he called Duluth, Minnesota, then a small settlement, "the Zenith City of the Unsalted Seas." That speech became a classic, but he wasn't always able to hold audiences spellbound. One evening he was the last speaker on such a long, dreary program that people were hungrily eying the nearest exit. When his turn finally came and he launched into his address, several people got up and headed sheepishly down the aisle. Knott stopped, looked at them sympathetically, and began to laugh. "I don't blame you for leaving," he said. "I'd go, too, only I'm the speaker!"[47]

Haf Dit

Once the mayor of a small town in Wisconsin who had a German background presided over a political meeting at which Republican Senator John C. Spooner was the key speaker. When it came time to begin, the mayor got up and went to the podium. "Mine friends," he said, "I haf been asked to introduce Senator Spooner, who is to make a speech, yes. Vell, I haf dit so, und now, he vill do so."[48]

LaFollette's Alarm Watch

Wisconsin's insurgent Republican Senator Robert M. LaFollette was a riveting speaker; people flocked from afar to hear him denounce the "special interests" controlling city councils, state legislatures, and Congress itself and blocking legislation in the public interest. His speeches were lengthy, and when he finished he came off the platform bathed in perspiration and then insisted on shaking hands with nearly everyone in the audience. Sometimes, he told his wife, his exertions made him feel dizzy and at times he almost lost the thread of his thought while speaking. Mrs. LaFollette urged him to shorten his speeches; and she finally bought him an alarm-watch so he could time his speeches, and she made him promise not to speak for more than two hours.

The alarm-watch didn't help. Whenever the alarm went off while LaFollete was speaking, startling the audience, he stopped, began gathering up his papers, and explained in mock-despair that his wife had given him the watch to prevent his talking too long, that she imposed a two-hour limit on him, and that he didn't dare utter another word. The people invariably laughed and cheered, and insisted he go on with his talk; and he always yielded, on condition they not tell his wife about it. Once, when he was shaking hands with some people afterwards, a woman exclaimed in a high-pitched voice: "Mr. LaFollette, I wish you would tell your wife for me that I think she wasted her money when she invested in that alarm watch!"[49]

Louder

Virginia Senator A. William Robertson liked to tell about the Virginia Congressman who had a problem when addressing a group of mountaineers on a windy day outdoors. Though the Congressman prided himself on the power of his voice, someone on the outer fringe of the audience kept yelling, "Louder, louder!" no matter how much he raised his voice. Finally he stopped and exclaimed: "My friends, on that great day of judgment, when Gabriel blows his horn to summon the quick and the dead, some d----d fool is going to yell, 'louder, louder'!"[50]

John Crisp's Admirer

Once Missouri Congressman John T. Crisp, an orator of force and fire, made a speech in Holden, Missouri, which produced great applause. Afterward an old fellow rushed up and pronounced it the greatest speech since the days of Patrick Henry—in fact, since the time of Demosthenes and Cicero. Crisp was of course immensely pleased and thanked his admirer profusely. "Where do you speak next?" asked the old man, for he knew Crisp was making the rounds. "At Warrensburg, tonight," Crisp told him.

Warrensburg is about fifteen miles from Holden and Crisp arrived there in plenty of time for his engagement. To his surprise, when he got up to begin his speech he saw his ardent admirer sitting in the front row of the auditorium. Not wishing to repeat himself too much in front of the old man, he changed the order of his remarks and made some other minor changes in the speech. When he finished, the man came forward again, showered him with compliments, and then asked: "Colonel, where do you speak tomorrow?" "At Webb City," said Crisp, realizing, with some relief, that Webb City was about one hundred miles away. To his astonishment, however, when he began speaking in Webb City, the first person he saw in the audience was the same old man. Restraining his irritation, he chopped his speech up, put the last part first and the first part last, and did his best to make it sound like a new speech. At the finish, his enthusiastic admirer rushed up again, slapped him on the back, and cried: "Great, Colonel! Greatest speech ever delivered! Beats your Holden and Warrensburg speeches all hollow; never enjoyed myself so much in my life." Then he added: "My dear Colonel, where do you speak next?" Wild with anger by this time, Crisp could no longer contain himself. "I speak next in Sheol, you blankety-blank old fool!" he roared. "And I hope that the first blankety-blank idiot I see sizzling in the bottomless pits will be you, you blankety-blank old rascal!"[51]

LaFollette's Ordeal

Even excellent speakers like Senator Robert M. LaFollette, the great Wisconsin Progressive, have their bad moments. In February 1912, LaFollette delivered a speech to the Periodical Publishers' Association in Philadelphia that effectively killed his campaign for the Republican nomination for President that year.

The publishers' dinner was an important event. Several hundred of the nation's leading newspaper and magazine publishers, editors, and writers were present, along with celebrities like Alexander Graham Bell and Rear-Admiral Robert F. Peary, and some of LaFollette's best friends in the Senate. Unfortunately, LaFollette was worn out from a speaking tour at the time and suffering from acute indigestion. He was also under a strain because his little girl was in the hospital scheduled for surgery.

LaFollette arrived late for the banquet; as he entered the hall, Woodrow Wilson, then governor of New Jersey, was speaking, and LaFollette stood quietly in the back until he finished. Then he walked to the speakers' table, shook hands with Wilson, and after being introduced, told the audience that if a Democrat were to be elected President he hoped it would be Wilson. After this auspicious beginning—his compliment to a political rival brought laughter and cheers—things began to go downhill. For one thing, it was late in the evening and when LaFollette picked up his manuscript, sixty pages long, a deep melancholy pervaded the room. For another, when LaFollette explained why he wanted to read the manuscript rather than extemporize, he did so ineptly. "For fear there may be some here who will not report what I say correctly," he declared, "and because I am going to say some things I consider important, I want to have a record of them." The way he phrased his apology for using the manuscript alienated most of the people in the audience at the outset and he never won them back.

Worst of all was LaFollette's delivery. Ordinarily a dynamic speaker, he botched everything he did that night. He read his manuscript for a while, then realized he was not winning his audience and put it down and began talking off the cuff. But this didn't seem to work so he returned to the manuscript and soon found himself repeating points he had already made. At one point, when he was discussing the evils of corporate control of American newspapers, he asked rhetorically: "Is there a way out?" At this, one man jumped up, shouted, "We hope so!" and headed for the exit. LaFollette became increasingly angry—at himself and at his audience—as he went on, and his tone became strident and his attacks on newspaper publishers heavy-handed. "The face of Wilson was a picture as LaFollette went from one blunder to another," the reporter for the *Philadelphia Public Ledger* noted. "He was the most attentive listener the Wisconsin radical had from beginning to end. At first he took notes of what Senator LaFollette said but soon desisted. His face grew graver and graver . . . and he, perhaps, understood better than anyone else in the room what terrible blunders LaFollette was making. Governor Wilson was looking on a tragedy, in a way, and his face showed it."

When LaFollette finally sat down, after an hour and a half, the toastmaster, Don Seitz of the *New York World,* got up and announced slowly and emphatically: "I want to apologize to the newspaper press of the country in general for the foolish, wicked and untruthful attack that has just been made on it." It was one in the morning by this time and hardly anyone spoke to the Wisconsin progressive as he left the banquet hall. When he got back to his hotel room he went immediately to the bathroom and threw up. A little later he caught the last train to Washington and arrived there in time for his daughter's operation.

For days afterward newspapers across the country ran stories about LaFollette's "collapse" at the Philadelphia banquet and about his "mental-breakdown." There were even false stories that he had been drunk, fallen across the table at the conclusion of his address, and even frothed at the mouth. Whatever chances LaFollette may have had at the Republican convention later that year were lost that unhappy evening in Philadelphia.[52]

Now or Later

Once Congressman Clarence Hancock of New York was scheduled to speak at a large political meeting which opened with band music. After the band had played a couple of numbers, the chairman of the meeting turned to Hancock sitting beside him on the platform and said, "Do you want to speak now, or shall we let the audience enjoy themselves a little longer?"[53]

Light and Heat

Once Democratic Senator Henry F. Ashurst of Arizona made an impressive speech for a cause he cherished and thought was dear to the hearts of his constituents. In his speech he quoted the Prophets, Shakespeare, Dante, and other notables in order to underscore his oratorical points. But when, a little later, the roll call came, he quietly voted against the cause he had defended so eloquently. One of the Senators who had opposed him during the debate rushed over after the vote, grasped his hand, and congratulated him on his change of mind. "Thank God, Henry," he cried, "you have seen the light!" "Oh, no," said Ashurst frankly, "I didn't see the light. I felt the heat!"[54]

Divine

Of Mississippi's Democratic Senator John Sharp Williams, one of the Senate's most eloquent speakers from 1911 to 1923, it was said: "When John had a pint of good liquor, he was fine. Give him a quart and he was divine!"[55]

Miracle

At the Republican presidential convention in 1920 the delegates at one point began calling for a speech by former New York Senator Chauncey M. Depew, then in his eighties, but still famous for his lively speeches. Depew's voice was still powerful and his speech to the convention was an enormous success. "Chauncey Depew," cried one of the delegates who met him in a hotel lobby afterward. "I have for over twenty years wanted to shake hands with you. Your speech was a wonder. I was half a mile off, way up under the roof, and heard every word of it, and it was the only one I was able to hear. That you should do this in your eighty-seventh year is a miracle. But then," he added thoughtfully, "my [own] father was a miracle [too]. On his eighty-fifth birthday he was in just as good shape as you are today, and a week afterwards he was dead."[56]

Senator Swanson's Opportunities

One evening Senator Claude A. Swanson of Virginia made a particularly long and rambling speech at a banquet. Afterward an old lady came up to him to shake his hand. "How did you like the speech?" Swanson asked her. "I liked it fine," she replied, "but it seems to me that you missed several excellent opportunities." Swanson looked puzzled. "Several opportunities for what?" he asked. "To quit," she snapped.[57]

Ain't Missing Nothing

When Senator James E. Watson, Republican of Indiana, was speaking at a political rally one night, a bunch of boys standing in back created such a racket that he finally stopped and cried: "Those boys back there are making so much noise, I can't hear the sound of my own voice." Yelled one of the boys: "You ain't missing nothing, Mister!"[58]

Borahdom

During the first part of the twentieth century Idaho's independent-minded Republican Senator William E. Borah was regarded as one of the best speakers on Capitol Hill. "Borah is the ablest man who has been in Congress in many years," acknowledged one of his conservative colleagues. "He is the quickest man on his feet I have ever seen. No one else is his equal in debate."

Borah took speech-making seriously. His models were Burke, Pitt, Fox, Webster, and Lincoln, and he studied their speeches carefully when he was perfecting his own style. His prescription for a speech was simple: know your subject, believe in it, and have the courage to say what you think. In preparing his major addresses, he gathered notes from a wide variety of sources, made an outline of what he intended to say, and then memorized quotations he wanted to cite. After that, he waited for the right moment to deliver his speech. The news that "Borah is up" sent flocks of reporters and crowds of visitors to the gallery. Thomas R. Marshall, who as Woodrow Wilson's Vice President listened to Senate speeches for eight years, thought Borah was unequaled as a speaker. "I have many times heard fall from his lips," he wrote in his memoirs, "specimens of oratory which, if they had been uttered by Cicero, or Webster, or Burke, would have become the common heritage of the school boys of today for declamation purposes."

But even Homer nods. Sometimes Borah belabored a subject, talked too long, and became tiresome. During one of his overlong harangues a weary Senator slipped out of the Senate chamber and headed for the cloakroom. "How is Borah's speech going?" one of his colleagues asked. "Just fine," sighed the Senator. "When I left, he was reaching new heights of Borah-dom!"[59]

Huey Long

Louisiana's Huey Long, who became a Senator in 1930, was famous for his speeches: sarcastic, vehement, funny, but at times filled with detailed information and preceptive comments. "Huey Long," said a Louisiana Congressman, "can make a more intelligent and more eloquent speech when drunk than any other Senator can when sober."

Long supported Franklin Roosevelt for the 1932 nomination, campaigned for him, and gave him his support for a while after he became President. Soon, however, he became convinced FDR was being too soft on the wealthy and he started blasting him and his New Deal policies in Senate speeches. In one speech he compared Herbert Hoover to a hoot owl and FDR to a scrootch owl. "A hoot owl," he said, "bangs into the nest and knocks the hen clean off, and catches her while she's falling. But a scrootch owl slips into the roost and scrootches up to the hen and talks softly to her. And the hen just falls in love with him, and the next thing you know, *there ain't no hen!*"

Long was merciless in his ridicule of the administration's efforts to raise agricultural prices by paying farmers to limit production. "A man came in to see me the other day," he said in one tirade against the New Deal, "and said to me, 'I ask you to consider what good I have done for this country. I am the man who taught two trees to grow where one used to grow before.' I said, 'You are the worst citizen we have in this state under our system of things. You are the man who ought to be condemned and hung tomorrow morning. The idea of your coming in here and asking for consideration because you taught two trees to grow where one used to grow! We want a man who fixes it so that none can grow. We want a man who can teach the people how none could be raised. That is what we want in this year of our Lord 1935, of Franklin Delano Roosevelt the little!"

In 1935 Long spoke for fifteen and a half hours—one of the longest filibusters on record—against a New Deal bill. During the course of his talkathon he read the Senate the complete Constitution of the United States. "At that he pulled the biggest and most educational novelty ever pulled in the Senate," quipped Will Rogers. "Most of the Senators thought he was reviewing a new book!"

Roosevelt's supporters fought back. Oklahoma's elderly Congressman Percy L. Gassaway called Long a "tomtit," which he defined as a very small bird that "tries to imitate the woodpecker," and attacks the "biggest tree in the forest," i.e. F. D. R. Roosevelt's Secretary of the Interior Harold L. Ickes said Long was suffering from "halitosis of the intellect, that is, presuming Emperor Long has an intellect." Even Virginia Senator Carter Glass, no friend of the New Deal, got his licks in. He announced that the Senate had outdone Caligula; where Caligula had made his horse a consul the Senate had made the posterior of a horse a U.S. Senator.

Roosevelt himself was fascinated by Long's demagogic pyrotechnics, though he looked on him as a real threat in the forthcoming 1936 presidential race. But on Sunday night, September 8, 1935, as Long stepped out of the House Chamber in Baton Rouge, he was suddenly confronted by Dr. Carl A. Weiss, who shot him (and was himself killed by Long's bodyguards). Long staggered down the steps, murmuring, "I wonder why he shot me," and died about thirty-one hours later.[60]

Alben Barkley's Speech

Kentucky Senator Alben W. Barkley enjoyed telling about his experience when reading a prepared speech to the Alumni Association of Marvin

College, his alma mater. He thought he had done a pretty good job, but when he asked the chairman of the Alumni Association about it afterward, the latter told him: "Well, I have three criticisms. In the first place, you read it. In the second place, you read it poorly. And in the third place, it was not worth reading."[61]

Something Different

Congressman Clarence E. Hancock (R, N.Y.) was one of several speakers at the meeting of a woman's club in his district, and when his turn came the woman introducing him announced: "Members, this is our last meeting of the year. We have enjoyed a splendid program. Our speakers have been both entertaining and instructive. Today we have something quite different. I present Congressman Hancock."[62]

Wayne Morse as Persuader

Oregon Senator Wayne Morse, an independent Republican who turned Democrat in 1952, had a profound grasp of basic issues and a persuasive way of communicating his point of view to other people. "He can convince the average audience that black is white," asserted Palmer Hoyt, editor and publisher of the *Denver Post*, "and in the same speech put the switch on and make them believe that white is black after all." Once Oregon trade-publication editor Carl Crow refused to attend a Republican rally where Morse was scheduled to speak. "That S.O.B. has changed my mind twice," he explained, "and I am not going to let him do it again."[63]

Ford's Longhorn Speech

One day, when Michigan's Republican Congressman, Gerald R. Ford, was a junior member of the House Committee on Appropriations, he made a long speech opposing any more funds for river, harbor, and flood control projects, and, when he finished, felt rather proud of himself. Glowing with self-satisfaction, he started down the aisle and ran into a Texas Democrat who was a good friend of his. "Jerry," said the Texan, "that was the best Texas longhorn speech I ever heard." When Ford looked puzzled, the Texan explained: "Well, Jerry, a longhorn speech is one that has two points, far, far apart, with plenty of bull in between!"[64]

Advice for Joe Martin

When Dr. Paul Dudley White treated Massachusetts' Joe Martin, then Republican Speaker of the House, for a blood clot and assured him that he was in good health, he also said: "I want to give you some advice: talk less, walk more." "Doctor," wailed Martin, "that's a hell of a piece of advice to give to a politician!"[65]

Sam Rayburn's Advice

Speaker Sam Rayburn liked to advise new members on how to be more effective in the House. One Congressman, who had been a judge, asked him if he was talking too much. "Yes," said Rayburn. "What should I do about it?" the man asked. "Quit it!" advised Rayburn frankly. "I have sat in the Speaker's chair," Rayburn once told a reporter, "and watched many a Congressman talk himself out of Congress."[66]

Norris Cotton's Loquacity

When he was beginning his career in politics, Senator Norris Cotton was asked to address a Republican rally in a town some distance from his home, so he took a friend along to keep him company. As he delivered his speech, he got carried away with his eloquence and suddenly realized he had spoken too long and was beginning to lose his audience. Apologizing for his loquacity, he announced that he would quickly wind up his speech. At this, his friend, hoping to give him a little lift, yelled from the back of the crowd: "That's all right, Norris. Tell us all about it! We want to hear all about it!" The moderator, somewhat deaf, looked up at once and whispered to Cotton: "Don't pay any attention to that damn fool. He's drunk all the time."[67]

Congressional Record *Fiction*

Illinois Senator Paul Douglas maintained that every speaker had three speeches: the one he intended to make, the one he actually made, and the one he wished he had made. But North Carolina's Sam J. Ervin, Jr., insisted that the *Congressional Record,* by permitting a Congressman to revise his remarks before they appeared in print, actually enabled him to make the speech he wished he had made. For Ervin the *Record* was thus "more of a work of fiction than one of fact."[68]

William Moorhead's Superfluous Speech

William S. Moorhead, Pennsylvania Democrat, was one of the House's topflight orators. During the 1960 presidential campaign he gave what he thought was a good speech on "Housing for the Elderly," and afterward an older woman rushed up to him, bubbling with enthusiasm, and cried: "Oh,

Congressman, your speech was superfluous! Simply superfluous!" "Thank you," Moorhead replied, not quite sure whether she was pulling his leg, "I'm thinking of having it published posthumously." "Oh, that's wonderful!" the woman exclaimed. "The sooner, the better!"[69]

Hubert Humphrey's Five-minute Speech

Congressman Gerald ("Jerry") Ford liked to tease Minnesota Senator Hubert H. Humphrey about his long-windedness. "Hubert is a dear friend of mine," he said. "I still remember when I came to Congress and attended something. It was the first time I ever heard him talk. He was in the second hour of a five-minute speech. I didn't have a program, so I asked the fellow next to me what followed Senator Humphrey. The fellow looked at his watch and said, 'Christmas.'"[70]

Olin Johnston's Filibustering Feet

In April 1953, Oregon Senator Wayne Morse began a filibuster against the tidelands-oil bill sponsored by the Eisenhower administration that broke all records. As he spoke all day and all night, he first broke Huey Long's record (fifteen and a half hours against a New Deal bill in 1935), then caught up with and surpassed the record of Robert M. LaFollette (who spoke for eighteen hours and thirteen minutes against a currency bill in 1908), and finally became the new filibuster champion when he sat down the following day after holding forth for twenty-two hours and twenty-six minutes. In 1957, however, South Carolina's Strom Thurmond beat him by two hours (twenty-four hours and eighteen minutes) in a filibuster against a civil-rights bill.

In the next civil-rights battle, Thurmond's colleague Olin D. Johnston told reporters he had a 400-page speech ready to deliver that would outdistance both Morse and Thurmond combined. But when the time came for his marathon talk session, the South Carolina Senator lasted only ninety minutes. When a disappointed reporter told him it looked as though he had been "bought off," Johnston said indignantly: "Ah have not been bought off. Mah feet got tired and so ah quit."[71]

Introducing Senator Cooper

At a large meeting Kentucky's Republican Senator John Sherman Cooper and another Senator were seated on the platform awaiting their turns to address the crowd. The master of ceremonies arose at the appointed time to make the introductions and went on for some time talking about the great virtues, outstanding statesmanship, and wonderful accomplishments of the next person to address the assembly. Then, when he finished, he turned to Cooper and his colleague and asked in a loud voice: "And now which one of you would like to speak first?"[72]

Humphrey's Three Minutes

Scheduled to speak at a banquet one evening, Senator Hubert H. Humphrey had to wait hours until his turn came. There were preliminary announcements, brief remarks by all the people at the head table, speeches by local politicians, and, finally, a lengthy introduction by the master of ceremonies. When Humphrey finally got to the microphone, he smiled and announced: "I'm just tickled to be here, though I hadn't planned to stay the weekend!" But the Minnesota Senator, as he cheerfully admitted, could take up a lot of time himself when he got going. Once Arizona Congressman Morris ("Mo") Udall told him that because of a crowded schedule for a meeting at which Humphrey was to speak, he would have to limit the Minnesotan's remarks to three minutes. "Three minutes!" wailed Humphrey. "Mo, I can't clear my throat in three minutes!"[73]

Muskie on Silence in Maine

Maine Senator Edmund Muskie believed that "silence is golden." He liked to tell about the man who visited a little coastal town in Maine, tried to start a conversation with the townspeople, and couldn't get anyone to respond. Finally he asked whether there was a law against talking in the town. "Not exactly a law," one man said, after a long pause. "But we have an understanding not to speak unless it improves on silence."[74]

V

On the Campaign
Trail

* 🖋 *

In 1954, shortly after Minnesota Democrat Hubert H. Humphrey won a second term in the Senate, he agreed to an interview with reporter Sam Shaffer. The interview was going along nicely when suddenly a Senate page came running up and handed Humphrey a note saying that one of his constituents was waiting to see him. Humphrey at once jumped up, excused himself, and started hurrying away. "For heaven's sake, Hubert," wailed Shaffer, "I haven't finished. You can let your constituent wait. You're not up again for six years." "I know that, Sam," said Humphrey, as he kept moving, "and I'm off and running for the next time right now!"[1]

Humphrey wasn't the only Senator who felt obliged to keep on running between elections. Even Senators who had served several terms and achieved national recognition could meet a sudden rebuff at the ballot box when the winds of opinion shifted and they discovered, too late, that they had lost touch with their constituents. Members of the House of Representatives felt even more hard-pressed, for they had to seek the approval of the voters every two years. Even Congressmen from "safe" districts were usually careful not to take their constituents for granted. A major part of the life of every Senator and every Representative was the campaign trail. From the beginning members of Congress were candidates for re-election and "ombudsmen" for their constituents (as Texas Congressman Jim Wright was fond of pointing out) as well as lawmakers for the nation.

American political campaigns have never been models of propriety, even in the early years of the republic. From the 1790s to the 1980s there has been a great deal of low-level gut-fighting in both Presidential and Congressional contests: appeals to prejudice and bigotry, cynical flag-waving, witch-hunting, and emphasis on the voters' narrowest range of interests. There has always been a lot of hoopla, too, on both the national and local levels, with torchlight parades, gaudy posters, snappy slogans, boisterous barbecues, steamy oratory, rambunctious rallies, and noisy songfests frequently overshadowing reasoned discussions of public issues. But Congressional campaigns, like campaigns for the Presidency, had their serious side, too, with candidates often exploring the issues thoughtfully and outlining their own views with some precision. Few Presidential contests, in fact, could match the high seriousness of the debates on slavery between Abraham Lincoln and Stephen A. Douglas in the Illinois Senatorial race in 1858.

Local contests, however, have necessarily been more down-to-earth and personal in nature than national contests, for Congressional candidates had closer encounters with the voters than Presidential candidates did, particularly in races for the House and in rural areas. Sometimes the crowds a Congressional hopeful faced in local churches, town halls, and school auditoriums were friendly and sometimes they weren't. There might be a good-natured give-and-take between candidate and audience in one town; but in another there might be heckling, hostile questions, and disconcerting interruptions during speeches. In local races, moreover, there were more direct confrontations between opposing candidates than in Presidential races; and this put a premium on quick thinking, skillfulness in debate, and the ability to establish rapport with audiences.

Many Congressmen have been justifiably proud of their campaign skills. In their memoirs, they tend to dwell more on their deftness in handling local crises—fielding tough questions, making snappy comebacks, and turning unexpected developments to their advantage—than on the correctness of the positions they took on the issues at stake. They admire this *ad hoc* skill in their colleagues, too, and are even willing to award kudos to their competitors if the latter display superior talents on the campaign trail.

Campaigns can be ordeals; it is impossible for Congressmen to express their opinions on the issues without alienating some of the voters. Not surprisingly, some of the most popular campaign stories on Capitol Hill have to do with the adroit way Congressional candidates avoid going out on a limb when asked leading questions by the voters. One old favorite involved Ohio Senator Tom Corwin. "What about the tariff question?" someone asked him at a rally at a time when the tariff was a controversial issue. "Glad you asked that, mister," Corwin exclaimed; and then, looking serious, he declared: "I know some in this audience are for a high tariff and others are against a high tariff. After considerable thought on the subject, I want everyone in this hall to know—so am I!"[2] Even more popular is the story about how nicely Texas' Tom Connally handled a tricky question during one of his campaigns for the Senate. He was in East Texas, perched on the back of a pickup truck in a little cotton-farming town, making a studiedly imprecise speech one afternoon, and when he finished, a man in the audience yelled: "How do you stand on the cotton issue?" Connally paused a moment and then said confidently: "I'm okay on that one. Are there any other questions?"[3]

It is significant, however, that the all-time favorite campaign story—it has been told and retold through the years—centers on the fickleness of the voters. Lyndon Johnson used to tell the tale; so did Emanuel Celler, Alben Barkley, and heaven knows how many others. But perhaps Sam Rayburn's version is as good as any. A freshman member of the House, according to Rayburn, received a letter from one of his staunchest supporters letting him know he was going to oppose him for re-election. The Congressman was extremely upset, and he hurried home to discuss the matter in person. "Isn't it true," he asked his constituent, "that not too long ago I helped you get your son out of jail?" "Yes," admitted the man. "And isn't it true," the Congressman went on, "that I helped you get a scholarship for your daughter?" "Yes," said the man. "Then why," cried the Congressman, "why are you opposing me in the coming election?" The man looked hurt. "But Congressman," he exclaimed, "what have you done for me *lately?*"[4]

☆   ☆   ☆

Henry Clay and the Kentucky Hunters

In 1816, Henry Clay was running for re-election, and while making the rounds he met an old Kentucky hunter who had once been his supporter but was now disaffected because Clay had endorsed a pay raise for Congressmen earlier that year. When the hunter told Clay he was going to vote for his opponent, Clay sighed and asked: "Have you a good rifle, my friend?" "Yes," said the hunter. "Does it ever flash?" Clay went on. "Only once," replied the hunter. "What did you do with it—throw it away?" Clay wanted to know. "No," said the hunter. "I picked the flint, tried it again, and brought down the game." "Have I ever flashed but upon the compensation bill?" Clay exclaimed. "No," admitted the hunter. "Will you throw me away?" Clay pressed his point. "No, no!" cried the hunter, excitedly. "I will pick the flint, and try you again!"

During the same campaign, Clay came across another hunter, who was carrying a rifle he called "Old Bess," and solicited his vote. "Are you a good shot?" the hunter asked. Thinking the man spoke figuratively, Clay said, "Try me, and see." "Very well," said the hunter, "here's Old Bess, try her once." A bit surprised, Clay reluctantly agreed to the test; and after the mark was set up and the distance taken, he was fortunate enough to hit the center. "Oh, a chance shot! a chance shot!" cried some of the hunter's friends. "Let him try it over—let him try it over!" "No," said Clay firmly; "beat that, and I will." At this, the hunter caved in and urged everyone to vote for Clay. Clay won the election, but later confided to friends: "I had never fired a rifle before, and never have since."[5]

Davy Crockett's Coons

In one of his best-known tales, "A Useful Coon Skin," David Crockett described his experience campaigning for Congress one day in the Tennessee backwoods during the early 1830s. The people in one place, he recalled, were refractory. "They could not listen to me on such a dry subject as the welfare of the nation until they had something to drink." Crockett had neither booze with him nor the means wherewith to purchase any, but by good fortune he succeeded in shooting a coon, trading its skin for some whiskey, and generously treating his audience to drinks. Then he mounted the stump, "and a clear majority of the voters followed me to hear what I had to offer for the good of the nation." But after a while the crowd became restless. "Before I was halfway through," he said, "one of my constituents moved that they would hear the balance of my speech after they had washed down the first part [of the speech] with some more of Job Snelling's extract of cornstalk and molasses. The question being put, it was carried unanimously. We adjourned to the shanty, and on the way I began to reckon that the fate of the nation pretty much depended upon my shooting another coon."[6]

Lincoln Goes to Congress

When Abraham Lincoln ran for Congress as a Whig in 1846, his Democratic opponent was Peter Cartwright, a popular Methodist circuit-rider. During the campaign, according to legend, Lincoln attended a camp meeting at which Cartwright preached a stirring sermon and then invited all those who wished to go to heaven to stand up. A few people got up somewhat self-consciously. "Now," cried Cartwright, "all those who do not wish to go to hell will stand!" All the rest of the people in the congregation, except Lincoln, stood up at this point. Cartwright looked solemnly over at his Whig opponent. "May I inquire of you, Mr. Lincoln, where you are going?" he asked. Rising to his feet, Lincoln replied: "I came here as a respectful listener. I did not know I was to be singled out by Brother Cartwright. I believe in treating religious matters with due solemnity. I admit that the questions propounded by Brother Cartwright are of great importance. I did not feel called upon to answer as the rest did. Brother

Cartwright asks me directly where I am going. I desire to reply with equal directness; I am going to Congress."

Lincoln won the election, served one term in the House, and became known for his opposition to the Mexican War and his good-natured ridicule of Democratic candidate Lewis Cass, the Michigan Senator, who ran against the Whigs' Zachary Taylor in 1848.[7]

Tom Corwin's Color

Because of his dark, swarthy complexion Ohio's Whig Congressman Thomas Corwin was called "Black Tom" and he didn't mind joking about it. Once, when he was addressing a great open-air meeting in southern Ohio as a candidate for Congress, a man in the crowd interrupted to ask: "Are you in favor of a law permitting colored people to eat at the same table with white folks, in hotels and on steamboats?" Realizing that if he said, "Yes," he would lose the pro-slavery vote and if he said, "No," he would alienate the abolitionists, Corwin replied cagily: "Fellow citizens, I submit that it is improper to ask that question of a gentleman of my color!" His answer amused the audience and he carried the day and later the election.[8]

Brother Vance and the Baptists

Once North Carolina's Zebulon B. ("Zeb") Vance was out in the back country of his state campaigning for Congress and at a sudden turn in the road found himself in the midst of some church people having lunch outdoors after their worship service. When he appeared, the leader of the little flock greeted him cordially and invited him "to light and take a bite with us." Vance accepted the invitation, fastened his horse to a tree, approached the congregation, and introduced himself as "Zeb Vance, Whig candidate for Congress." All the time he was wondering, "What denomination is this? Methodist? Baptist? *What?*" But when he scanned the faces about him, he failed to get any light on the all-important question. "Mr. Vance," said the leader of the flock as Vance sat down at the table, "what persuasion are you of?" Vance did some quick thinking. "My sainted grandfather was, during the later years of his long and useful life, a ruling elder in the Presbyterian church," he said tentatively, but as he saw frowns and head-shakings, he went on: "But my father during long years of faithful service in the Master's cause was an equally devout member of the Methodist Episcopal Church." The frowns and headshakings continued, so he rallied himself for the last charge. "But, when *I* came to maturity," he continued, "and was able, after prayer and meditation, to read and understand that blessed book myself, I came to the conclusion *that the old*

Baptist church was right." "Bless God!" exclaimed the old preacher, seizing Vance by the hand. "He is all right, brethren! Oh, you'll get all the votes in these parts, Brother Vance!"[9]

Lincoln-Douglas Debates

Until 1913, when the Seventeenth Amendment (popular election of U.S. Senators) was adopted, the various state legislatures picked members of the upper house. But there were campaigns anyway, for voters elected members of the state legislatures, and the party capturing the legislature succeeded at the same time in winning votes for its Senatorial candidate. One of the most famous Senatorial campaigns took place in 1858, when Illinois Republicans ran Abraham Lincoln against Senator Stephen A. Douglas, the Democratic candidate for the Senate.

Some people were surprised when Lincoln challenged Douglas, one of the most skillful debaters in Congress, to a series of debates in various election districts in Illinois. But Douglas took Lincoln's challenge seriously. "I shall have my hands full," he told Philadelphia journalist John W. Forney. "He is the strong man of his party—full of wit, facts, dates, and the best stump-speaker, with his droll ways and dry jokes, in the West. He is as honest as he is shrewd; and if I beat him, my victory will be hard won."

The Lincoln-Douglas debates—there were seven of them between August 21 and October 15—centered on slavery, with Douglas bypassing the moral issue and Lincoln attacking slavery as "a moral, a social, and a political wrong." The debates became famous for their high level of intellection, and they made Lincoln a national figure. Lincoln impressed people with his thoughtfulness but also with his gentle humor and what Douglas called "his droll ways." In one exchange Lincoln said that Douglas' argument was "as thin as the homeopathic soup that is made by boiling the shadow of a pigeon that had been starved to death." And on another occasion he compared Douglas to an old steamboat. "When I was a boy," he said, "I spent considerable time along the Sangamon River. An old steamboat plied on the river, the boiler of which was so small that when they blew the whistle, there wasn't enough steam to turn the paddle wheel. When the paddle wheel went around, they couldn't blow the whistle. My friend Douglas reminds me of that old steamboat, for it is evident that when he talks he can't think, and when he thinks he can't talk."

During the debates Douglas made continual references to Lincoln's lowly station in life, and in one speech he said the first time he met Lincoln it was across the counter of a general store in which Lincoln was selling whiskey. "And an excellent bartender he was, too," Douglas added, knowing there were temperance people in the audience. When the laughter died down, Lincoln (a teetotaler) got up and said: "What Mr. Douglas says is quite true.

I did keep a general store and sold cotton and candies and cigars and sometimes whiskey, and I particularly remember Mr. Douglas, as he was a very good customer. Many a time I have been on one side of the counter and sold whiskey to Mr. Douglas on the other side. But now there's a difference between us: I've left my side of the counter, but he sticks to his as tenaciously as ever!"

Lincoln lost the election, but by no means ignominiously. His party carried districts with a larger population than those the Democrats carried, but inequitable apportionment returned a Democratic majority to the legislature, which went on to elect Douglas as Senator. Asked how he felt after the election, Lincoln said: "Like the boy who stubbed his toe. I am too big to cry, and too badly hurt to laugh."[10]

Cartwright on the Enemies of the Democratic Party

At the Democratic state convention in Springfield, Illinois, in the spring of 1860, a resolution instructing the Illinois delegates to the forthcoming national Democratic convention to support Senator Stephen A. Douglas for nomination as President was adopted amid great enthusiasm. Immediately after its adoption, one delegate rose to call attention to the fact that the venerable Methodist circuit-rider who had run against Lincoln for Congress in 1846 was present and went on to say he knew the convention would be happy to hear a word from him. At once cries of, "Cartwright! Cartwright! Cartwright!" went up, and from his seat near the central part of the hall Peter Cartwright arose, and, with deep emotion, declared: "My friends and fellow-citizens, I am happy to be with you here on the present occasion. My sun is low down upon the horizon, and the days of my pilgrimage are almost numbered. I have lived in Illinois during the entire period of its history as a State. I have watched with tender interest its marvellous growth from its feeble condition as a Territory, until it has reached its present splendor as a State. I have traveled over its prairies, slept with only the canopy of heaven for a covering; I have followed the trail of the Indians, fought the desperadoes, swam the rivers, threaded the almost pathless forests, in order that I might carry the tidings of the blessed Gospel to the loneliest cabin upon the border. Yes, my friends, for seventy long years, amid appalling difficulties and dangers, I have waged an incessant warfare against the world, the flesh, the devil, *and all the other enemies of the Democratic party!*"[11]

Douglas Campaigns in 1860

In June 1860, the Democrats, meeting in Baltimore, nominated Illinois Senator Stephen A. Douglas for President on a popular-sovereignty platform (permitting slavery in the Federal territories). By this time the Southern Democrats had left the party; their choice for President was James Buchanan's Vice President, John C. Breckinridge of Kentucky, and their platform demanded Federal protection of slavery in the territories. The split in the Democratic party made the election of the Republican candidate, Abraham Lincoln, almost a certainty; and it was also clear that Lincoln's election would touch off a secession movement in the South. During the 1860 campaign Senator Douglas did something unusual: he took to the stump. It was not considered dignified in those days for presidential candidates to go out hustling for votes, but Douglas considered the crisis so grave that he felt impelled to travel around the country, particularly in the South, encouraging sectional harmony and warning against the perils of disunion.

In August, when Douglas spoke in Norfolk, Virginia, people in the audience asked whether the Southern states would be justified in seceding from the Union if Lincoln became President, and he cried: "To this I emphatically answer no. The election of a man to the presidency by the American people in conformity with the Constitution of the United States *would not justify any attempt at dissolving this glorious confederacy.*" The question was then repeated in a somewhat different form and Douglas exclaimed: "I tell them 'no—never on earth!'"

When Lincoln's election in November produced secession despite Douglas' best efforts, he remained staunchly loyal to the Union. One day a devoted Douglas man announced he was going to raise a regiment for the Confederates and was on his way to seek Senator Douglas' approval. When he got home that night, however, he had another announcement to make. He had received Douglas' blessing for the regiment, he said, but the Senator "had told him to take it into the Union Army," and so he had decided "he would take it there!"[12]

Cornstalks

According to an old story, a man by the name of Lex Johnson ran for Congress just before the Civil War and told the voters: "Elect me. We can lick those yellow-livered, soft Yankees with cornstalks!" After the war he ran again, announcing: "Folks, elect me, and I'll get this state back on its feet." "Just a minute, Lex," yelled a man in one of his audiences. "Before the war you said we should elect you and we'd lick those Yankees with cornstalks." "Yes, that's right, man," cried Johnson, "but those Yankees wouldn't fight with cornstalks!"[13]

Ben Butler's Apple

During his run for Congress on the Republican ticket in 1866, Massachusetts' Ben Butler was invited to speak at a huge political rally in New

York City, but to his surprise he encountered a great deal of hostility. When it came his turn to address the audience he was greeted with boos, catcalls, and hisses; and suddenly an apple flew through the air and hit him on the forehead. Butler at once whipped out his knife and some of the people nearby were afraid he was going to start slashing the hecklers. Instead, he calmly leaned over, picked up the apple, pared it, and began eating it. "Not a bad apple at that," he said pleasantly, as the crowd watched quietly. When he finished eating the apple, he threw the core away, wiped his mustache, and went into his speech. There was no more heckling.[14]

Thad Stevens' Scoundrel

In close Congressional elections the losers usually challenged the right of the winners to take their seats in the House, but the majority party almost invariably awarded the election to its own candidate, regardless of the merits of the case. One day Republican Congressman Thaddeus Stevens of Pennsylvania arrived late for a meeting of the Committee on Elections and asked about the case under investigation. "There is not much point to it," one of his colleagues told him. "They are both damned scoundrels." "Well," said Stevens, "which is the Republican damned scoundrel? I want to go for him!"[15]

Speak Afterwards

In 1874, when J. C. S. Blackburn of Kentucky was a candidate for Congress for the first time, he attended a public hanging in one of the counties in his district. The sheriff invited him to occupy a seat on the gallows along with the prisoner and his spiritual adviser, and, as the fatal hour approached, told the prisoner he had five minutes still to live and that it was his privilege, if he so desired, to address the crowd gathered below. The prisoner meekly declined, whereupon Blackburn stepped promptly to the front of the scaffold and announced: "As the gentleman does not wish to speak, if he will kindly yield me his time, I will take this occasion to remark that I am a candidate for Congress, regularly nominated by the Democratic convention." At this point the prisoner interrupted. "Please hang me first," he pleaded, "*and let him speak afterwards!*"[16]

Private Allen and the General

In 1884, John M. Allen of Mississippi took on former Confederate General Tucker in a race for the House of Representatives. One night during the campaign General Tucker ended a speech by telling the audience: "My fellow citizens, twenty years ago last night, after a hard fought battle on yonder hill, I bivouacked under yonder clump of trees. Those of you who remember, as I do, those times that tried men's souls will not, I hope, forget their humble servant when the primaries are held." When Allen's turn-came to speak he picked up on his opponent's theme. "My fellow citizens," he said, "what General Tucker says to you about having bivouacked in yonder clump of trees on that night is true. It is also true, my fellow citizens, that I was a vidette picket and stood guard over the general while he slept. Now then, fellow citizens, all of you who were generals and had privates stand guard over you while you slept, vote for General Tucker, and all of you who were privates and stood guard over the generals while they slept, vote for Private John Allen!" The audience roared with delight and on election day Allen swamped the General at the polls. From that time forward he was known as "Private" John Allen.[17]

Fair Election

Once, when some disputed election cases came before a House committee, Mississippi's John Allen began defending the way elections were conducted in his state, and, noticing amusement on the faces of the other Congress-man, stopped, looked embarrassed, and finally exclaimed: "Well—well, it is true that we have fair elections in Mississippi, but every election morning, just before the polls open, we fire off a few guns and cannon, just to let the negroes know that it is to be a fair election!"[18]

Worried

During one of John Allen's Congressional campaigns in Mississippi, one of his constituents asked him: "Private John, what are you going to do if you are elected?" "Hell, man," said Allen, "what I'm worried about is what I'm going to do if I'm not elected!"[19]

Pregnant

One year, when "Private" John Allen was running for re-election, he agreed to debate one of his challengers, W. B. Walker, at a political rally in Kirkville, Mississippi. Walker spoke first. "Gentlemen, I want you to notice my opponent, Mr. Allen," he cried. "Just look at him sitting over there, big and fat, why, he's literally pregnant on the people's money, he has been in Congress so long." When Allen's time came to speak he arose, patted his large stomach, smiled, and said: "My fellow citizens, what Mr. Walker said is true about me being pregnant on the people's money. I've been exposed. I will promise you one thing, that when I am in labor and delivered of the child, if it's a girl I will name it Martha Washington, if it's a boy I will name it George Washington, and if it's a jack-ass I will name it W. B. Walker!"[20]

Promise

In 1887, just before the Pennsylvania legislature elected Republican political boss Matthew Quay to the U.S. Senate, his cynical friend and associate Boies Penrose threw a big party for the state legislators that lasted two nights and required huge quantities of food and drink to keep the guests happy. Late the second night one of the legislators broke down in tears at the thought of breaking a promise he had made to his mother. "What did you promise her?" asked Penrose sympathetically. "I promised her," sobbed the legislator, "that I'd never vote for Matt Quay." "Well, you haven't—yet," consoled Penrose. "No," wailed the man, "but I feel I'm going to." "That's fine," said Penrose. "Be sure and vote for Mr. Quay. Then write your mother and tell her you were too drunk to know what you were doing. She'll understand."[21]

Moral Character

A Congressman from the West began receiving a great deal of criticism in his district for his behavior in Washington, and, since he was up for election again, he hastened home to get right with his constituents. When he reached his home town, he was met at the station by a large number of his supporters. Quickly alighting from the train and stepping on the platform, he delivered himself of the following remarks with a beaming countenance: "Fellow-citizens, my heart is deeply touched as my eyes behold this splendid assemblage of my constituents and friends gathered here before and around me. During my absence in Congress my friends have spoken in my vindication. I am here now to speak for myself. Vile slanders have been put in circulation against me. I have been accused of being a defaulter. I have been accused of being a drunkard; I have been accused of being a gambler; but, thank God, fellow-citizens, *no man has ever dared to assail my moral character!*"[22]

Sends a Document

Massachusetts Congressman James Buffington prided himself on the fact that he never missed a roll call in the House and that he kept in touch with his constituents by sending at least one document under his frank each year to every voter in his district. His conscientiousness served him well. In a closely contested election one year he received four more votes in one town on Cape Cod than any other candidate. Curious about it, he looked into the matter and discovered that an old farmer and his three sons, who lived in an out-of-the-way place and kept mostly to themselves, had cast the crucial votes. The four men never came to town meetings, he learned, but for that particular election they had appeared in town, voted for Buffington and for no other candidate, and then disappeared. Just before they left, however, one of the aldermen asked the farmer why he had voted for Buffington. "Did you know him?" he asked the farmer. "No," said the old fellow. "He knows me." Then he explained: "He sends me and each of my sons a document every winter."[23]

Division on Shakespeare

One evening the celebrated tragedian John McCullough performed scenes from two of Shakespeare's masterpieces at a Washington theater and received great applause. The following morning, when Kentucky Congressman J. Proctor Knott was on his way to the Capitol, a rather solemn-looking individual stopped him on the street and said: "Mr. Knott, I would like to have your judgment as to which is the best play, *Hamlet* or *Macbeth*." Knott gazed thoughtfully at the man for a moment and then replied: "My friend, don't ask me that question. I am a politician, and a candidate for re-election to Congress; my district is about equally divided; Hamlet has his friends down there, and Macbeth his, and I am unwilling *to take any part between them!*"[24]

Invitation

When Speaker Thomas B. Reed was making a campaign speech in a town in Maine during one presidential contest, a Democrat sat in the front row to heckle him. He kept asking impertinent questions, to which Reed answered courteously, and it soon became obvious that the Democrat wanted to goad him into losing his temper. Finally, despairing of upsetting the Speaker's equanimity, the man cried: "Aw, go to hell!" Said Reed at once: "I have traveled in many parts of the State, and have spoken at many meetings, but this is the first time I have received an invitation to the Democratic headquarters."[25]

Reed's Knockdown Argument

During one of his campaigns, Thomas B. Reed was speaking in South Berwick, Maine, and when he came to the peroration, with the audience hanging onto every word, a man in the audience had his seat suddenly collapse and he went down to the floor with a great crash. "Well," said Reed calmly, "you must at least credit me with making a knockdown argument!" He had the audience with him again.[26]

Not Sure

One blistering hot afternoon, an old Senator stood on the rear platform of a campaign train, orating at length to an increasingly restless crowd gathered at the station. Before he finished, the train started to pull out and the crowd broke into thunderous applause. As the shouts faded, the Senator poured himself a drink and confided to a reporter: "You know something? I'm not sure whether they were applauding me or the engineer."[27]

Divided

When North Carolina Senator Zebulon Vance was on the campaign trail and asked where he stood on the subject of Prohibition, he exclaimed: "I will reply to the gentleman's question by saying that my head is strongly inclined to the great policy of prohibition, but my stomach yearns the other way. I may say therefore I truthfully declare myself as being divided on the issue."[28]

Hurts

In 1890, Joseph G. Cannon, William McKinley, and Benjamin Butterworth were all defeated for re-election to the House, and a few days after the election happened to meet in Chicago and had dinner together. During the course of the evening McKinley and Butterworth remarked that they did not regret the result of the election; they were glad, in fact, for they now had time to attend to their private affairs. "Oh, hell, boys!" scoffed "Uncle Joe" Cannon, "tell that to the marines. There's no use for us to lie to one another! It hurts, and it *hurts damned bad!*"[29]

Wooden-shoe Statesman

During his first run for Congress, Indiana's James E. Watson was scheduled to speak at a place called Spades. Accompanied by a friend, Dr. G. B. Vincent, he started off in a buggy, but got so chilled by the cold biting wind that he told his friend, "Doctor, my feet are cold, and my legs clear up to my knees." "Let's go back," said Dr. Vincent. "I'll show you something." When they arrived at the doctor's house, he brought out a pair of wooden shoes with a thin lining of wool in them. "Put them on," he instructed, "and I promise you won't be cold any more." Watson put the shoes on somewhat reluctantly, for they made his feet look "like a pair of gondolas." Then they drove to Spades, entered the country store, which was full of people, all German-Americans, and Watson got up on a coffee sack and made them a Republican speech in German. "The combination of language and shoes was irresistible," he said later, "and the result was that, while that township normally had but twenty Republican votes, that I fall I got eighty-seven. Time and again after that day I was called 'the Wooden-Shoe Statesman' all over the countryside."[30]

Well-known Figure

During one campaign year Democratic Congressman William Jennings Bryan of Nebraska, known for his oratory, stumped the length and breadth of a neighboring state, campaigning against a Republican candidate for governor, but the Republican won the election anyway. Months later Bryan found himself unexpectedly in an embarrassing situation; he shared the platform with the newly elected governor at a St. Patrick's Day celebration. Worse still, the Governor was called on to introduce him to the crowd. "I went forward," Bryan said later, "wondering if the gentleman held a grudge against me for my ardent campaigning in opposition to him. He stood at the front of the platform, prompted by another man, and said, 'Now, let me introduce that well-known figure in this state, W. J. Bryan.' Well, I felt much relieved that he didn't harbor any resentment, for he grasped my hand warmly, drew me to him, and whispered, 'Quick, do you speak, sing or dance?' He had never heard of me!"[31]

Senator Allison's Reply

According to the *Baltimore Herald*, if there was one Senator better at concealing his position on public questions from the voters than Rhode Island's Nelson W. Aldrich, it was Iowa's William B. Allison. One day Allison dictated a long letter to his secretary in answer to some pointed questions sent him by one of his constituents. When he finished, he asked thoughtfully: "What do you think of that reply?" The secretary hesitated, and then said politely: "To be entirely candid, Senator, it is difficult to gather exactly what you mean." "Admirable!" exclaimed Allison gleefully. "Admirable! That's precisely the idea!"[32]

McKinley's Changing Views

When William McKinley was in the House, he favored the free coinage of silver, but by 1896, when he ran for President, he had become a firm advocate of the gold standard. During the 1896 contest Walter P. Brownlow, Republican Congressman from Tennessee, stumped his state for McKinley but whooped it up for free silver as well. When Republican National Committee Chairman Mark Hanna heard about it, he wrote at once asking Brownlow to stop talking about free silver since McKinley was running as the sound-money candidate on a gold-standard platform. "Dear Mr. Chairman," Brownlow replied, "I regret exceedingly if I have offended. The most eloquent Silver speech I ever heard fall from human lips was made by Major McKinley some years ago. I did not know he had changed his views, and I was going up and down quoting his remarks on the coinage question. I will, however, conform my speech to your suggestions, but I beg of you that, should he again change his views, you will telegraph me notice in advance, so that I can still work in harmony with our great leader!"[33]

Platt's Sense of Humor

New York's Republican Senator Thomas C. Platt had a "singular sense of humor," it was said, and it was never more evident than the night he entertained a large number of newspapermen at a dinner party soon after a political campaign in which they had attacked him sharply as a reactionary. After the feast, when the time for the speech-making arrived, Platt got up, reached under the table, and, to the consternation of everyone there, pulled out two horse pistols and aimed them at his guests. Then, calling the newsmen up, one by one, with the pistols aimed at their heads, he made them take back all the mean things they had said about him during the campaign. The party ended in a lovefest.[34]

Doublecrossed

When one of North Dakota's Senators died, the leaders of the state legislature decided to pick one of their likable but mediocre colleagues from a rural district to fill out his term. The man they chose knew he was no great shakes, but he was excited by the possibility of being a Senator even for a short time, and on the day the legislature was to vote he sat expectantly in the back of the assembly eagerly awaiting the nominating speech. The man chosen to nominate him was given to flowery language and he went into action at once. "My colleagues," he began, "I nominate for the vacancy in the United States Senate, that man among us of noble character, of outstanding ability, of unimpeachable integrity, of impressive achievements. . . ." But as his language mounted, the old fellow he was nominating got a look of surprise on his face, then became angry, and finally leaned over to the man next to him and snarled: "Well, the dirty double-crosser! He promised to nominate *me!*"[35]

Friend of the People

Pennsylvania's reactionary Republican Senator Boies Penrose took a vigorously unsentimental view of democratic politics that, for all its cynicism, had the merit of demolishing the windy bombast that became so popular in American political contests in the nineteenth century. "Friend of the people?" he once jeered, when his campaign managers used the phrase on posters setting forth reasons why he should be re-elected to the Senate in 1902. "Friend of the people? Who says so?" "Well—of course, Senator—you are. Aren't you?" said one of his campaign workers. "After all, it's just the customary—" "Politicians don't have any friends," said Penrose firmly. "I don't know that I have any. There are a hell of a lot of people who'll vote for me that I wouldn't think of being friends with. If you think that sort of stuff fools anybody, you're a damn fool!"[36]

Americanism

"Once," said Boies Penrose, "I thought success in politics required ninety percent brains and ten percent guts. Now I know it's just ten percent gall and ninety percent wind." On the eve of one campaign, a Republican boss almost as cynical as Penrose himself asked him what the issue was going to be. Penrose thought for a moment and then replied: "Americanism." "Yeah?" muttered the boss. "And what is this Americanism?" "Something to get votes with," explained Penrose. "Outside of that, what do you care?"[37]

Time to a Hog

Once the Democrats held a big rally in Washington just before an important campaign and picked New York Congressman Charles A. Towne, known for his oratorical prowess, to give the address. But to add zest to the meeting they picked Bourke Cockran, another New York Congressman, to introduce Towne because he too was famed for his speech-making. "Now Cockran and Towne were as jealous of each other as two prima donnas," a Republican Senator who knew them both noted amusedly. "It is well-known that no two songbirds will sit on the same limb and sing at the same time." The inevitable happened that evening. Cockran completely forgot his role as the curtain-raiser and proceeded to spend close to two hours on his introduction.

By the time Towne got to speak he was boiling mad. But, keeping control of his temper, he walked to the front of the stage when Cockran finished and announced: "Ladies and gentlemen, this introduction reminds me of an incident out in a little town in Minnesota. A man there owned a hog which he kept in a pasture in one corner of the town. Every morning and every evening he drove this hog entirely through the town out to his home where he lived in another corner of the town, fed him, and then drove him back to the pasture. This finally excited the curiosity of all the people who noticed it, and one day someone asked him why he did such a thing as that, and he responded that he simply took him out there to feed him. 'Well,' said the inquisitor, 'but it takes so much time to do that.' 'Oh, well,' said the owner, 'what the hell is time to a hog?'" And that was all Towne said, and he sat down amid long and uproarious applause. Needless to say, the two Congressmen never spoke to each other again.[38]

Cannon's Profanity

When Joseph Cannon was campaigning for re-election to Congress in 1906, he asked one of the campaign workers in his home town, Danville, Ohio, whether there was any special phase of the campaign that should be called to his attention. "Yes," said the man, "one thing." "What is that?" asked Cannon. "Your everlasting and insistent profanity," said the man. "People who have known about this all their lives, and large numbers who have heard it themselves as long as they can remember anything, have suddenly flared up about it and seem to be all agog over it. There is a kind of moral wave going over the country at this time, and it has taken possession of a lot of our people, and there are many mutterings about sending a man who is so outlandishly profane to represent their district."

Cannon was amused. "Well," he said, good-naturedly, "I guess these folks are right about my cussin', but they must remember that I belong to a different age. I was born at a time when about everybody swore and about everybody drank liquor and even preachers had it on their sideboards. I suppose that, boylike, when I started swearin' I thought it was smart and kept it up for that reason; but now it has become such a fixed habit with me as to be an ineradicable part of my nature, and in private conversation I can't even emphasize if I don't put in a few cuss words to show my real feeling. Everybody who knows me knows that I would not injure anyone and especially that I would not call on our common Maker to damn any of his creatures." He paused for a moment, and then, thinking of a local preacher named Jones who was considered short on piety, he summed it all up: "Oh, I'm with my cussin' a great deal like Brother Jones is with his prayin'; don't mean a damned thing by it!"[39]

Democratic Gain

Republican Congressman Charles Grosvenor of Ohio and Democratic Congressman Champ Clark of Missouri met for the first time after a

Congressional campaign in which the Republicans had done very well. "Hello, Champ! How did you get through the campaign?" asked Grosvenor. "Splendidly," said Clark. "I gained twenty-five pounds." "Well, I congratulate you," said Grosvenor. "That is the first Democratic gain of which I have heard!"[40]

All Stood Up

Defending his record one day before some of his constituents in Kansas, Republican Congressman Victor Murdock angrily deplored the unscrupulous attacks on his character by his opponents and said disgustedly: "Why, they even say I'm crazy!" Then he added: "How many of you think I'm crazy? All of you who do, stand up!" "And, by Gad," he said ruefully afterward, "you know, they all stood up!"[41]

Never Make It

In 1912, when Kentucky Congressman Ollie M. James, a huge man physically, vacated his seat in the House to run for the Senate, Alben W. Barkley, not quite thirty-five years old, entered the race for the House. One day during the campaign he introduced himself to a country storekeeper and announced: "I'm running to fill Ollie James' place." "Son," said the storekeeper, looking the slender young man over carefully, "you'll never make it!"[42]

Didn't Know Him

During Alben Barkley's first race for Congress in 1912, he took his son Bud along when campaigning one day near his home town, Paducah, where the Baptist church was having a doctrinal dispute of some kind. At one point the two pulled into a service station and, while the attendant was filling the tank, Barkley decided to do a little politicking. "My name's Barkley," he announced, sticking his head out of the car. "Barkus?" said the attendant, putting his hand out for a shake. "No, Barkley. Alben Barkley." Glad to know you, Mr. Allen," said the attendant. "No!" cried Barkley. "The name is Barkley. Barkley—of Paducah." "Oh, yes—Paducah," said the attendant, his face lighting up. "That's where the Baptists are having all that trouble, isn't it?" "Bud," sighed Barkley as they drove away, "I don't believe that man knew me."[43]

Inquiry or Invitation

A temperance advocate queried a candidate for Congress: "Do you ever take alcoholic drinks?" "Before I answer that question," responded the candidate cautiously, "I want to know whether it is put as an inquiry or as an invitation."[44]

Hate to Lose

Like many Congressmen, New Jersey Republican Charles Wolverton won automatic re-election to the House every time he ran. But during one of his sixteen successful campaigns he became ill for a time. "I hope he doesn't die," his opponent was supposed to have said, "because I would hate to lose to a dead man!"[45]

Tillman's Help

During one election the Republicans were worried about black voters in Newcastle, Indiana, James E. Watson's Congressional district. For some reason the blacks were out of sorts with the Republican party and Watson's managers were afraid they might stay away from the polls. There was another problem, too, for the Republicans in that district. Up in Crawfordsville, General Lew Wallace, Civil War hero and author of *Ben Hur*, who had great influence with the voters, was hostile to President McKinley's expansionist policies during the Spanish-American War and was distancing himself from the party. Party leaders were anxious to get him back in line.

Congressman Watson finally came up with a solution to both problems. He persuaded South Carolina Senator Ben Tillman ("Pitchfork Ben"), an unrepentant rebel and an outspoken white supremacist, to give some speeches (at $250 per lecture plus expenses) at Chautauqua meetings in his district and assured him he could speak on any topic he chose. Needing the money, Tillman eagerly accepted the engagement. The blacks turned out in great numbers at the Newcastle Chautauqua; but they were so shocked by Tillman's blatant racism and his blasts at the Republicans for coddling black people that they all flocked to the polls on election day and voted straight Republican. Tillman also helped unintentionally with Lew Wallace. When he spoke at the Chautauqua in Crawfordsville, Wallace was in the audience and he, too, was offended by the South Carolina Senator's tirade against Republicans. He was even more angered, if anything, by the way Tillman defended the Confederates and blasted General Sherman for wreaking havoc in the South during the Civil War. Early the next morning, General Wallace walked into the Republican headquarters in Crawfordsville and told the officials there to sign him up to give speeches every day from then on until election day. That November there was a big turnout and the Republicans carried every county in Watson's district by huge majorities.[46]

Special Interests

Democratic Senator Henry F. Ashurst of Arizona once said frankly: "When I have to choose between voting for the people or the special interests, I always stick to the special interests. They remember. The people forget."[47]

Not in the Race

In one of his speeches when running for Congress for the first time in 1912, Texas' Sam Rayburn announced modestly: "I will not deny that there are men in this District better qualified than I to go to Congress." Then, as consternation spread among the people in the audience, he grinned and added quickly: "But these men are not in the race!" There was a storm of applause.[48]

Knutson's Balky Car

In 1916, when Minnesota Republican Harold Knutson ran for Congress the first time, he had little money, was facing a candidate who had a lot of it, and decided at the outset that he would have to do something different (and inexpensive) if he was to have a chance at winning. His solution was to take his automobile along on campaign tours and fix it so he could unobtrusively throw the carburetor or something else out of kilter, whenever he needed to. Approaching a prospective voter, he would have his machine wheeze to a halt and appeal to the voter for help. The voter would fix it, without much trouble, since nothing was seriously wrong, and then Knutson would congratulate him warmly on his knowledge of mechanics, mention casually that he was running for Congress, and then pass on to the next voter. His tactics worked. When the votes were counted on election day, his opponent, who made the rounds in a high-powered car that gave no trouble, went down to defeat.[49]

Heflin on the Phone

In 1918, when Alabama's J. Thomas ("Tom") Heflin was preparing his last run for Congress, he heard that a politician with a great deal of popular appeal was thinking of running against him and he was extremely upset, for he planned to try for the Senate some day and needed the House as a springboard. About a week before the deadline for entering the Alabama primary he sent an assistant down to Montgomery, the state capital, to follow developments. When the crucial evening, with its midnight deadline, arrived, the House was having a night session, and Heflin was so nervous that he left the floor periodically, went to the cloakroom telephone booth, called Montgomery, and in a loud voice that everyone in the cloakroom recognized, anxiously bombarded his assistant with queries. "That you, Jim?" he yelled. "Well, how is it down there? . . . Well, has he filed? Has he filed against me? What! You say he has? . . . He hasn't? . . . Oh, he hasn't? . . . All right, old boy, thank you. . . . Stay right there!" This went on, about every half hour, until midnight, Alabama time, when the deadline arrived and Heflin went out to make his last call. "Did he file?" he cried. "What! He *filed!* You say he filed! He filed against me! . . . Oh—Oh, you say he *didn't* file! He hasn't filed yet. Too late now, eh? It's after twelve, and he didn't file against me, and he can't file now! . . . Well, all right, old boy, thank you, thank you, good-bye, see you later!" Then he came out of the phone booth, drew himself up proudly, and told the Congressmen there who had overheard everything: "Damn his hide! I wish he had filed. I'd have beat the hell out of him!"[50]

No Compromise

Whenever his constituents asked Republican Congressman Fred Schwegel of Iowa about his views on Prohibition, he had a standard reply to make. "Dear Friend: I had not intended to discuss this controversial subject at this particular time. However, I want you to know that I do not run away from a controversy. On the contrary, I will take a stand on any issue at any time, regardless of how fraught with controversy it may be. You have asked me how I feel about whiskey. Here is how I stand on this question:

"If when you say 'whiskey' you mean the devil's brew, the poison scourge, the bloody monster that defiles innocence, dethrones reason, destroys the home, creates misery and poverty, yea, literally takes the bread from the mouths of little children; if you mean the evil drink that topples Christian men and women from the pinnacles of righteous, gracious living into the bottomless pit of degradation and despair, shame and helplessness and hopelessness—then certainly I am against it with all of my power.

"But if, when you say 'whiskey,' you mean the oil of conversation, the philosophic wine, the ale that is consumed when good fellows get together, that puts a song in their hearts and laughter on their lips and the warm glow of contentment in their eyes; if you mean the drink that enables a man to magnify his joy and his happiness and to forget, if only for a little while, life's great tragedies, heartbreaks and sorrows; if you mean that drink the same of which pours into our treasuries untold millions of dollars to provide tender care for our little crippled children, our blind, our deaf, our dumb, our aged and infirm, and to build highways, hospitals, and schools— then, certainly, I am in favor of it.

"This is my stand, and I will not compromise."[51]

Garner's Game

Texas' John Nance Garner refused to abandon his opposition to Prohibition even after Texas voted to ratify the Eighteenth Amendment. During one of his campaign speeches a prohibitionist heckler wanted to know whether Garner, in addition to being a "wet," also played cards. "Yes," said Garner promptly. "Game in Room 5, Starr Hotel, directly after this meeting!"[52]

Buttering up the Voters

Republican Congressman William C. Cramer of Florida liked to tell the story of the young Congressman campaigning for re-election in the mountainous western part of Virginia who was determined to shake hands with everyone in his district. One day he even spent several hours climbing a mountain in order to reach the farmhouse on top and solicit votes among the people there. When he reached the farmhouse he found an elderly woman chopping wood in the front yard. Eager to make a favorable impression, he introduced himself, took the axe from her hands, and began chopping the wood himself. After he had accumulated a sizable pile, the woman thanked him heartily, and, to impress her further, he lugged the wood into the house for her. But as he entered the house with an armful of wood, convinced he had her vote in the bag, he heard a noise in the chimney corner. He looked over and met the eyes of his opponent in the contest, who was busily at work churning butter.[53]

Bacon

When New York's Sol Bloom, an orthodox Jew, was running for re-election to the House in 1924, his friend New York Senator Royal S. Copeland offered to help out in the campaign. On election eve he spoke for Bloom at a big rally of orthodox Jews, and made a lot of good points in his speech, Bloom thought, until he came to the end. Then, to Bloom's amusement, Copeland exclaimed: "And with your loyal support, I confidently predict that by this time tomorrow your good friend and mine, Sol Bloom, will have *brought home the bacon!*"[54]

Getting Out of the Senate

Soon after Indiana's Republican Senator Harry S. New was defeated in a primary contest which was both vigorous and expensive, he was walking down the stairs in the Capitol to the long tunnel that leads to the Senate Office Building, and a woman visiting the Capitol who was bewildered by the network of passageways rushed over when she saw him. "I am trying to get out of the Senate," she cried. "Can you tell me how to do it?" "Madam," said New, bowing low, "I advise you to run in an Indiana primary!"[55]

Name of Opponent

When Kentucky's Alben W. Barkley was running for the Senate in 1926, he took his daughter Wahwee along as chauffeur and campaign helper. It was a strenuous race; he made as many as sixteen speeches a day. But Wahwee took good care of him. She wrapped him in a blanket to keep him warm, wound a scarf around his throat to protect his voice, and, whenever he dozed off while doing some of the driving himself, she yelled the name of his opponent in his ear, and he instantly woke up and started spouting some campaign oratory.[56]

Not Ruthless

"Whatever else it may be, the new Congress will not be Ruthless," quipped the *Springfield Union* shortly after the 1928 election. The Massachusetts newspaper was referring to the fact that three Ruths—Ruth Bryan Owen (D, Fla.), daughter of William Jennings Bryan, Ruth Baker Pratt (R, N.Y.), and Ruth Hanna McCormick (R, Ill.), daughter of Ohio Senator Mark Hanna—had just been elected to the House. "If women's place is no longer in the home," said the *Cleveland Plain Dealer,* "it at least appears to be in the House." The *Houston Chronicle* noted that four women had also been re-elected to the House and that there were now seven "women Congressmen" on Capitol Hill. "All are interesting and intelligent," declared the *Chronicle.* "Their . . . prominence in politics brings a fresh viewpoint from which to attack the growing problems affecting the national life of America. The hand that rocks the cradle helps to rule the nation."

Illinois' Ruth Hanna McCormick probably conducted the most interesting campaign of the three Ruths. Her slogan was "No Promises and No Bunk," and she took a no-nonsense approach to her race for the House. "Usually," she told audiences, "when a candidate announces his candidacy, we read in the papers that owing to the demand of his constituency and the pressure of his friends he has reluctantly agreed to make this great sacrifice and run for office. In all candor and honesty I must say that nobody has asked me to run. I have no demand upon me from constituents, friends, enemies, neighbors or family, and as far as I know, nobody wants me to run. But I hope at the end of the campaign that I am going to find a sufficient number of people who think I ought to run." She achieved her hope. Not only did she run first in the primary election in a field of eight; she also led all the Republicans on the ticket, including Herbert Hoover, in 1928's general election.[57]

Connally's Daughter

In 1928, when Texas' Tom Connally ran for the Senate, he denounced the Ku Klux Klan (then riding high) vigorously and the Klan threw its support to his opponent. The Klan also tried to take advantage of anti-Catholic prejudices by saying that Connally had a daughter in a Catholic convent school in San Antonio. When Connally heard the story, he began taking his son, an only child, along on campaign tours, and introducing him at rallies before launching into his speech. "Now, folks," he said, "this is my daughter, who is attending a Catholic convent school for girls in San Antonio." Then his big, gangling son stepped forward, Connally wrapped his arms around the grinning kid's shoulders, and the crowd always roared with laughter. He won the election.[58]

The Heathen

Mississippi Congressman Ross A. Collins' diligence in securing for the Library of Congress the world-famous Vollbehr Collection of historic volumes, including one of the three extant copies of the Gutenberg Bible, almost cost him his seat in the 1930 elections. During the campaign his opponent violently attacked him for wasting the people's money" by getting the Federal Government to pay $1,500,000 for a bunch of "foreign books." So serious did the situation become that Collins finally felt obliged to explain to his constituents that the large sum of money was required by the need to get the Bible that "Moses wrote" out of the hands of "the heathen."[59]

Dog-catcher

After North Carolina Senator Lee S. Overman died in office in 1930, a Democratic primary was held in North Carolina to name a candidate for the unexpired remainder of his term. Several persons, including Frank Grist, qualified as candidates in the primary. But an editorial writer for the *Greensboro Daily News*, who had taken a strong dislike to Grist, wrote a scathing editorial about him, declaring that "Frank Grist is not qualified to be a dog-catcher." On the advice of his attorney, Grist sent a telegram to the *News* threatening a libel suit unless it retracted the editorial. At that point the editorial writer wrote a retraction: "Frank Grist is fit to be a dog-catcher, but instead of running for that office he is seeking the post of United States Senator."[60]

Until I See Him

Back in the days before television, an extremely ugly Congressman from Kentucky was running for re-election after serving four terms in the

House. One day he went to a town he had never visited before, walked up to a man, shook hands, and introduced himself. The man looked him over skeptically and then said: "Are you the fellow I have been voting for these eight years?" "Yes, sir," beamed the Congressman, "I sure am!" "Well!" exclaimed the man. "This teaches me a lesson. I'll never vote for another man until I see him!"[61]

Regret

New Hampshire's Democratic Senator Thomas J. McIntyre liked to tell about the Democratic candidate for the U.S. Senate who was campaigning in a densely rural and Republican part of northern New England. Everywhere he went he received a cool reception by people who had never even seen, much less voted, for a Democrat before. In one general store, amid the general chilliness, an old man sitting in the corner, suddenly hollered at him: "I voted for a Democrat once." With a big smile on his face, the candidate walked over to the man, put out his hand, and began to introduce himself. "Yes," interrupted the old man, "I voted for a Democrat about twenty-five years ago, and I've regretted it ever since!"[62]

Just One Riot

In 1932, Speaker John Nance Garner received a great deal of support for the Democratic nomination for President, but in the end he threw his support to Franklin D. Roosevelt and received second place on the ticket. During the campaign, however, he made only one speech. Pressed by one campaign worker to do more, he told him about the Texas ranger and the riot. Only one ranger showed up at the seat of disturbance, said Garner, and when someone frantically inquired, "What, just one ranger responded to our call?" the redoubtable Texan said calmly: "Just one riot, ain't there?" To FDR, Garner put it a little differently: "Hoover is making speeches, and that's enough for us!"[63]

Applause

Three sets of Louisiana delegates arrived in Chicago for the Democratic Convention in 1932, and one of them, headed by Louisiana Senator Huey Long, backed Franklin Roosevelt for the nomination. But when Long appeared before the Credentials Committee he gave such a crude speech that he antagonized all the members and they recommended seating one of the other slates. The pro-FDR faction at once appealed to the Convention as a whole to override the committee's recommendation and seat the Long delegates. When Long took the dais to present his case to the Convention, the booing started at once. But Long put his mouth close to the microphone and yelled: "Don't applaud me! Don't applaud me! My time is limited and I don't want applause!" Then, as he plunged into his speech, the crowd quieted, and when he finished it did applaud him, and voted to seat his pro-Roosevelt delegates. Afterward, Long came across Montana Senator Burton Wheeler and said with a smile: "You thought I thought they were applauding me when they were actually booing me, didn't you?" Wheeler admitted that was what he thought. "Well," said Long, "I knew they were booing but I also knew the people down in Louisiana, hearing all that noise over the radio would take my word for it that it was applause."[64]

Bilbo's Dirt

Pat Harrison and Theodore ("The Man") Bilbo, both Senators from Mississippi, cordially disliked each other. In 1936, when Harrison was running for re-election, Bilbo supported his opponent and in speeches attacking Harrison, he "reached into the substrata," it was said, for dirt to throw at him. "When Bilbo dies," said Harrison, "the epitaph on his gravestone should read: 'Here lies Bilbo, deep in the dirt he loved so well'!" Harrison also began telling a story at rallies which centered on Bilbo's nickname ("The Man") that always brought the house down. "Two gentlemen and A MAN," he said, "once made a wager as to who could remain longest in a closed shack with a skunk. The first gentleman stayed a minute; the second, two minutes." Then, drawled Harrison, "THE MAN went in with the skunk and the door was bolted behind him. A couple of hours later the men outside heard a frantic scratching from inside the shack. They looked at each other and agreed to open the door and see what had happened to THE MAN." Shaking his head, Harrison cried: "And what do you think happened? Why, that poor skunk shot out the door like a bolt of lightening, raced pell-mell toward the woods about a hundred yards away and dropped stone-dead." Harrison won the primary.[65]

Spell it

When the Republicans held their national convention in 1940, Massachusetts Congressman Joe Martin, who was presiding, became concerned by the mounting tension in the auditorium as supporters of Wendell Willkie, Robert A. Taft, and Thomas E. Dewey fought bitterly for ascendancy. On the fourth ballot Willkie went into the lead, but without the 501 votes needed for the nomination, and his backers began putting pressure on Kansas, one of the important states in the Midwest, to switch to him, hoping it would induce delegates in other states to switch too. On the fifth ballot, when Kansas was reached, the head of the Kansas delegation announced: "Mr. Chairman, Kansas casts her eighteen votes for Wendell

Willkie," and this touched off a great tumult. As the balloting proceeded, Martin became desperate to find some way of relieving the increasingly unbearable tension that was building up. At last a delegate with a Scandinavian background from North Dakota gave him the opportunity he was seeking. "North Dakota," the delegate announced, "casts four votes for Senator Taft and four votes for Vendell Villkie." "For whom?" asked Martin impishly. "For Vendell Villkie," repeated the delegate. "Spell it," cried Martin in mock-bewilderment. The delegate's response was drowned in a gale of laughter. The convention went on to pick Villkie on the sixth ballot.[66]

How to Vote

In 1946, when Thruston B. Morton of Kentucky was first running for Congress, he prepared a high-minded speech on the important issues of the postwar world and delivered the speech in one precinct after another in his Congressional district. One day, after he had addressed a crowd on the problems of postwar Europe, the precinct captain, a woman, arose to explain how to vote on one of the new-fangled voting machines which used symbols to distinguish parties. "Now, it's all really simple," she declared. "When you go into the booth you'll see an old rooster. He'll be wiry, skinny, and scrawny, and tough-looking. You'll know you couldn't even make soup out of him. Then you'll see a nice little log cabin. It will be the kind of cozy place where you could find protection from the wildest winter storm or the worst of summer heat. You'll feel right at home with that little log cabin. So when it comes to voting, you just take the lever beside the log cabin and pull and pull and pull." Then she added: "Electing a Congressman is just like flushing the toilet."[67]

Hickenlooper and Rickenbacker

Sometimes a name can be an asset. Iowa's Bourke B. Hickenlooper found that out when he was running for the Senate as a Republican against Al Loveland, the Democrat candidate, in 1944. In one town Loveland approached a voter, identified himself, and said, "I am a candidate for Senator, and I hope I will have your support." "Nope," said the man instantly. "I'm going to vote for that other feller." Then he added: "He's a prayin', God-fearin' man." "Yes, he is a good man," said Loveland, somewhat dismayed, "but what is it about him that impresses you to this extent?" "Well, now," said the man, "everybody ought to know that. The papers was full of it. That airplane went down in the Pacific and a bunch of 'em was in the raft with him. He got out the Bible and read to 'em and prayed—yes, sir—he's a prayin', God-fearin' man. That's what pulled 'em through."

Astonished, Loveland exclaimed: "Man, that wasn't Hickenlooper. That was Eddie Rickenbacker." "I don't care what you call him . . . Hickenbacker, Rickenbacker . . . ," said the voter. "I tell you he's a prayin', God-fearin' man, and I'm fer him." Relating the incident to friends afterward, Loveland sighed: "What can you do with a handicap like that?"[68]

Kefauver's Coonskin Cap

In 1948, when Estes Kefauver ran for the Senate, Memphis boss Ed Crump placed advertisements in the newspapers charging that Kefauver was "soft on Communism" and had voted the party line when he was in the House. This was preposterous, of course, but when Kefauver issued a denial, Crump came up with another advertisement comparing him to "the pet coon that puts its foot in an open drawer in your room, but invariably turns its head while its foot is feeling around in the drawer," as if to say: "You have me wrong—I have made a mistake, look at my turned head. I am sorry about my foot. I couldn't see what I was doing."

Kefauver quickly turned the tables on Crump. The coon, he said in a radio address, "the most American of all animals, has been defamed. You wouldn't find a coon in Russia. It is one of the cleanest of all animals; it is one of the most courageous. . . . A coon . . . can lick a dog four times its size; he is somewhat of a 'giant-killer' among the animals. Yes, the coon is all American. Davy Crockett, Sam Houston, James Robertson and all of our great men of that era in Tennessee history wore the familiar, ring-tailed coon-skin cap. Mr. Crump defames me—but worse than that he defames the coon, the all-American animal. We coons can take care of ourselves. I may be a pet coon, but I 'ain't' Mr. Crump's pet coon."

Kefauver's riposte brought such praise from around Tennessee that his managers acquired a live coon, persuaded him to take it along on his campaign trips, and soon made it his campaign symbol. "This is a pedigreed West Tennessee coon," Kefauver told audiences. "Notice his big bushy tail. This coon has rings in his tail, but I want you to remember I have no ring in my nose." Unfortunately the coon became nervous and balky from all the noise at rallies so Kefauver finally released him. But about this time the head of a Chattanooga bank which used a coonskin cap as its emblem sent Kefauver a nice coonskin cap and he began donning it just before speeches and announcing: "I may be a 'pet coon,' but I'm not Mister Crump's 'pet coon.'"

The coonskin cap was a powerful campaign symbol. It represented independence from Boss Crump; it called up images of Tennessee's old frontier days; and it was so thoroughly "American" that it made the Communist charge sound silly. At rallies people chanted, "Put it on," Kefauver recalled, and "I'd have to stick the coonskin cap on my head and give a big grin before they'd let me go on with my speech." Naturally he won the election.[69]

Over That Way

In 1948, when Maine Republican Margaret Chase Smith ran for the Senate the first time, she stopped in a little town to introduce herself to the owner of a grocery store and his customers and made a little pitch for their votes. The grocer listened quietly as she talked and then inquired: "What are you running for, Madam?" "The United States Senate," she replied. "From where?" he asked. "Maine, of course," she answered, a bit annoyed. "Well, lady, you are in New Hampshire," he said, as his customers tittered. "Maine is over that way." It was one of Senator Smith's favorite stories.[70]

Came Back to Vote

In 1948, Lyndon B. Johnson won his election to the Senate by such a narrow margin that his enemies referred to him sarcastically as "Landslide Lyndon" and charged that his supporters had stuffed the ballot boxes. Shortly after the election, according to a popular joke, a man taking a walk in San Antonio came across a little Mexican boy he knew seated on the curb crying bitterly. "José," he said, "why are you crying?" "My daddy doesn't like me," wailed the boy. "But José," said the man, "your daddy is dead." "But," sobbed the boy, "he came back to vote for Lyndon Johnson and he didn't come to see me."[71]

The Sins of Claude Pepper

In 1950, when George Smathers ran against incumbent Democratic Senator Claude D. Pepper in the Florida primary, his victory was attributed, at least in part, to the misleading attacks on Pepper which his campaign managers sponsored. "Are you aware," went one of the Smather campaign pitches, "that Claude Pepper is known all over Washington as a shameless extrovert? Not only that, but this man is reliably reported to practice nepotism with his sister-in-law, and he has a sister who was once a thespian in wicked New York. Worst of all, it is an established fact that Mr. Pepper, before his marriage, habitually practiced celibacy."[72]

Senator Smith's Apology

When Senator Margaret Chase Smith's name was mentioned in 1952 as a possible Republican vice-presidential candidate, a radio interviewer asked her: "Suppose you woke up some morning and found yourself in the White

House, what would you do?" "I'd go straight to Mrs. Truman and apologize," she said. "Then I'd go home."[73]

Much Better

When Democratic Congressman Mike Mansfield was running for the Senate in 1952, Wisconsin's egregious Senator Joseph R. McCarthy went to Montana to campaign for Mansfield's Republican challenger, Zales Ecton, and in his usual demagogic fashion called Mansfield a "Communist dupe." After Mansfield won the election, McCarthy decided to mend fences with him; and when the two met on Capitol Hill for the first time after the election, he went up to the Montanan, grabbed his arm, and cried: "Mike, how good to see you. How is everything in Montana these days?" Pulling himself away, Mansfield said coldly: "Much better since you left, sir," and walked off.[74]

No Landslide

After John F. Kennedy won his first Senate race in 1952, his critics charged that he had bought his victory with his father's money. To tease JFK about this, reporters at the annual Gridiron Club meeting in Washington soon after the election introduced him with a song they called, "For the Bill Goes to Daddy." Responding to the serenade, Kennedy brought the house down by reading a telegram he said came from his father: "Dear Jack: Don't buy a single vote more than necessary. I'll be damned if I'll pay for a landslide!"[75]

Ada

When Minnesota Senator Hubert H. Humphrey was running for re-election in 1954, some people criticized him for belonging to the Americans for Democratic Action (ADA), a liberal organization. Asked by a reporter what the farmers in his state thought about his membership in ADA, he replied: "I simply declare to them in answer that things had come to a sad pass when a man could be so abused for belonging to that fine old American institution, the American Dairyman's Association!"[76]

Senator Green's Tip

Once Rhode Island's Democratic Senator Theodore Green got into a Washington taxi with a friend, and when they reached their destination, paid the driver, and, as the cab pulled away, remarked, "Well, there's one vote we can count on." "Why?" asked the friend. "Did you give him a big tip and tell him to vote Democratic?" "No, indeed," said Green, "I didn't tip him at all and told him to vote Republican."[77]

A Favor for a Voter

It's an old story, but Democratic Majority Leader Lyndon B. Johnson enjoyed updating it. Once, he said, one of his constituents came to ask a favor and pointed out he had voted time and again for LBJ in his races for the House and Senate. "So naturally," said Johnson, "Ah thanked the man for his fine support and Ah said, 'Mah friend, what can Ah do for you?' And mah visitor said, 'Well, Senator, after all Ah did to hepp you, Ah wonder if you could hepp me become a citizen?'"[78]

Ask Lyndon

In the summer of 1956, just before the Democrats met in Chicago to pick their presidential candidate, Lyndon B. Johnson, the powerful Senate Majority Leader who was beginning to have presidential aspirations, got *Newsweek* reporter Sam Shaffer on the phone and practically ordered him to come to his office. When Shaffer appeared, Johnson blistered him for having quoted a Democratic politician on LBJ's plans at the convention in a piece Shaffer did for *Newsweek*. "If you wanted to know what Lyndon Baines Johnson was going to do at the national convention," he yelled, "why didn't you come to Lyndon Baines Johnson and ask him what Lyndon Baines Johnson was going to do?" "All right," said Shaffer calmly, "what is Lyndon Baines Johnson going to do?" "I don't know," admitted Johnson.[79]

What it Takes

In 1956, when liberal Democrat Joseph S. Clark of Pennsylvania was running for the Senate, he promised voters that if he won he would vote against Mississippi's James Eastland, a foe of civil rights, for chairman of the Judiciary Committee, which had jurisdiction over civil-rights legislation. After his victory, however, Clark began having second thoughts about his effectiveness as a Senator after having attacked one of the Senate's leading members. At lunch in New York shortly after his election he asked Minnesota's Hubert Humphrey what he should do, and Humphrey suggested that he get in touch with Eastland as soon as he got to Washington and try to mollify the Mississippi conservative. Clark decided to take Humphrey's advice. But a few days later when he appeared in Eastland's office and began to explain his campaign strategy, Eastland interrupted him. "Hell, Joe, don't worry," he said, waving his cigar at Clark. "I know what it takes to get elected in Pennsylvania."[80]

Handshake

When Kentucky Congressman William H. Natcher, a Democrat, was campaigning in one of the Republican counties in his district, he stopped a man on the street, told him he was a candidate for re-election, and held out his hand. The man asked what party Natcher belonged to, and when Natcher said he was a Democrat, the man reluctantly held out his hand and said: "Well, all right, but just press it light!"[81]

On the Doubtful List

One of Nevada Senator Alan Bible's favorite stories was about the Congressman who was thinking of running for re-election, but sent a friend out to make the rounds in his district to find out what his chances were. Pencil and pad in hand, the friend went into action. "Say," he said to the first person he met on the street. "Old John Smith is thinking of running for Congress again. What do you think of him?" "Smith," cried the man, "is an unscrupulous scoundrel devoid of intellect, decency and integrity, and an infamous plunderer whose sole aim in life is to feather his nest at the expense of the taxpayer." "Thanks a lot," said the Congressman's friend, busily jotting the man's remarks down on his pad. "I'll put you down on the doubtful list."[82]

Inconceivable

In one Oklahoma campaign a Republican who was a minister of the gospel entered the lists against Democratic Senator Robert Kerr, agreed to debate Kerr, and got to speak first at the rally. "I believed in times past," he said in his speech, "that seeking public office was incompatible with my holy profession. I became a candidate for the Senate only after I spent the night wrestling in prayer with the Lord and being told by Him that it was my duty to run for the office." When Kerr's turn came, he told the audience: "A Senator holds a most important office. If he is rightly motivated, he can do much good for God and country. Hence, I can conceive of the possibility that the Almighty might urge an individual to run for the Senate." He paused for a moment and then went on: "It's inconceivable, however, that the Almighty would tell anyone to run for the Senate on the Republican ticket!"[83]

Joke

Texas' Sam Rayburn always campaigned on serious issues. He never slapped a voter on the back, kissed a baby, bragged about himself, or told funny stories in his campaign speeches. "I tried to tell a joke once in a speech," he confessed, "but before I got through I was the joke!"[84]

Might Vote for You

In 1958 Ernest Gruening made his first successful run for the Senate from Alaska, which Congress had just voted into the Union as the forty-ninth state. Since Gruening, a former governor, had spent the previous two years in Washington lobbying for statehood, he was afraid there might be a lot of newcomers in Anchorage who didn't know him, so he decided to walk up and down the city's main thoroughfares soliciting votes. His practice was to stop a passerby, hold out his hand, and say, "My name is Gruening. I'm a candidate for the United States Senate and I'd appreciate your vote." One heavy-set fellow whom he stopped pulled his hand away and growled: "You're Gruening? I'd rather vote for the devil!" "You know, he'd be a tough guy to beat," said Gruening, holding back his temper. "But if he decides not to run, do you suppose you could switch to me?" The man stared at Gruening for a moment and then started laughing. "Why, you son of a bitch," he cried, "I might vote for you yet!"[85]

Right Between the Eyes

In 1960, when Oklahoma Senator Robert Kerr learned that JFK had offered LBJ the vice-presidential nomination at the Democratic Convention in Los Angeles, he stormed over to Johnson's hotel room and exclaimed: "Lyndon, I hope you're not thinking about running with that liberal Irish boy from Boston!" Then he added: "If you *are*, Lyndon, I feel like taking my thirty-thirty rifle and shooting you right between the eyes." At that point Speaker Sam Rayburn went over and asked Kerr to step into an adjoining room with him. "Bob," he said, when they were alone, "you're in a campaign of your own down there in Oklahoma, aren't you?" "Yes, I am," said Kerr. "It could be a tough one, couldn't it?" said Rayburn. "It could be," admitted Kerr. "Could be tougher to run with Kennedy at the head of the ticket?" Rayburn went on. "It *will* be," said Kerr emphatically. "Now," said Rayburn, "wouldn't it be better for you to have a neighbor like Lyndon on the ticket?" Kerr thought for a moment and then hurried back to LBJ's room. "Lyndon," he cried, "if you *don't* take that vice-presidential nomination, I'm gonna take my thirty-thirty rifle and shoot you right between the eyes!" LBJ enjoyed telling the story.[86]

LBJ

In July 1960, soon after Lyndon Johnson lost the Democratic presidential nomination to John F. Kennedy and accepted second place on the ticket, he proudly pointed to the button on his lapel and annouced: "Someone asked me this morning what LBJ on the Johnson lapel button means. And I said, 'Let's Back Jack'!"[87]

Haven't Missed Anything

In the spring of 1960, when Senator Hubert Humphrey was running against Senator John F. Kennedy in the West Virginia primary, Humphrey made much of the fact that JFK was a millionaire's son who had never done a day's work in his life. One day, when JFK was shaking hands with some coal miners, one of them said, "Just a minute, Senator Kennedy, is it true that you are a millionaire's son and have never done a day's work in your life?" Grinning, Kennedy said, "Yeah, I guess so." The old man slapped him on the back and cried: "Let me tell you something, Mister, you haven't missed a damned thing!"[88]

JFK's Record on Farm Issues

Toward the end of the Wisconsin primary race in 1960, Minnesota's Hubert Humphrey attacked John F. Kennedy's voting record in the Senate on agricultural issues, seemed to score points with the voters, and had JFK worried. Just before the voters went to the polls, Kennedy happened to run into Senator Gene McCarthy, pulled out a Humphrey brochure about his farm votes, brandished it at McCarthy, and said angrily: "This is outrageous!" With a deadpan expression, McCarthy ignored the point of JFK's remark and, glancing at the brochure, said: "Jack, it's not so bad a record for a man from Massachusetts!"[89]

JFK Endorses LBJ

At the Democratic Convention in 1960, during the wooing of delegates for the presidential nomination, Lyndon Johnson invited John F. Kennedy to visit the Texas delegation and debate with him in front of the pro-Johnson audience. To everyone's astonishment, Kennedy accepted. Facing the Johnson loyalists, JFK stunned the crowd by announcing that he had come to endorse Lyndon Johnson; that he admired him, had great affection for him, and strongly supported him—for Senate Majority Leader. Even the Texas loyalists laughed.[90]

Affection

In September 1960, Illinois Republican Everett Dirksen paid his respects to his Senate colleagues, John F. Kennedy and Lyndon B. Johnson, who had been picked to head the Democratic ticket that year. "I extend to the Senators who are candidates the warm hand of fellowship," he announced. "We want to keep them here. I want to keep them here. It would be lonesome without my distinguished friend, the Majority Leader, and without my distinguished friend from Massachusetts, with whom it has been my honor and pleasure to work on the Senate Labor Committee. My affection is as high as the sky and it is as deep as the sea—and I do not want sixteen blocks to intervene!"[91]

Tom

In 1960, when Rhode Island millionaire Claiborne Pell was running for the Senate on the Democratic ticket, he asked an aide for a pair of rubbers one rainy day, and the aide rushed off to the nearest Thom McAn store, bought a pair of galoshes, and brought them back to Pell. At the end of the day Pell peeled them off, handed them back to his aide, and asked: "Where did these come from?" "Thom McAn," said the aide. "Well, give them back to Tom," said Pell, "and thank him very much."[92]

Let Me Go

One evening, during the 1964 campaign, Arizona's Senator Barry Goldwater, Republican candidate for President, was winding up a speech on the meaning of freedom and was so exhausted that he was almost asleep when he came to the close of his address. "There are no heights to which our people can't go," he said wearily. "There is no limit to the heights, no limit to their expense, if we go as a free people. I say, as a great man once said, 'Let my people go!' Thank you." Then he turned to Denison Kitchel, his campaign manager, and exclaimed: "You heard the speech. Let me go—to bed!"[93]

Episcopalian

Senator Goldwater's father was Jewish but he married a Gentile and Barry was raised as an Episcopalian. During the 1964 presidential campaign, when it looked for a time as though the Arizona Senator had a chance of beating Lyndon Johnson, North Carolina journalist Harry Golden exclaimed: "Somehow I always knew that our first Jewish President would be an Episcopalian!"[94]

Goldy

When he was running for President in 1964, Senator Goldwater was highly amused when the head of a women's club got so excited when she introduced him that she announced: "Ladies and gentlemen, the next President of the United States, Goldy Bearwater!"[95]

TV

During the 1964 campaign an elderly woman is said to have told a reporter that she intended to vote against Senator Goldwater because "he's the guy who's going to get rid of TV." "But, madam," said the reporter, "I think you're making a mistake. Senator Goldwater is talking about getting rid of the Tennessee Valley Authority, TVA." "Well," persisted the woman, "I'm not taking any chances!"[96]

Ruthless

Before his successful run for the Senate from New York in 1964 Robert F. Kennedy's "image" was that of a tough, ruthless politician, and during the campaign he worked hard to change that image. After the election, when a reporter asked him if he was glad it was all over, Kennedy said he was and added: "Now I can go back to being ruthless again."[97]

Not Much of a One

In 1964, when William L. Hungate, a Missouri Democrat, ran for Congress for the first time he learned that to carry one of the counties in his district he needed to get the endorsement of an influential elderly newspaper editor. So he called on the man and spent an hour or so doing his best to make a good impression on the old-timer. "Son," said the editor, as Hungate was about to leave, "I like you, and I think we're going to endorse you, but one thing first—I hope you're not one of those goddamned lawyers!" Hungate hesitated for a moment, and then ventured: "Well, sir, yes, I am. But if it helps, I'm not much of one."[98]

Can Do Better

When New York Senator Robert F. Kennedy was running in the presidential primaries in the spring of 1968, reporters traveling with him enjoyed teasing him about some of the pet phrases he used in his campaign speeches. "I think we can do better," he frequently told audiences; "I think we can turn this city [or town or industry] around . . ." In Indianapolis, where the hotel the reporters stayed in was on the sleazy side, they mocked RFK: "I think we can do better. I think we can turn the Indiana hotel industry around." In restaurants where the waiters were sloppy they would announce: "The service is unacceptable. I think we can do better. I think we can turn this restaurant around."

The reporters also teased Kennedy about his propensity for ending a speech with a favorite quotation: "As George Bernard Shaw once said. . . ." After they had heard the Shaw quote twenty or thirty times it became the signal to head for the bus, train, or plane scheduled to take them to the next place. Once RFK forgot to quote Shaw and the campaign train started off leaving all the reporters stranded on the platform. When they finally caught up with Kennedy, they asked him always to include the Shaw cue after that. So at the next stop Kennedy ended his speech with the words: "As George Bernard Shaw once said, 'run for the bus'!"[99]

For the Farmer

When Senator Robert F. Kennedy was running in the Democratic presidential primaries in 1968, he happened to walk into a room full of farmers at the wrong time and couldn't help overhearing one of them grumbling about what a drain it would be on the Federal budget if all those nine or ten Kennedy children got into the White House. "Yes, I've got ten kids that drink milk," said Kennedy triumphantly. "Tell me anyone else who's doing that much for the farmer!"[100]

Immortal

During the 1968 campaign, Hubert Humphrey, the Democratic presidential candidate, promised his friends and advisers he would cut short his speeches so his campaign trains would run on time, but he never did. One hot night, when he was talking on and on, and the audience was getting more and more restless, his wife Muriel sent a small note up to the podium. "Dear," she had written, "Remember that for a speech to be immortal it need not be eternal."[101]

A Few Words

In 1972, when Maine Senator Edmund Muskie was campaigning for the Democratic presidential nomination in the New Hampshire primary, his wife Jane helped him out even though she was somewhat shy in public. "Oh, I think I'm going to faint," she cried, clutching the microphone in front of a large crowd in one town. "But before I do," she added quickly, "I'd like to say a few words about my husband."[102]

One of the Planks

Once when Henry ("Scoop") Jackson, Democratic Senator from Washington, was campaigning, he fell through a rotten floor, but as the audience started laughing, he quickly looked up and cried: "I'm standing on one of the planks from the Republican platform!"[103]

Laughing About It

During the Democratic primary campaign in 1976, Arizona Congressman Morris ("Mo") K. Udall went into a barbershop in a little New Hampshire town one day, shook hands with the barber and his customer, and cried: "Hi, I'm Mo Udall. I'm running for President." "Yeah, we know," said the barber. "We were laughing about it this morning." Udall enjoyed telling the story.[104]

Lightning

In 1976, Idaho Democratic Senator Frank Church was on a list of six men whom Jimmy Carter was considering as his running mate, but when he wasn't chosen he took it philosophically. "I should have known two days ago that I wasn't going to get the Vice-Presidency," he said. "That's when I got the news that my house in Bethesda had been struck by lightning—I should have known that lightning never strikes twice."[105]

Spirited

When Wyoming's Alan Simpson was running for the Senate as a Republican in 1978, he found himself in a debate of sorts in which his opponent had first shot at the microphone. The Democratic candidate began raving about what a terrible person Simpson was, what a terrible record he had, how unfit for public office he was, and what an incompetent job he would do in Washington. It was one of the most vehement speeches a Wyoming audience had heard in years and when the Democrat finished, his face flushed and the audience thunderstruck, the spotlight turned to Simpson. Simpson got up, stepped to the mike, and then drawled: "Spirited rascal, ain't he?"[106]

VI

★   ★   ★   ★   ★   ★   ★   ★

Comedy

★ 🖾 ★

Ohio's Thomas Corwin thought his sense of humor had hurt his Congressional career. "If you would succeed in life," he told his young colleague James A. Garfield, "you must be as solemn as an ass. All the great monuments on earth have been built to solemn asses."[1] Garfield was solemn, all right, and he eventually moved all the way from the lower house to the White House. But "Corwin's Law," as it was called, was by no means implacable. From the outset there was hilarity as well as high seriousness in both House and Senate, and there is no reason to think the funsters were handicapped. Henry Clay's admirers reveled in his puns; so did Everett Dirksen's.

Clay's puns were in fact outrageous. When the House voted on a tariff bill he was sponsoring in 1824, he expected both Connecticut's Samuel Foote and New York's Charles Foote to support the bill, but to his disappointment, both voted against it. When the bill passed anyway, one Congressman went up to the Speaker's chair afterward to congratulate him. "We have done pretty well today," he said. "Yes," nodded Clay, "we made a good stand, considering we lost both our Feete."[2] Dirksen's puns were, if anything, even more atrocious than Clay's. In 1933, when the House was discussing the sale of beer in Washington after the repeal of Prohibition, the Illinois Republican took to the floor to have some fun. "I assume, of course," he announced, "that if Hamlet could come in here from Denmark with a New York accent, he might say, 'To *beer* or not to *beer,* that is the question.'"[3] Dirksen's colleagues found this well-nigh unbeerable.

Most of the time Congressional humorists, including both Clay and Dirksen, wanted to be more than punsters. They prided themselves on the witty remark, the clever riposte, *le mot juste,* the retort courteous, and the

141

cockamamie chronicle illuminating the points they were pressing on their colleagues. During the Gilded Age, an opponent of Virginia Congressman John S. Wise ended an argument on a bill before the House by reveling in oxymorons: "In a crowd I once saw a man who towered above the rest like a redwood above sage brush. His name was Short. Another I knew so thin that the summer breezes blowing in his face kept flies from alighting on his back. His name was Stout. A Negro I know blacker than the crime of '73, and his name is White. Ah, Mr. Speaker, we know that nature delights in these sarcasms, for is not the principal opponent of this measure called Wise?"[4] And about this time Massachusetts Senator George F. Hoar (whose name gave punsters a field day) did even better, at least, so he thought. When Nevada's John P. Jones, in the course of an interminable speech on the money question, mentioned an ancient society which used oyster shells as a medium of exchange, Hoar, begging pardon for the interruption, livened things up by declaring these were an excellent substitute for gold and silver coins and greenbacks, because "with oyster shells as money, a man could order half a dozen oysters on the half shell, and pay for them with the shells."[5]

Some lawmakers, like North Carolina Senator Sam Ervin, Jr., had a penchant for telling amusing stories to make their points during debates. In 1954, when Wisconsin's reckless Republican Senator Joseph R. McCarthy was riding high, and the Senate was considering a resolution of censure, the debate got so heated that two Senators almost came to blows. At this point Ervin got up and said the scene reminded him of the time old Uncle Ephraim, crippled with arthritis, attended a church service in which the preacher was having the older members of the congregation stand up and testify to their religious experiences. One after another, according to Ervin, all the old-timers got up and talked at length about how the Lord had blessed them. Finally the preacher looked over at Uncle Ephraim, bent double in one of the pews, and cried: "Brother Ephraim, suppose you tell us what the Lord has done for you." Slowly and painfully, Ephraim got up, stood there for a moment, and then croaked: "Brother, he has mighty near ruint me!" "And that," added Ervin, "is what Senator McCarthy has done to the Senate."[6] Abraham Lincoln would have loved Ervin's ploy.

Much Congressional comedy is of course inadvertent. When the man nominating John W. Kenna of West Virginia for Congress called him "the peer, sir, *of no man* in the State of West Virginia," everyone but Kenna himself found the statement pretty funny.[7] Even more amusing was the episode involving South Carolina's Benjamin ("Pitchfork Ben") Tillman and the young Senate page who was new on the job. One day Tillman called the page over and asked him the name of the new Senator sitting on the Republican side of the Chamber. But the page was not only ignorant of the new Senator's name; he didn't even know who Tillman was, though he noticed the South Carolinian had a bad eye. Puzzled as how to proceed, the boy went over to the Senate clerk and asked: "Who is the man with one eye?" "Cyclops," said the clerk without looking up. The boy rushed back to Tillman. "Now Senator Cyclops," he said triumphantly, "I will go and find out the other Senator's name!"[8]

There were gaffes and gaucheries as well as unintentional comic scenes in the House and Senate chambers. In a place where so many words were exchanged it is not surprising that a fair number of tongue-slips tumbled out during Congressional debates. Indiana's Homer Capehart called his Omnibus Farm Bill the "Ominous Farm Bill," and Massachusetts' Joseph W. Martin, Jr., talked about fighting in "Indigo China." An old-time favorite was a Senator's announcement on Independence Day: "The Fourth of July is a peculiarly American institution." Much liked, too, was one Congressman's opposition to high tariffs on wool imports: "If you don't stop shearing the wool off the sheep that lays the golden egg, you'll pump it dry." In more recent times Gerald R. ("Jerry") Ford of Michigan came up with an instant classic in a House debate: "If Lincoln were alive today he'd be turning over in his grave." And of the latest Middle East crisis Missouri Congressman Richard Gephardt said one day that he didn't see why the Arabs and Jews "couldn't sit down and settle this like good Christians."[9]

For a time—the 1940s and early 1950s—the master malapropist was Senator Kenneth S. Wherry of Nebraska. A former funeral director, he was called "the Merry Mortician" and, then, when his talents became known, as "the Sam Goldwyn of Capitol Hill." Wherry not only talked about "Indigo China" the way Joe Martin did; he also referred to Chinese Nationalist leader Chiang Kai-shek as "Shanghai Jack" and to his Communist foe, Mao Tse-tung, as though it was spelled "Mousey Tongue." For Wherry, Oregon's Wayne Morse, then the junior Senator from Oregon, was "the distinguished Senator from Junior," and Florida's Spessard Holland was "the distinguished Senator from Holland." He accused President Truman of "sugarcoating his red ink," said "the issue is clear and indistinct to me," urged Republicans to become "bell-door ringers" during campaigns, talked of the "anti-Sherman Trust Act," and spoke of the Joint Chiefs of Staff as "the Chief Joints of Staff." During a debate in 1949 he assured William Langer that "the Senator from North Dakota will have opple ampertunity to speak." Talking about the American system one day he announced: "There are four departments." Enumerating: "There's the executive, and the legislative, and the judicial, and—" After a pause and some pondering: "And the Bill of Rights."[10]

There were misadventures as well as *lapsi linguae* on Capitol Hill. South

Carolina Senator Burnet Rhett Maybank probably had more of them than just about any other Congressman. Maybank always drove his own car to Capitol Hill and parked it in the underground garage of the old Senate Office Building. Close by the garage entrance was the entrance of a street car tunnel. Late one night, though very tired, the conscientious Senator decided to return to his office and catch up on his work. He mistook entrances and drove into the trolley tunnel instead of the Senate garage. About midway through the subterranean tunnel he saw a streetcar coming toward him. Both he and the motorman applied their brakes and avoided a head-on collision by inches. The motorman was wild-eyed with rage, but he almost went out of his mind when Senator Maybank climbed out of his car and demanded imperiously: "What are you doing in the Senate garage?"[11]

A fair number of Congressional stories are what might be called generic. The casts of characters and the settings they present vary with each generation, and their genesis in fact is highly dubious. "Clay," Daniel Webster said (according to a popular tale), when a man passed with a pack of mules, "there goes a number of your Kentucky constituents!" "They must be going up to Massachusetts to teach school," retorted Clay. But the same tale involving South Carolina's John C. Calhoun and Ohio Congressman Thomas Corwin has also made the rounds. "There go some of your constituents," Calhoun is said to have remarked, pointing to a drove of mules just in from Ohio. "Yes," Corwin is reported to have responded, "they are going down South to teach school."[12]

Even more improbable—but delightful all the same—is the story about the Lord's Prayer first appearing in an anthology of humorous tales published in 1871. One day, according to the old account, several Congressmen got to chatting in the lobby and one Congressman criticized another for putting so much piety into his speeches. "I'll bet you five dollars," he said, "that you can't even repeat the Lord's Prayer, if you try." "Done," said the other Congressman promptly. "Done." He looked serious, racked his brains, and then recited: "Now I lay me down to sleep, I pray the Lord my soul to keep, if I should die before I wake, I pray the Lord my soul to take." "Well, I give up the beat," sighed the other Congressman, handing him the money. "I wouldn't have thought you could do it!"[13] Years later, the same tale was told of Harry Cohn, the profane head of Columbia Pictures in Hollywood. Some day—who knows?—it may even be told of Ronald Reagan.

Some of the best humor, political or otherwise, involves self-teasing. During the debates accompanying the Illinois Senatorial race in 1858, Stephen A. Douglas accused Abraham Lincoln one day of being two-faced. "I leave it to my audience," responded Lincoln good-naturedly. "If I had another face, do you think I would wear this one?"[14] Like Lincoln, the best Congressional humorists laugh at themselves as well as at the world.

☆ ☆ ☆

Two Barbours

In the early years of the American republic there were two Barbours from Virginia in Congress: Philip Barbour, a Senator, who was a logic-chopper, and James Barbour, a windy orator who gave lengthy speeches in the House. John Randolph, also a Virginian, once said that Phil could split a hair but Jim couldn't hit a barn door. A little later some wag wrote the following on one of the House chamber's walls:

Two Barbers to save our Congress long did try;
One shaves with froth, the other, he shaves dry.[15]

Bad Roads (1828)

Francis P. Blair, editor of the *Frankfort Argus,* was once a warm Clay supporter, but in 1828 he threw his support to Andrew Jackson, Clay's political foe, and helped carry Kentucky for Old Hickory in the presidential race that year. Shortly after Jackson's inauguration, Clay rode over to Frankfort from Lexington and happened to run into his former friend. "How do you do, Mr. Blair?" he said politely. "Pretty well, I thank you, sir," murmured Blair, a bit embarrassed. "How did you find the roads from Lexington to here?" "The roads are very bad, Mr. Blair," said Clay, with a sigh; "very bad; and I wish, sir, that you would mend your ways!"[16]

Ins and Outs (1829)

When Andrew Jackson "went IN" on March 4, 1829, wrote one of Henry Clay's supporters, President John Quincy Adams and Secretary of State Clay "went OUT." Clay on his way back to Kentucky after Jackson's inauguration, stopped in a little Pennsylvania town. To the surprise of some of his friends there, he was sitting outside on the box next to the coachman when he arrived in town, instead of inside with the other passengers. Queried about it, he said he had chosen that seat as the most comfortable, on account of the roughness of the roads. "You see, my friend," he added, as they headed for the hotel, "I am one of the OUTS; but I can assure you, that the INS behind me, have the worst of it."[17]

The Worst On't

One summer day Daniel Webster went off on a fishing excursion on Cape Cod with his son Fletcher. The two drove through the pine woods and at last reached a stream they had heard about, a few miles from Sandwich, and approached the owner of the property, a man named Baker. "Well,

Mr. Baker," said Webster, "with your leave, we thought we would like to try and take a trout in your brook." "Oh, yes, sir," said Baker, "very welcome to." He then showed the Websters a spot where they could begin fishing, but it was thickly overhung with alders and the ground was very miry. "Rather miry here, Mr. Baker," murmured Webster as he sank into the mud half-way up his leg. "Yes," agreed Baker, "that's the worst on't." "The alders are rather in the way, Baker," said Webster a little later, after throwing several times and catching his hook on the shrubs. "I know it," said Baker. "That's the worst on't." "These mosquitoes are pretty thick and very hungry, Mr. Baker," remarked Webster a few minutes later, as he and his son tried to cope with the new problem. "I know it," said Baker. "That's the worst on't." A minute or two later Webster started wiping his forehead. "It is very hot down here in these bushes, Mr. Baker," he sighed. "I know it," said Baker. "That's the worst on't." After an hour or so of struggling with the heat, the bushes, the mud, and the mosquitoes, Webster finally gave up. "There seem to be no fish here, Mr. Baker," he exclaimed. "I know it," said Baker. "That's the worst on't."[18]

Shootin' Little Birds

One warm August day Webster went out to shoot some birds near his home in Marshfield, and in the course of his rambles he came to a river and beckoned to a farmer on the opposite bank to take him over in his boat, which lay moored nearby. The man at once left his work, came over with the boat, and paddled Webster across the stream. When Webster offered to pay him, the man declined; and then, after some hesitation, he said: "This is Daniel Webster, I believe." "That is my name," said Webster, pleased at being recognized. "Well, now," the farmer went on, "I am told that you can make from three to five dollars a day, pleadin' cases up in Boston." Webster acknowledged he sometimes received that much for his legal services. "Well, now," mused the farmer, "it seems to me, I declare, if I could get as much in the city, pleadin' law cases, I would not be a-wadin' over these marshes this hot weather, shootin' little birds!"[19]

Webster's Fame

Once, when Daniel Webster was at the height of his fame, he was riding in a stage in New Hampshire and got to talking to an old gentleman. When he learned the man was from Salisbury, his home town, he asked: "Did you know Mr. Webster?" "Old Captain Ed Webster? Sure," said the old man. "I knew him and all his family. They were my neighbors and friends; and a nice old man he was." "Did you know him intimately?" Webster asked. "Very intimately," said the man. "He had a son who was a very extraordinary man. Ezekiel Webster was a son of Captain Webster, and was the greatest man New Hampshire ever raised. I was in the Concord Courthouse, where I was a juryman at the trial, when he fell dead. He was arguing a case very eloquently, when he suddenly fell to the floor. It caused much excitement among the people. He was a great man, and there is nobody left like him. He was a powerful, noble-looking person. We were all proud of Ezekiel Webster, yes, very proud of him. We would have sent him to Congress, if he had lived. There were one or two girls, but they died young, I believe; and there were one or two other sons." "Do you remember anything about any of Ezekiel's brothers?" Webster asked. "He had a brother, I think—a younger brother," the old man said. "What was his name?" asked Webster. "Let me see," mused the man. "Oh, yes; I recollect his name was Daniel." "Did you ever see him?" asked Webster. "Yes, when he was a boy." "Well, is he living?" asked Webster. "Well, I guess so," said the old man. "I never heard of his dying. I never thought anything about it, but I believe he is a lawyer down about Boston somewhere." Webster enjoyed telling this one on himself.[20]

Vox Populi

At the end of a speech on the admission of Oregon to the Union in 1859, Georgia's Alexander Stephens spoke of the states being "all bound together for general objects under a common thread, as it were, 'a wheel within a wheel,'" and concluded dramatically: "Then, indeed, may the nations of the earth look with wonder at our career, and when they hear the noise of the wheels of our progress in achievement, in development, in expansion, in glory and renown, it will appear to them not unlike the noise of great waters, the very voice of the Almighty—*Vox populi, vox Dei.*"

With applause ringing in his ears, Stephens left the House chamber, and as he went down the corridor he overheard a man telling a friend: "You should have been there and seen him, his slight form quivering, yet erect, his shrill voice ringing through the hushed hall in that grand climax—*Vox populi, vox Dei!*" "Yes, no doubt," said the friend, who hadn't been in the gallery for the speech, "but I'll bet you ten dollars you can't tell what *Vox populi, vox Dei* means." "I'll bet I can," said the first man. "Put up your money." So the two men put up the money and the second man said: "Well, what does it mean in English?" "Why," said the Stephens enthusiast, "it means, 'My God, My God! Why hast thou forsaken me?'" "That's right," said his friend disappointedly. "The money is yours. I didn't think you knew."[21]

Cracking

During the prolonged fight over the Speakership in 1859, Thaddeus Stevens said he would never vote for anyone but Galusha Grow. Later on, though, he cast his ballot for someone else and a colleague reminded him of his promise to support Grow "until the crack of doom." Replied Stevens, "I thought I heard it cracking!"[22]

A Bull Run

Late in January 1862, Ohio's Republican Congressman John A. Gurley made a speech in the House vehemently criticizing General George B. McClellan, who had taken command of Union forces soon after the rout at the first Battle of Bull Run in July 1861. Samuel S. Cox, Ohio Democrat with a flair for satire, thought the attack on McClellan unfair; and in rising to defend the General, he decided to mingle a little *ad risum* with *ad hominem* in his response to Gurley. He remembered that Gurley was one of the Congressmen who had accompanied Union troops headed for Richmond one fine summer day, almost as if on an outing, and then fled with the others in their precipitous panic after the encounter with Confederate forces at Bull Run.

"Sir, my colleague, Mr. Gurley," began Cox, "compels me to examine into his merits as a military critic . . . and also into the propriety of criticizing military 'movements' here in Congress and elsewhere by civilians." Gurley was not a professional soldier, Cox observed; nor was he "a soldier, like Falstaff, on instinct." Whence, then, came his military expertise? Apparently from his experience at Bull Run. "He admits being at Bull Run," said Cox. "His masterly activity on the retreat he admits." Cox went on to give details. "My colleague," he said, "after his fatiguing race to Centreville, and having passed that point with the speed of Gilpin—and not having the benefit of a carriage like the Congressman who kicked out of it the tired soldiers besmirched with their cartridges in battle—was scampering along like the devil in Milton . . . until luckily he met—what think you, noble Representatives?—a herd of stampeded cattle, which were from my own beloved district—Texas cattle, Sir, wintered in the Scioto valley, and selected by their drover for their stampeding propensity. Seizing upon the extreme rear of a noble bull, the Reverend and Honorable gentleman was borne from the field, holding on with vigorous prehension to the tail of that animal! There was a Bull Run indeed!" Cox then urged Gurley, a former preacher, to have a little faith in McClellan.[23]

Third Commandment

Pennsylvania Congressman Thaddeus Stevens, Radical Republican who led the move to impeach President Andrew Johnson in 1868, frequently exploded in profanity when he was upset. Once, hearing the crash of dishes

in his dining-room, he shouted angrily to his black servant: "Well, ————
it, what . . . thing have you broken now?" "I bless de Lawd," said the
black woman, "that it am not de third commandment!"[24]

Poor Commissioner

Once Thaddeus Stevens' vote was solicited during a general election in
Lancaster, Pennsylvania, by an impecunious and incompetent man who
was candidate for Poor Commissioner. "Certainly," said Stevens amiably.
"We should make you Poor Commissioner, for I know of no one in all
Lancaster county who would make a poorer Commissioner than you."[25]

Dead and Gone

In Stevens' later years, his health was so poor that he had to engage two
sturdy young blacks to carry him in a chair to his seat in the House so he
could continue his work each day. "Thank you, my good fellows," he said
one day. "What shall I do when you are dead and gone?"[26]

Disappearance

When Thaddeus Stevens was in his last illness, a friend visited him and said
cheerily: "Thad, you look well—your appearance is good." "Ah, John!"
Stevens said with a weak smile. "It's not my appearance, but my disap-
pearance that troubles me."[27]

Greatest Men

One day, several years after the Civil War, South Carolina's Wade Hampton and Massachusetts' Charles Sumner got to talking about Reconstruction in the rotunda of the Senate Chamber. At one point Hampton began
praising the people of Virginia and South Carolina. "They are great
states—," he said, "and a brave people live in Virginia and South Carolina."
Just then Ohio's Ben Wade joined the two Senators. "Yes," said Wade, who
had overheard Hampton's remark, "I have known a good many people
who went down there myself, and splendid people they were, too, as brave
and high-toned as the Huguenot." "You did, sir?" said Hampton, surprised
and pleased. "Oh yes, sir," said Wade. "I knew some of the greatest men
Virginia and South Carolina ever saw, sir—knew them intimately," and he
drew closer to Hampton. "Who did you know down there, sir—in the old
Palmetto State?" asked Hampton."Well, sir," said Wade, "I knew General
Sherman, General Grant, and General Kilpatrick, who went—" "Great
guns!" cried Hampton, and fled to the bar-room.[28]

Black Heart

Massachusetts Congressman Ben Butler, a vigorous champion of civil rights for the blacks during the Gilded Age, arranged for his son, a West Point graduate, to serve for a time with a regiment of blacks on the Western Plains. And when the first black Congressman met with a cold reception on his arrival in Washington, Butler went out of his way to make him feel at home in the House. His concern for blacks was so great that when he went to Richmond to deliver an address to a black convention, the master of ceremonies, a black preacher, introduced him with the words, "General Butler may have a white face, but he has a black heart!"[29]

Lower House

Members of the House resented the expression, "lower house." They said the Senate was called the "upper house," only because it continually "upped" House appropriation bills. They also pointed out, more seriously, that the House of Representatives came to be called the "lower house" only because in 1789, when Congress first met in New York, the House occupied the lower floor of Federal Hall there and the Senate met on the upper floor. But Representatives could joke about it on occasion. At the close of an annual session in the 1870s, Pennslyvania's Samuel Randall told Massachusetts' Ben Butler: "I expect to meet you some day, Butler, in another and better world." "Oh no, Sam," said Butler at once, "you will be there, as you are here, a member of the lower house!"[30]

Interviews

One day Nebraska's Senator Alvin Saunders vigorously opposed a bill, and, following the debate, a reporter approached him and asked: "Haven't your views changed on that bill, Senator?" "No," replied Saunders. "But, sir," said the reporter, "how about the views you expressed to me for publication a couple of weeks ago?" "Son," smiled Saunders, "those were not my views. Those were my interviews."[31]

Ask for Sam

Congressman William A. Smith, former president of the North Carolina Central Railroad, visited New York, went into a nice restaurant his first night there, and when the waiter gave him the menu, he tossed it aside and handed him a dollar. "Bring me a good dinner," he instructed. The dinner was excellent, so he continued this way of ordering his food the rest of the time he was in New York. When he had his last dinner just before leaving the city, he told the waiter he was returning to Washington. "Well, sir," said the waiter, "when you or any of your friends that can't read the bill of fare come to New York, just ask for Sam!"[32]

Ultra Vires

When a Congressional committee was grilling Central Pacific Railroad president Collis P. Huntington about his company's practices, the latter asked to make a statement about his railroad's relation to the Federal Government. The committee granted his request and he made a long speech reminding the Congressmen of all the Central Pacific had done for the country by connecting two oceans with a great railroad across the continent and thus saving American merchants millions of dollars in travel expenses. Besides that, he went on, his railroad had more than paid the Government back for all the money it had advanced by preventing Indian wars. One winter, he said, his railroad had fed a hostile Indian tribe when Government supplies failed to arrive and thus prevented starvation and probably a bloody and costly Indian war. "Was that not *ultra vires* [beyond authority] for a railroad corporation?" Senator George F. Hoar wanted to know. "No, sir! No, sir!" cried Huntington excitedly. "We never gave them anything as strong as that!"[33]

Private John Allen of Tupelo

In the late nineteenth century, Mississippi Congressman John Allen was one of the House's real funnymen. He became nationally known as "Private John" and liked to boast that he never even got a corporal's stripe out of his service to the Confederacy during the Civil War.

Allen came from Tupelo, and he used to joke that his hometown was the real cause of the Civil War. When the trouble started, he told the House, Abraham Lincoln's Secretary of War rushed into the President's office and shouted: "Mr. President, the South has seceded!" Lincoln shrugged his shoulders and said calmly: "Well, let it secede." "But, Mr. President," wailed the Secretary of War, "Tupelo is in the South." "My God!" cried Lincoln, jumping up. "We can't give up Tupelo!" And that, said Allen, was how the Civil War began.

In Mississippi, the Allens and the Bilbos were implacable political enemies and Private Allen once made the rash promise that if Theodore Bilbo were re-elected governor he would leave the state at once. When Bilbo was re-elected, he sent Allen a wire reminding him of his promise, and received this answer: "Mississippi has gone to hell and I'm going to St. Louis." But Allen soon returned to Mississippi, though he never again acknowledged that he was a Mississippian. He always signed himself: "Private John Allen, Tupelo, U.S.A."[34]

First Speech

In 1885, when John Allen first entered the House, he tried to get the floor to make a speech, but the Speaker, taking a dim view of speeches by freshmen members, refused to recognize him. Allen then asked for permission "to print some remarks in the *Record,* and insert 'laughter' and 'applause' in appropriate places." This amused the Speaker and he let Allen have the floor. In his maiden speech, Allen called for money to improve the Tombigbee River in his state, and when he finished, he announced: "Now, Mr. Speaker, having fully answered all the arguments of my opponents, I will retire to the cloakroom for a few moments to receive the congratulations of admiring friends." The House rocked with laughter, and after that looked forward to Allen's performances.[35]

Repeater

With the end of Reconstruction in 1876 and the return of the Southern states to local rule the South soon became solidly Democratic. The time came when John Allen could amuse his colleagues in the House by telling amusing stories about political conditions in Mississippi. There was a man in his part of the state, he once said, who hankered for public office, turned up whenever there was a Democratic primary, seeking the nomination for one position or another, but was always turned down. Finally he left the Democratic party, saying the Democrats didn't recognize real merit when they saw it, and turned Republican. "At the next election," said Allen, "he entered himself as candidate for sheriff on the Republican ticket. Well, sir, that fellow certainly made a spirited campaign. If ever a man worked to bring out the full strength of the white Republican vote he was the man. He canvassed the county from end to end. He spoke at every cross-roads blacksmith shop and every county schoolhouse. He left no stone unturned." Finally election day arrived; he got exactly two votes "and was arrested that night for repeating!"[36]

Rather Fight than Feed

At a banquet in honor of New York Congressman John R. Fellows, John Allen decided to have a little fun with the honoree, who, during the Civil War, had led an Arkansas regiment. "There is one thing I would like to have Colonel Fellows explain," said Allen toward the end of his eulogy. "He was captured the first year of the war, and never exchanged, but held as prisoner by the Federals until the war was over. I was taken prisoner five times, and always promptly exchanged. I would like Colonel Fellows to explain how it was that he was kept in a place of safety, while I was always at the front."

When the laughter died down, Fellows arose and told the audience: "I am grateful to my friend from Mississippi for giving me an opportunity to explain that part of my military record which I apprehend has never been sufficiently clear. It is true, I was taken prisoner the first year of the war, and the enemy, well knowing the danger of my being at large, persistently refused to release me until peace was restored. Had I been promptly exchanged, *the result of that war might have been different!*"

Fellows then decided to tease Allen a bit. "But why was it," he went on, "that my friend from Mississippi was so repeatedly and promptly exchanged is a question that until yesterday I have never been able to understand. It has given me deep concern. I have pondered over it during the silent watches of the night. Yesterday, however, my mind was completely set at rest upon that question by reading the correspondence . . . between President Lincoln and President Davis relating to the exchange of Private John Allen of Company C, Fourteenth Mississippi Volunteers. The correspondence covers many pages . . . , but I will read only the closing communication." Then, as Allen and the other guests listened intently, Fellows continued: "The letter I will read from President Lincoln concluded the correspondence, and is as follows: *'Dear Jeff:* With this I return you Private Allen of Company C, Fourteenth Mississippi. I require no prisoner exchange. The Lord's truth is, Jeff, *I had rather fight John than feed him!*"[37]

Would Have Been Killed

One day when Congressman John Allen was speaking to some hostile voters, someone threw a heavy stone at him, but as he happened to bend over at that instant, it passed over his head. "You see," he told friends afterward who congratulated him on his narrow escape, "if I had been an upright politician, I would have been killed!"[38]

Befo' the War

John Allen was struck by how popular the phrase, "before the war," became in his part of the country in the years following the Civil War. He liked to tell about how he heard the expression used when he was campaigning for Congress in a rural community inhabited mainly by hard-shell, predestinarian Baptists. He gave his campaign speech on Saturday, he said, stayed all night with one of the elders, and then went to church on Sunday. During the sermon, he recalled, the preacher was holding forth on the doctrine of predestination, and suddenly turned to a stranger who somehow had gotten crowded into the amen corner, and cried: "My brother, when were you predestinated to eternal salvation or eternal damnation?" Startled, the stranger mumbled: "I don't adzactly remember, Parson, but I think it was befo' the war."[39]

Romanism

Republican Senator James G. Blaine lost the election of 1884 to Grover Cleveland partly because a New York preacher referred to the Democratic party of "Rum, Romanism, and Rebellion," thus offending Irish Catholics in New York City on whose support Blaine had been counting. Some years afterward North Carolina Senator Zeb Vance, a former Confederate, whose first wife, a Presbyterian, had died, married a devout member of the Roman Catholic church. Soon after the wedding he was taken to task by an old Presbyterian friend, who expressed great surprise that he should marry a Catholic. "Well," said Vance good-naturedly, "the fact is, Uncle John, as I had tried Rum, and tried Rebellion, and I just thought I would try Romanism too!"[40]

Noah

One day, while eulogizing Daniel Webster, Kansas Congressman Jerry Simpson referred in complimentary terms to his dictionary. Another Congressman pulled his coattails and whispered, "Noah made the dictionary." Simpson scornfully whispered back: "Noah built the ark!"[41]

Mrs. W.

Massachusetts' rough and ready Benjamin F. Butler didn't think much of Boston Brahmins like Senator George F. Hoar. Knowing that Harvard College (where Hoar studied) was in the habit of naming its undergraduate houses for students after prominent Massachusetts figures, he once declared: "They certainly will never name a house after Senator Hoar." There's another old (Hoary?) story—undoubtedly apocryphal—about how Senator Hoar was once greeted effusively by a man he barely knew but who recognized him at once. "How are you, Senator?" the man inquired. Then he added: "And how is Mrs. W.?"[42]

B-U-R-D

Once George Hearst, millionaire California Senator and father of William Randolph Hearst, entered a restaurant in San Francisco and saw the word, bird, on the blackboard listing the specialties of the day. "See here, Sam," he called out to the restaurant owner, "that's a devil of a way to spell

bird! Don't you know any better than that? You ought to spell it *b-u-r-d!*"
The restaurant owner was irked. "I would have you understand, George
Hearst, that I am just as good a speller as you are," he cried, and then
decided to make a bet. "I'm willing to leave it to the best scholar in the room
that you don't know any more than I do," he said. "I bet you a basket of
champagne that you can't spell *bird* the right way." "Done," said Hearst.
"All right," said the owner, "and there is a piece of paper for you to put it
down in black and white." Hearst took the paper and pencil and immediately wrote the word *b-i-r-d.* "But," said the restaurant owner in dismay,
"you spelled it with a *u* before." "Now, Sam," laughed Hearst, "did you
really think that I was damn fool enough to spell *bird* with a *u* when there
was any money in it?"[43]

Time Flies

In 1888, former Minnesota Congressman Ignatius Donnelly published a
book entitled *The Great Cryptogram,* in which he claimed to have discovered
a cipher running through Shakespeare's plays revealing that Francis Bacon
was the real author of the plays. Soon after the book appeared, he attended
a dinner in Washington and bored all the guests, including several members of Congress, by droning on about his theory. Finally Kentucky's
Colonel Dick Wintersmith, an incorrigible jokester, decided to have a little
fun with the humorless Minnesotan. "I have been reading your book,
Donnelly," he said, "and I don't believe a word of it." "What?" cried
Donnelly, somewhat taken aback. "Oh, that book of yours," said Wintersmith, "in which you tried to prove that Shakespeare never wrote
'Hamlet' and 'Macbeth' and 'Lear' and all those other plays." "My dear sir,"
said Donnelly with great dignity, "I can prove beyond all peradventure that
Shakespeare never wrote those plays." "He did," said Wintersmith emphatically. "He did write them. Donnelly, *I saw him write three or four of them
myself.*" "Impossible!" exclaimed Donnelly, "impossible, Colonel, that you
could have seen Shakespeare write those plays; they were written three
hundred years ago." "Three hundred years, three hundred years," repeated Wintersmith lugubriously, "is it possible that it has been so long?
Lord, how time does fly!"[44]

Not Enough Debate

When Missouri's James S. Green was in the Senate, he lived in the old
National Hotel, where he was popular with the other guests, but continually teased by the women there for not attending church on Sunday. Finally
he made up his mind to put an end to the teasing; and he showed up late for
dinner one Sunday. When one of the women at the table asked why he was
late, he said proudly: "Been to church." "What church?" she asked. "Don't

know," he admitted. "Who preached?" she persisted. "Don't know," he said. "I went up the avenue several blocks, turned up Four and a Half Street a few blocks, and entered a big brick church on the left-hand side" (which Green's dinner companions recognized at once as an Episcopal church). "And how did you like the services, Senator?" asked the woman. "In my judgment," said Senator Green thoughtfully, "there was too much reading of the Journal and not enough debate!"[45]

Profitable

One day, several months after the Panic of 1893, Republican Congressman Nelson Dingley, former governor of Maine, famous for his humorlessness as well as for his devotion to high tariffs, was riding on the streetcar in Washington with "Private" John Allen, the Mississippi Democrat. Soon Dingley began talking about the depression that had swept the country, blamed it on the Cleveland administration, and lamented the bad situation to which the Democrats had brought the land. "Governor, you are entirely too blue over this thing," Allen finally said. "It is not true that good, profitable investments cannot be made. I made a small one this morning on which I realized handsomely, clearing about twenty per cent!" Dingley was impressed; he said he would like to invest some money in such a thriving institution, and asked Allen how he did it. "I purchased six street-car tickets for two bits," Allen told him with a straight face, "whereas usually they cost a nickel each!" Dingley, according to a colleague, "was in a huff for a week" after that.[46]

Talkative

One day a reporter called on Senator Thomas C. Platt at his office in New York City to interview him about a political contest in Brooklyn. "I want your views on the Brooklyn fight," the reporter told him. "I'm busy today," said Platt. "You know how I feel about that matter. Write a little piece about it for me, and I'll stand by it. Goodbye," So the reporter went back to his office and the editor asked him what he had. "A little talk with Platt," said the reporter. "Is it a good one?" asked his editor. "First class," said the reporter. "How much do you want of it?" "Let it run," said the city editor. So the reporter turned out a two-column interview. The next day he met Platt uptown in a hotel corridor. Said Platt: "I was rather talkative yesterday, wasn't I?"[47]

Faith Healer

Pennsylvania's hard-bitten Senator Matt Quay was riding a train in Florida during a vacation there, and the farmer sitting next to him started a conversation with him. "Don't belong to these parts, do ye?" he said. "Don't know much about Floridy, do ye?" "I have been here several times in my wanderings," Quay assured him. "And what might be the reason ye air wanderin'?" the farmer asked curiously. "I am trying to ameliorate the condition of man," said Quay, with mock solemnity, "the inner man." The farmer moved to another seat and remarked to the man beside him: "Talked to that feller back thar a good bit 'fore I found out he was one 'o them dern faith healers!"[48]

Signal

During a debate in the Senate one hot afternoon West Virginia's Henry Gassaway Davis, then in his seventies, fell sound asleep, dreaming, no doubt, of the days he had been a brakeman on the Baltimore and Ohio Railroad, as a young man. Suddenly Vermont's George F. Edmunds, who had just taken a pinch of snuff, pulled out his large red bandanna handkerchief and blew an unusually large blast. As the sound reverberated throughout the Senate Chamber, Senator Davis, recognizing the signal for down brakes, jumped to his feet, grasped the top of his mahogany desk, and nearly twisted it off the floor before he realized what had happened.[49]

Digestion

Ohio Senator Mark Hanna, influential Republican conservative, suffered severely from indigestion and had to watch his diet. Dining with a Democratic Senator in the Senate restaurant one day, he looked at the menu, scanned the lists of all the good things he was forbidden to eat, and sighed. "Say," he said to his Democratic friend, "I'd like to be able to eat anything I wanted on this bill of fare—and leave the digestion to you Democrats!"[50]

Doesn't Polyg

In 1903, when Reed Smoot went to Washington to take his place as one of Utah's first Senators, there was a delay in his swearing-in because of rumors that he practiced polygamy, outlawed by the Edmunds Act of 1882. Smoot was not, in fact, a polygamist, though as a good Mormon he had supported the practice when it was good church doctrine. As the debate over his situation went on, one old Senator is said to have looked around and, spotting some notorious womanizers in the Senate chamber, murmured: "Gentlemen, I would rather have a polygamist who does not polyg, than a monogamist who does not monog!"[51]

Latest Wife

After Reed Smoot was sworn in as Senator, there was considerable teasing about his Mormon beliefs, but he took it in good humor. He enjoyed telling about the Washington guide who informed some tourists passing Smoot's house on Connecticut Avenue that the iron bars in the lower-story windows were there to keep his wives from escaping. He wasn't so amused, though, by the way some women used Mormonism to talk their way into the special section in the gallery set aside for the Senators' wives. One day, when one of the Senate debates was attracting large numbers of visitors and it was hard to obtain admission, the Senate doorkeeper sought out Vice President Thomas Marshall and asked him how many wives Senator Smoot had. Marshall assured him the Utah Senator had only one. "Well, now, don't that beat the dickens!" exclaimed the doorkeeper. "I have let in seven already, and I told the last one she was the seventh, and she said yes, she was his latest wife!"[52]

The Page and the Britishers

One day a Senate page took a British admiral and his wife on a tour of the Capitol. The boy was an American history buff, knew a lot about the War of 1812–15, and decided the visitors would be particularly interested in hearing about how the British invaded Washington in 1814 and sacked and burned the Capitol. Once or twice, as he was giving a vivid description of the burning, the admiral's wife murmured that she was sorry at what the British had done; but as the page went on talking about it, she finally interrupted and exclaimed: "You don't have to worry. We don't have a match with us today!"[53]

Senator Davis' Fortune

In 1904 the Democrats picked West Virginia's Henry Gassaway Davis as their Vice-Presidential candidate, even though he was in his eighties, because he was wealthy and they hoped he might contribute handsomely to the party. But Davis didn't come through with much money, despite his large fortune, and the Democrats lost the election to Theodore Roosevelt by a large margin.

Soon after the election the Gridiron Club held its annual meeting in Washington, and, with Davis and several other members of Congress in the audience, presented a couple of skits teasing Davis about his stinginess. In a "dead letter" skit, a letter from the Democratic National Committee turns up acknowledging a receipt of $7.39 from Senator Davis. And in a fortune-telling skit, a man dressed up to represent an ancient gentleman of dignity and character, wearing an old-fashioned suit and out-of-date high hat, is introduced to the fortune-teller as "Mr. Davis." "What Davis?" the fortune-teller asks. "Henry Gazaway Davis," the man answers; "and I would like to have my fortune told." The fortune-teller then asks: "The late candidate for Vice President?" And the man answers, "The same." Thereupon the fortune-teller says he is happy to tell Davis' fortune; and he takes his hand, looks at it carefully for a few seconds, drops it, and solemnly announces: "Mr. Davis, your fortune is precisely the same as it was before you were nominated!" No one seemed to enjoy the ribbing more than Davis himself.[54]

After-Dinner Speeches

When the celebrated oratorical wit New York Senator Chauncey Depew introduced Joseph H. Choate, ambassador to Britain, as guest speaker at a dinner, he had this to say: "Gentlemen, permit me to introduce Ambassador Choate, America's most inveterate after-dinner speaker. All you need to do to get a speech out of Mr. Choate is to open his mouth, drop in a dinner, and up comes a speech." When Depew finished, Choate arose, thanked the Senator for the compliment, and remarked: "Mr. Depew says that, if you open my mouth and drop in a dinner, up will come a speech. But I warn you that, if you open your mouths and drop in one of Senator Depew's speeches, up will come your dinners!"[55]

Relations and Affairs

A bright young man joined the staff of Joseph G. ("Uncle Joe") Cannon, then Speaker of the House, and worked hard at learning the ropes. After a while he noticed that in the Senate there was a Committee on Foreign Relations, while in the House, doing the same kind of work, was a Committee on Foreign Affairs. "Why," he asked Cannon one day, "does the title read 'Affairs' in the House and 'Relations' in the Senate?" "Well," said Cannon, taking on a confidential tone, "since you are old enough to ask about such things, I suppose it's all right to tell you. You see, the House Committee, being junior to the Senate Committee, is not old enough to have relations; it can only have affairs."[56]

All They Need

In 1912, when Arizona Democrat Henry F. Ashurst made his maiden speech in the Senate, he spoke movingly about the glories of his state, which had just been admitted to the Union. "Mr. President," he cried,"this great new baby state is magnificent, this great new baby is destined to join the pantheon of other splendid states in our fair union, this great new baby state is poised to become a veritable paradise. We only need two things:

water and lots of good people." Interrupted an old Senator from New England: "If the gentleman from Arizona will forgive me, that's all they need in Hell!" It's an old story, told about Ben Wade as well as about Ashurst.[57]

Congressman at the Front

Toward the end of World War I, Alben E. Barkley visited France as a member of a House Committee investigating the conduct of the war. On a trip to the front lines in the Ypres sector, the committeemen went into the trenches about seventy-five feet from the German front lines, and a tough but good-natured sergeant led them through the narrow, muddy excavation. For the fun of it, Barkley asked the sergeant to stop, and then took a rifle, stuck a helmet on it, and raised it above the trench level. Zing! Before he could pull it back eleven enemy bullets hit the helmet and whanged it around. "Man," said the sergeant, looking disgustedly at Barkley, "I wish the German Army knew there was a Congressman within seventy-five feet of 'em—they'd just walk over here and surrender!"[58]

Ideal Candidate

In 1919, when it seemed likely the Republicans would return to power, a Washington reporter asked Senator Boies Penrose what kind of presidential candidate his party would look for in 1920. "We shall elect a man of lofty ideals," said Penrose gravely. "Get that? Lofty. He shall be a man familiar with world problems. Very important, world problems. Lots of them to deal with now. He will be a man who will appeal warmly to the young voter—the young men and women of our country. A man of spotless character, of course. That's important, so don't forget that. A man whose life shall be an inspiration to all of us, to whom we may look as our national hero. A man who understands us all and whose heart beats with—" He paused at this point, as if searching for words, and the reporter interposed to ask whether the Republicans had located such a paragon. "We have just such a man," said Penrose. "That's fine," said the reporter. "I don't suppose there's any use in my asking the name of this next President, is there?" "I don't see why not," said Penrose. "The man I have in mind is the late Buffalo Bill."[59]

Eight Years

Pennsylvania Senator Boies Penrose went to the White House soon after Warren G. Harding succeeded Woodrow Wilson as President. "Senator," said the President's secretary, "I hope you won't mind waiting a few minutes." Replied Penrose: "I've been waiting eight years to see a Republican President; a few minutes longer won't hurt."[60]

Never Read It

During the late 1920s the Senate Majority Leader was Indiana's James E. Watson, a large, handsome Old Guard Republican who worked hard at his job and was an effective speaker. Writing, though, was not his forte; he once signed his name to a book that had been ghost-written. When he appeared at Antioch College to deliver an address and the president of the College said, "I read your book and I certainly enjoyed it," Watson said frankly, "Well, I'm glad to hear that, because I never read it."[61]

Heflin and the Catholics

Alabama's Senator Tom Heflin, virulently anti-Catholic as well as anti-black, frequently charged that the Pope was plotting to take over the United States. But Catholic Senators like David I. Walsh of Massachusetts found it hard to take his fulminating seriously and sometimes found themselves chuckling rather than cringing at his tirades. Once, according to a popular story, someone in the Democratic National Committee who didn't know Heflin, asked him to speak at a Democratic state convention in the Bay State. Heflin accepted the invitation; and when he arrived in Boston Senator Walsh met him and took him to Young's Hotel to wait in the lobby until the time came for presenting him to the convention. Meanwhile the Holy Name Society was getting ready for its own convention in Boston, and while Walsh and Heflin were chatting in the hotel lobby, hundreds of its members marched down the street outside. Finally Heflin burst out: "I didn't know there were so many Catholics in the world!" "Hell, Tom," Walsh is reported to have said, "these are just the ones who don't swear!"[62]

Borah as Guide

Idaho Senator William E. Borah, a Republican known for his rugged independence, took horseback rides almost every day before going to work and when it was raining he wore an outfit that made him look very much like a policeman. One nasty day when he was riding in the park a woman hailed him. "Officer," she cried, "can you direct me to the Zoo?" Somewhat surprised, Borah reined in his horse and gave directions. Not quite sure she had spoken to an officer after all, the woman said uncertainly: "I take it that you are a guide." Returned Borah: "Many people don't think so, Madam."[63]

Deportation

After visiting the Soviet Union in 1930, Massachusetts-born and reared Burton K. Wheeler, Democratic Senator from Montana, urged that the United States abandon its isolationist policy and extend diplomatic recognition to Russia. He had learned that Britain and France were buying U.S. cotton and selling it to the Russians, and thought that doing business directly with Russia might help pull the United States out of the growing depression. When a weekly newspaper in Red Lodge, Montana, said that Wheeler ought to be deported for urging recognition of a Communist government, the Senator exclaimed: "Where would you deport me—back to Massachusetts?"[64]

Maury Maverick Replies

Texas Congressman Maury Maverick's outspoken championship of liberal causes during the 1930s produced many letters filled with anger and abuse. Like his friend H. L. Mencken, another iconoclast, Maverick usually gave such letters short shrift. His response to a two-thousand-word tirade from an Illinois conservative became a classic: "Dear Sir: Ph-t-t!! Very truly yours, Maury Maverick." He was wordier when responding to another blast from a Minnesotan calling him a rabble-rouser: "Dear Friend Smith: Go jump in the lake, you old bull frog. I mean any one of the beautiful ten thousand lakes in Minnesota. Very truly yours, Maury Maverick. P.S. Don't do it—it will ruin the lake!"[65]

Wisdom

Kentucky's Alben W. Barkley, Senate Majority Leader in the 1940s, liked to quote an old hillbilly he called Uncle Zeke, who was famous for his wisdom. Asked why he was so wise, according to Barkley, Uncle Zeke responded: "Waal, I've got good judgment. Good judgment comes from experience; and experience . . . waal, that comes from bad judgment."[66]

C'est la Clare

Of the sharp-tongued Clare Boothe Luce, who entered the House in 1943, Harriet Hughes Crowley wrote in the *Detroit Free Press;*

> A lawmaker, wily and fair . . .
> Wore bows on each side of her hair . . .
> Of velvet her clothes . . .
> And with voice like a dove's . . .
> She cooed as she knifed . . . c'est la Clare. . . .[67]

Distraction

During World War II, a national public-opinion poll picked Clare Boothe Luce, anti-New Deal Connecticut Republican serving in the House, as one of six women, including film star Marlene Dietrich, with the most beautiful legs in the United States. One Congressman was incensed. "Don't you think," he cried, "it's beneath the dignity of the House to have one of its members voted among the six women in America with the most beautiful legs?" "Don't you realize, Congressman," replied Mrs. Luce, "that you are just falling for some subtle New Deal propaganda designed to distract attention from the end of me that is really functioning?"[68]

Mind of Man

One Congressman, intending to flatter Clare Boothe Luce, said of her in the House of Representatives one day, "She has the best mind of any woman in the House." Mrs. Luce was enraged by the patronizing tone of the compliment. "The mind knows no sex," she retorted. "If the lady believes that," remarked another Congressman, "she doesn't know the mind of man."[69]

Prices, Fixed and Unfixed

When Congress passed an act in 1945 extending the life of the wartime Office of Price Administration (OPA), President Truman deemed the act ineffective, vetoed it, and appealed to the nation to call on Congress to enact an adequate law on the subject. North Carolina's Sam J. Ervin, who had just entered the House for the first time, received an avalanche of letters from his constituents on the subject, some of them from producers who demanded the removal of the price controls and others from consumers insisting that price controls be retained. His favorite letter came from a small businessman in Charlotte who suggested that Congress ought to remove price ceilings from the things he sold and keep them on the things he bought.[70]

China Stop

One day North Carolina's long-winded Robert Reynolds was rambling on about the fascinating places he had visited around the world, and Majority Leader Alben Barkley, anxious to conclude some Senate business, listened impatiently. Finally, as Reynolds finished with the beauties of the Far West and headed for the islands of the Pacific, Barkley tapped him on the shoulder and interrupted: "Senator, let me off when you get to Shanghai!"[71]

Only Way

F. Edward Hébert, chairman of the House Committee on Armed Services for a time, once insisted: "The only way we'll ever get a volunteer army is to draft 'em."[72]

Uncovered

California Democrat Helen Gahagan Douglas produced unintended laughter when she fought hard for a revision of the Fair Labor Standards Act because it "leaves two million women uncovered."[73]

Teeth

One day a woman in the House gallery jumped up and started screaming: "Mr. Speaker, damn you, I want you to put some teeth in this bill!" When the guards got to her they found she didn't have a tooth in her head.[74]

Quotient

Asked by a reporter to comment on Oregon Senator Wayne Morse's move in the 1950s from the Republican to the Democratic party, former Congresswoman Clare Boothe Luce, known for her tart tongue as well as for her partisanship, exclaimed: "Whenever a Republican leaves one side of the aisle and goes to the other, it raises the intelligence quotient of both parties."[75]

Sitting on It

Once New York's Emanuel Celler, long-time chairman of the House Judiciary Committee, was asked how he stood on a bill recently sent the committee. "I don't stand on it," laughed Celler. "I am sitting on it. It rests four-square under my fanny, and will never see the light of day!"[76]

Virgins

Thor C. Tolletson of Washington State hired a new stenographer. Answering a constituent's query about a bill, he dictated: "The House version differs from the Senate version, and they will have to go to conference to settle their differences." When the stenographer finished typing up the dictation, she turned to the other woman in the office and asked: "Who is the House virgin and who is the Senate virgin?"[77]

Boyish

To some people John F. Kennedy looked like a college boy when he first entered the Senate in 1953. When he went to see the Secretary of the Senate about his office space after being sworn in, the receptionist reportedly said, "Sit down, sonny. The Secretary will be able to see you in about an hour." JFK sat down and while he was waiting a clerk came along, mistook him for a page, and gave him some letters to mail. A little later the receptionist said, "Secretary Biffle is very busy starting the session. What do you want to see him about?" "Well," said Kennedy, "I'm Senator Kennedy, and I'd like to see about my office."

Carl Albert, the short, boyish-looking Oklahoma Congressman, who became Speaker in 1971, had similar problems. One day he was headed for the Speaker's stand and a newly elected Congressman, mistaking him for a page, snapped his fingers and cried: "Boy!" Amused, Albert stopped, looked around, and when the Congressman thrust some papers at him and told him to take them over to another Congressman, Albert did as he was told. Then, as he took his place at the desk on the top level of the three-tiered Speaker's stand, he paused before rapping his mallet and cast an impish glance at the freshman Congressman. But the newcomer was hard to see. He had "slumped down in his seat," someone observed, "shrinking to the smallest size possible."[78]

Disregard

In the spring of 1954, when a Senate committee was examining Senator Joe McCarthy's reckless charge that the U.S. Army was soft on Communism, the committee's counsel, Ray Jenkins, had to follow an impartial course and it was not at all easy. When he was conducting his direct examination of Secretary of the Army Robert Stevens (who was defending the Army), a woman wired him: "YOU ARE FAIR AND IMPARTIAL. MAY GOD GIVE YOU STRENGTH." But when he put on one of his other hats, and began a vigorous cross-examination of Stevens, the woman sent another telegram: "DISREGARD WIRE ASKING GOD TO GIVE YOU STRENGTH."[79]

Unheard Of

Angrily stalking out of a committee meeting one day Wisconsin Senator Joseph R. McCarthy ran into some reporters, and when they asked for his reaction to a surprising allegation that had just been made, he sputtered: "Why, it's the most unheard-of thing I've ever heard of!"[80]

Southern Accent

In 1954, shortly after entering the Senate, North Carolina's Sam J. Ervin, Jr., initiated a weekly radio program, with the help of Harry Gatton, one of his aides, to keep people in his state informed of his official activities. Soon afterwards he was driving back to North Carolina with Gatton and they turned on the car radio and heard a speaker describing the salient features of a revenue bill then being considered by the Senate. "Harry," said Ervin, "I don't know who is talking, but I recognize by his accent that he's a Southerner." "That's you, Senator," cried Gatton. Ervin, who had never heard his recorded voice on radio before, was surprised, but he exclaimed: "If that's right, I can say for the first time since I went to the Senate, I agree with everything that's being said!"[81]

Absolved

When the North Carolina legislature contemplated banning the teaching of evolution in the state's public schools, the state's Senator, Sam Ervin, was scornful. "I can think of only one thing that can come of this," he declared. "The monkeys in the jungle will be pleased to know that the North Carolina legislature has absolved them from any responsibility for humanity in general and for the North Carolina legislature in particular."[82]

Afraid

Soon after the Supreme Court handed down its decision banning prayer in the public schools, Senator Sam Ervin presided over a luncheon attended by Chief Justice Earl Warren and several other members of the Supreme Court. In remarks he made as master of ceremonies, Ervin told about the North Carolina schoolteacher who entered her classroom a few minutes early one morning and found some of the schoolboys down on their knees in a huddle in the corner of the room. "What are you boys doing?" she asked sharply. "We're shooting craps!" one of the boys yelled back. "Oh," she sighed with relief, "that's all right. I was afraid you were praying!"[83]

Topknot Come Down

In speaking to the Senate in favor of the recommendation of the Watkins committee that the Senate censure Joseph R. McCarthy, Sam Ervin told a story to illustrate McCarthy's technique of lifting things out of context to disparage others. "The McCarthy technique of lifting statements out of context was practiced in North Carolina about seventy-five years ago," he declared. "At that time the women had a habit of wearing their hair in topknots. This preacher deplored that habit. As a consequence, he preached a rip-roaring sermon one Sunday on the text, 'Top Not Come Down.' At the conclusion of his sermon an irate woman, wearing a very pronounced topknot, told the preacher that no such text could be found in the Bible. The preacher thereupon opened the Scriptures to the seventeenth verse of the twenty-fourth chapter of Matthew and pointed to the words 'Let him which is on the housetop not come down to take anything out of his house.' Any practitioner of the McCarthy technique of lifting things out of context can readily find the text 'top not come down' in this verse."[84]

Handmaiden

When a special committee headed by conservative Republican Senator Arthur V. Watkins of Utah recommended censuring Wisconsin's Joseph R. McCarthy for disorderly behavior in his Senatorial office, McCarthy at once charged that the committee was "the unwitting handmaiden of the Communist Party." In response, North Carolina's Sam Ervin, one of the committee members, declared that if McCarthy made his charge knowing it to be untrue, he might well be expelled from the Senate for moral incapacity, but if he made it believing it to be true, he might well be expelled for mental incapacity. Colorado's big, burly Edwin C. Johnson took a different tack. "I've been accused of many things during my long public career," he snorted, "but this is the first time I've ever been accused of being anybody or anything's handmaiden!"[85]

Enthusiasm

Once an older, experienced Congressman advised a younger colleague on campaigning. "You've got to speak loud to audiences so they don't fall asleep," he told him. "Be enthusiastic. Open your mouth and throw yourself into it!"[86]

Politician

When Congressman Hardin Peterson of Florida retired, Charles E. Bennett, his Florida colleague, drove down to Lakeland, Florida, for a celebration in his honor, stopping overnight in an old hotel in central Florida. The next morning, when he went out to resume his journey, he found he had accidentally locked his keys in the car. Some of the men sitting on the whittling bench nearby became interested in his plight, and all but one of them had suggestions to make about getting into the car. But none of them was a constituent, so Bennett did the job himself; he simply used a wire coathanger to get one of the car doors open. Then he got in the car and started to drive off; but then, curious about the old fellow who had offered no advice, he stopped the car, backed up, looked out the window, and cried: "Say, how is it you didn't have a suggestion on how I could get into my car?" "Well, son," said the man, "I seen that Congress sign on the back of your car, and I figured you was a politician; and a politician can wiggle in or out of any place he wants to."[87]

Bag of Bones

When the nomination of Clare Boothe Luce, former Congresswoman, as ambassador to Brazil ran into difficulties in the Senate, Illinois Republican Everett Dirksen defended her stoutly against her Democratic critics. "Why thrash old straws," he cried, when they quoted cracks she had taken at President Roosevelt years before, "or beat an old bag of bones?" As the Senators began laughing at Dirksen's unfortunate phrase, Democratic Senator Hubert Humphrey leaped to his feet and cried mischievously: "I must rise to the defense of the lady." "I am referring to the old bag of political bones," stammered Dirksen in embarrassment. Mrs. Luce won confirmation, but resigned when a crack she took at Senator Wayne Morse, one of her opponents, angered most of the Senators.[88]

Pronunciation

When Hawaii's Japanese-American Daniel Inouye first entered the Senate, his colleagues had trouble pronouncing his last name. But one day, at a meeting of the Commerce Committee, one of the Senators, angry about an amendment just made to a bill under discussion, blurted out: "I will not accept that amendment—*in no way!*" "Gentlemen," said Senator Inouye triumphantly, "that is exactly how you pronounce my name!"[89]

The Other Phone

As Republican Minority Leader, Everett Dirksen used some of the same methods that Lyndon Johnson employed as leader of the Senate's Democrats. He polled members of his party before important votes were taken, tried to persuade them to go along with the party on issues, delayed votes until the time was favorable for his side, and worked on members of the other party to join him on votes. "Dirksen doesn't stand on principle so much," observed one Republican Senator; "he gets on the phone and lines up the votes for our side."

Dirksen also insisted on the same "perks" as Majority Leader Johnson enjoyed. After much effort, according to one tale, he finally managed to get a telephone installed in his official limousine, just like the one LBJ had, and immediately called up Johnson, who was in his limousine at the time. "Hello, Lyndon," he is supposed to have announced triumphantly. "This is Everett Dirksen. I'm calling you from my limousine with my new phone." "Just a minute, Ev," LBJ supposedly shot back. "Hold the line. My other phone is ringing!" The story is apocryphal. Dirksen in fact had the telephone taken out of his limousine so he could work without interruption when traveling to and from his office.[90]

Against Them

Oklahoma's Democratic Senator Robert Kerr loved to take cracks at Republicans, and one of his favorite stories was about a die-hard Oklahoma Republican who was interviewed by a reporter on his ninety-sixth birthday. "You've lived a long time," said the reporter, "and have seen many changes." "Yes," said the ancient Republican, "and I was against every damned one of them!"[91]

Job for George

One day Kentucky Senator John Sherman Cooper received a letter from his old friend George, who resided with his wife Mandy on a little farm in Sleepy Hollow, Kentucky, reminding him of his loyal support for Cooper and the Republicans through the years, informing him that he and his wife were getting older and suffering from arthritis, and asking him to persuade President Eisenhower to appoint him as ambassador to Great Britain. Cooper at once sent the letter to Thruston Morton, a former Kentucky Senator then serving as Assistant Secretary of State, begging him to arrange for a tactful reply turning down the man's request. But Thruston returned the letter to Cooper and told him no diplomat in the State Department possessed sufficient skill to frame such a reply and said Cooper would have to perform the task himself.

Cooper thought it over for a while and at length drafted a letter himself. "Dear George," he wrote, "the Republican Party owes you any office within its gift, and I'll be glad to help you obtain any office you want. As your friend, however, I want to warn you that being ambassador to the Court of St. James isn't always a bed of roses. I'm going to tell you about some of its drawbacks. . . . The ambassador to the Court of St. James can't get much rest in the daylight hours because he is annoyed all day by trivial demands of Americans visiting England, and he can't get much sleep at night because he lies awake worrying about the sad state in which international affairs find themselves. The Court of St. James is located in London, where the winters are long and dreary, and the fog and dampness soak into the bones of those who suffer from arthritis. Mandy and you will have to attend the social functions of the royal court at Buckingham Palace, where Mandy will have to bend her arthritic knee to the Queen, and you'll have to expose your arthritic knees to the gaze of all present by wearing knee breeches. After Mandy and you have considered all these drawbacks, let me know whether you still want me to go to the White House and ask President Eisenhower to give you the job of ambassador to the Court of St. James."

On receipt of Senator Cooper's letter, George wrote back at once: "Dear John Sherman, As always you're right. The job of ambassador to the Court of St. James wouldn't suit Mandy and me at all. I'll settle for the postmastership of Sleepy Hollow."[92]

Columbus Day

It was Columbus Day, and some Senators were needling Rhode Island's John Pastore at a committee meeting by suggesting that it was Leif Ericsson, not Columbus, who first discovered America. "Yes, yes, gentlemen," said Pastore finally; "of course Ericsson discovered America. That is why we are meeting today in the District of Ericsson."[93]

Honk

Whenever Arkansas Democrat William Fulbright, chairman of the Senate Foreign Relations Committee for many years, received an embarrassingly glowing introduction before making a speech, he liked to tell the story of a farmer and the calf. The farmer was leading a bawky calf across a bridge, he said, and halfway over, the calf froze and stood there stiff-legged and nothing would budge it. Finally a car came along and stopped, unable to get by. The farmer explained the problem and suggested the driver honk his horn to see if the noise would scare the calf into moving. The driver obliged; but he honked the horn so loudly that the calf panicked, leaped into the air, plunged over the bridge railing, and drowned. When the farmer started bawling out the driver, the latter protested. "But you asked me to honk," he said. "Sure," said the farmer, "but you didn't have to honk so *big* for such a *little* calf!"[94]

Friends

Conservative Senator Barry Goldwater and liberal Senator Hubert Humphrey disagreed on just about every social issue, but liked and respected each other and teased each other good-naturedly. After one of Humphrey's long-winded harangues, Goldwater remarked that the Minnesotan "had probably been vaccinated with a phonograph needle." Humphrey responded by saying that Goldwater "would have been a great success in the movies working for Eighteenth Century-Fox."[95]

Principle

Most people visiting Congress are unaware of the fact that the floor on which the House of Representatives meets is sometimes called the "principal floor" of the Capitol Building. One day the young man running one of the elevators started up. "Anybody for Principal?" he asked. No one answered, but one of the women on the elevator looked shocked. "Young man," she said, "I came all the way from Tennessee to see these Congressmen at work. I certainly hope some of them are for principle!"[96]

English Blood

Hawaii's Republican Senator Hiram Fong, an American of Chinese ancestry, had an impassive face but a keen sense of humor. Once he accompanied some Senators to London to attend a conference and was at the dinner which a member of Britain's House of Commons gave in their honor. The toastmaster introduced the Senators, one by one, and when he reached Fong, he said: "I am pleased to introduce the next of our guests. He is the first American Senator of Chinese ancestry. Unlike many—perhaps most—Americans, he has no English blood." Fong got up to respond, and, with a deadpan expression, announced: "I must correct our good host. He said I have no English blood. I must tell him that my great-grandfather ate Captain Cook." This brought down the house.[97]

Udall's Bill

The first bill that Arizona Democrat Morris K. ("Mo") Udall sponsored that became law was intended to settle the question of whether the illegitimate children of civil servants are eligible for benefits. The courts had made varied rulings and the Civil Service Commission was eager to have the matter settled one way or the other. Udall's bill saw to it that illegitimate children were "children" for the purposes of civil-service retirement, and the bill was soon being called the "poor bastards bill." Despite the facetious nickname, Udall's bill sailed through Congress and became law with President John Kennedy's signature. The following weekend Congressman Udall was in Arizona and happened to meet a member of the ultraconservative John Birch Society at some gathering. "Congressman," said the Bircher belligerently, "you guys are throwing our money away in Africa, Europe, and everywhere else. What I want to know is, when are you going to do something for the poor bastards in this country?" "Sir," said

Udall triumphantly, "I'm glad you asked that question. Why, just last week. . . ."[98]

Angel's Kiss

When Morris K. Udall became chairman of the House Interior Committee, an Irish colleague told him: "There is an old Irish legend that when an infant is placed in his cradle immediately after birth, an angel of the Lord hovers over him and kisses him. If the angel kisses him on the forehead, the child will grow up to be a great thinker or philosopher; if the kiss is on the throat, a great singer or orator; if on the heart, a great humanitarian." Then he got to the point. "The angel has kissed you in several places," he told Udall, "including one which will make you a great chairman."[99]

One Less

Right after Thomas N. Downing was elected to Congress as a Democrat from Virginia's First District, he triumphantly asked his wife: "How many great men has the First District of Virginia produced since this country began?" "I don't know," she said, "but, sweetheart, it's one less than you're thinking!"[100]

Hard to Tell

Soon after entering the House, Lucien N. Nedzi of Michigan approached an elevator near which a pre-teen boy was standing. As he pushed the "up" button, the boy told him he had already pushed it. Nedzi thanked him and they waited in silence for the elevator to arrive. Suddenly the boy broke the silence. "Are you a Congressman?" he asked. When Nedzi said he was, the boy sighed: "You know, I can't tell a Congressman from a regular man!"[101]

Bob Doyle

In 1960, Kansas' Robert Dole, World War II veteran who lost the use of his right arm after being seriously wounded in battle, ran for Congress and won by a comfortable margin. Soon after entering the House he agreed to speak at a dinner in a small town in Indiana. Since his name had "little marquee value" in those days, he recalled, the G.O.P. dinner committee arranged for an interview at the local radio station to publicize the dinner and boost attendance. "The guest at this evening's dinner," announced the interviewer, "will be Congressman Bob Doyle [sic]. He will speak at the American Legion Hall. Tickets have been slashed from three dollars to one dollar. A color television set will be given away. You must be present to win,

and we're not going to draw till Congressman Doyle gets through talking."
Then the interviewer gave biographical details: "Doyle was born in Kansas,
raised in Kansas, educated at the University of Kansas. Prior to World War
II, he was a pre-medical student. He fought in Italy, where he suffered a
serious head injury. Then he went into politics."[102]

Pigs

On April 22, 1969, Congressman Frederick D. Schwengel, Republican of
Iowa, delivered a eulogy to pigs and the pork industry. "I like pigs," he told
his colleagues, "and I honestly believe that most pigs like me. Hogs are
beautiful. Some of my best friends are hogs. To amuse ourselves, let us take
a look at some of the uncomplimentary terms and phrases being heaped
upon the poor pig. Consider these image-makers, for example:

> She is *pigheaded*.
> Her apartment is as dirty as a *pigsty*.
> On weekends, she goes *hog wild*.
> She knows as much about politics as a *hog* knows about Sunday.
> She is always *hogging* the show.
> What's more, she is a *road hog*.
> Her Congressman is nothing but a *pork-barrel* politician who feeds at the
> Government trough.
> I've never met her, but they say she is as *fat as a pig*.
> Who wants to buy a *pig in a poke*?
> Maybe she is all *lard*, who knows?
> I've heard rumors that she casts her pearls before *swine*.
> Does she have a cute little *piggy* bank?
> Yes, I know, but you can't make a silk purse out of a *sow's ear*.
> On the dance floor, she was awkward as a *hog on ice*.

"Now that we have a pig's eye image of this girl, how would you like to go
whole hog and hire her as a member of your congressional staff?"

Having finished talking about the "semantics of swine slang," Schwengel
went on to pay tribute to the noble pig for its nine hundred years of noble
service to humanity. "Yes, sir," he exclaimed, "pigs are versatile creatures—
and smart, too. Sometimes they are smarter than we think. For example, I
recall a story I heard as a boy on my father's farm in Franklin County, Iowa,
about the city slicker from Boston who bought a farm near ours. He wanted
to get rich quick raising hogs. For a start he had one sow. He wanted some
baby pigs so he loaded his sow into the wheelbarrow and pushed her up the
road a couple of miles to the nearest neighbor to visit a boar. Then he
wheeled the sow home again. Next morning he went to the barn bright and
early, but to his surprise there were no little pigs. So he hoisted the sow into
the wheelbarrow and repeated the journey. Next morning he went to the

barn again—and still no little pigs. But there was the sow sitting in the wheelbarrow! Yes, sir; pigs are smart. . . ."[103]

Moving to Virginia

Republican Senator John G. Tower of Texas liked to tell a story about George Washington when the latter, he said, was growing up on his daddy's ranch in the High Plains of West Texas. On that ranch, said Tower, there was a beautiful mesquite tree, which George's daddy loved, not only because it was a beautiful tree but also because it was the only tree for fifty miles in any direction. One day, when his daddy was out on the range rounding up a few mavericks and strays, George pulled on his boots, picked up his Bowie knife, and went out and whittled down that mesquite tree. When his daddy got home, he took little George out behind the corral and asked him: "George, who whittled down my mesquite tree?" "I did it, Daddy," said George. "I cannot tell a lie." "Pack your things, son," his daddy said. "We're moving to Virginia. You'll never get along like that in Texas!"[104]

Can't Miss It

Once Senator William Proxmire of Wisconsin, due in another city for an important appointment, got caught in a traffic jam in Washington on his way to the airport, and, spotting a police car, pulled alongside, rolled down the window, and cried: "Pardon me, officer, but I am Senator Proxmire of Wisconsin. Could you get me to the airport?" "You bet your life," said the policeman confidently. "Go to the stop sign, turn left; then turn right; follow the signs, and you can't miss it."[105]

Inspiration

While speaking at a rural school in his Congressional district in Oklahoma one day, the diminutive Carl Albert (five feet, four inches) gave the audience everything he could. When he finished a little boy came running up and cried: "Mister, you sure inspired me today!" Beaming, Albert asked the boy what he had said that inspired the lad so much. "It isn't anything you said," replied the boy. "I just figure if a little squirt like you can be elected to Congress, I can become President of the United States."[106]

Next One

In Congress, New York's Bella Abzug was a vigorous champion of the Equal Rights Amendment (ERA). She was extremely upset when Brooklyn

Congressman Emanuel Celler insisted that women had always been un-equal since Adam and Eve and were likely to remain so. But she was even more upset when Celler declared: "Why, women weren't even at the Last Supper." "We may not have been at the last one," she told him icily, "but we sure as hell will be at the next one!"[107]

Not in Cincinnati

During the course of Senate hearings on the Watergate scandal in 1973–74, committee chairman Sam J. Ervin, Jr., had occasion to go to Cincinnati to deliver the commencement address at the University of Cincinnati. When he returned to his motel suite afterward, he found two Cincinnati police officers awaiting him. Their chief, it seemed, had received an anonymous call threatening to kill the Senator, and the two police officers were instructed to spend the night in his suite and look after him while he was in Cincinnati. "I don't know how much the chief is concerned with your assassination," one of the policemen told Ervin, "but I am absolutely convinced he doesn't want it to happen in Cincinnati!"[108]

Deep Into

Once a Congressman was talking at length to the Texas delegation about the high price of fertilizer. After listening to him for a time Barbara Jordan, a member of Congress from Texas herself, got tired of his long-windedness. "Congressman," she finally said, "it's refreshing to hear you talking about something you're really deep into."[109]

Morally Repugnant

When proposals were made to have a national lottery, New York's Demo-cratic Congressman Alfred Santangelo indignantly declared that such a thing "was morally repugnant to millions of people, not only in the United States, but also in the Twenty-fourth Congressional District."[110]

Beef

On October 2, 1975, Republican Congressman Silvio A. Conte of Massa-chusetts delivered a speech in the House objecting to a bill dealing with farm supports. "Mr. Chairman," he announced, "I rise to assure my colleagues that I would not 'steer' them wrong, but I must 'raise a beef' about this bill. This 'choice' legislation is a 'prime' example of what can make Congress 'stew in its own juices.' It drips with excess 'fat,' while it 'strips' the consumer. This 'beef-doggle' would raise retail meat prices by

$60 million a year. No matter how you 'slice' it, consumers are having their 'flanks' attacked. They are being 'slaughtered.' It was not my intent to 'roast' the sponsors of this 'bum steer.' But I must remind them that consumers have a 'stake' here too. But if this bill is 'herded' through the House, many consumers will no longer have 'steak.' You have all heard of Britain's 'Rump Parliament' under Lord Cromwell. I fear that if this private interest bill for the beef industry passes, history will hereafter refer to us as the 'Rump-Roast Congress.' I ask my colleagues to take this 'bull by the horns,' kill this bill, cut the fat off the bone, and 'render' it back to the committee. It 'butchers' lean consumer pocketbooks, and makes 'mince-meat' of fiscal responsibility. While I do not want to 'rib' my friends from the cattle raising States, I think that someone is trying to pull the cowhide over our eyes. I urge my colleagues to reject this 'hunk of fat.' It bleeds the American consumer. And I do not know a 'knock wurst' than that."[111]

Scotch

Sometimes, when Congressional sessions dragged on until late at night, members liked to have a drink or two to fortify themselves. One night Alaska's Republican Senator Theodore F. ("Ted") Stevens charged that the Democrats were riding roughshod over the Republicans, and exclaimed: "There's just enough Scotch in me to demand that I get my fair rights!" A little later, when some of his colleagues expressed surprise that he would admit publicly to being a little tipsy, he at once sought the floor again to explain that he had been referring to "his Scottish heritage."[112]

VII

★　★　★　★　★　★　★　★

On the Floor

★ ◪ ★

One day, when Vice President Alben W. Barkley was presiding over the Senate, Tennessee's Kenneth D. McKellar angrily addressed the chair to complain that Illinois' Scott Lucas had dared to "yawn" while he was speaking. Barkley took the objection under consideration, and then solemnly ruled: "The yawn of the Senator from Illinois will be stricken from the record."[1]

There was plenty to yawn about through the years. Sometimes the issues brought to the House and Senate floors were trivial; and sometimes, even with serious issues on the agenda, long-winded orators reduced their colleagues (and visitors in the galleries) to somnolence. "We knew a member," wrote Henry G. Wheeler, author of a book on Congress published in 1848, "whose rising with intent to make a speech was a signal at which the benches, in every quarter of the Hall, were precipitately vacated."[2] Wheeler may have been thinking of Virginia's garrulous Alexander Smyth. In the midst of one of his interminable speeches in the House, Smyth suddenly noticed Henry Clay was getting restless, and, looking him straight in the face, announced loftily: "You speak for the present generation; I speak for posterity." "Yes," sighed Clay, "and you seem resolved to continue speaking until your audience arrives."[3]

Clay himself spoke at length on occasion, but never bored anybody, for he was lucid, forceful, and at times witty. He was also good at repartee. When Tennessee Congressman Felix Grundy, a hard-money man known for his ingenious reasoning, delivered a tirade against paper money one day, Clay sarcastically remarked that he didn't doubt that "his honorable friend furnished himself with United States banknotes to travel from Nashville to Washington." "No, sir," said Grundy stoutly, "I always travel on *specie.*" "Ah!" dried Clay, seeing his opening, "my old friend is always *specie-ous!*"[4]

In his memoirs, Missouri's Champ Clark pronounced repartee one of the delights of Congressional debates. A favorite of his—and of other Congressional memoirists—was a heated exchange, just before the Civil War, between Georgia's diminutive Alexander Stephens (five feet tall, eighty pounds avoirdupois) and a great, big, huge fellow from the West who was making his maiden speech in the House. After Stephens had interrupted several times to ask some probing questions, the Westerner finally exploded: "Why, you little shrimp! I could swallow you whole!" "If you did," Stephens shot back, "you'd have more brains in your belly than you ever had in your head!"[5] Equally popular with Clark—and with other Congressional retrospectators—was the Reed-Springer tilt. One day Illinois' William M. Springer got into an argument with Maine's Thomas B. Reed and at length declared with finality: "I'm right. I know I'm right, and I say, with Henry Clay, I'd rather be right than President." Drawled Reed: "The gentleman from Illinois will never be either."[6]

Sometimes the exchanges were in fun; Congressmen enjoyed teasing as well as taunting each other. Once, when a great many members of the House were interrupting a speech Massachusetts' Benjamin F. Butler was giving and Ohio's Samuel S. ("Sunset") Cox— a little fellow (like Alexander Stephens)—joined in, Butler good-naturedly waved him off and quoted from a popular song dating from the Civil War: "Shoo, fly! Don't bodder me! Shoo, fly! Don't bodder me!" ["For I belong to Company G!"] Cox didn't mind the teasing; he and Butler were on good terms.[7] On another occasion Cox made a speech taking issue with some of Butler's opinions, and to emphasize his points he held his right hand high above his head and radiated his fingers like the spokes of a wagon wheel. When Cox finished, Butler got up, stood quietly in the aisle for a minute, and then began: "Mr. Speaker." Then, as the room became still, he suddenly raised his right hand, extended his fingers, and wriggled them around the way Cox had done. Then he let his arms fall again, and stood still and silent again for a moment or two. "That is all, Mr. Speaker," he finally announced. "I just wanted to answer the gentleman from Ohio."[8]

Like his friend Butler, "Sunset" Cox went in for joshing himself now and then. Once, when he was delivering a speech in the House, Clarence Cannon, his hefty colleague from Ohio, interrupted. "Will the gentleman yield?" he asked. "Oh, no," said Cox. "I cannot yield. The gentleman shakes his finger and he scares me." Then he smiled and exclaimed: "Yes, I will yield." "For what time?" asked Speaker James G. Blaine. "As long as the gentleman keeps his hands in his pockets," said Cox, well knowing that Cannon simply could not speak without gesticulating. Cannon accepted the yielding and started in; but he had not talked half a minute before his left hand went up like a catapult. "Time's up!" cried Cox triumphantly; and the laughter rocking the House almost cracked the glass roof.[9]

Congressional funsters prized well-timed put-downs, as well as whimsical leg-pulls and impertinent interruptions, especially when a speaker became too pompous, sentimental, tendentious, or self-important. One day Ohio's Jim Bingham made a speech in the House so full of pathos that when he finished his colleagues sat in rapt silence for a moment or two. Then Ben Butler broke the spell. "I always did like that speech," he remarked loud enough for everyone to hear.[10] Tom Reed similarly spoiled a speech his colleague Jasper Talbert of South Carolina was giving one fine day. To underscore a point Talbert began telling a much-told tale about the preacher who startled his congregation by reading some strange passages from the Bible after a mischievous boy had glued two of the pages together. When Talbert was about halfway through the story, Tom Reed came ambling down the aisle and interrupted. "Mr. Speaker," he said, "I would like to inquire, for the sake of information, if the statute of limitation never runs [out] against an anecdote."[11]

Jonathan P. Dolliver's experience with a speech was even more deflating. Scheduled to address the House on the tariff, the conscientious Iowan worked hard on what he was going to say. "I had written and rewritten it," he recalled, "boiled it down, polished it up, and committed it to memory. There was one passage with which I was particularly pleased. As an argument in favor of the tariff as a generator of prosperity I drew as graphic a picture as I could of how foreign-born citizens of Iowa would come into my law office at Fort Dodge, employ me to write to the old folks across the sea, and include money [in their letters] to promote their comfort and happiness, and how, while [I was] engaged in this kindly duty, tears would roll down their cheeks." Just as Dolliver launched into what he regarded as the most moving passage of his speech, Kentucky Congressman Asher Caruth arose and exclaimed: "Mr. Speaker, what did I understand the gentleman from Iowa to say those people were crying about?" The House broke up in laughter and Dolliver sat down in frustration.[12]

Not all Congressional repartee of course has been good-humored. In the heat of debate the "retort churlish" was just as common as the "retort courteous." In 1894, when Missouri's John J. O'Neill was making a speech, a Congressman noted for his acidulous tongue interrupted him so often that he finally turned on him savagely and snarled: "If the gall which you have in your heart could be poured into your stomach, you'd die instantly of the black vomit!"[13] There are injunctions against indulging in personalities, however, and insults employed during Congressional debates are usually euphemized. Once, in the midst of a heated exchange, Indiana Congressman Henry Johnson called a Congressman from Illinois a jackass, producing an immediate legislative "point of order," and a requirement by the Speaker that he retract his statement. "While I withdraw the unfortunate word, Mr. Speaker," he said, "I still insist that the gentleman from Illinois is out of order." "How am I out of order?" cried the Illinois Congressman. "Probably a veterinary surgeon could tell you," was Johnson's acid reply.[14] Years later Democratic Majority Leader John McCormack neatly disposed of a Republican Congressman who was needling him: "I have a minimum high regard for the gentleman."[15]

Some observers thought there was less insult-hurling in the Senate than in the House, but the record does not bear them out. In the Senate, as in the House, members sometimes "gave the lie direct, without any circumlocution whatever" in the midst of debates, Champ Clark reported, and on occasion Senators came to blows.[16] One day, during the debates on the Compromise of 1850, Mississippi's Henry S. Foote called Missouri's Thomas Hart Benton a "calumniator," and the latter at once jumped up, violently pushed his chair aside, and headed stormily in Foote's direction. The Mississippian then took out a big pistol and aimed it at Benton. "Let him fire!" screamed Benton, as two Senators tried to restrain Foote. "Stand out of the way! I have no pistol! I disdain to carry arms! Stand out of the way, and let the assassin fire!" But the Senators managed to disarm Foote and restore order, and Foote said afterward he thought Benton was armed too. A select committee which investigated the incident criticized both Benton and Foote, but recommended no action; its hope was that the report it issued would be "a sufficient rebuke and a warning not unheeded in the future."[17]

But the future was much like the past, with ferocity as well as frivolity appearing in debates, and fistfights erupting at times. Champ Clark regarded Congress as basically a tough arena for debaters. "Men don't stand on ceremony there," he wrote in 1920. "Quarter is neither asked nor given. It is every fellow for himself, and the devil take the hindmost. The fittest survive in that field of fiercest competition. It is an unequaled arena for intellectual slugging-matches. . . . To succeed in that species of discussion, a man must keep a clear head; must have a nimble tongue; must think rapidly; must strike from the shoulder; must not lose his temper; for it is true, as James G. Blaine states in his *Twenty Years in Congress*, that 'usually to lose one's temper in debate is to lose one's cause.' In it every kind of mental weapon is used—the claymore, broadsword, Damascus blade, battle-ax, knife, stiletto, sledgehammer, club, small arms, rifled cannon, and mortar guns. Attacks are made front, flank, and rear."[18]

During the twentieth century, debates in the House and Senate steadily declined in importance. Critical work on legislation took place increasingly in committees, and the discussion of measures in the House and Senate chambers came at times to be largely pro forma. "In the twenty-eight years that I have been a member of one or the other branches of Congress," said Virginia Senator Carter Glass, back in the 1930s, "I have never known a speech to change a vote."[19] Glass may have exaggerated the irrelevance of debates, but it is certainly true that they had ceased to be the center of things the way they had been in the earliest years of Congress.

Still, Congress continued to contain members who were skilled in debate and good at repartee and who enjoyed taking to the floor from time to time to display their talents, just as Congressional debaters enjoyed doing in the nineteenth century. New York's lively Congresswoman, Bella Abzug, for one, refused to dismiss Congressional debates as anachronisms. "There is a theory around here . . . that to attend a debate on the floor is a waste of time," she wrote in 1972. "Since everybody has his mind made up in advance, the theory goes, what's the point of going to a debate? Insert what you have to say in the *Record,* which doesn't even require you to be on the floor, and distribute it to your constituents. If you're seen hanging around the Floor listening to others, you're considered overearnest. You should be up in your office answering mail. To stay on the Floor is to be unsuave and unsophisticated. Well, that's the theory, and I, obviously, don't buy it. I hardly ever leave the Floor when the House is in session, because what I was sent here to do is sit and watch and participate. Besides, I don't think debate is a waste of time. I have seen my own arguments sway votes."[20]

It would be wrong, of course, to think that when Congress met there was a great deal of the kind of excitement on the floor pictured in Frank Capra's famous film, *Mr. Smith Goes to Washington* (1930), which most Senators, in fact, found distasteful when it was first released; but it would also be a mistake to think that Congressional sessions consisted only of highly technical and (to the uninitiated, at least) deadly dull parliamentary maneuvers. There were still lively debates, and, with members of Congress like Bella Abzug in attendance, sparkling moments and splendid repartee in the late twentieth century.

☆ ☆ ☆

Pennsylvania Dutch

Virginia's John Randolph knew the classics and loved to fill his House speeches with erudite Latin and Greek quotations. But Pennsylvania's George Kremer got tired of it all and finally rose one day and poured forth a torrent of Pennsylvania German in response to a Randolph declamation. When he took his seat, covered with perspiration, the startled Randolph sought the floor and begged the honorable gentleman from Pennsylvania to enlighten the House and the country by translating what he had just uttered. "I have only to say in reply to my friend from Virginia," said Kremer, "that when he translates the dead languages which he is constantly using for the benefit of us country members, into something like English, I will be equally liberal in translating my living Pennsylvania Dutch into something that the House can understand!" The laugh was on Randolph.[21]

Vacancy

One day a Congressman who had just been elected to fill a vacancy caused by a death made a fierce attack on John Randolph, and, to everyone's surprise, the short-tempered Virginian had nothing to say in response. Two or three days later, however, while discussing a bill which the deceased Congressman was sponsoring at the time of his death, Randolph remarked casually: "This bill, Mr. Speaker, lost its ablest advocate in the death of my lamented colleague, whose seat," he added pointedly, "is still vacant."[22]

The Misery Debate (1818–21)

When Missouri applied to Congress for admission into the Union in December 1818, she touched off the nation's first big sectional crisis. "'Missouri' is the only word ever repeated here by the politicians," Virginia Congressman John Tyler wrote a friend at the height of the crisis. "You can have no possible idea of the excitement which prevails. Men talk of a dissolution of the Union with perfect nonchalance and indifference." For months the "Misery Debate," as it was called, raged in Congress over the status of slavery in Missouri and the other Federal territories, and it wasn't until early 1821 that North and South finally reached an uneasy compromise on the issue. "The Missouri question is the most portentous that ever threatened the Union," said the aging Thomas Jefferson in retirement at Monticello. "In the gloomiest moments of the Revolutionary War I never had any apprehension equal to that I feel from this source."

The Missouri crisis ended when Kentucky's Henry Clay, Speaker of the House, took the lead in sponsoring bills coupling the admission of Missouri to the Union as a slave state with the admission of Maine as a free state (thus preserving the balance of free and slave states in the Union) and prohibiting slavery in the Federal territories north of the line, 36°30′, the southern boundary of Missouri. "He uses no threats, or abuse," wrote one Congressman admiringly of the way Clay went about his work, "but all is mild, humble & persuasive—he begs, entreats, supplicates, & beseeches us to have mercy upon the people of Missouri. . . ." While some people on both sides of the dispute charged that the Missouri Compromise forged by Clay was a sell-out, most Americans hoped the sectional agreement had laid the slavery issue to rest. "It was a painful scene," sighed a New Hampshire Congressman, "& I hope a similar discussion will never again take place in our walls."[23]

Previous Question

During debates on the Missouri Compromise Ohio's Philemon Beecher became so impatient with John Randolph's long tirades against the North that, to cut him off, he rose to move the previous question every time the Virginian paused to catch his breath, hoping thus to cut off debate. Each time, however, the Speaker ruled these interruptions out of order and Randolph went merrily on. Finally, after several such interruptions, Randolph looked up from his notes, and, pointing his long, bony finger at the Ohioan, exclaimed: "Mr. Speaker, in the Netherlands a man of small capacity, with bits of wood and leather, will, in a few moments, construct a toy that, with the pressure of the finger and thumb, will cry 'Cuckoo! Cuckoo!' With less ingenuity, and with inferior materials, the people of Ohio have made a toy that will, without much pressure, cry, 'Previous Question, Mr. Speaker! Previous Question, Mr. Speaker!'" Randolph's sally brought the House down with laughter and ended the interruptions.[24]

Randolph's Venom

In the House and then the Senate John Randolph was famous for his epithets. During debates he called John Quincy Adams, then President, "a traitor," Daniel Webster, "a vile slanderer," John Holmes, "a dangerous fool," and Edward Livingston, "the most contemptible and degraded of beings, whom no man ought to touch, unless with a pair of tongs." One day, when he was hurling abuse at Daniel Webster, then a member of the House, another Senator whispered to him that Webster's wife was in the gallery. This did not deter Randolph, however, for he continued his excoriation of the New Englander for a few minutes longer. Then he turned his wrath on New York's John W. Taylor, then Speaker of the House, and when he finished with him he looked at the Senator who had told him about Mrs. Webster's presence, and asked sarcastically: "Is Mrs. Taylor present also?"[25]

Animal Faculty

When Rhode Island's Tristam Burges taunted John Randolph, a beardless bachelor with a high-pitched voice, with being "impotent of everything but malevolence of purpose," Randolph retorted: "You pride yourself on an animal faculty in respect to which the slave is your equal and the jackass infinitely your superior!"[26]

Wit and Logic

Not all of John Randolph's exchanges with his colleagues were acerbic. One day he got into an argument with his Virginia colleague, Daniel V. Sheffey, during the course of which the latter made some playful remarks about him. Randolph then offered Sheffey some advice; logic, he said, was Sheffey's forte, and he ought therefore to confine himself to logic and avoid wit, for which he had no talent. Sheffey at once thanked Randolph for the advice, but went on to say he didn't like to be in debt and had some advice of his own to offer in return. Nature, he went on, had been bountiful to Randolph in bestowing on him "extraordinary wit," but she had at the same time "denied him any powers of argument," and his advice therefore was for Randolph "to confine himself to the regions of wit, and never attempt to soar into those of logic." Amused by the rejoinder, Randolph announced that he had no alternative but to retract what he had said about Sheffey, for "he had shown himself to be a man of wit as well as of logic!"[27]

Randolph's Quips and Quiddities

Randolph could be bitingly *ad hominem* in Congressional debate. "Fellow citizens," he said, when talking about Andrew Jackson's Secretary of State, Edward Livingston, "he is a man of splendid abilities, but utterly corrupt. He shines and stinks like rotten mackerel by moonlight." Of Congressional colleagues Robert Wright and John Rae he said that the House exhibited two anomalies: "A Wright always wrong; and a Rae without light." When Richard Rush was appointed Secretary of the Treasury, he remarked: "Never were abilities so much below mediocrity so well rewarded; no, not when Caligula's horse was made Consul." He described political operator Martin Van Buren as a man who habitually "rowed to his object with muffled oars." He called Samuel Dexter, a Congressman who shifted his position on an issue, "Mr. Ambi-Dexter." Of an ambitious man with little native ability he once said his mind was "like the lands at the headwaters of the Monongahela, naturally poor and made still poorer by excessive cultivation." Of Henry Clay: "Clay's eye is on the Presidency; and my eye is on him."

Randolph was a coiner of epigrams as well as an epithet-tosser, and some of his remarks circulated widely. Discussing primogeniture, he observed: "An English noble had but one son; all the rest are bastards." Defending states' rights, he declared: "Asking one of the States to surrender part of her sovereignty is like asking a lady to surrender part of her chastity." On education: "All of us have two educations: one which we receive from others; another, and the most valuable, which we give ourselves." On power: "You may cover whole skins of parchment with limitations of power but power alone can limit power." On spending: "That most delicious of all privileges—spending other people's money." On time: "Time is at once the most valuable and the most perishable of all our possessions." He used the expression, doughfaces, to describe Northern Democrats with Southern sentiments, and the name stuck. Told that someone had launched an attack on him, he exclaimed: "Denounce me! That is strange. I never did him a favor." He was undoubtedly flattered to be quoted so much, but he once protested: "All the bastard wit of the country has been fathered on me!"[28]

Clay Interrupted

One afternoon, when Henry Clay was replying to some heated remarks by another Senator, a sudden squall came up and started rattling the window curtains in the Senate Chamber. Clay stopped abruptly, looked around to see where the noise was coming from, and then declared: "Storms seem to be coming in upon us from all sides."[29]

Out of Order

When Daniel Webster was holding forth one day, the Senate clock suddenly began striking, and after it had struck fourteen or fifteen times, Webster stopped and addressed the presiding officer. "The clock is out of order, sir," he exclaimed. "I have the floor." He then stood there silently until the Sergeant-at-Arms had silenced the "refractory time-piece."[30]

On the Brink

Once, in 1834, when Webster was speaking in the Senate, a clerical-looking man in one of the galleries arose and shouted: "My friends, the country is on the brink of destruction! Be sure that you act on correct principles. I warn you to act as your consciences may approve. God is looking down upon you, and if you act on correct principles you will get safely through." He then left the gallery before the guards could reach him. Surprised at the interruption, Webster remained standing and waited until the man disappeared and then announced: "As the gentleman in the gallery has concluded, I will proceed with my remarks."[31]

Buchanan's March

Henry Clay liked to tease his colleagues on occasion, and one of his favorite targets was Pennsylvania's fussy and humorless James Buchanan. One day Buchanan got up in the House to defend himself against charges of disloyalty during the War of 1812, and he reminded his colleagues that he had entered a company of volunteers at the time of the Battle of North Point and marched to Baltimore. "True," he added, he "was not in any engagement, as the British had retreated before he got there." "You marched to Baltimore, though?" observed Clay. "Yes, sir," said Buchanan. "Armed and equipped?" asked Clay. "Yes," said Buchanan, "armed and equipped." "But the British had retreated when you arrived?" said Clay. "Yes," said Buchanan. "Will you be good enough," cried Clay, moving in for the kill, "to inform us whether the British retreated in consequence of your valiantly marching to the relief of Baltimore, or whether you marched to the relief of Baltimore in consequence of the British having already retreated?"[32]

Bible Quotes

Thomas Hart Benton was scrupulously honest, but his enemies periodically revived an old story that he had stolen some money when he was in college, even though it was untrue. One day, Senator James S. Green, fellow Missourian, launched an attack on him so filled with venom that Benton started to shake his fist at him and shouted: "It is written, 'Thou shalt not bear false witness against thy neighbor.'" Quick as a flash Green retorted: "In the same document it is written, 'Thou shalt not steal!'"[33]

John Quincy Adams and the "Gag Rule"

John Quincy Adams was the only President to become a member of the House of Representatives after leaving the White House. His Presidency (1825–29) was a disappointment, and his defeat for re-election by Andrew Jackson in 1828 had plunged him into gloom. But in September 1830, when Adams' neighbors asked him if he would run for Congress from the Plymouth district, even though he had once served as President, he perked up. "No person," he said, "could be degraded by serving the people as a Representative to Congress. Nor in my opinion would an ex-President of the United States be degraded by serving as selectman of his town, if elected thereto by the people."

Adams took his seat in the House in December 1831 and served until his death in 1848. "My election as President of the United States," he once declared, "was not half so gratifying to my inmost soul. No election or appointment conferred upon me ever gave me so much pleasure." When he arrived in the Capitol to take the oath of office, Henry Clay asked how he felt at "turning boy again," and told him he would find the situation in the House extremely laborious. "I well know this," Adams responded; "but labor I shall not refuse so long as my hands, my eyes, and my brain do not desert me." He soon won fame as a Congressman far exceeding his reputation as a one-term President. Though no abolitionist, he found himself within a few years prominently identified with the anti-slavery cause. And he became the center of one dramatic scene after another during debates in the House chamber.

By the mid-thirties, anti-slavery petitions were flowing into Washington by the thousands. The Senate adopted a policy of receiving the petitions and then rejecting them without referring them to the appropriate committees for consideration. The House was even more restrictive; in May 1836 it adopted a "gag rule" which provided that all anti-slavery petitions "be laid upon the table" without any action whatsoever being taken on them. Adams refused to vote on the gag resolution when his name was called. "I hold the resolution to be a direct violation of the Constitution of the United States," he announced, "of the rules of this House, and of the rights of my constituents."

For the next nine years Adams waged a determined fight against the "gag rule," as a violation of the Constitutional right of petition, and he soon won the nickname, "Old Man Eloquent." Since the "gag rule" had to be renewed at each new session of Congress, he had plenty of opportunities to work for its repeal. At the beginning of each session he arrived with scores of petitions to present to the House, and doggedly read as much as he could from them amid yells, screams, threats, and repeated shouts of "point of order!" To silence him and his supporters the House voted to impose the gag on the first petition day of each new session; then it went further: it voted to prohibit the very reception of anti-slavery petitions, and made the gag one of the standing House rules. But after that, when the House was ready to adopt its standing rules at the start of each session, Adams regularly proposed an amendment repealing the gag rule, thus opening the way for a renewed discussion of the issue. And even after the House rejected the amendment each time and approved all its standing rules again, Adams resorted to every parliamentarian trick he could think of to get around the restriction on anti-slavery petitions.

On February 7, 1837, Adams was particularly ingenious. "Mr. Speaker," he declared, "I have in my possession a petition of a somewhat extraordinary character. I wish to inquire of the Chair if it is in order to present it." "If the gentleman from Massachusetts will inform the Chair what the character of the petition is," responded the Speaker, Tennessee's James K. Polk, somewhat uncertainly, "it will probably be able to decide on the subject." "Sir," said Adams, "the petition is signed by eleven slaves of the town of Fredericksburg. It is signed partly by persons who cannot write, by making their marks, and partly by persons whose handwriting would manifest that they have received the education of slaves. The petition declares itself to be from slaves and I am requested to present it. I will send it to the chair." Taken by surprise, Polk said he needed time to consider it and would have to consult the "sense of the House."

Adams' maneuver produced explosions of fury. "Expel him!" Southerners shouted. "Expel the old scoundrel!" "Put him out!" "Censure him!" "By God, sir," fumed Alabama's portly Dixon H. Lewis, "this is not to be endured." Lewis went on to sponsor a resolution censuring Adams for destroying the dignity of the House by presenting a petition from slaves calling for the abolition of slavery. Adams then quietly corrected Lewis. The petitioners had not called for abolition, he revealed; on the contrary, they preferred slavery to freedom and had petitioned the House not to interfere with slavery. Adams' ironic revelation produced four days of fierce debate, during the course of which he spoke movingly of the importance of the right of petition, especially among the poor and lowly, in a just and decent society. In the end the resolution to censure Adams failed to pass: 137 nays and only 21 yeas.

Adams received many scurrilous letters and even death threats during his long fight for ending the gag rule, but he refused to be intimidated. And he was by no means alone in his opposition to the "gag rule." Each time he forced a vote on the issue he was able to count on the support of all the Northern Whigs, four Southern Whigs, and some of the Northern Democrats. In December 1844 he finally won enough votes from Northern Democrats (miffed because slaveholder James K. Polk rather than Martin Van Buren received the Democratic nomination for President that year) to ensure victory. After the House voted, 180 to 80, to repeal the "gag rule," Adams wrote in his diary: "Blessed, forever, blessed, be the name of God!"

Adams' courage won admiration even among Congressmen who detested his views. In 1847, a year before he died, when he returned to the House chamber after a long illness, the House voted to suspend debate, and William Moseley of New York and Isaac Holmes of South Carolina each took him by an arm and escorted him to his seat. Then Congressmen from both sections gathered around to congratulate him on his return to the House, and the aging Adams made a brief address in his feeble voice thanking his colleagues for the honor they had paid him.[34]

Old Bull

In 1842, after Adams presented a petition to the House from some citizens of Massachusetts calling for the dissolution of the Union, there was an effort, led by Southerner Thomas F. Marshall, to pass a resolution of censure against him, but it failed of passage. A few days later, some Southern members of Congress, irked again by something Adams had said in the House, were dining in a Washington hotel, and Marshall joined them. "Well, Marshall," said one of them, "the old devil has been at work again; you must take him in hand." "Not I," said Marshall, shaking his head decisively; "I have been gored once by the d----d old bull, and have had enough of him. If there is to be any more of this kind of work, it must be undertaken by somebody else. The old devil, as you call him, is a match for a score of such fellows as you and I!"[35]

So Much Knowledge

Thomas Hart Benton, Democratic Senator from Missouri, liked to say, "What are the facts?" or "Give us the facts!" He did careful research, wrote out his speeches, saw that the grammar and punctuation were correct, and then delivered his addresses in the Senate slowly and deliberately. When he had an important point to make, he repeated it three times. First, he announced it to the President of the Senate; second, "Through you, sir, I tell the Senate," sweeping his eyes around the Senate chamber to get his colleagues' attention; and, third, "Through you, sir, I tell the people of this Country," looking up at the gallery.

Full of facts and figures, Benton was extremely pleased whenever one of his colleagues consulted him about a historical reference. And whenever one of the Senators got his facts wrong while delivering a speech, Benton called for a page and sent him to the library for a book containing the correct information; and then, finding the passage he wanted, sent the book, with the passage marked, over to the Senator. One day, one of the Senators criticized him for using the word "bamboozle" in a speech, which he called "not appropriate, or obsolete, or vulgar." The next morning Benton marched into the Senate chamber followed by several pages carrying stacks of books which they piled on Benton's desk. "It was a good word, sir," he announced, as soon as he got the floor, and then spent the next half hour reading definitions from Noah Webster, Joseph Addison, and John Arbuthnot.

Henry Clay admired Benton's diligence but couldn't help teasing him about it. One day, after Benton made a speech complaining that his colleagues didn't fully recognize his achievements, the great Whig leader took to the floor and began showering him with praise. "There is no man," he said, "whom we could not better spare—our arithmetic, our grammar, our geography, our dictionary, our page, our date, our ever-present library, our grand labor-saving machine. What would these little pages do when we sent them for books without the Senator to tell them upon what

shelves they may be found? How much would it curtail our social enjoy-
ment if we did not realize, whilst we were attending the evening entertain-
ments of our friends, that the Senator was laboriously investigating every
question that might be sprung upon us, and we did not see the light in his
windows at the latest hours of our return home!"

As Clay continued, everyone listened intently, wondering where he was
headed. "We must not, we cannot, we will not spare him," Clay went on. "Of
all men who ever occupied a seat in this body, posterity will most wonder at
his labors and his knowledge acquired thereby." Then he reached his
point: "And there is but one thing that posterity will more wonder at, and
that will be how a man who had acquired so much knowledge *could put it to
such a terribly bad use!*"[36]

The Morse Bill (1843)

In February 1843, when the House took up a bill calling for an appropriation of $30,000 to permit Samuel F. B. Morse to construct an experimental
telegraph line from Washington to Baltimore, some Congressmen made
fun of the proposal. One Congressman suggested spending half the money
for making experiments in Mesmerism; another proposed using the
money to build a railroad to the moon. As the debate proceeded, Morse
stood nearby listening nervously, and when Nathan Sargent, Washington
correspondent for the *U.S. Gazette*, told him he looked anxious, the
inventor exclaimed: "I have reason to be; and if you knew how important
this is to me, you would not wonder. I have spent seven years in perfecting
this invention, and all that I had: if it succeeds, I am a made man; if it fails, I
am ruined. I have a large family, and not money enough to pay my board
bill when I leave the city." Sargent said he thought the bill would pass. "Are
you sure of it?" asked Morse. "Yes, perfectly," said Sargent; "all this ridicule
goes for nothing."

Sargent was right. In May 1843 the Morse bill passed the House by a
narrow margin and sailed through the Senate without debate. By May 1,
1844, when the Whigs met in Baltimore to nominate their presidential
candidate, the line was partially completed, and an operator there was able
to flash the news of Henry Clay's nomination to Washington an hour before
a train reached the Capitol with the news. Later that month, the Democrats
held their convention in Baltimore, too, and the Morse line, now completed, sent periodic reports of the proceedings to the Washington ter-
minus of the line in a room under the Senate chamber. Morse read the
dispatches coming in from Baltimore with an air of triumph to the
members of Congress gathered there, and to the people crowding around
the windows outside. First came James K. Polk's nomination; then the
balloting; and finally Polk's selection on the eighth ballot. "This talking with

Baltimore was something so novel, so strange, so extraordinary, and upon a matter of such intense interest," wrote Sargent, "that we could hardly realize the fact. It seemed like an enchantment, or a delusion, or a dream."[37]

Webster on Tariffs

In 1846, shortly after Congress passed a low-tariff measure sponsored by Democratic Congressman Robert J. Walker, Daniel Webster addressed a fancy Whig banquet in Philadelphia. Webster had once been a free-trader but was now a devout Whig protectionist, and his talk that evening was an attack on the Walker tariff and a paean to protectionism. But when John W. Forney reported the event for the *Pennsylvanian,* a Democratic paper, he decided to have a little fun; instead of running the speech Webster made that evening, he got out an old free-trade speech Webster had made in Congress in 1824, labeled it, "Webster's Great Speech on the Tariff," and issued it as a special supplement to his newspaper the following day. The Whigs bought thousands of copies for distribution and many of them were furious when they discovered the leg-pull. But Webster took it in good humor. When his friend George Ashmun handed him a copy, he laughed: "I think Forney has printed a much better speech than the one I made last night."[38]

Lincoln Teases Cass

In 1848, the Whigs ran General Zachary Taylor, Mexican War hero, for President and the Democrats ran Michigan Senator Lewis Cass. But when the Democrats, citing Cass' record in the War of 1812, tried to build him up into a military hero like Taylor, Abraham Lincoln, an Illinois Whig, got up in the House on July 27 and delivered a hilarious speech ridiculing Cass' military exploits. Lincoln, reported the *Baltimore American,* "is a very able acute, uncouth, honest, upright man, and a tremendous wag, withal. . . . Mr. Lincoln's manner was so good natured, and his style so peculiar, that he kept the House in a continuous roar of merriment for the last half hour of his speech. He would commence a point in his speech far up one of the aisles, and keep on talking, gesticulating, and walking until he would find himself, at the end of a paragraph, down in the centre of the area in front of the Clerk's desk. He would then go back and take another head, and work again, and so on, through his capital speech."[39]

Lecturing

On June 13, 1850, when the Senate was discussing the so-called Compromise of 1850 that Henry Clay was trying to put together, Missouri's

Thomas Hart Benton accused Clay of "lecturing" the Senators, all of whom, he pointed out, were over thirty years old, the limit prescribed by the Constitution for Senate membership. Clay responded at once. "Now, with respect to lecturing the Senate, it is an office which I have never sought to fill," he said hotly. "There are many reasons I do not like to do it. In giving a lecture, the person lecturing ought to have some ability to impart instruction, and the person to whom it is addressed should have the capacity of receiving it. In this case, as between the Senator and myself, both of these conditions are wanting. Therefore I do not aspire to the office of a lecturer." The Senate exploded with laughter.[40]

Classical Quotations

Massachusetts' scholarly Edward Everett once concluded an elegant speech in the House with a long quotation in Latin from Tacitus and then took his seat. No sooner was he seated than up sprang a burly Congressman from the West. Obviously irritated by Everett's erudition, the Westerner, a former Indian agent, began pouring out a vehement harangue in Choctaw. After a while the Speaker called him to order. "I don't see why my freedom of speech should be abridged," protested the Westerner. "You let the gentleman from Massachusetts run on, and I didn't understand the first word of his lingo any better than he does mine." Reporting the incident, one journal expressed the belief that "it struck the death-knell of further classical quotations in Congress."[41]

Noisome

Abolitionist Charles Sumner was outraged by Stephen A. Douglas' compromises with slavery and the two exchanged many bitter words in the Senate. One day, after Sumner declared that a "planter will one day take a slave for his harlot, and sell her the next as a . . . beast of burden," Douglas accused him of "lasciviousness and obscenity." Furious, Sumner charged Douglas with uttering falsehoods and added that "no person with the upright form of man can be allowed—" At this point he hesitated. "Say it," cried Douglas. "I will say it—" Sumner continued. "No person with the upright form of man can be allowed without violation of all decency, to switch out from his tongue the perpetual stench of offensive personality. . . . The noisome, squat, and nameless animal to which I now refer is not the proper model for an American Senator. Will the Senator from Illinois take notice?" "I will," said Douglas, "and therefore will not imitate you, Sir." "Mr. President," said Sumner, "again the Senator switches his tongue, and again he fills the Senate with his offensive odor."[42]

Black Mammy

One day, during the debates on the Kansas-Nebraska bill (1854), Senator George Badger of North Carolina spoke sentimentally about slavery from the Southern point of view. In his childhood, he said, he was nursed by an old black woman and he grew to manhood under her care. He loved his "old black mammy," he said, and she loved him. But if the anti-slavery opponents of the Kansas-Nebraska bill had their way, he said, and he ever wanted to go into either of those Territories, he wouldn't be able to take his "old black mammy" with him. Turning to Ohio's Benjamin Wade he exclaimed: "Surely, you will not prevent me from taking my old black mammy with me?" Returned Wade drily: "It is not that he cannot take his old black mammy with him that troubles the mind of the Senator, but that if we made the Territories free, he cannot sell the old black mammy when he gets her there."[43]

Ancestors

Once, when a Senator taunted Louisiana's Judah P. Benjamin, who entered the Senate in 1853, about his Jewishness, Benjamin is said to have retorted: "It is true that I am a Jew, and when my ancestors were receiving their Ten Commandments from the immediate hand of the Deity, amidst the thunderings and lightnings of Mount Sinai, the ancestors of the distinguished gentleman who is opposed to me were herding swine in the forests of Scandinavia!" The Senate, it was reported, was "electrified" by Benjamin's statement, and "the carping Senator was quite effectually silenced."[44]

Benjamin's Cigar

One day, at the end of a speech on the Kansas imbroglio, Senator Judah Benjamin made a bitter attack on New York's William T. Seward, leader of the Republicans in the Senate. When he resumed his seat, Seward rose, turned to his assailant, and said calmly: "Benjamin, give me a cigar, and when your speech is printed, send me a copy." Then he retired to the cloakroom to smoke Benjamin's cigar.[45]

Code of Morals

Illinois' Stephen A. Douglas and Ohio's Ben Wade were on good personal terms but disagreed violently on the slavery issue. One day, in discussing a measure, Douglas declared: "Mr. President, that proposition is contrary to my code of morals." Wade jumped up at once and shouted: "Against his code of morals! Good God! Mr. President, his code of morals! I didn't know he had any!"[46]

Apology

In a tiff with another Senator, Alexander Stephens is said to have called out: "My opponent is not fit to carry swill to swine. . . ." There were cries of "Order! Order!" and Stephens was called on to apologize. "Mr. Speaker," said Stephens meekly, "I do apologize. The Senator is absolutely fit for the duty to which I referred!"[47]

Good Example

Propriety enjoined members of the House against taking cracks at the Senate, but there was nothing to prevent their teasing about it. In August 1861, the House had enacted a mass of important legislation and was ready to adjourn, but New York Congressman Charles Van Wyck warned that if the house adjourned, the Senate might "follow its example" and adjourn, too, instead of going to work on the measures received from the House. "No," exclaimed Thaddeus Stevens, "I never knew the Senate to follow a good example!" So the House voted to adjourn.[48]

Feeble Remarks

Once West Virginia's Kellian Whaley, a Congressman who expressed great humility about the value of his opinions but always spoke at length anyway, asked Thaddeus Stevens to yield him time to discuss a measure pending in the House. "I now yield to my honorable colleague," said Stevens resignedly, "who will make a few feeble remarks."[49]

Turkey Gobbler Strut (1866)

In 1866, two of the House's best-known members—New York's Roscoe Conkling and Maine's James G. Blaine—got into a feud that lasted for the rest of their lives. The two men clashed temperamentally; Conkling was fastidious, conceited, and imperious, while Blaine was affable, expansive, and outgoing. They also clashed over legislation in the House and over eminence in the Republican party. At a dinner party they got into an argument over who wrote a couplet which Conkling liked because it represented the Utica district in New York:

> No pent-up Utica contracts our powers,
> But the whole boundless continent is ours.

Conkling thought the lines came from Joseph Addison's *Cato,* but Blaine bet him a basket of champagne that they were from Sewall's "Epilogue to Cato." Conkling lost the bet and sent Blaine the champagne, but he was so disgruntled about being wrong that he refused to attend the dinner Blaine gave to serve the champagne.

The quarrel in the House was more serious. On April 24, 1866, Conkling attacked legislation creating a permanent Provost Marshal's Bureau in the War Department and also cast aspersions on General James B. Fry, the officer who was to head the Bureau. The bill, he said, "creates an unnecessary office for an undeserving public servant." Blaine, a member of the Committee on Military Affairs, defended the bill; he also accused Conkling of misrepresenting General Grant's views about the Bureau, of seeking to get even with General Fry after having "come out second best" in some quarrels he had had with him, and of having acted unethically in accepting a fee of $3000 as temporary judge-advocate while drawing his regular salary as a Congressman. Conkling listened to Blaine with disdain. Then he shot back: "If General Fry is reduced to depending for vindication upon the gentleman from Maine, he is to be commiserated certainly. If I have fallen to the necessity of taking lessons from that gentleman in the rules of propriety or of right or wrong, God help me." Blaine's rejoinder was equally contemptuous. "As to the gentleman's cruel sarcasm," he exclaimed, "I hope he will not be too severe. The contempt of that large-minded gentleman is so wilting; his haughty disdain, his grandiloquent swell, his majestic, supereminent, turkey-gobbler strut had been so crushing to myself and all members of the House that I know it was an act of the greatest temerity for me to venture upon a controversy with him." The House roared with delight at Blaine's description of the New Yorker's pomposity.

The Blaine-Conkling exchange went on for three days, and in the end Conkling succeeded in killing the proposal for a permanent Provost Marshal's Bureau. But he was not appeased. Blaine's reference to his "turkey gobbler strut"—Conkling did, in fact, strut around on the House floor and display imperious manners—cut him to the quick and he came to view the Maine Congressman with loathing. Blaine was willing to forgive and forget, but Conkling turned down all overtures for ending the feud.

Once, at an informal gathering, Conkling was handing out some candy to his colleagues, came unexpectedly to Blaine, and instinctively pulled back. Afterwards, a friend asked Blaine: "Would you have taken it if he had offered it?" "Certainly," said Blaine, "if it had choked me!" Conkling wouldn't have minded choking him. After 1866 he did all he could as Republican boss in New York to block Blaine's political ambitions. When Blaine received the Republican nomination for President in 1884 and

Conkling was asked to campaign for him, he sneered: "No, thank you. I don't engage in criminal practice."[50]

Butler and the Salary Grab

Early in 1873, when James A. Garfield introduced an appropriations bill into the House, Ben Butler added a rider which doubled the President's salary and increased the salary of Congressmen from $5000 to $7500 and gave each of them a two years' retroactive pay gift of $5000. When an Ohio Congressman objected, Butler declared: "I can suggest a remedy to any gentleman who does not think this increase of salary is right and proper; let him come up and sign a pledge that he will not take the increase. Virtuous men and true, come up and sign it!" He went on to say that any Congressman not worth the increase shouldn't be in Congress: "He ought to resign!"

Butler, a millionaire, thought that Congressmen less affluent than he badly needed the raise. He observed that many Congressmen couldn't afford to bring their families to Washington or, if they did, had to borrow heavily to meet living expenses and stay in tawdry boarding houses unbecoming a member of Congress. There were financial temptations, too, for underpaid Congressmen. "I see them exposed day by day," he said, "to the pressing temptations of whoever should offer them other means of getting money to supply their wants, and I know that some of them had yielded, and disgraced themselves and their country by so doing."

Butler's arguments failed to win public support. The passage of the bill on March 3 produced tremendous public indignation. Critics called it the "Salary Grab" and the "Back Pay Steal." The financial collapse in the fall (the Panic of 1873) and the hard times that followed increased the clamor against the bill, and finally, in January 1874, Congress repealed the pay raises (except those for the President and Supreme Court justices). Through it all Butler was unmoved by the protests. When one of his constituents wrote to denounce the salary bill, Butler sent him a three-cent piece for his share in the increased taxation to pay for the raises. But he and many other Congressmen who had voted for the pay raises fell by the wayside in the Congressional elections later that year.[51]

Kansas

Senators from the East liked to tease about Kansas, but that ended when John J. Ingalls joined the upper house in 1873 as Senator from Kansas. When a Delaware Senator ventured to say something flippant about the Prairie State Ingalls flashed back: "Mr. President, the gentleman who has just spoken represents a state which has two counties when the tide is up—and only three when it is down."

Ingalls took on Pennsylvania too. When a Pennsylvania Senator made some remarks comparing "bleak Kansas" with his own wonderful Keystone State, Ingalls exclaimed: "Mr. President, Pennsylvania has produced only two great men—Benjamin Franklin of Massachusetts and Albert Gallatin of Switzerland!"[52]

Question of Privilege

Once Massachusetts Congressman Ben Butler was making a long speech on the tariff. Everyone was tired, but he gave no sign that he was ever going to stop talking. After he had gone on for an hour or so, Ohio's Samuel Cox got up and said loudly: "Mr. Speaker!" "The gentleman from Ohio," responded the Speaker looking in Cox's direction. "I arise on a question of privilege," said Cox. "I wish to ask the gentleman from Massachusetts a question." "The gentleman from Ohio," said the Speaker turning to Butler, "wishes to ask the gentleman from Massachusetts a question." "Very well," said Butler, "go on!" "The gentleman from Ohio has the floor," announced the Speaker. Cox then rose and said solemnly: "Mr. Speaker, I wish to ask the gentleman from Massachusetts a question. I wish to ask him if he hasn't—got m-o-s-t t-h-r-o-u-g-h?" The laughter sweeping the House upset Butler and he at once closed the debate.[53]

Feats

In the heat of debate the talkative Ben Butler would sometimes fill his speeches with references to his military exploits during the Civil War. Once, when he was "chasing rebels" this way, a fellow Congressman remarked, loud enough for everyone to hear, "Every time Butler opens his mouth, he puts his feats in it!"[54]

Immense Domain

Sumner's colleagues liked to tease him about his egotism. "He identifies himself so completely with the universe," Senator Carpenter once declared, "that he is not at all certain whether he is part of the universe, or the universe is part of him. He is a reviser of the decalogue. You will soon see the Sermon on the Mount revised, corrected, and greatly enlarged and improved by Charles Sumner." During one Senate debate Roscoe Conkling looked over at Sumner and exclaimed: "Ah, I fell into an error by supposing the Senator was paying me attention. His mind is roving at large in that immense domain which it occupies!"[55]

From Earth to Moon

Kentucky's J. Proctor Knott was stupefied by the size of the country's national debt in 1875: $2,500,000,000. "Have you sir, any conception of the magnitude of that sum?" he asked the House one day. "Sir, it is not within the power of the human intellect. The brain reels beneath the immensity of the conception. You had as well undertake to number the seconds on the dial of eternity." He went on to calculate that if one were to put $2,500,000,000 in a line, it would be over 250,000 miles long. "Geographers tell us it is 25,000 miles around the earth," he noted. "Our public debt would therefore make a band of greenback dollars that could encircle this globe more than ten times. It is said to be 240,000 miles from the earth to the moon. If this is so, our debt would make a rope of greenback dollars long enough to cable the moon to the earth, and have over 10,000 miles to sag!"[56]

Thoroughly Wounded

There was always a full House when Samuel S. Cox, a Democratic Congressman from Ohio and then New York, was scheduled to speak. Once he delivered a colorful speech describing the setting of the sun in the west that won him the nickname of "Sunset" Cox. Sometimes, though, when he appeared on the House floor he was a bit "spifflicated," as they used to say, and opened himself up to some teasing. On one such occasion he was appealing for the passage of a private pension bill for a soldier in his district and was in such an expansive mood that he poured out a torrent of words describing the terrible manner in which his constituent had been wounded, the agonies he had suffered, and the tortures he had endured from his wounds, and soon had his colleagues wondering how any man in such a frightful condition could have lasted for a single day. Suddenly, a Republican prankster, observing Cox's condition, got up, expressed interest in the case, and, apparently with utmost seriousness, interrupted to ask: "Did I understand the gentleman from New York to say that his constituent had been wounded?" As the House roared with delight, Cox was taken by surprise; then he recovered himself and exclaimed in a loud voice: "I want to say to the gentleman in reply to his question that my constituent was thoroughly wounded in every respect!"[57]

Free Sunshine

Like most Democrats, "Sunset" Cox favored low tariffs. One day he delighted his colleagues by a humorous attack on William "Pig-Iron" Kelley of

Pennsylvania, the House's leading champion of protective tariffs. To tease Kelley, Cox proposed a resolution against free sunshine: "Resolved, that all windows, skylights, inside and outside shutters, curtains, and blinds shall be permanently closed, as also all openings, holes, chinks, clefts, and fissures through which the light and heat of the sun have been allowed to enter houses to the prejudice and injury of meritorious miners and dealers in gas-coal to protect domestic industry." His main argument for the proposal: "The sun is a foreigner. He comes from abroad. . . ."[58]

Names

In 1885, when the House was considering a rivers and harbors bill which provided, among other things, for the improvement of the Skag, Steilaguamish, Nooksack, Snohomish, and Snoqualmie Rivers in Washington Territory, Michigan Congressman Byron M. Cutcheon offered an amendment: "Mr. Speaker, I move an amendment in the nature of a proviso, that at least one thousand dollars of the money hereby appropriated shall be used in straightening out the names of said rivers."[59]

Watchdog

Elihu B. Washburn of Illinois was known as the "Watchdog of the Treasury." Few questionable claims against the Federal Government escaped his vigilance or prevailed over his strenuous opposition. One day, though, a private bill sponsored by his brother Cadwallader passed the House while Elihu kept entirely silent. Cried one Congressman: "The watchdog don't bark when one of the family goes by!"[60]

Pairing

As early as the 1820s the custom of "pairing off" had developed to accommodate Congressmen who had to miss formal House votes. A Congressman who had to miss a vote arranged beforehand with a Congressman on the opposite side of the issue to make a "pair" with him, whereby the two agreed not to vote and thus cancelled each other out. Despite objections to the practice by men like John Quincy Adams and Thomas Hart Benton, it gradually became a normal part of House procedures and persisted into the twentieth century. But it produced many jokes. One day a Congressman who seemed to have no convictions on any question and often confessed that he seldom investigated a subject without finding himself a neutral, asked for a leave of absence and a pair. "Mr. Speaker," said Thaddeus Stevens, "I do not rise to object, but to suggest that the honorable member need not ask this favor for he can easily pair off with himself!"

The Senate developed "pairing," too, and Massachusetts Senator George F. Hoar couldn't resist teasing Ohio's solemn John Sherman about it on one occasion. One hot summer day Sherman told Hoar: "Hoar, I think I shall go take a ride; I am rather tired. When a vote comes up, will you announce that I am paired with my colleague?" Hoar at once called over to Senator Edward Rollins of New Hampshire, who was sitting nearby: "Rollins, there will be no vote this afternoon, except on a funeral resolution in honor of Mr. Allen of Missouri. Will you kindly announce that Mr. Sherman is paired with his colleague?" Sherman hastily jumped up, went over to Rollins, and said earnestly: "Mr. Rollins, Mr. Hoar entirely misunderstood me. I never should think of announcing a pair on a funeral resolution!"[61]

Outstanding Member

Private John Allen was showing some Mississippians around the Capitol one morning and one of them asked, "Who is the outstanding member of the House at the present time?" "Well, my friend," said Allen, "being a member at the present time, I hesitate to say, but you will be in the gallery at noon when the roll is called. It is called by name according to ability. Just watch the roll call and you will get the answer to your question." They were in the gallery at noon and of course soon heard Mr. Allen's name called first.[62]

More Than Six Years

Eli Saulsbury always boasted that he was the only man who ever served more than six years after being elected to the Senate for one term. His explanation: when the hands of the clock marked the hour of twelve noon—at which time his term expired—he was on his feet making a speech, and the presiding officer couldn't choke him off until he had spoken twenty minutes beyond his Senatorial life.[63]

LaFollette As Bolter

In 1889, toward the end of his service in the House, Wisconsin's Robert LaFollette took out after a ship subsidy bill which was so full of giveaways to private interests that he said it would "subsidize every fishing smack in New England." He canvassed vigorously among his Republican friends and finally succeeded in persuading enough of them to vote with the Democrats (who opposed the measure) so that the bill went down to defeat. But the bill lost by only a narrow margin; and when the clerk was recapitulating the roll call, supporters of the measure bustled about trying to persuade Republican dissenters to change their votes. One of their targets was LaFollette's Wisconsin colleague Myron McCord, and, to LaFollette's dismay, they seemed to have won him over. As the clerk was droning on, McCord suddenly rushed out of the cloakroom and started yelling, "Mr. Speaker—Mr. Speaker." LaFollette at once jumped up, slipped through the crowd, seized McCord by the collar, jerked him backward, and kept him going until he had him back in the cloakroom. "Tell me, Myron," he cried, "what do you mean? Why are you trying to change your vote? You promised to vote against the bill." "Bob," said McCord sheepishly, "I've got to change my vote." Wisconsin Senator Philetus Sawyer, he explained, had sent a page over from the Senate to insist on his voting for the bill. "I've got to do it," McCord wailed. "He has loaned me money; he has a mortgage on everything I possess. And he is on his way over here now. He seems to have a personal interest in the passage of the bill."

Lafollette resolved to stay on top of things. "Myron," he said firmly, "here is your hat and coat. Get off the floor as quickly as you can." He then pushed McCord out into the corridor behind the Speaker's desk, and returned to the House chamber, only to see Senator Sawyer rushing down the aisle toward him. White with rage, Sawyer ran up to LaFollette, jabbed him in the cheek with the ends of his stubby fingers, and roared: "Young man, young man, what are you doing? You are a bolter. The Republican platform promises this legislation. You are a bolter, sir; you are a bolter." "Senator Sawyer," said LaFollette angrily, "you can't tell me how to vote on any question. You've no business on this floor seeking to influence legislation. You are violating the rules. You get out of here, or I will call the Speaker's attention to you." Then he turned to the Speaker's desk and Sawyer left without another word. In the end LaFollette triumphed; the House turned down the ship subsidy bill and passed a substitute measure.

A day or two later LaFollette happened to run into Sawyer in a corridor of the Capitol. To his surprise the Wisconsin Senator stopped and apologized. "I am sorry for what I said the other night," he told LaFollette. "You were right and I was wrong. You have a perfect right to vote as you please." He was always cordial to LaFollette after that.[64]

Name in My Speech

Once when Thomas B. Reed was in the full tide of eloquence, New York's redoubtable Amos Cummings interrupted him. Reed looked at him in a fatherly sort of way for a moment and then, with mock pathos, asked: "Now Amos, must you, must you really get your name into my speech—must you?" The smiles in the House left Cummings speechless.[65]

202 • CONGRESSIONAL ANECDOTES

Made in London

Speaking on behalf of a tariff bill one day, Maine's Nelson Dingley, the great champion of protectionism in the House, had harsh words for Americans who evaded the rigors of the customs laws by making their purchases abroad. While he was sounding off, Kansas' Jerry Simpson suddenly reached under Dingley's desk, pulled out the latter's silk hat, and held it up so everyone could see the label: "Made in London."[66]

Talked to Death

In March 1901, just before the end of Montana Republican Thomas H. Carter's term in the Senate, he became convinced that a rivers and harbors bill adopted by both houses and awaiting final touches was extremely wasteful and deserved to be defeated. So about midnight, March 3, he looked at the Senate clock and announced his determination to talk the bill to death, even if it meant talking until noon, the hour set for President McKinley's second inauguration. "This bill cannot become a law," he announced, "unless my strength fails between this time and twelve o'clock on the 4th of March, and I will say to the Senate that I am in a pretty fair state of health." Then he began his talkathon. A Maryland Senator spelled him briefly while he got something to eat; and, toward dawn, a quorum disappeared for a time and he was able to get a little rest. But with only a few interruptions after that he continued to talk and soon came close to beating all records in the Senate up to that time for filibustering.

Inauguration Day dawned, workmen swept the Senate chamber, rearranged the furniture, and got things ready for the ceremonies, while Carter talked on. Senators favoring the bill shifted impatiently in their seats and muttered curses, and some even took the floor to criticize the filibusterer, but this only helped him. He was still talking when the gallery doors were opened and the inauguration guests began pouring in. "The spectacle which met their eyes," one reporter noted, "was one never seen before on a similar occasion. Here was the sombre Senate chamber prepared for the inauguration of the President and Vice-President, with seats arranged for the President and his Cabinet, the Supreme Court of the United States, the Diplomatic Corps, the officers of the army and navy, the House of Representatives and other distinguished guests. Some of the Senators were grouped upon one side of the chamber and there, near the front row of desks, stood Carter denouncing the rivers and harbors bill." When the time arrived to bring in the first guests, Carter ceased talking. It was too late to secure action on the bill; he had talked it to death.[67]

Objection

Judge William S. Holman of Indiana became nationally famous because he got up and exclaimed, "I object," just about every time a money bill was called up in the House. Some of his colleagues called him stingy and short-sighted, but he probably saved the taxpayers millions of dollars by his constant repetition of those two little words.

One day, however, Holman had his words thrown back at him. A young Congressman came up with a bill he wanted to present to the House, but he was so afraid of rejection that he asked one of the older members of the House if there was any way he could get the bill past Judge Holman. For the fun of it, the old-timer assured him that Holman was really a kind and generous man, who just wanted to be coddled, and if he talked things over with him, all would be well. With fear and trembling the young man approached the Judge, and to his surprise found him extremely hospitable. "My young friend," said Holman after looking over the bill, "that is a very meritorious measure. I will indorse it. Indeed, if it will be of any assistance to you, I will myself ask unanimous consent for its consideration."

A day or two later the Congressional tenderfoot introduced his bill. Judge Holman at once rose sedately in his place, received recognition from the chair, and said gravely: "Mr. Speaker, I ask unanimous consent for—" At that instant some three hundred voices shouted in unison: "I object!" with such vehemence, it is said, that it "caused the bronze Goddess of Liberty on top of the dome to shake like an aspen leaf."[68]

Sly Old Judge

Judge William Holman may have been a chronic objector to money bills, but once he had a small appropriation bill of his own which he needed to get passed if he was to keep on good terms with his constituents. He knew that for him to ask unanimous consent meant certain defeat, so after thinking it over he decided to ask a friend to call the bill up and then go through the motions of raising the usual objections before giving his approval. Everything went swimmingly. His friend presented the bill, Holman asked questions about it, and made some objections, and then announced benignly: "Mr. Speaker, as this appears to be a decidedly meritorious measure, and carries only a small appropriation for a necessary purpose, I withdraw all objections." As he spoke, his colleagues rubbed their eyes in amazement. Could Judge Holman really be approving a money bill? Their astonishment turned to anger, however, when they discovered the trick the sly judge had put over on them.[69]

Tantalus Club

In 1901, Ohio's Robert Nevin, a newly elected member of the House, sought to question Eugene Loud of California, chairman of the Post Office Committee, during a floor debate on one of Loud's bills. "I assume that the gentleman who asked me that question is a new member," said Loud scornfully, "and that he has asked the question for no other purpose than to get his name in the *Congressional Record*." And he went on with his speech.

Loud's rebuff outraged Nevin and the other freshmen Republicans, and they decided to organize what they called the "Tantalus Club" to work together and support each other as much as possible in the House. "The new member of Congress," said one of them, "was very much in the situation of Tantalus. Everything he wanted was just out of his reach." Vermont's David Foster was the first member of the club to make a speech on the House floor. By advance agreement, the other members of the club clustered around him as he spoke, hanging onto every word, and when he finished, they gave him a great ovation, rushed up to shake his hand, and congratulated him enthusiastically on his speech. The older members of the House had ignored Foster's speech, but they were taken aback by the ovation he received. Thinking he must have made an important speech, many of them rushed over to compliment him, too, including New York's Sereno Page (majority floor leader) and Pennsylvania's John Dalzell (chairman of the Rules Committee). The freshmen had tricked the old-timers into recognizing their existence.[70]

The Company He Keeps

New York's William Sulzer ("Old Bill") dressed as much as he could like Henry Clay, strode into the House through the door beside the Speaker's desk as though he were a famous actor appearing on the stage, and, if the galleries were crowded, always found some way, no matter how contrived, to get into the debate going on in the House. One day, when the House was discussing a bill to appropriate $5000 to erect a monument to Baron Steuben, Prussian officer who had drilled George Washington's troops during the American Revolution, Sulzer got the floor and proposed an amendment substituting Washington's name for Steuben's. Someone quickly made a point of order against the amendment on the ground that it was not germane, and Speaker Cannon sustained it. "Mr. Speaker," roared Sulzer dramatically, "am I to understand that George Washington is out of order in this House?" Visibly irritated, Cannon brought his gavel down heavily and cried: "He certainly is when he is in the company he is keeping today!"[71]

Travel Expense

In a fight with Speaker Joe Cannon and his machine in March 1909, Democratic party whip Champ Clark went to a lot of trouble to bring all the Democrats to the House floor to vote, including one Congressman who was sick. The ailing member complained that he was lame and couldn't walk to the House chamber, so Clark paid someone two dollars to roll him onto the House floor in a wheelchair. But to Clark's chagrin, when it came time to vote, the man voted the wrong way, thus swelling the Republican majority. "How he returned to his hotel," said Clark afterwards, "I know not. One thing cocksure—he did not travel at my expense!"[72]

Only $100,000

During a Senate debate on the Armor Plate bill, Missouri's James A. Reed objected to Pennsylvania's George T. Oliver's voting on the bill because, he said, Oliver owned half a million dollars stock in the U.S. Steel Corporation. Vice President Thomas Marshall overruled the point of order, noting that Senate rules had no such provision and that it was up to Oliver himself to decide whether he should cast his vote or not. The next morning Oliver rose to a question of personal privilege and launched into an attack on Reed. Reed, he said, had insulted and maligned him, and his charge about owning half a million dollars stock in U.S. Steel was utterly unfounded. "It is not true," he cried angrily. "I have only one hundred thousand dollars of the stock!"[73]

Patriotism (1917)

In April 1917, Senator Robert M. LaFollette of Wisconsin spoke impassionedly against going to war against Germany and cast his vote against the war declaration; and, once the United States entered the war, he fought hard against legislation conscripting young men and on behalf of "conscripting wealth," as he put it, to pay for the war. So fervent was the war fever at this time that most of LaFollette's colleagues began avoiding him and there were insistent demands for expelling him from the Senate.

When LaFollette entered the Senate chamber on the day set aside to discuss expulsion, most Senators looked the other way. But not Republican Senator Boies Penrose of Pennsylvania. Penrose may have been a reactionary—he disagreed with the progressive LaFollette on just about every public issue, including entry into World War I—but he despised hypocrisy and cant and respected LaFollette's courage and independence. So when Penrose saw LaFollette coming in, he jumped up, went to his side, put his arm around him, and walked him down the aisle to his seat. A hush fell over the Senate; it was clear that Penrose, influential Republican party boss, would support no such foolishness as expulsion, and the proposal to expel LaFollette from the Senate died a-borning.

"Sentiment?" wrote Penrose's biographer, summing up the Pennsylvania boss's view. "Not at all! Just sheer honesty. Why not let every fellow think and act as he pleased? Speaking of patriotism, what about all those fellows in the training camps ready to go to the trenches? They were the ones who were patriotic. As for the rest of the shouters they were mostly interested themselves in maintaining the security of Allied bonds. If we didn't have several billions of dollars invested in Europe to be saved from default, how patriotic would some of the Senators be? . . . As for himself, he was perfectly willing that we should fight Germany, but let's be honest about it! Nothing very patriotic in the whole mess . . . just good business."[74]

Jeannette Rankin

Elected to the House in 1916, Jeannette Rankin, Montana Republican, was the first woman to serve in Congress. And as a pacifist, she turned out to be the only member of Congress to have voted against entry into both World War I and World War II.

In 1916, there was a great deal of curiosity about the first woman to enter the nation's legislature. Reporters wanted to know her opinions about many things; companies asked her to endorse their products; bachelors sent her proposals of marriage from all over the country. "I feel a tremendous reponsibility," she told a *New York Times* reporter soon after her election. "As Representative of the state of Montana, I shall represent to the best of my ability the men, women and children of my state. But in a certain sense I feel that it is my special duty to express also the point of view of women and to make clear that the women of the country are coming to a full realization of the fact that Congress is a body which deals with their problems." From writer Christopher Morley came some teasing lines:

> Her maiden speeches will be known
> For charm and grace of manner
> But who on earth will chaperone
> The member from Montana?

In March 1917, when Jeannette Rankin took her oath of office, she was greeted with cheers and applause from Congressmen of both parties as well as from relatives and friends in the gallery. But the following month things turned unpleasant. On April 4, President Wilson appeared before a joint session of Congress to call for a declaration of war on Germany, and the following day the House met to consider the war resolution. Rankin's pacifist views were well known, but there was considerable pressure on her to vote for war. The suffragettes were afraid she might hurt their cause if she cast an anti-war vote; and her own brother warned that a vote against war would end her career in politics. Her mail from Montana, however, ran 16 to 1 against involvement in the war in Europe.

At 10:00 a.m. on April 5, the House began debating the war resolution, a debate that went on until after midnight, but the vote didn't come until the following day. When the first roll call came on April 6, Rankin was silent when the clerk came to her name, for she knew she did not need to vote until the second roll call. "It was a different roll call from any I had ever seen from the gallery," she said afterward. "Every vote was watched with intensity. When they called my name there was a hush, and I didn't say a word." Former Speaker "Uncle Joe" Cannon hurried over to her seat. "Little woman," he said, "you cannot afford not to vote. You represent the womanhood of the country in the American Congress. I shall not advise you how to vote, but you should vote one way or another—as your conscience dictates." The second roll call came soon after; and when the clerk read her name, all eyes in the gallery turned toward her, and the room became still. She rose to her feet. "Mr. Speaker," she said, "I want to stand by my country. But I cannot vote for war. I vote no." The tally clerk looked uncertainly at Speaker Champ Clark; she had violated the time-honored custom of refraining from comments during roll calls. Clark picked up the gavel, then changed his mind, and put it down again. "Resume the call," he told the clerk. The final tally was 324 for war, 50 against, with 9 not voting. The *New York Times* reported that Rankin was weeping when she voted, but she wasn't. "I had wept so much that week," she said later, "that my tears were all gone by the time the vote came." Of her vote, Fiorello LaGuardia, New York Congressman, wrote later: "It was stated at the time Miss Rankin was crying. I have been asked the question so many times I do not know, for I could not see because of the tears in my own eyes." In Montana the *Helena Independent* called Rankin "a dagger in the hands of the German propagandist, a dupe of the Kaiser, a member of the Hun army in the United States, and a crying schoolgirl." In 1918, Rankin ran for the Senate, met defeat, and retired from politics.

Twenty-two years later Rankin returned to politics. In 1940 she made a successful run for a seat in the House on a campaign to "Keep Us Out of War." But in January 1941, when she took her oath of office, the country was once more on the brink of war; and on December 8, the day after the Japanese attack on Pearl Harbor, she was faced again with having to vote on a war resolution. This time she stood alone. When the House met to take up the joint resolution declaring war on Japan, she was determined to speak. As soon as the resolution was read she rose and cried, "Mr. Speaker! I object!" "You're out of order!" Speaker Sam Rayburn told her. Again and again, during the forty-minute debate that followed, she rose to address the

Chair: "Mr. Speaker, I would like to be heard! Mr. Speaker, a point of order!" But Rayburn refused to recognize her, and there were cries from some of her colleagues, "Sit down, sister!" Several Congressmen went over to urge her to vote with them. "They really did bomb Pearl Harbor!" one of them told her. "Does it have to be?" Illinois' Everett Dirksen asked her. "Yes," she said. "Well," he said, "we'll stand by you."

When the roll call came, Rankin voted "nay" in a quiet but firm voice and then added: "As a woman I can't go to war, and I refuse to send anyone else." There were hisses and boos; and the final vote was 388 to 1. When she left the House chamber some soldiers in the corridor hurled angry remarks at her. And when she left the Capitol some people in the crowds outside were so hostile that Capitol policemen were afraid she might be hurt. The Republican national committeeman from Montana sent her a wire: "I URGE AND BESEECH YOU TO REDEEM MONTANA'S HONOR AND LOYALTY. CHANGE YOUR VOTE AS EARLY AS POSSIBLE." She refused; but she did not run for re-election in 1942, knowing she had no chance of winning.

Press reaction to her "nay" vote was hostile. But William Allen White, editor of Kansas' *Emporia Gazette,* couldn't help admiring her spunk. "Probably 100 men in Congress would have liked to do what she did," he wrote in the *Gazette* on December 10. "Not one of them had the courage to do it. The *Gazette* entirely disagrees with the wisdom of her position. But, Lord, it was a brave thing! . . . When, in one hundred years from now, courage, sheer courage based on moral indignation is celebrated in this country, the name of Jeannette Rankin, who stood firm in folly for her faith, will be written in monumental bronze not for what she did but for the way she did it."

Years later, Senator John F. Kennedy, author of *Profiles in Courage* (1956), a book about members of Congress who had bucked public opinion to follow their consciences, published an article in *McCall's* (1958) entitled "Three Women of Courage," in which he singled out Jeannette Rankin for special praise. Although "many of us may have disagreed with the conclusions of her conscience," wrote JFK, "few of us would disagree with the appraisal once given her by the colorful Fiorello LaGuardia: 'This woman has more courage and packs a harder punch than a regiment of regular-line politicians.'"[75]

Hot Time

Once Virginia's John Sharp Williams, very deaf, got into a heated debate with Illinois Senator Lawrence V. Sherman, who was also hard of hearing, and they flung angry words at each other for several minutes. Finally Indiana's James E. Watson went over to the side of Sherman on which his good ear was located and said: "Lawrence, you seem to be having a pretty hot time here." "Yes," said Sherman, turning to Watson, "Williams and I are having a hell of a debate. Neither of us hears a word the other fellow says, and neither of us gives a damn!"[76]

Faculties

One day Virginia's John Sharp Williams walked into the Senate chamber and started down the center aisle while Alabama's J. Thomas Heflin was making a speech. Because he was deaf, Williams had the habit of placing his left hand behind his left ear and forming a support for his left elbow with his right hand. On this occasion he stopped, caught a sentence or two of Heflin's speech, and then made some comment about it. "Well," cried Heflin, angry at the interruption, "whatever may be said of me, when I come into the Senate chamber, I always come in full possession of my faculties!" At this Williams, who had drunk a good lunch, flashed back: "What difference does that make?"[77]

Borah's New Suit

Idaho Senator William E. Borah's wife Mamie complained a lot about the careless way he dressed. One day he went out and bought what she later called a new "cheap" suit, wore it proudly to the Senate, and, when he got home that night, announced triumphantly: "Mamie, I was told today I was the best-dressed man in the Senate." Mrs. Borah said nothing, and he then asked whether she wanted to know who had paid him the compliment. "I don't need to be told," she said shortly. "Of course, it was Senator Gore." Thomas P. Gore was Oklahoma's blind Senator.[78]

Borah's Birthday

One year, when Idaho's William E. Borah celebrated his birthday, some of the older Senators got up, made speeches praising him, and made him feel pretty good. Then to everyone's surprise a freshman Senator—he had only been there three or four months—got to his feet and started in on a eulogy. He was an excellent speaker; but in between each of his laudatory references to the Idahoan, Borah loudly whispered, "that son-of-a-bitch, that son-of-a-bitch!" Borah didn't dislike the man personally; he just didn't think a Senator should make a speech so soon after taking office.[79]

Blindfold

Democratic Senator Thomas P. Gore, a populist turned conservative, was totally blind; and when his grandson, writer Gore Vidal, was a boy, he guided him around Washington and read to him excerpts from the

Congressional Record as well as from newspapers and books on monetary theory. Tough, hard-nosed, and outspoken, Gore was known for his humorous barbs in Senate debates. One day he got into a heated exchange with another Senator and the latter became so enraged that he muttered under his breath: "If you weren't blind, I'd thrash you within an inch of your life!" But Gore heard the remark, got into a fighting posture, and yelled: "Blindfold the son of a bitch and point him in my direction!"[80]

Lady Chatterley and the Senate (1930)

In October 1930, during a debate on the new tariff bill sponsored by Utah's Reed Smoot, Senator Bronson M. Cutting, New Mexico Republican, proposed deleting the section giving the Customs Service the authority to ban the importation of any books or pictures it considered obscene. In 1928, he observed, the Bureau had banned 739 books, all but 114 of which were in foreign languages, and some of the books were admissible in one language but not in another. "This blacklist," he told the Senate, "reaches the depths of absurdity. Gautier's *Mademoiselle de Maupin,* for example, is admissible in French and English editions, but not in the Spanish. Only an expurgated edition of *All Quiet on the Western Front* is permitted entry. Many of the forbidden volumes may be found in identical American editions in almost any good public library. The Congressional Library across the park contains practically all of them." Montana's Burton K. Wheeler sided with Cutting, as did Idaho's William E. Borah and several other Senators in both parties. "If the morals of the people of the United States are so easily corrupted," said Wheeler, "then surely the keeping out of a few volumes of classics and works of that kind is not going to save them."

Some of the Senators tried to have a little fun with "Smoot of Ut." They wanted to know, among other things, whether there was one customs official who sat around all day reading "dirty books." But Smoot saw nothing funny about the matter. The customs agents were banning books, he said, "such as I did not believe were in the world—books lower than the beasts. . . . If I were a customs agent," he shouted, "they would be admitted only over my dead body." To impress his colleagues with the seriousness of the situation, he offered to read aloud certain passages from D. H. Lawrence's novel, *Lady Chatterley's Lover,* at a secret session of the Senate. Cutting pretended to be shocked. "I tremble," he said, "to think of the effect of my colleague's proposed performance on the Senators' morals!"

The Senate rejected the proposal for a closed session, so Smoot arrived in the Senate chamber one day carrying an armful of books, with all the obscene passages clearly marked for inspection. "The reading of these books," he announced, "would so disgust the Senators that they would never dream of agreeing to the amendment of the Senator from New Mexico. You need only read a page or two to know how damnable they are!" Smoot's colleagues seemed eager to read. One after another, they marched up to Smoot's desk, and, as people in the galleries tittered, picked out books to study, and returned to their desks.

While the Senators were doing their homework, Smoot went after *Lady Chatterley's Lover* again, and after he had raved about it for a time, Cutting cut in to charge that Smoot was publicizing the book. "As a result," he said, "the Senator has made a classic of it. . . . It appears now to be the Senator's favorite work. He has brought it into the chamber with him after giving it nation-wide advertising, and he has been going around reading passages from it to Senators on the floor." Smoot was outraged. "I suppose the Senator is judging me by himself," he sneered. "I haven't spent ten minutes on that book, outside of just looking at the opening pages. After the speech the Senator has made today, I would hesitate even to think of reading anything he would recommend." "I was just going to refer to the Bible," said Cutting mischievously. "Oh," cried Smoot, "if the Senator will read the Bible altogether, he will not stand on this floor defending any such rotten stuff as he appears to be defending." "That is exactly the point," Cutting returned. "Anyone who will read the Bible altogether will be entirely in favor of the Bible, but there are certain passages in the Old Testament which can be misconstrued. All books have to be read as a whole." Smoot was not persuaded. "I deny it with all the force at my command," he shouted, pounding his desk and shaking his long finger at *Lady Chatterley's Lover,* which New York's Copeland was then looking over. "That book there," he said, "hasn't anything in it but the rottenest kind of stuff that can be thought of by a human being! That book was written by a man with a soul so black that he would even obscure the darkness of hell! It would corrupt anybody." "Why doesn't the Senator rescue the Senator from New York?" Michigan's James Couzens cut in at this point, as the galleries roared with laughter.

In the end Cutting won a partial victory. Scores of books, including *All Quiet on the Western Front,* once barred, were finally admitted to this country, and the United States, as one observer put it, "has been officially lifted out of the infant class." But it was another thirty years before the Customs Service decided that the American people could read *Lady Chatterley's Lover* without deleterious effects.[81]

Worst Demagogue

Once, after denouncing the Hoover administration for wasting the taxpayers' money during the Great Depression, Mississippi Democrat Pat Harrison strolled across the Senate floor to the Republican side and whispered to Indiana's James Watson: "Jim, ain't I the worst demagogue you ever heard?" "No, Pat," Watson replied impishly. "I am!"[82]

Gunman in the Gallery (1932)

One afternoon in 1932, as members were filing down the aisle of the House chamber to be counted in a teller vote, one of the page boys pointed to the gallery and started shouting: "He's got a gun! He's got a gun!" This was the Al Capone era, and at the word, gun, all the Congressmen from the Chicago area hit the floor at once. Others lunged for the doors and scrambled under desks. Connecticut's Edward W. Gogg, an athlete in his youth, went whizzing past Massachusetts' Joe Martin, shouting, "Make room for a fellow to run who knows how to run!" South Carolina's Thomas S. McMillan was in the chair at the time and started to leave it, but Lewis Deschler, the parliamentarian, rushed up to hold him back. "You can't leave," he cried. "You're presiding." Amid all the commotion, the cause of the furor, a young department-store clerk from Allentown, Pennsylvania, stood in the gallery, swinging a huge revolver in a wide arc and saying, "I want twenty minutes to address the House." Meanwhile Representative Melvin J. Maas of Minnesota, a fighting marine in World War I (and, later, World War II), threaded his way across the floor to a point near the deranged gunman, and the latter asked him: "Will you give me twenty minutes to make a speech?" "Sure, sure," Maas replied, "you can make a speech, but it's against the rules to speak with a gun in your hand. Come on, buddy, give me your gun and you can make your speech." Instead, the gunman cocked the revolver and pointed it straight at Maas' head. But Maas continued asking for the revolver. Suddenly, after terrible suspense, the young man leaned over and dropped the weapon. Maas caught it, cocked and loaded. By this time New York's Fiorello LaGuardia who had gotten up to the gallery behind the gunman, grabbed him and, with the help of a policeman and a spectator, overcame him. Maas was later awarded a Carnegie Silver Medal for his bravery.[83]

Unwarranted Remark

Once Huey Long was engaged in one of his famous filibusters—raving, storming, mimicking, pacing the floor—and the peppery Senator Kenneth McKellar of Tennessee was trying to take him on. Long kept making satirical remarks about McKellar, which made the galleries roar and McKellar angrier and angrier. Finally the presiding officer banged the gavel and threatened to clear the galleries if the demonstrations didn't cease. At this point Senator Alben Barkley arose to see if he couldn't calm things down with a little humor. "Mr. President," he said, "I do not think the chair ought to be too hard on the galleries today. When the people go to a circus, they ought to be allowed to laugh at the monkey." Barkley meant Long, of course, but the "Kingfish" pretended he didn't. "Mistuh President!" he boomed, leaping to his feet. "I resent that unwarranted remark on the part of the Senator from Kentucky, directed toward my good friend, the Senator from Tennessee." Even McKellar laughed at that one.[84]

Maury Maverick and Dr. Hegel

When someone introduced a resolution in the House to permit U.S. officers to accept foreign medals, Texas' Maury Maverick, irked that the House should be wasting time on trivialities when the welfare of the nation was at stake during the Great Depression, prepared a tongue-in-cheek report on the resolution. "Since this matter of medals touches all the heights and depths of civilization . . . ," he declared, "it is not to be treated lightly. It must be treated philosophically. Now, the heaviest philosophy for the occasion is that of Hegel who handled everything dialectically. This method calls for the division of every . . . argument into three parts: thesis, antithesis, and synthesis. It may not be generally known, but thesis, antithesis, and synthesis form the basis of all argumentation. . . . This was proved beyond any doubt by Dr. Hegel, a distinguished philosopher."

Maverick then went on to reveal the "Hegelian Truth" about the problem of foreign medals facing Congress:

Thesis
1. If a citizen is not worthy, he should not have a medal, and if he is worthy, he does not need it.
Antithesis
2. To insist on his having it is . . . the antithesis.
Synthesis
3. Don't let him have the medal.[85]

Reds

In April 1936, the American Legion publicly disavowed a booklet on Americanism prepared by its New York chapter because it contained "a cut that is supposed to resemble the American Legion emblem . . . done up in red rather than black or legitimate color." The Legion also denounced the booklet because it pictured a raised torch, "with its striking similarity to the left wing socialist emblem."

When the Legion's plaint hit the news, Maury Maverick couldn't resist having a little fun over the matter in the House. In a speech there he first asked whether the Legion's objections to the flaming torch would lead it to recommend sawing off the arm of the Statue of Liberty in New York harbor. Next, he wondered whether the Legion's protest against the booklet's use of red was prefatory to an effort to seek the complete elimination of that color from American life. "Since red in itself is a sin," he said, "a logical dissertation of its effects is in order. If red should be entirely removed, however, there might be trouble." Some of the troubles:

"Congressman Sirovich, of New York, cannot wear his red carnation on the lapel of his coat. . . .

"Red wines are prohibited. . . . No use going to Italian restaurants.

"Seeing 'red' will also be abolished. In this many red baiters will suffer severe inhibitions and mental maladjustments.

"Lure of the red-headed girls; handsomeness of red-headed boys to be eradicated by Federal law. Will cause importation of nonfading German dyes to make color of hair different. This will hurt 'Buy American' campaign; in this case, the importation will be a metamorphosis from communism to fascism.

"Red herrings cannot be drawn across issues. This will also be a blow to red baiters.

"Red tape must be made blue; however, the change in colors will not affect red-tape psychology or human nature.

"The high curtains in the Supreme Court, which are red, or near red, must be substituted at once.

"Bulls will not get mad any more."

Maverick found only one good result of the ban on red. "Red ink will be abolished," he noted; "and this is really good, for then there would be no depression. With only black ink the profit system would be assured ad infinitum."[86]

Bigotry (1940)

Mississippi's John Rankin was probably the most bigoted man in the House; he was anti-Semitic as well as anti-black. He particularly enjoyed baiting Morris Michael Edelstein, Jewish Congressman from New York, calling him a "friend of the *Daily Worker,*" questioning his patriotism, and, in the months before Pearl Harbor, denouncing him as a warmonger.

"Mr. Speaker," cried Rankin one day, "Wall Street and a little group of our international Jewish brethren are still attempting to harass the President of the United States into plunging us into the European war unprepared; and at the same time the Communistic elements throughout the country are fomenting strikes by harassing industry and slowing down our defense program. . . ." Then he went on raving about the Jews for a time, and Edelstein finally rose to ask for a minute to answer. "Mr. Speaker," cried Edelstein, "Hitler started out by speaking about 'Jewish brethren.' It is becoming the ploy and the work of those people who want to demagogue to speak about 'Jewish brethren' and 'international bankers.' The last speaker, speaking about international bankers, coupled them with our Jewish brethren. The fact of the matter is that the number of Jewish bankers in the United States is infinitesimal. . . . I deplore the idea that any time anything happens, whether it be for a war policy or against a war policy, men in this House and outside this House attempt to use the Jews as their scapegoat. I say it is unfair and I say it is un-American. As a Member of this House I deplore such allegations, because we are living in a democracy. All men are created equal, regardless of race, creed, or color; and whether a man be a Jew or Gentile he may think what he deems fit."

When Edelstein finished, the House burst into applause, but it was the last sound he heard. For he walked off the floor and fell dead. The strain had been too much for him.[87]

Just One Vote (1941)

In the fall of 1941, the House took up a bill to extend the draft (first enacted in 1940 for one year's duration) for another year. The bill's sponsors knew the vote would be close; there was much opposition to a "peacetime draft," even though the United States was already heavily involved in the war raging in Europe. Amid mounting tension, Foreign Affairs Committee chairman Sol Bloom of New York recorded his vote in favor of draft extension and then retired to the cloakroom to quiet his nerves. There, to his dismay, he encountered a Congressman who had voted, "Aye," on the measure, but was now planning to change his vote to "No," before Speaker Sam Rayburn announced the final vote. "Over my dead body," said Bloom determinedly. "Sol, I won't have this on my conscience," wailed the Congressman. "You can't stop me." "Maybe not," retorted Bloom, "but I'm going to try." "Sol," persisted the Congressman, "I'm going to change my vote. It might make all the difference." "That's why you'll have to knock me through the doorway if you want to return to the floor," said Bloom firmly. "I'm going to stand right here." And stand he did, in the doorway, until Rayburn announced the final count: the draft had been extended by a margin of just one vote.[88]

Inferences and Implications

In November 1942, playwright Clare Boothe Luce was elected to Congress from Connecticut and in her maiden speech in the House she dismissed

Vice President Henry A. Wallace's plea for "freedom of the skies" after the war as "globaloney." Arkansas Democrat, J. William Fulbright, a onetime Rhodes scholar, at once challenged her. The Representative from Connecticut, he said, had "inferred that Wallace's plan for free skies would endanger the security of the United States," and she was clearly wrong. "I inferred nothing," Luce shot back, "I *implied* and the gentleman from Arkansas did the *inferring.*"

Years later, when President Eisenhower nominated Mrs. Luce to be ambassador to Brazil and she appeared before the Senate Foreign Relations Committee, Senator Fulbright, the chairman, started off by saying: "I am implying certain defects and drawbacks I recognize in this nomination and Mrs. Luce can infer whatever she likes from my implication."[89]

Getting Things Straight

One day Senator Rufus Holman, Oregon Republican, decided to make use of the Senatorial privilege of "pairing," but couldn't seem to get things straight. The bill at stake was a minor one, but Holman took it very seriously. During the roll call, he announced that he was paired with "my great good friend who graces the other side of the aisle, the able and distinguished senior Senator from Virginia," i.e., Democratic Harry F. Byrd. To make things perfectly clear, he added: "If Senator Byrd were here, he would vote 'No.' And if I were here, I would vote 'Aye.'" He then resumed his seat; but as his fellow lawmakers began chuckling, he bethought himself for a moment or two and then arose again and requested permission to amend the pair. "Mr. President," he explained, "I said that if Senator Byrd were here he would vote 'No,' and that if I were here, I would vote 'Aye.' I wish to correct that, Mr. President. What I meant to say was that if Senator Byrd were here he would vote 'Aye,' and that if I were here, I would vote 'No.'" It was a long time before laughter in the House subsided.[90]

Maiden Speech

H. R. Gross, Iowa Republican, entered the House in 1949 and worried about the time he would make his maiden speech in the House. When he mentioned his concern to Clare Hoffman of Michigan, an old-timer, the latter said: "Nothing to it. I'm making a long speech tomorrow, and somewhere in it you stop me and ask a question. I'll answer it, and that will take care of your first speech." Elated by Hoffman's suggestion, Gross rehearsed with the Michigander the question he was to ask and the point in Hoffman's speech where the question was to come. All went as planned the next day. Hoffman spoke as scheduled, and at the agreed-upon moment

Gross rose, asked if the Congressman from Michigan would yield for a question, and Hoffman courteously yielded. Gross then posed his question and sat down to await the answer. He never forgot Hoffman's reply. "I cannot understand what possessed the gentleman from Iowa to ask such a stupid question!" Hoffman exclaimed. Gross learned the hard way: freshmen Congressmen have many pitfalls to avoid when making their way around Capitol Hill.[91]

Not a Yes Man

One day Kentucky's Alben Barkley spent a great deal of time answering a question Ohio's Robert Taft had asked. When he finished Taft said: "I thank the Senator. It seems to me that the word 'yes' might have answered the question." "Well, Mr. President," said Barkley, "knowing the Senator from Ohio has always boasted that he is not a 'yes' man, I hesitated to use that term."[92]

Not Mad

During a heated argument over continuing the Office of Price Administration (OPA), a World War II agency, Republican Senator Kenneth S. Wherry of Nebraska goaded Democratic Senator Alben Barkley of Kentucky into a high rage and then asked innocently whether Barkley was too mad to yield for one more question. Red in the face, Barkley stormed, "I'm not mad! I'm not mad! I'm not mad!" and slammed his fist down hard on his desk each time. As the Senate rocked with laughter, Barkley himself finally managed a grin.[93]

Consideration

When California Republican Senator William Knowland pressed Texas' Tom Connally, chairman of the Senate Foreign Relations Committee, to act on a Knowland proposal which foreign-policy leaders considered unwise, Connally responded: "I assure the Senator from California that his matter will have in the Foreign Relations Committee *exactly* the consideration that it so richly deserves." Then the colorful Texan looked up at the press gallery, grinned, and passed his index finger across his throat.[94]

Small Audience

During an exchange with another Senator when the Senate chamber was almost deserted, Texas' Tom Connally declared frankly: "I am not trying to argue with the Senator. I do not want to get into any controversy with him because the audience is small."[95]

Conscience (1950)

Outraged by the way Wisconsin Senator Joseph R. McCarthy hurled reckless charges of Communism and treason at people in and outside of government, Maine Republican Margaret Chase Smith, the only woman in the Senate at the time, drafted a "Declaration of Conscience," persuaded six other Republican Senators to sign it, and then rose in the Senate on June 1, 1950, to read it to her colleagues. "I speak as briefly as possible," she said, "because too much harm has already been done with irresponsible words of bitterness and selfish political opportunism. I think it is high time for the United States Senate and its members to do some soul-searching . . . on the manner in which we are using and abusing our individual powers and privileges. . . . I think that it is high time that we remember that the Constitution . . . speaks not only of freedom of speech but also of trial by jury instead of trial by accusation. . . . Those of us who shout the loudest about Americanism in making character assassinations are all too frequently those who, by their own words and acts, ignore some of the basic principles of Americanism. . . . The American people are sick and tired of seeing innocent people smeared. . . . I don't want to see the Republican Party ride to political victory on the four horsemen of calumny—fear, ignorance, bigotry, and smear."

Senator McCarthy sat tight-lipped as Senator Chase was speaking, and when she finished he left the Senate without saying a word. A little later, New York's Herbert Lehman told reporters that Senator Smith had "said things which had to be said and should have been said a long time ago"; Maryland's Millard Tydings called for a new word, "States-womanship"; and Missouri Democrat Stuart Symington exclaimed: "Senator Smith represents just about all that is best today in American public life—even if she is a Republican." The letters pouring into Senator Smith's office were overwhelmingly in favor of what she had done.

Senator McCarthy and his followers were of course extremely upset by the "Declaration of Conscience." In 1952 two McCarthyite reporters published a book called U.S.A. Confidential charging that Senator Smith (whom they called "Maggie") hobnobbed with "left-wing writers and reporters" and was "pals" with a woman who was a "security risk." They also made much of the fact that she was the only woman in the Senate and quoted a Senate doorman who had heard her speech as saying: "There's too many women in the Senate!" Expanding on this theme, the two reporters exclaimed: "She is a lesson in why women should not be in politics. When men argue matters of high policy they usually forget their grudges at the door. She takes every opposing speech as a personal affront and lies awake nights scheming how to 'get even.' She is sincere—but a dame—and she reacts to all situations as a woman scorned, not as a representative of the people." Only after Senator Chase brought a suit against the reporters did they acknowledge publicly that she was not a "Communist sympathizer." As for McCarthy himself, in 1954, when Senator Smith was running for a second term, he encouraged a dynamic young man, Robert L. Johnson, to run against her in the Republican primary and helped him out financially too. But Mrs. Smith beat Johnson by better than five-to-one and was returned to the Senate that fall. By that time McCarthy's colleagues had censured him for his behavior as a Senator.[96]

Pandemonium in the House (1954)

On March 1, 1954, as Speaker Joe Martin was counting the 243 members on the floor after a quorum call, two young men and an attractive young woman suddenly jumped up in the gallery, shouted, "Free Puerto Rico," pulled out Luger automatics, and began shooting. "Those shots are just in play," someone shouted. "The hell they are!" cried Louisiana's George S. Long (brother of Huey). "Those are real bullets!" And as the panic-stricken Congressmen began ducking behind their seats or making a dash for the exits, Martin yelled: "The house stands recessed!" Then he ducked behind a marble pillar near the Speaker's desk.

On the Democratic side of the House, Alabama's Kenneth Roberts gasped, "I'm hit," and, as blood oozed from his left leg, crawled on hands and knees to the end of his row of seats, where Tennessee's Percy Priest took off his tie and applied it above the wound as a tourniquet. Maryland's George H. Fallon was shot in the hip, tried to get up, but toppled to the floor behind some seats and lay helpless until the shooting was over. When the firing began, Tennessee's Clifford David slid off his chair to take cover behind his desk, but he was too late, and a bullet passed through the calf of his leg.

On the Republican side, Michigan's Alvin M. Bentley was walking down the aisle when the shooting started, dropped to his knees, seeking protection, but a bullet struck him underneath the right armpit, went through his chest and into his liver, and he toppled over unconscious onto the floor. Iowa's Ben J. Jensen, standing at his seat, waiting to be counted, had just turned to speak to his Iowa colleague, Thomas E. Martin, when a bullet hit him between his neck and right shoulder, and ripped through the back muscles to lodge near his left shoulder blade. "They got me!" Jensen gasped, steadied himself against a chair, and then tottered toward an exit. Just as he reached the door, he collapsed and fell across the threshold to the floor of the Speaker's lobby. Another Congressman, headed for the same door, saw Jensen fall, thought he had been shot from the lobby, and yelled: "My God, they're in here too! They're in the corridor!"

During the uproar, Pennsylvania's James E. Van Zandt managed to get out of the chamber. He raced up to the gallery, and pinned one of the assailants to the floor, while Capitol guards seized and disarmed the other two. Meanwhile, two Congressmen who were physicians—Minnesota's Walter H. Judd and Nebraska's A. L. Miller—rushed over to administer first aid to Bentley, who seemed to be the most seriously wounded of the five Congressmen who had been hit. Fortunately, all five eventually recovered, though Roberts' leg gave him a great deal of trouble, and he was in a wheelchair for the next two years. Bentley was back in action after about six weeks.

The attackers turned out to be members of the terrorist Nationalist Party of Puerto Rico (the same group that tried to assassinate President Truman in 1950) and—together with a fourth member of the gang, who was picked up in a bus station a little later—were sentenced to prison for terms of 15 to 25 years. Ironically, most Puerto Ricans opposed independence, favoring continued association with the United States.

Soon after the assault, the House took measures to tighten security, but rejected a proposal calling for the installation of bullet-proof glass around the front of the galleries. "For one thing," Speaker Martin explained later, "I was advised that the weight of the glass would be too great for the galleries. For another, I felt that, danger or not, Americans do not want their Congress walled off from the people by glass."

There was some teasing later on. The sight of two overweight Congressmen—Frank Boykin and Martin Dies—scrambling to get through the same door, unable to move—produced much retrospective mirth. But the two took it in good humor. "Say, Martin," said Boykin afterward, "who was that guy that got caught between us in the doorway?" And when the house discussed security measures Dies told his colleagues that "the safety measure needed most around here is bigger doors!"

The favorite story, probably apochryphal, centered on the Congressman who raced out of the House chamber as the bullets started flying, down one of the corridors, and out of the Capitol. "Congressman, where are you going?" a friend called, as he flew down the street. "I'm going to get my gun," puffed the Congressman. "And where is your gun?" the friend asked. "Mobile, Alabama!" shouted the Congressman, without slackening his pace.[97]

Westminster Abbey

When Hubert Humphrey became chairman of the liberal organization, Americans for Democratic Action (ADA), he became a target of Republican conservatives for whom ADA was a dangerous leftist group, which they said took its program from the British socialists. One day Senator Homer E. Capehart was raving about the organization and he charged that the ADA wanted to do to America what the British Labour party was doing to Britain. Suddenly he shouted at Humphrey furiously: "Just name me one thing that Great Britain has that we don't have!" Said Humphrey quickly: "Westminster Abbey." Senators and galleries exploded in laughter and Capehart sputtered and sat down.[98]

Freshman Senators

In their eagerness to get off to a good start, some newly elected Congressmen make the mistake of trying to do too much too soon. During Senator John F. Kennedy's first year in the Senate he was anxious to make a good impression on his elders and on occasion outdid himself. One afternoon, in a burst of energy, he rushed to the Senate floor, offered a flurry of amendments, held a news conference, made some remarks on two or three bills, issued some press statements, and finally sank, exhausted, into a chair next to Carl Hayden, who had been in the Senate for more than forty years. "Well," said JFK, looking earnestly at the venerable Arizonan, "I guess you must have seen lots of changes in the time you've been here." "Yes," said Hayden shortly. "What are some of the more important ones?" asked Kennedy. "Well, for one thing," said Hayden, "in those days freshmen Senators didn't talk."[99]

Quorum Call

In the House, quorum calls were taken seriously. It took time to call the roll, and once it was started it always went through to the end. And since on a member's record it counted as if it were a vote, House members dropped everything to get to the floor for such calls.

The Senate was different. Whenever sponsors of a bill wanted a little time to negotiate or needed a Senator on the floor, someone would suggest the absence of a quorum, the bells rang, and the clerk started calling the roll. But as soon as the absent Senator arrived or the matter was adjusted, the quorum call was withdrawn. Most Senators who had previously served in the House were unaware of the difference in procedures at first. During his first week or two in the Senate, New Hampshire's Norris Cotton, formerly in the House, nearly ran his legs off rushing from his office to the Senate Chamber to answer quorum calls, only to find that the call had been withdrawn. Eventually he learned that unless a third bell rang, indicating a "live" quorum, he didn't need to rush back to the Senate floor.

One of Cotton's favorite stories was about the old Senator who was in his office watching a baseball game on television with some guests while the Senate was in session. In the midst of the game the bells rang twice. One of the guests looked over at the Senator, surprised that he didn't head for the floor. "What's the matter with you?" the Senator asked him. "I thought I heard a quorum call," said the guest. "No doubt you did," said the Senator carelessly. "This is their mating season."[100]

Own Judgment

One Congressman made wide use of questionnaires and referred to results of the polls in every speech about issues he made on the House floor. One day somebody asked him: "How would you vote on a bill if one of your polls showed an exact 50–50 division on it?" "In that case," he replied, "I would use my own judgment."[101]

Motion

"A quorum is present," announced the presiding officer in the Senate on December 4, 1980. "Vote," moved Robert C. Byrd. "The question," announced the presiding officer, "is on agreeing to the motion to lay on the table the motion to reconsider the vote by which the motion to lay on the table the motion to proceed to the consideration of the fair housing bill was rejected. On this question, the yeas and nays have been ordered, and the clerk will call the roll." The legislative clerk called the roll and announced the result: Yeas, 61, nays, 31. So, according to the *Congressional Record,* "the motion to lay on the table the motion to reconsider the vote by which the motion to lay on the table the motion to proceed to the consideration of the fair housing bill (H.R. 5200) was rejected was agreed to.[102]

VIII

* * * * * * *

In the Chair

* 👑 *

The Vice President of the United States presides over the Senate and the Speaker presides over the House of Representatives, but there the resemblance ends. The Vice President, elected by the people, is little more than a presiding officer, though the Constitution does give him authority to cast a vote when there is a tie in the Senate. The Speaker, by contrast, has considerable power. Elected by members of the House, he retains the right to speak and vote on issues; he also preserves order in the chamber, has unlimited power of recognition during debates, decides points of order, and has authority to appoint Speakers *pro tempore*.

Some Speakers became "czars"; most Vice Presidents have been mere nullities. Vice Presidents have, to be sure, varied a great deal in forcefulness, but even the most assertive has never approached the Speaker in power and influence. The "chief embarrassment in discussing his office," Woodrow Wilson once wrote, "is, that in explaining how little there is to be said one has evidently said all there is to say."[1] Benjamin Franklin suggested addressing him as "Your Superfluous Excellency."[2] If the VEEP, as he came to be called, moved into first place upon the death of the President, the Senate quickly elected its own presiding officer to fill the vacancy he left behind, and seems always to have gotten along nicely without a Vice President in the chair. John Nance Garner, who held second place during Franklin D. Roosevelt's first two terms, called the Vice President "the Spare Tire in our Government."[3]

John Adams, the first Vice President, was irked by his powerlessness. "My country," he grumbled, "has in its wisdom contrived for me the most insignificant office that ever the invention of man or his imagination conceived."[4] Still, he tried to wrestle special meaning out of his designation

223

as President of the Senate. For Adams it became a metaphysical (ontological?) question: how to behave as President of the Senate whenever the President of the United States entered the Senate chamber. "Gentlemen, I feel great difficulty how to act," he told the assembled Senators a few days before George Washington's inauguration. "I am possessed of two separate powers; the one *in esse* and the other *in posse*. I am Vice President. In this I am nothing, but I may be everything. But I am President also of the Senate. When the President comes into the Senate, what shall I be? I cannot be [President] then. No gentlemen, I cannot, I cannot. I wish Gentlemen to think what I shall be."[5]

Adams' concern seemed like a mountainous molehill to Pennsylvania Senator William Maclay; he thought the earnest New Englander protested too much. "Here, as if oppressed with the sense of his distressed situation," wrote Maclay in his journal, "he threw himself back in his chair. A solemn silence ensued. God forgive me, for it was involuntary, but the profane muscles of my face were in tune for laughter in spite of my indisposition."[6] Possibly to Adams' chagrin, George Washington's first appearance before the Senate produced no crisis. Adams introduced Washington and the latter gave his inaugural address, acknowledged the ovation, and withdrew. Adams then went on to preside competently over the ensuing Senate proceedings as the Constitution-framers had intended for him to do.

But Adams wanted to do more than preside. Not only did he cast numerous tie-breaking votes (twenty-nine) in the Senate; he also made suggestions for the agenda and interrupted debate to express his own opinions. Adams simply couldn't keep still. "It is, to be sure, a punishment to have to hear other men talk five hours every day, and not be at liberty to talk at all myself," he told his wife, "especially as more than half I hear appears to be very young, inconsiderate, and inexperienced."[7] Senator Maclay found Adams too obtrusive as well as too regal in manner and filled his journal with notations on Adams' repeated interventions: "The Vice-President, as usual, made us two or three speeches from the Chair"; "The Vice-President made a harangue on the subject of order"; "The Vice-President made a speech, which really was to me unintelligible"; "And now the Vice-President rose to give us a discourse on the subject of form"; "The Vice-President made a remarkable speech"; "I saw Mr. Adams begin to fidget with a kind of eagerness or restlessness, as if a nettle had been in his breeches. He could not restrain himself long, and he got to tell us all about ambassadors, Ministers, and other consuls. . . ." Maclay found Adams maddening at times. "Adams, Adams," he wrote at one point, "what a wretch art thou!"[8]

During his eight years as the Senate's presiding officer, gradually John Adams came to exercise self-restraint. But he never really reconciled himself to the passive role for the Vice President apparently contemplated by the Constitution-makers. He once complained to his wife that he did not possess "the smallest degree of power to do any good either in the executive, legislative, judicial departments." The Vice President, he lamented, was "a mere Doge of Venice . . . a mere mechanical tool to wind up the clock."[9]

Most of Adams' successors accepted their inconsequence with good humor and rarely intervened in Senate debates. They dozed, daydreamed, wrote letters, or recovered from hangovers during the speech-making. William A. Wheeler, Rutherford B. Hayes' Vice President, told a reporter that "any man is foolish to be Vice President, unless he cares nothing for active life, and is willing to be a nonentity in the great debates which go on in his presence, without being able to express an opinion."[10] When Thomas R. Marshall, Woodrow Wilson's Vice President, first assumed the chair in 1913, he begged leave to make a few remarks to the Senate "before he enters upon a four-years' silence." A little later, at the end of a two-week debate on the tariff, he said he had been "like a man in a cataleptic state; he cannot speak; he cannot move; he suffers no pain; and yet he is perfectly conscious of everything that is going on about him." To his successor, Calvin Coolidge, he sent a telegram in 1921: "Please accept my sincere sympathy."[11] Harry Truman, Franklin Roosevelt's third and last Vice President, said Vice Presidents "were about as useful as a cow's fifth teat."[12] His own Number-Two Man, Alben W. Barkley, liked to tell about the man with two sons: "One went to sea, the other was elected Vice President; he never heard of either of them again."[13]

Texas' John Nance Garner was the only public figure to serve as both Speaker and Vice President, and he saw no comparison between the two positions. The Vice-Presidency, he said, was "not worth a pitcher of warm spit [sic?]."[14] This, despite the fact that the Chief, as he called FDR, did more for Garner than any previous President had ever done for the Vice President. Roosevelt, who liked to break precedent, invited Garner to sit in on Cabinet meetings, used him as liaison with the Senate on legislative matters, and sent him abroad several times on official business. But Garner was never under any illusions about his importance. "A great man may be a Vice President," he once said, "but he can't be a great Vice President, because the office in itself is unimportant."[15] But the Speakership was an entirely different matter. Garner thoroughly relished his years as Speaker of the House before becoming Vice President, for the position did, in fact, amount to something.

It was Kentucky's Henry Clay who had made the Speakership the important position it was when Garner took over the post in 1930. In November 1811, soon after entering the House as a freshman, young Clay was chosen Speaker by a large majority and at once set about making the post one with both power and prestige. "Decide, decide promptly," he advised one of his successors years later, "and never give your reasons for the decision. The House will sustain your decisions, but there will always be men to cavil and quarrel about your reasons."[16] There was plenty of caviling and quarreling while Clay was Speaker, but his charm, tact, courtesy, articulateness, and sense of purpose enabled him to carry the House with him time and again.

First of all, though, Clay insisted on enforcing discipline in the House. Not only did he call to order members who violated the rules or simply dozed off during debate; he also forced Virginia's obstreperous John Randolph of Roanoke to behave when he became too unruly. Randolph was in the habit of bringing a dog with him into the House chamber, and Speakers before Clay were never able to restrain him. Once, when a peevish Congressman complained about the noise the dog was making, Randolph began pummeling him with his hickory cane. There was no more pummelling with Clay in the chair. "Our Speaker is a fine man, gives universal satisfaction, and not even Randolph himself has as yet attempted to embarrass him," noted New Hampshire's John Adams Harper. "He is a gentleman who commands respect and esteem, & keeps good order. . . . *Mr. R. has brought his dog into the House only once this Session,* and then the Speaker immediately ordered the Doorkeeper to take *her* out."[17]

Once, when Clay reprimanded the long-winded and frequently rambling Randolph for his conduct on the floor, the Virginian complained that the Speaker wasn't paying any attention to his speeches. "Oh, you are mistaken, Mr. Randolph," cried Clay. "I frequently turn my head, it is true, and ask for a pinch of snuff . . . but retentive as I know your memory to be, I will wager that I can repeat as many of your speeches as you can."[18] Randolph fell silent at this polite put-down. Even the Federalists, Clay's political foes, were impressed with his deft way with recalcitrants. "The new Speaker is quite popular," one of them reported. "He possesses fine talents and presides with dignity."[19]

But Clay did more than preside with dignity and firmness. He filled committees with Congressmen who shared his views. He also pushed for legislation he favored in informal conferences with his confreres and took to the floor to make stirring speeches when the House was in the Committee of the Whole. Clay and his allies in the House—the young "War Hawks" from the West and South—called for forcible resistance to British depredations on American shipping; they also favored strong action against Canada, where British officials were inciting Indians across the border to attack American settlements in the West. President James Madison was reluctant to go to war; but Clay succeeded in persuading him to sponsor preparedness, then an embargo, and finally, a call for war. Massachusetts Federalist Josiah Quincy, a Federalist who opposed war, thought Clay was "the man whose influence and power more than any other produced the War of 1812.[20] But when Britain indicated willingness to discuss a settlement of the conflict, Clay accepted Madison's appointment to the peace commission and went to Europe with the other peace-makers to negotiate the Treaty of Ghent ending the war. At the conclusion of the treaty, Clay spent three months sight-seeing in Europe and then returned to Washington to become Speaker again and start pushing for his nationalistic "American system"—a program of protective tariffs, internal improvements, and industrial development—in the House. As his fame increased, he acquired several nicknames along the way: "the Mill Boy of the Slashes" (he came originally from a region in Virginia known as The Slashes), "the Kentucky Hotspur," "Harry of the West," "Prince Hal," "The Western Star," and then, after his diligent labors in the House, and later the Senate, to subdue the increasing sectional tensions among the lawmakers, "the Great Compromiser" and "the Great Pacificator." He was far better known and far abler, too, than most of the Presidents with whom he served, though, to his enormous disappointment, he never made it to the Executive Mansion.

Clay left the House in 1825 to become Secretary of State for John Quincy Adams, but the precedents he built up as Speaker continued to govern the House, and succeeding Speakers, even the less able ones, never doubted thereafter that the Speakership was one of the most prestigious positions in the American system of government. When Massachusetts' Robert C. Winthrop became Speaker in 1847, he asked John Quncic Adams, former President, but now serving in the House, for his advice on his social duties. "The Speaker of the House of Representatives, as representative of the people's representatives is next to the President and Vice-President," Adams told him. "Call upon no one else."[21] Missouri's Thomas Hart Benton was a Senator, but he, too, insisted on the high status of the Speaker of the House. "Be as modest as you please," he advised Winthrop, "but don't compromise the House of Representatives."[22]

Some of Clay's successors carried their refusal to compromise to great lengths. When one President invited Speaker Thomas B. Reed to the White House to discuss legislation, Reed flatly refused; he thought it would detract from the dignity of the office he held. The Speaker, Reed declared, had "but one superior and no peer" in the American government.[23] Joseph Cannon, another no-nonsense sort of fellow like Reed, refused Theodore Roosevelt's invitation to dine at the White House when he learned he had been assigned a seat at the table below the Attorney-General. T.R. then hastily arranged a special dinner for Cannon, and after that the Speaker's dinner became a regular part of the White House routine. Years later, Sam Rayburn exploded when a reporter remarked that the Texan had served as Speaker under eight Presidents. "I never served *under* any President," snapped Rayburn. "I served *with* eight."[24]

While serving with eight Presidents (from FDR to JFK), Sam Rayburn also served as host for an informal group known as "the Board of Education" that came into existence in the late 1920s. The so-called Board began almost by accident. In 1928, when John Nance Garner became Democratic Minority Leader, he got into the habit of meeting regularly with the Republican Speaker, Ohio's Nicholas Longworth, in a small hideaway in the Capitol for both conferences and conviviality. Neither Garner nor Longworth took Prohibition seriously; and they liked to "strike a blow for liberty" (Garner's phrase) with some of the other Congressmen after a hard day's work in the House.[25] Sometimes Longworth took his Stradivarius (he was a fine musician) to the sessions to entertain his colleagues. Other times the lawmakers played poker, drank "bourbon and branch water," as Garner put it, and swapped stories.

But the Garner-Longworth get-togethers had a serious as well as a recreational purpose. They were convenient occasions for deciding the next day's agenda, discussing the new bills facing them, and for ironing out the difficulties in moving legislation along in the House. "Hell, don't tell me what the bill says," Garner frequently said. "Tell me what it does." The meetings also gave old-timers like Garner and Longworth an excellent opportunity to instruct new Congressmen in the ways of the House. "You got a couple of drinks in a young Congressman," said Garner, "and then you know what he knows and what we can do. We pay the tuition by supplying the liquor."[26] Alabama's John McDuffie, a regular member of the group, began calling the meetings the "Board of Education," and the name stuck. Other regulars in the 1920s: New York's Bert Snell, Connecticut's John Tilson, and Texas' Sam Rayburn.

At one meeting Longworth and Garner got into a big argument about J. P. Morgan's gift of his London residence for an embassy residence. It was valued at around $300,000, and the State Department was asking for an appropriation of $150,000 for repairs. The penurious "Cactus Jack" Garner attacked the proposal on the floor of the House, saying it violated the Lowden Act restricting the cost of embassies to $150,000, but Longworth favored accepting the Morgan gift. In meetings of the "Board of Education," Garner called the Morgan offer a "white elephant," while Longworth charged that Garner wanted ambassadors to live in "dugouts." Later a reporter asked Longworth how the argument came out. "Oh, we got that settled," he replied airily, "and are working on one in South America now. We're deadlocked on the plumbing. I want running water and he is holding out for bowls and pitchers."[27]

When the Board of Education adjourned its meetings, Longworth usually gave Garner a ride home in the Speaker's official automobile. Garner called it "our" car; he told Longworth to take good care of it since he expected to be using it himself some day. When the 1930 election returns, disastrous for the Republicans, came in, Longworth sent Garner a telegram from Cincinnati: "WHOSE CAR IS IT?" Garner's reply: "THINK IT MINE. WILL BE PLEASURE TO LET YOU RIDE."[28] But it turned out that the Republicans still had a slender majority; and it wasn't until there were a few deaths, including that of Longworth himself, that the Democrats gained control of the House. In December 1931, when the 72nd Congress was organized, Garner became Speaker and took over as host for the Board of Education.

Garner was as solicitous a host as Speaker Longworth had been. His custom was to motion to his cronies on the House floor to come up to the Speaker's stand just before adjournment and tell them: "Boys, it's almost five o'clock. Let's get this House adjourned so you fellows can lead me down the steps. And on the way, after the first landing, let me stick my finger in the mouth of my pet snake and see if he'll bite me this afternoon. Because if he does, as he has in the past, I will be in need of the cure, and we will have to go to the Board of Education room and take care of the situation pronto."[29] Then, when the four bells rang for adjournment, Garner and his buddies would go off to the hideaway room for the cure: bourbon and branch.

Sam Rayburn carried on the tradition established by Garner and Longworth when he became Speaker in 1940 and he even permitted Vice President Harry Truman to join the powwows during World War II. After the war, however, the Board of Education stopped meeting for a time when the Republicans took control of the House after the 1952 elections and Massachusetts' Joe Martin replaced Rayburn as Speaker. Martin didn't smoke; he didn't drink; "he didn't *anything*," some people complained.[30] But when the Democrats recaptured the House in 1954 and Rayburn became Speaker again, the Board of Education resumed its meetings and continued to meet until Rayburn's death in 1961.

☆　☆　☆

Reins

Once, according to an old story, Henry Clay was asked, on leaving a party at sunrise, how he could expect to preside competently that day over the House of Representatives. "Come up," he said airily, "and you shall see how I will throw the reins over their necks!"[31]

Harbor of Yankee Democracy

In August 1814 the British invaded Washington (just after all government officials fled to Virginia) and set fire to the Capitol, the President's House, and most of the department buildings. Before setting the torch to the House of Representatives, however, according to an old account, the British commander, Sir George Cockburn, mounted the Speaker's dais and put this question to a vote for his troops: "Shall this harbor of Yankee democracy be burned? All for it say 'aye.'" And they voted to burn.[32]

Declines His Acquaintance

Henry Clay's charm disarmed even his political foes; some people even tried hard not to fall under his spell. When Georgia Democrat Thomas Glascock went to Washington after his election to the House, he resolved to have nothing to do with the great Whig leader. "General," said a friend at a reception, "shall I make you acquainted with Mr. Clay?" "No, sir," said Glascock promptly. "I choose not to be fascinated and moulded by him, as friend and foe appear to be, and I shall therefore decline his acquaintance."[33]

Sine Qua Non

Henry Clay liked to tell a story about one of his constituents in Kentucky known as "Old Sandusky." When he was helping negotiate the Treaty of Ghent ending the War of 1812–15, he said, "Old Sandusky" and his neighbors followed newspaper reports of the proceedings with great interest, but were puzzled by the appearances of the words, *sine qua non,* in the news coverage, from time to time. "Sine qua non," murmured Old Sandusky, when a friend asked him what the words meant. Then suddenly his face lighted up. "Why," he cried, "sine qua non is three islands in Passamaquoddy Bay, and Harry Clay is the last man to give them up!"[34]

The Latest News

When Clay was in Brussels helping to negotiate the Treaty of Ghent, he more than held his own with the British negotiators. One day Henry Goulbourn, one of the British commissioners, sent him a London newspaper containing an account of the British invasion of Washington, apologized for "this *disagreeable* intelligence," but said he presumed Clay would like to know the latest news from the United States. Clay promptly thanked Goulbourn for his thoughtfulness; then he sent him a Paris newspaper containing the first news of the American destruction of the British fleet on Lake Champlain. He, too, apologized for the *"disagreeable* part of the news," but presumed the Britisher, too, "would like the *latest."*[35]

Clay and the Duke

In the spring of 1815, when Clay was in Paris he attended a ball given by an American banker to celebrate the conclusion of peace and met the celebrated Madame de Staël. "Ah!" she cried, "Mr. Clay, I have been in England, and have been battling your cause for you there." "I know it, madam," said Clay; "we heard of your powerful interposition, and we are grateful and thankful for it." "They were very much enraged against you," said she; "so much so, that they at one time thought seriously of sending the Duke of Wellington to command their armies against you!" "I am very sorry, madam," responded Clay, "that they did not send his grace." "Why?" she asked, surprised. "Because, madam," said Clay, "if he had beaten us, we should have been in the condition of Europe, without disgrace. But, if we had been so fortunate as to defeat him, we should have greatly added to the renown of our arms." Madame de Staël was so enchanted by Clay's response that she couldn't resist telling the Duke about it when she introduced him to Clay a few days later at a dinner party she hosted. The Duke was tactful. "If I had been sent on that errand," he told Clay, "and been so fortunate as to be successful against so gallant a foe as the Americans, I should have regarded it as the proudest feather in my cap!"[36]

Half Right

When Henry Clay said he would rather be right than President, John C. Calhoun (who became Vice President in 1825) exclaimed: "Well, I guess it's all right to be half right—and Vice-President!"[37]

Aversion

John C. Calhoun, like Henry Clay, had presidential ambitions, but unlike Clay he never got to run for first place. That was fine with Virginia's acerbic Senator, John Randolph of Roanoke. When Calhoun was Vice President during Andrew Jackson's first term and was presiding over the Senate one day, Randolph began a speech by exclaiming: "Mr. Speaker! I mean, Mr. President of the Senate and would-be President of the United States, which God in His infinite mercy avert!"[38]

Pinch of Snuff

In September 1833, when President Jackson instructed his Secretary of the Treasury to stop using the Bank of the United States (B.U.S.) as a depository for government funds and start distributing them among state banks, the Whigs, stout supporters of the B.U.S., were up in arms. Day after day, Whig leaders in the Senate, especially Daniel Webster and Henry Clay, blasted the President, charging not only that he was behaving like a despot, but also that his anti-B.U.S. policy was bringing financial ruin on the country. One morning in March 1834, toward the end of a vehement harangue on the subject, Clay addressed himself directly to Vice President Van Buren, imploring him to leave the Senate chamber at once, hurry over to the White House, and, on bended knees, beg the President to restore the deposits to the B.U.S. without an hour's delay. When Clay finished talking, Van Buren called a Senator to the chair, strolled down to Clay's seat, and said: "Mr. Senator, allow me to be indebted to you for another pinch of your aromatic Maccaboy." Clay resignedly waved his hands toward the gold snuff-box on his desk and sat down, while Van Buren took a delicate pinch and then calmly returned to the Vice President's chair.[39]

Ready for Business

Before James K. Polk became President, he represented Tennessee in the House for several terms and served as Speaker from 1835 to 1839. One morning there was some important news in the newspapers and all the Congressmen were busily reading when Polk called the House to order. After the Journal was read, Polk announced that the House was ready for business, but no one paid the slightest attention to the announcement. Suppressing his irritation, Polk picked up a newspaper, turned his back to the House, and began reading himself. Ten, fifteen, twenty minutes passed; by then all the Congressmen had finished their papers and were beginning to wonder what was holding things up. "Mr. Speaker! Mr. Speaker!" shouted one member after another, as Polk sat absorbed in his newspaper. Finally one Congressman rose and addressed the Clerk of the House: "There does not seem to be any Speaker present, and I move, Mr. Clerk, that we proceed to a choice of Speaker *pro tem.*" Instantly Polk turned in his chair and cried: "The Speaker is present, and begs to say to the honorable House that, in accordance with established custom, he notified the House that it was ready for business, but found it was not ready, and trusts it is now ready to proceed." Everyone burst into laughter at Polk's rebuke and they all agreed he had given them a good lesson in politeness.[40]

Plagiarism

At the end of one session, the Kentucky Whig, John White, Speaker of the House from 1841 to 1843, delivered an eloquent address, only to have it discovered that he had plagiarized it from a speech that Vice President Aaron Burr had delivered thirty-eight years before. The ridicule heaped on him after the discovery eventually drove him to suicide.[41]

Clay and the Actor

When Clay was visiting Philadelphia in 1850, John W. Forney, editor of the *Washington Daily Union,* called on him at his hotel with his friend the actor Edwin Forrest and soon got into a lively discussion with him about the Compromise of 1850. But when Forney happened to mention that he had heard one of Louisiana Senator Pierre Soulé's speeches and thought it was an able presentation of the case against the Compromise measures, Clay lost his temper. "He is nothing but an actor, sir—" he cried, "a mere actor!" Then, suddenly recalling Forrest's presence, he lowered his voice, turned to the editor, waved his hand, and added: *"I mean, my dear sir, a mere French actor!"* As Forney and Forrest left the hotel a little later, the latter mused: "Mr. Clay has proved, by the skill with which he can change his manner, and the grace with which he can make an apology, that he is a better actor than Soulé!"[42]

The Crisis of 1859–60

On the eve of the Civil War Congress itself seemed on the verge of a bloody riot. At times feelings were so strong that legislation ground to a halt while "belligerent Southrons glared fiercely at phlegmatic Yankees," according to one observer, and the House of Representatives "seethed like a boiling caldron."

When the Thirty-sixth Congress met in December 1859, the Capitol was like an armed camp. "Every man on the floor of both Houses is armed with a revolver," reported South Carolina Senator James Hammond, "some with two revolvers and a Bowie knife." Ohio Senator Benjamin Wade carried a sawed-off shotgun to his desk for everyone to see. "The members of both sides are mostly armed with deadly weapons," wrote Iowa Senator Grimes, "and the friends of both are armed in the galleries. The Capitol resounds with the cry of dissolution and the cry is echoed through the city."

The contest for the Speakership in 1859–60 was the bitterest in Congressional history. It raged eight weeks and was punctuated by vilification and near-violence on the House floor and by applause, hisses, cheers, boos, hand-clapping, and foot-stomping in the galleries. The Republicans put Ohio's John Sherman forward and the Democrats picked Virginia's Thomas S. Bocock as their candidates. After the first ballot, which put Bocock slightly ahead, Missouri slaveowner John B. Clark surprised his colleagues by proposing a resolution declaring that no Congressman who had endorsed Hinton R. Helper's book, *The Impending Crisis of the South— How to Meet It,* published in New York in 1857, was fit to be chosen Speaker. Clark was fully aware of the fact that sixty-eight Republican Congressmen, including Sherman, had signed a statement endorsing the book, and that the Republicans had cited extracts from the book during the 1858 Congressional campaign. Helper's book, banned in the South, attempted to show by graphs and charts that slavery benefited only a small minority of Southern whites while impoverishing the rest and reducing the South as a whole to a state of "comparative imbecility." Clark read from the book to show how incendiary he thought it was.

Clark's strategy put the Republicans on the defensive. Many of those who had endorsed (without reading) the book got up to deny any sympathy with abolitionism. Sherman himself said frankly: "I do not recollect signing the paper referred to; but I presume, from my name appearing in the printed list, that I did sign it. I therefore make no excuse at all." Came then violent attacks on Sherman as the "Abolition candidate for the Speakership," and a vituperative exchange between South Carolina's Lawrence Keitt and Pennsylvania's Thaddeus Stevens that led some Congressmen to start reaching for their pistols. "The clerk has no power to enforce order," shouted the clerk above the din. "He is powerless and therefore throws himself upon the generosity of the gentlemen on both sides to assist him in enforcing order." The sergeant-at-arms marched through the milling crowd, holding the mace high, but it was some time before order was restored.[43]

It was, though, a typical day during the long Speakership battle. The balloting—and the near-rioting—continued, day after day, with Sherman taking the lead but lacking a majority to win. On December 26, after the 21st ballot, the House chaplain prayed for a "spirit of conciliation, of kindness, of peace, of patriotism, of piety. . . ."

But the bitter fighting continued into the new year. On January 17, 1860, New York's John Haskin and Mississippi's John McRae got into a fight that produced an uproar when Haskin's pistol suddenly fell out of his pocket, hit the floor, and bounced down the aisle. "Take your seats! Sit down!" yelled the clerk frantically, while people in the galleries hooted and hollered and the sergeant-at-arms rushed down into the melée with his mace. When order finally returned, Louisiana's Davidson declared: "I desire to say that if these things are to continue in the future I must bring a double-barrelled shotgun into the House with me."

In the end the House reached a compromise. On January 30, by prearrangement, Sherman withdrew from the race, and the Republicans threw their support to William Pennington, former Whig governor of New Jersey, whom the Democrats also agreed to support. And on February 1, on the 44th ballot, Pennington won the contest with 117 of the 223 votes cast. Clark, who had started all the trouble, was triumphant. "Sir," he exulted, "that Resolution of mine has worked its effect, so far, at least, that it has smoked out before the American people the fact that an endorser of the Helper book cannot be Speaker of this House."

At the height of the contest Sherman's brother, William T., wrote to ask him how he had come to endorse the Helper book, and the Ohio Congressman wrote back to say it was a "thoughtless, foolish, and unfortunate act" on his part. General Sherman then wrote back: "Disunion would be civil war, and you politicians would lose all charm. Military men would then step on the tapis, and you would have to retire."[44]

Consultation

After Kentucky Senator John C. Breckinridge had been James Buchanan's Vice President for a time, a friend asked whether it was true that the President never bothered to consult him about anything. "Yes, sir, it is only too true," said Breckinridge resignedly. Then he reflected. "No, that is not just right," he corrected himself. "He did consult me once." He went on to explain. "He sent for me one evening to come to the White House." And, said Breckinridge, as he entered the White House library, Buchanan solemnly took a document out of his pocket and announced: "Mr. Vice President, I have here my Thanksgiving Proclamation, the phraseology of which I desire to submit to your critical opinion and judgment."

Years later, Adlai E. Stevenson, Grover Cleveland's Vice President, recalled the Breckinridge story when dining with Senator Thomas Gorman, and when he finished Gorman inquired: "Has Mr. Cleveland consulted you to that extent, Mr. Vice President?" "Not yet," replied Stevenson, eyes twinkling. "But there are still a few weeks of my term remaining."[45]

One Vote

In July 1861, when Congress convened at President Lincoln's call, Thaddeus Stevens nominated Galusha Grow for Speaker. Appointed teller, Stevens declined, pointing out, "I cannot write." He knew whereof he spoke; his handwriting was so execrable that an old Quaker friend once told him he "would be very willing to know what thy opinion is, if thou could write so I could read it."

In the contest for the Speakership, Grow received 99 votes on the first ballot and Moss Blair of Missouri received 40 votes. When the results were announced, Blair withdrew his name and asked his supporters to vote for Grow. At that point Stevens, who had received one vote, got up and announced: "I have the same remark to make. I will not be a candidate any longer and request my friend who voted for me to withdraw his vote." The remark drew much laughter, and on the next ballot Grow was elected.[46]

Saved His Life

Maine Republican James G. Blaine, who entered the House in 1863, didn't like Abraham Lincoln's Vice President, Hannibal Hamlin (also from Maine), but never criticized him openly. He professed, in fact, to admire him. "Why, Hamlin saved the life of a dear friend once," he told his friends. "Yes, he saved my poor friend Brooks from sure death." "How was that?" his friends asked. "Well, Brooks says Hamlin saved his life three distinct times in the Mexican War," Blaine replied, "and that he could never repay him the debt of gratitude he owed him." Then Blaine went on to give details. "It was this way," he said; "Brooks says he always kept his eye on Hamlin during an engagement. And whenever Hamlin ran, he ran, too, and three times Hamlin saved his precious life!"[47]

Evasion and Escape

When Congress began its spring session in 1869, Massachusetts' Benjamin Butler whipped up support among Southern Republicans (whom he controlled) for Maine's James G. Blaine as Speaker, hoping in return to become chairman of the Committee on Appropriations himself. But Butler's strident ways made him unpopular in the House, and having won the Speakership Blaine had no intention of backing Butler. When Butler suspected something was amiss—just before the committee chairmanships were to be announced—he went around to the Speaker's office to press his claim. He found Blaine's messenger stationed by the door and the latter said Blaine was busy and couldn't see anybody. "Very well," said Butler, "I will wait." So he took a chair and sat down by the door hoping to intercept the Speaker as he came out. Learning that Butler was outside, Blaine hastily climbed out of the window in his office, went around the portico, and entered the House chamber from the other side. A little later one of the Congressmen came down the hall and, seeing Butler sitting in front of Blaine's office, cried: "What are you doing here, General?" "Waiting for Blaine," said Butler. "Blaine is in the chair in the House," the Congressman told him. "It isn't possible!" exclaimed Butler. "Yes," said the Congressman. "He is just announcing the committees." Butler rushed at once back into the House chamber just in time to hear the clerk read the name of Henry L. Dawes (whom Butler had helped defeat for the Speakership) as chairman of the Appropriations Committee.[48]

Common Sense

One day, when Iowa's Edwin H. Conger vehemently protested a ruling which the Speaker, Pennsylvania's Samuel J. Randall, made, the latter said indignantly: "Well, I think the Chair has a right to exercise a little common sense in this matter." "Oh," said Conger, "if the Chair has the slightest intention of *doing anything of that kind,* I will immediately take my seat!"[49]

Speaker Reed and the Disappearing Quorum

In December 1889, Maine's Thomas B. Reed became Speaker of the House and soon made it clear that he intended to play a forceful role in the conduct of business in the Republican-dominated chamber. On January 29, 1890, Congressman John Dalzell reported a resolution from the Committee on Elections which proposed to award a disputed Congressional seat in West Virginia to the Republican candidate. When Reed demanded a roll call on whether to consider the resolution, the Democrats sat silently in their seats, refusing to vote. There was nothing unusual about this. It was a time-honored method of filibustering in the House known as "the disappearing quorum," by which members of the minority party stymied action by the majority party by preventing a quorum from being reached for discussing legislation. In this instance there were 161 yeas (Republicans), 2 nays, and 165 not voting (Democrats). "No quorum," cried Georgia's Charles Crisp, Democratic leader, triumphantly.

To the consternation of the Democrats and the delight of the Republicans, Reed broke precedent at this point. "The Chair directs the Clerk to record the following names of members present and refusing to vote," he announced. Interjected Crisp sharply: "I appeal from the decision of the Chair." But Reed flatly ignored him and began reading the names of all the Congressmen present; but when he came to Kentucky's William P. Breckinridge, the latter yelled angrily: "I deny the power of the Speaker, and denounce it as a revolution!" Reed ignored him and went calmly on with the roll call, while the Democrats roared their protests with mounting indignation. When he got to the name of J. B. McCreary of Kentucky, the latter noisily interrupted him. "I deny your right, Mr. Speaker, to count me as present," he cried, "and I desire to read from the parliamentary law on that subject." "The Chair is making a statement of fact that the gentleman from Kentucky is present," Reed responded firmly. "Does he deny it?" Then he resumed the roll call, amid shouts, yells, boos, hisses, and catcalls, until he got to the end, and then announced that he would make a quorum ruling. "There is a provision in the Constitution which declares that the House may establish rules for compelling attendance of members," he told the House. "If members can be present and refuse to exercise their functions and cannot be counted as a quorum, that provision would seem to be entirely nugatory. Inasmuch as the Constitution only provides for their attendance, that attendance is enough. If more was needed, the Constitution would have provided for more." His ruling: "The Chair thereupon rules that there is a quorum present within the meaning of the Constitution." Illinois' Joseph G. Cannon backed him up. "I say that a majority under the Constitution is entitled to legislate," he declared, "and that, if a contrary practice has grown up, such practice is unrepublican, undemocratic, against sound policy and contrary to the Constitution."

For three days the contest raged. "The House resembled a perfect Bedlam," reported the *New York Tribune,* but "in the midst of this pandemonium," Speaker Reed "remained calm and self possessed, not for an instant losing his presence of mind. He delivered his decisions in the calmest way possible, but in a voice that could plainly be heard above the din." At one point Joe Wheeler, former Confederate officer, got so excited that he climbed on a desk, yelling and screaming, and began leaping from desk to desk, headed toward the Speaker's chair, like a wild goat.

Toward the end of the battle, some Democrats tried to escape Reed's eye by hiding under their desks and behind screens or even heading for the exits. Reed finally ordered the doors locked. But Texas' Constantine Buckley Kilgore, determined to leave, kicked out the panels of a door leading into the lobby, bumped into Maine's Nelson Dingley, who was standing outside, and injured his nose. From then on he was known as "Kicking Buck" Kilgore. He "made more reputation with his foot," it was said, "than he ever will with his head!"

The Democrats blasted Reed as a czar, despot, tyrant, usurper, bully, and coward, but in the end he prevailed. And the West Virginia case finally appeared on the agenda and was decided, as the Democrats knew it would be, in favor of the Republican candidate. Four years later, when the Democrats gained control of the House, they found the old ways they had defended so frustrating that they, too, adopted Reed's method of counting a quorum.[50]

Peculiar Combination

Whenever Colonel W. L. Terry, Democrat of Arkansas, didn't want a quorum to be present, he didn't bother to leave the chamber; he simply crouched down behind his desk so he couldn't be seen. One morning, Speaker Reed, wanting to count a quorum, told the clerk: "Count Mr. Terry. He is hiding under his desk." Furious, Terry rushed down the aisle shaking his fist, and cried: "Mr. Speaker, it is strange to me that you can see me under my desk, but when I am wanting to make a speech and yelling to you at the top of my voice, you never know I am on the place. Sir, I want you to know that I am a Democrat and a gentleman." Reed leaned back in his chair and said calmly: "Well, you needn't blame me for the peculiar combination in your makeup!"[51]

Rights of Minority

At a Rules Committee meeting one day, Speaker Reed slammed a bill on the table and, looking over at the Democrats, announced: "Gentlemen, we have decided to perpetrate the following outrage!" "But what of the rights of the minority?" a Democrat once protested. "The right of the minority," returned Reed, "is to draw its salaries and its function is to make a quorum."[52]

Choate Did

Speaker Reed despised hypocrisy. At a dinner party in Washington one evening he was chatting with Colorado Senator Edward O. Wolcott and Joseph H. Choate, former Senator but about to become ambassador to Britain, and at one point Choate said he had never played cards, drunk whiskey, or chewed tobacco. "Lord," sighed Wolcott, "I wish I could say that." "Well, why don't you?" snapped Reed. "Choate did."[53]

Vindicated

Speaker Reed was scrupulously honest. "I do not expect by acting thus to escape public slander," he once announced. "I only expect not to deserve it." When Illinois Congressman Richard Townsend suggested there was some doubt about his integrity, Reed took to the floor to announce that there were only two sets of people whose opinions he respected: his constituents, who knew him, and the House, which knew Townsend. "It is hardly necessary to say," he added, "that I shall stand vindicated before both."[54]

Washout

Once, when the House was trying to secure a quorum, Reed sent telegrams to members who were absent demanding their presence. One Congressman who was held up by a flood on the railroad line, telegraphed, "Washout on the line. Can't come." Reed wired back: "Buy a new shirt and come at once."[55]

Antidote

One afternoon an aging Southern Congressman strode into "Czar" Reed's office for a chat. During the conversation Reed asked the old fellow to what he attributed his long and active life. "I always have a mint julep every afternoon," said the Southerner, "and vote a straight Democratic ticket." "Well," said Reed, a prohibitionist as well as an ardent Republican, "that explains it; one poison offsets the other!"[56]

Impossible

One morning Colonel James Hamilton Lewis, Congressman from Washington, went to Speaker Reed's room to secure recognition from the chair to call up a bill of interest to his constituents. After some talk, Reed drawled: "Well, I guess I will have to grant your request, Lewis. I am not so ugly as I look." "Impossible, Mr. Speaker," cried Lewis, bowing nearly to the floor; "utterly impossible!" This greatly amused Reed, though the joke was on him.[57]

Ain't Saying a Word

Colorado's James B. Belford tired his colleagues with his long-winded orations; according to Mississippi's John Allen, "every time he wanted to state a fact he put it in three ways." Once Belford was challenging an opponent and at one point exclaimed: "There he sits, dumb, mute and silent." "He ain't saying a word either," interposed Speaker Reed in his piping voice, bringing the House down.[58]

Money Out of Treasury

Speaker Reed took a dim view of requests for local expenditures. When Tennessee's Thetus W. Sims told Reed, soon after entering the House, that since the Tennessee River ran through his district he would like to serve on the Committee on Rivers and Harbors, Reed drawled: "How big a steal do you want?" A little later Florida's Robert W. Davis went to see Reed about a bill for improving a river in his state. "I am sorry," drawled the Speaker, "to see you joining the procession which is not happy unless it is taking money out of the Treasury." "But this is only $50,000," pleaded Davis. "Well," said Reed, "that is a good deal for a district where alligators form the largest part of the population."[59]

Reed Rules

After winning the quorum battle in 1890, Reed persuaded the House to adopt a new code of rules—popularly known as the "Reed Rules"—which greatly increased his powers as Speaker. One day, however, when he overruled a point of order made by a Democratic Congressman, the latter pulled out his copy of *Reed's Rules*, walked triumphantly up to the

Speaker's desk, and, pointing to a passage in the book, said Reed's ruling clashed with the book. "Oh," said Reed coolly, "the *book* is wrong."[60]

"Czar" Reed

Thomas B. Reed served as Speaker of the House during the administrations of Benjamin Harrison, Grover Cleveland, and William McKinley, ran the House with an iron hand, and came to be called "Czar" Reed. "Thank God," he said, after ramming through a rule limiting the time allotted to speakers during debates: "the House is no longer the greatest deliberative body in the world!" Though he favored woman suffrage, he was in the main a sturdy conservative. "Most new things," he said, "are not good." When appropriations reached an all-time high while he was Speaker and the Democrats talked ominously of "the billion-dollar Congress," he said airily: "This is a billion-dollar country."

Reed was famous not only for his resolute rule as Speaker, but also for his witty, though at times acidulous way of putting things. "A Statesman," he once said, "is a politician who is dead." Another time: "All the wisdom of the world consists of shouting with the majority." In 1896, when someone asked him whether the Republicans were going to nominate him for President, he responded: "They might go further and do worse; and they probably will." They did; they picked William McKinley, whom Reed disliked. Afterward he said: "They were for me until the buying started." Reed is said to have originated the remark about McKinley—"He has no more backbone than a chocolate eclair"—used later by Theodore Roosevelt. Roosevelt amused Reed. "Theodore," he once said to the chronically indignant T.R., "if there is one thing more than another for which I admire you, it is your original discovery of the Ten Commandments." Of his Maine colleague Nelson Dingley, Reed once remarked: "He'd rather have a pad and pencil on his knee than a pretty girl."

In debates, Reed was a master of the sardonic put-down. He had a tongue, someone said, "that at one stroke sliced the whiskers off his opponents' faces." Of two garrulous Congressmen who bored him he declared: "They never open their mouths without subtracting from the sum total of human knowledge." Once he apologized for his inability to "equal the volume of voice" displayed by a New York Democrat and added: "That is equalled only by the volume of what he does not know." When William M. Springer, Illinois Democrat, asked for "unanimous consent" to correct a statement he made attacking the Republicans, Reed exclaimed: "No correction needed. We didn't think it was so when you said it." One day J. Hamilton Lewis, the House's talkative Beau Brummel from the Pacific Coast, rushed down to the rostrum waving a newspaper. "Mr. Speaker," he cried, "I rise to a question of personal privilege. I have here a copy of this morning's *New York Sun* in which I am referred to as a thing of beauty and a joy forever." "The point is well taken," Reed shot back. "It should have been a thing of beauty and a jaw forever."

Reed liked to tease with reporters. When some of them in an interview asked him to clarify the money question for their readers, he drawled: "Well, there is something about the intimate study of finance that, if a man continues it long enough, disqualifies him from talking intelligently upon any other subject, and, if he continues it still longer, disqualifies him from talking intelligently upon that." Once a newspaper sent reporters to Capitol Hill to ask all the leading Congressmen what they thought the most important problem facing them was at the time. Speaker Reed's response: "Dodging bicycles."

Reed was of course a devout Republican. "We live in a world of sin and sorrow," he once remarked. "Otherwise there would not be any Democratic Party." He loved the House of Representatives the way Speaker Sam Rayburn did years later. The Senate for Reed was the "little" House and the lower chamber the "large" House. The Senate, he once said, was "a close communion of old grannies and tabby cats," a place "where good Representatives go when they die." He once facetiously pictured a future United States in which the Senate picked the President by secret ballot; and when the ballots were counted, there was one vote for each Senator.

One day Reed was lounging in one of the House lobbies with some of the other Congressmen and General Henderson started teasing him about his size. "How much do you weigh, Tom?" he asked. Reed said he weighed one hundred and ninety-nine pounds, though it was clear that figure was probably seventy-five pounds under his real weight. "Oh," laughed Henderson, "we all know better than that." "Well," said Reed, "I'll own up to two hundred pounds, but no gentleman ever weighs over two hundred."

In April 1899, when Reed retired from his long service in the House, the *New York Tribune* exclaimed: "Congress without Tom Reed! Who can imagine it?"[61]

Reed: Isolationist

Reed was an "isolationist." He thought that war was sometimes necessary, but he didn't think a great nation like the United States should pick quarrels with other nations, especially weaker ones. In 1891, when President Benjamin Harrison sent Chile a bellicose note after some American sailors got killed in a riot in Valparaiso, he was thoroughly disgusted. "I do not think the President ought to have written such a message to those little Chileans," he told a friend. "They do not wish to fight us, we do not want to fight them. What we ought to do is to charter a ship, not too large or too safe, put Harrison on board of it, and send him down to fight the Chileans. He's just about their size."

Reed also opposed war with Spain, the annexation of Hawaii, and the acquisition of the Philippines after the war. To stem the movement toward war in 1898 he sometimes acted arbitrarily. One day, when the Democratic floor leader sought recognition to offer a motion to recognize Cuban belligerency (which would ensure war with Spain), he calmly ignored him. With no one else seeking recognition, Reed then blandly announced that a motion to adjourn had been offered by Maine's Nelson Dingley. Dingley was in the House Chamber, all right, but he was busy studying tariff statistics (his specialty) and not paying any attention to the Speaker at the time. But Reed moved quickly. "The Gentleman from Maine moves that the House do now adjourn," he cried. "Do I hear a second? The motion is seconded. The question is now on the motion to adjourn. All in favor say 'aye.' Those opposed, 'no.' The 'ayes' have it. The House-stands-adjourned!"

In February 1898, when the battleship *Maine* blew up in Havana harbor, the clamor for war with Spain mounted, but Reed stood firm against it. He tried to restrain discussion of the war in the House by placing severe limits on the time allotted for general debate, and he was extremely upset by the way the Senate became a major forum for the hawks. On March 17, Vermont's Redfield Proctor read a report on the Senate floor that Reed considered inflammatory, and when a reporter asked him about it, he observed that Senator Proctor owned some large marble quarries and added: "Proctor's position might have been expected. A war will make a large market for gravestones."

When the war came and after it the annexation of the Philippines, Reed decided to resign from Congress and move to New York to practice law. When someone told him the United States had the obligation to take freedom to the Philippines, he said: "Yes, canned freedom." He was deeply depressed by the long struggle U.S. troops were forced to wage after the war to suppress rebel Filipino forces headed by Emilio Aguinaldo. One morning, when newspapers reported that American soldiers had captured Aguinaldo's young son, Reed went to his office and found his law partner at work at his desk. "What, are you working today?" he cried, pretending to be surprised. "I should think you would be celebrating. I see by the papers that the American Army has captured the infant son of Aguinaldo and at last accounts was in hot pursuit of the mother!"[62]

Another Outrage

While American newspapers were playing up Spanish atrocities in Cuba, hoping to whip up sentiment for American intervention, a South Carolina mob proceeded to murder a black postmaster. Reed saw the story, clipped it from the morning paper, and asked his clerk to paste it on a sheet under the caption:

Another Outrage in Cuba

Body of a Patriot Riddled with Bullets and Thrown
through the Burning Rafters of his Dwelling

He then handed it to a Congressman from South Carolina who was particularly militant in his demands for intervention in Cuba. The South Carolinian began to devour the article greedily. "Why," he suddenly exclaimed, "this isn't Cuba," as he read on. "No, it isn't," said Reed in tones of contempt that, it was said, "rasped like a file."[63]

Supernumerary

People regarded Vice President Charles Fairbanks as a supernumerary. When a chandelier tinkling in the White House disturbed President Roosevelt's sleep, he ordered the butler to remove it. When the butler asked where he should take it, T.R. said: "Take it to the Vice President. He needs something to keep him awake." Later on, when T.R. took a trip in a submarine and there was much criticism on the ground that the President shouldn't endanger his life in this way, one newspaper offered: "At least he should have taken Fairbanks with him."[64]

Uncle Joe's Ways

Illinois Republican Joseph G. Cannon, who became Speaker in 1903 and held the post until 1911, had several nicknames. At first he was known as "the Hayseed Member from Illinois," then as "Uncle Joe," and then, after a coarse speech he gave in August 1890, as "foul-mouthed Joe." He was known for his "Niagara-like profanity" and barnyard humor. He smoked cigars and chewed tobacco, and a spittoon had to be kept close by him. President William Howard Taft warned Alice Roosevelt (T.R.'s daughter) never to get between Cannon and his spittoon. She was amused by the advice until she spent an evening playing poker with him. When their hostess didn't have a spittoon, Cannon allowed as how the umbrella stand would do just fine and used it "freely and frequently."

When Cannon was elected Speaker, he started to read a speech expressing his gratitude, but since he was not good at reading speeches, he suddenly threw it down, turned to the House, and said: "Gentlemen, I propose to be just as fair and impartial in the performance of my duties here as the exigencies of politics will permit." This brought roars of applause, because everybody knew he was telling the simple truth.

At a White House dinner for visiting Chinese dignitaries, President Taft's aide Archie Butt approached the Speaker and asked if he wanted to meet the guest of honor. "You mean," said Cannon in a loud voice, "for me to go over there and meet that Chink?" "Not unless you desire to," said Butts, "but he is the guest of honor." "Oh, all right," said Cannon. "I will do as you say, but it goes against my pride for an American free-born citizen to cross a room to meet a heathen Chinese." As the evening progressed, however, he warmed to the Chinese visitors. "Later in the library," Butt recalled, "while the men were smoking . . . Uncle Joe, a little worse for dinner, amused the entire room by keeping one arm around the shoulder of the Prince and the other around the neck of Lord Li, with a cigar stuck at seventy degrees out of the corner of his mouth, telling them all about the Constitution and government in general and airing his ignorance of Eastern affairs."[65]

Bean Soup

Bean soup had been served in the House restaurant for years, but one hot day, when Speaker Cannon went there for lunch he couldn't find it on the menu. "Where is the bean soup?" he asked angrily. "I'm looking for the bean soup." The waiter explained that the chef had decided it was too muggy that day for bean soup, but Cannon was not appeased. "Hell and thunderation!" he cried. "I had my mouth set for bean soup. Get me the chef." When the chef appeared, Cannon gave him a severe dressing down. "From now on," he told him, "hot or cold, rain, snow or shine, I want bean soup on the menu every day." Since that day bean soup has appeared on the menu in the House restaurant every single day.[66]

A Few More

Once, when Cannon was Speaker, the Democrats discovered that most of the Republicans had left the House floor, so they called up for a vote on a bill they wanted passed. After the traditional callings of the roll of members, Cannon quietly asked the clerk to call the roll once more, a clear violation of House procedures. The Democrats angrily objected and demanded Cannon's justification for so unprecedented an act. "The Chair will inform the gentlemen," said Cannon calmly. "The Chair is hoping a few more Republicans will come in." The Democrats burst into laughter at Cannon's candor, and decided to let his lieutenants have the extra time to round up enough Republicans to defeat the bill.[67]

Cannon's Tour

Uncle Joe Cannon announced one summer that he would take a party of friends through Yellowstone National Park. That was an opportunity for which Hiram Martin Chittenden, the builder of the park's road system, had been waiting for a long time. When Cannon arrived in the park, Chittenden arranged to have four stagecoaches ready for Cannon and his party, saw to it that the Speaker sat in the last coach, and instructed the driver to keep as close to the coach ahead as he could without inviting disaster. During the sightseeing trip that followed, Cannon took a tremendous powdering, for the road was white with volcanic ash. "Why in the devil doesn't somebody do something about those blankety-blank roads?" fumed Cannon. Chittenden then gently reminded the Speaker there were plans drawn up for improving the roads, but no money available. "Well, let's see the plans," growled Cannon. And in the next Congress came generous appropriations for redoing the roads.[68]

Light the World with Gas

Speaker Joe Cannon was a Standpatter. "Everything is all right out West and around Danville," he once said. "The country don't need any legislation." Sometimes, when interviewed, he liked to quote some lines he came across in a newspaper that summed up his view of reformers:

> I'm thankful that the sun and the moon
>   Are both hung up so high
> That no pretentious hand can stretch
>   And pull them from the sky.
>
> If they were not, I have no doubt
>   But some reforming ass
> Would recommend to take them down
>   And light the world with gas.[69]

In Direct Line

Once, when Uncle Joe Cannon was on a campaign trip, a man boarded the train who insisted on arguing the Scriptures all the time. Cannon got up and left the smoking-car, but when he returned, the man was still there. As he stepped in the door, the fellow exclaimed: "Now, I'd like you to tell me why it was necessary for the Israelites to spend forty years in the wilderness going from Egypt over to the Land of Canaan, when in a direct line it is not more than two hundred miles straight across?" Unable to restrain his wrath any longer, Cannon savagely snapped back: "Well, I'd like for you to tell me why it is that the food a man eats has to go through thirty-five feet of intestines before it emerges from his body, when in no man is it more than three feet in a direct line from ingress to egress." At that the other people in the car shouted in such great glee that the man left and never came back.[70]

Damned Little Left

Once an eloquent young Methodist preacher in Washington visited Joseph Cannon in his House office and after they had talked a bit, the preacher said: "Well, Mr. Speaker, I now know you well enough to say that, if I had you to make all over myself, I would leave you just as you are except that I would cut out your profanity." At this, Cannon turned to him with a merry twinkle in his eye and said: "Well, Brother Moore, you would leave but damned little of me, wouldn't you?" And they both laughed.[71]

Same Hole

On one occasion an inexperienced young fellow began a speech at a banquet at which "Uncle Joe" Cannon was present. "Gentlemen," began the young fellow, "my opinion is that the generality of mankind in general is disposed to take advantage of the generality of—" "Sit down, son," interrupted Cannon. "You are coming out of the same hole you went in at."[72]

Revolt Against Cannonism

Like Speaker Reed before him, Uncle Joe Cannon came to be called a "czar." He was an "able man and a clever politician," observed a contemporary, who "owns the House of Representatives body, soul and conscience." When a constituent asked his Congressman for a copy of the House's rules and regulations the Congressman sent him a picture of Speaker Cannon. Once, a woman who was attending the opening of a House session with Cannon in the chair, was shocked to see Cannon stand and bow his head with the other members of the House as the chaplain gave the opening prayer. "Thar's old Joe Cannon," she whispered loudly to a friend. "And him a-prayin'. The old hypocrite!"[73]

Cannon rather enjoyed his reputation as an autocrat. "Behold Mr. Cannon, the Beelzebub of Congress!" he once exclaimed in a mock-triumphant air. "Gaze on this noble, manly form—me, Beelzebub—me the Czar!" But progressive Republicans found nothing amusing about what they called "Cannonism." Cannon's dictatorial power as Speaker—he chose the members of all the fifty-odd House committees and was chairman of the powerful Committee on Rules—enabled him to block all efforts at reform. There was mounting resentment, especially in the West, at his tyrannical ways. "Emma Goldman, in her palmiest days," observed Kansas journalist William Allen White, "never made so many anarchists as Cannon."

Republican Congressman George W. Norris of Nebraska was no anarchist, but like other Republican insurgents in the House, he was anxious to reduce the Speaker's power to dominate the legislative process. He finally framed a resolution cutting the Speaker down to size and began carrying it around with him at all times, looking for an opportunity to present it to the House. The moment finally arrived on St. Patrick's Day, March 17, 1910. The day before, a Republican regular took to the floor to call for the consideration of a resolution having to do with the U.S. Census. Both the Democrats and Republican insurgents objected; the census bill was way down on the list of bills on the calendar and was thus out of order. But Cannon overruled them; he pointed out that the census was mentioned in the Constitution and that the motion therefore enjoyed Constitutional privilege. He lost his point, but the following day the House voted to consider the census resolution anyway.

Norris at once saw his opening. On March 17, he sought recognition. "Mr. Speaker, I have a privileged resolution," he announced. "Mr. Speaker, I have a matter of privilege." When, after his third effort, Cannon finally recognized him, Norris declared: "Mr. Speaker, I present a resolution made privileged by the Constitution." Then he took the well-worn paper containing his resolution out of his pocket and sent it up to the clerk. As soon as the clerk finished reading it, one of Cannon's henchmen jumped up and cried: "I make the point of order that it is not in order! It is not privileged." Norris then pointed out that the House rules, like the census, were mentioned in the Constitution and were thus privileged. When a motion to adjourn at this point failed, showing that Cannon didn't have the votes to uphold a ruling against Norris, the Speaker decided to stall. The rest of the day his supporters sent telegrams to members back home for the holiday urging them to hurry back to Washington. Several regulars did show up. But a few hours later, when another motion was made to adjourn, the Cannon people lost again.

The Democrats joined Norris and the other Republican insurgents in putting pressure on Cannon to make his ruling on Norris' resolution. When one Republican regular complained, "These proceedings are absolutely unfair," Norris' supporters yelled back, "What do you know about fair dealing?" "I am inclined to think—" he began, but they interrupted him: "Why don't you?" Periodically they shouted at the Speaker: "Rule! Rule! Rule!" But Cannon continued stalling, and the House remained in session all through the night (with Cannon pouring ice water on his head to stay awake) and into the next morning and afternoon. At 4:00 p.m. on March 18 Cannon finally announced he was ready to rule, but, weary after twenty-six hours in session, the House voted to postpone business until the following day so members could catch up on their sleep.

At noon on March 19, the House assembled with more than 350 of its 391 members present and the galleries crowded with spectators. Cannon ruled, as expected, against Norris, but the Nebraska insurgent appealed the ruling, and the House joined him in voting to override the Speaker. Next came a vote on the Norris resolution itself, and, again, the House, by a vote of 193 to 153, voted to uphold Norris. Cannon then entertained a motion to declare the office of Speaker vacant so that the House could proceed to the election of a new Speaker. When a Texas Democrat offered such a motion, Cannon called the Republican floor leader to the chair and walked out of the house. Amid great excitement the House quickly voted to reinstate Cannon as Speaker and he resumed the chair to tremendous applause. "But Cannonism," he said later, "was dead, dead as a doornail, dead as a last year's birdnest, dead as a defeated presidential candidate—and is there anything deader than that?"

The Norris amendment to the House rules enlarged the Committee on Rules from five to ten members, removed the Speaker from it, and authorized the committee to pick its own chairman. This revision of the rules didn't go as far as Norris wanted (to garner support he had been forced to water down his original proposals), but he was convinced it was a big step forward. "We all know there is a change of atmosphere in the House," he said afterwards. "There is more individual freedom and less coercion. There is more individual liberty and less machine control. The result is better legislation, better laws, better government."

Shortly after his defeat, Cannon attended a banquet in New York City and told the guests he thought every insurgent ought to be hanged. "The Speaker said this *after* the banquet," observed Norris, when he heard of Cannon's remark, "which explains his probable condition."[74]

What the Country Needs

Thomas R. Marshall, former governor of Indiana, presided over the Senate during Woodrow Wilson's eight years in the White House, and, with his dry wit and fund of humorous stories, was one of the most popular men ever to serve as Vice President. One day Kansas Senator Joseph L. Bristow launched into a long, boring speech on "What This Country Needs," and after a while Marshall, unable to contain himself, leaned over to an aide and said in a whisper everyone could hear: "What this country needs is a really good five-cent cigar!"[75]

Agreement

Mississippi's two Senators, John Sharp Williams and James K. Vardaman, had no love for each other and very little mutual respect either. For a long time Vice President Marshall was able to predict how they would vote on a bill: if Williams voted "aye," Vardaman would vote "no"; and if Williams voted "no," Vardaman would vote "aye."

Williams was a bit hard of hearing and as a result sometimes thought he was entitled to the floor when he was not. On one occasion, Marshall had to tell him he was out of order, and he flounced out of the Senate chamber in high dudgeon. Shortly afterwards, Marshall had to treat Vardaman in the same way, and he, too, went off the floor in anger. Marshall then left the chair, went to the Democratic cloakroom and triumphantly told the Senators there that he had accomplished something that nobody else had ever been able to do: get Williams and Vardaman to agree on something. Asked what it was, he said: "They agreed that the presiding officer is a fool!"[76]

Wild Animal

In Washington there was an organization known as "Guides," whose members told visitors about the paintings, busts, and works of art in the Capitol, and who could talk knowledgeably about the history of the entire building, from the dome on top to the secret vault beneath, where Congress at one time contemplated putting George Washington's ashes. Sometimes, when the guides were passing the Vice President's Chamber, next to the Senate Chamber, they would stop, point out Indiana's Thomas Marshall, then Vice President, as though he were on display. Once Marshall ran to the door and exclaimed: "If you look on me as a wild animal, be kind enough to throw peanuts at me, but if you are really desirous of seeing me, come in and shake hands!"[77]

Hamlet

After the Republicans captured the House in 1918, James R. Mann, who had been Minority Leader for the past four terms, was regarded by many as the logical choice for the Speaker's chair. But Nicholas Longworth thought Mann was too much like the last Republican Speaker, Joe Cannon, to be suitable. Mann had been Cannon's right-hand man when "Uncle Joe" was Speaker; he even looked a little like Cannon, with his silver hair and beard. But he was so thoroughly a legislator, with a penchant for doing everything himself, that Longworth once declared: "The gentleman from Illinois undertakes to play the role of Hamlet in this House, and does it with skill, grace and tact, and I think no one will begrudge that role, but when . . . he undertakes not only to play Hamlet, but the fair Ophelia and the King and the Queen and the first grave digger and sometimes, as now, carries a spear, he might be criticized for carrying the thing too far." In the end, the anti-Mann forces, with Longworth as one of their leaders, picked Frederick Gillett, a Massachusetts Republican, rather than Mann as their candidate. But after Gillett became Speaker, he was so lethargic when presiding over the House that one newsman remarked that the Speaker avoided coffee in the morning "for fear it would keep him awake all day."[78]

Spats

In 1922, Ohio's Nicholas Longworth was a candidate for Republican floor leader. Popularly known as the "old" husband of "young" Alice Roosevelt, daughter of Theodore Roosevelt, Nick, as his friends called him, was a smooth, debonair, and well-tailored gentleman who enjoyed playing the piano and violin at parties, composed amusing verses during House debates, and moved in the highest social circles whenever he so desired. But some of his supporters in the House were bothered by his swanky dress and decided to talk to him about it. "You won't mind if we talk to you on a serious subject?" said their spokesman somewhat diffidently. "I'd like you to," said Longworth amiably. "It's this," said the Congressman. "We find there is a great deal of criticism about your clothes and particularly about those spats. Now we want to ask you, wouldn't you be willing to give up wearing spats? It would help a lot." Longworth was amused. "Go over to the Senate," he advised them, "and see LaFollette." It turned out that the Wisconsin insurgent, about as down-to-earth as anyone in Congress, wore spats too. The Congressman dropped the subject and Longworth became floor leader.

But in 1924, when Longworth was a candidate for Speaker, some of his supporters began worrying again. "For God's sake, Nick," they said, "don't change your suit tomorrow! These guys won't dare vote for a man who wears another suit every day." Longworth laughed and said nothing. The next day, when they saw him looking as spiffy as usual, one of them cried: "What's that, Nick, another new suit?" "Look," said Longworth; then, turning around, he proudly showed them two big patches in the seat of his trousers. He went on to become one of the most popular Speakers in the history of Congress.[79]

Not Too Strong

"I should like to see the Republican party well organized," Speaker Longworth once announced, "responsible for its candidates, proclaiming its platform, and strong in every branch. And I should like to see a strong Democratic party." He paused for a moment as his Republican audience looked startled, and then added: "But not too strong!"[80]

Longworth's Head

It was an open secret in Washington that Speaker Nicholas Longworth, husband of Theodore Roosevelt's daughter Alice, was a great womanizer.

One day a brash Congressman went up to him where he was reading in the House floor library, playfully ran his hand over the Speaker's shiny scalp, and exclaimed: "It feels just like my wife's backside." Longworth at once ran his own hand across his head and said thoughtfully: "So it does."[81]

Pure Democracy

"The great thing about Harvard University," said Speaker Longworth, a Harvard graduate, in one speech, "is that it is the best example of pure democracy that I know of. It is a place where true character always wins. The only other place I know of where pure democracy exists is in the House of Representatives of the United States." He went on: "Why, last year, an active member from the South, who retired after serving for ten years, said he had got everything he deserved but the Speaker's eye!"[82]

Republican Prosperity

One day Speaker Longworth stopped in Newark, Ohio, and when he got off the train a crowd gathered and demanded a speech. The Newark platform was triangular, bounded on one side by the Pennsylvania Railroad, on another by the Baltimore and Ohio, and on the third by the Big Four. "My fellow citizens," began Longworth, but at once a Big Four train drowned out his voice. The people on the platform waited impatiently for the train's departure and Longworth started in again. "My fellow cit"—and a switching engine backed up on the Baltimore and Ohio and began to let off steam. In a minute or two Longworth was able to resume, but before he got through his salutation this time, an almost endless freight train rode up on the Pennsylvania track. The crowd began tittering. "What is the use," Longworth yelled, "of my trying to uplift my voice against this great roar of Republican prosperity?"[83]

Dawes Slept Here

In March 1925, five days after his inauguration, President Coolidge nominated Charles F. Warren of Michigan to be Attorney-General, but there was considerable opposition to the appointment because he had been connected with the "Sugar Trust" and many Senators opposed having him head the Department of Justice, which was responsible for enforcing the Sherman Anti-Trust Act.

On March 9, when the Senate voted on Warren, Charles G. Dawes, the new Vice President, was not in the Senate chamber. Senate leaders had assured him there were a half-dozen more speeches coming up and that the vote wouldn't come until that afternoon, so he returned to the Willard

Hotel to take a nap. To his amazement, he was suddenly aroused by the violent ringing of the telephone and the banging of bellboys at the door with the startling news that the Warren vote was being taken after all and his presence urgently demanded.

Dawes leaped from his bed, threw on his clothes, and sped at breakneck speed to the Capitol. But he arrived too late. There was a tie in the vote on the Warren nomination—the first Senate tie in three years—and Dawes was not there in time to cast his vote for Coolidge's nominee. Republicans were furious; Democrats were elated. And reporters, amused by Dawes' wild ride to the Capitol, pointed out that one of the Vice President's ancestors was Rufus Dawes, who accompanied Paul Revere on his famous ride in 1775, and that "wild rides" were in Dawes' blood. It got to be a joke. When someone was absent a Senator would ask: "Where is that fellow anyhow?" And the reply was: "Oh, he's out Dawsing'!" At the Willard Hotel a prankster put up a big sign: "DAWES SLEPT HERE!"[84]

Dolly Gann and Alice Roosevelt

When Kansas Republican Charles Curtis was in the Senate, he was quiet, hard-working, and well liked. Even after he became Majority Leader everyone continued calling him "Charlie." In 1929, however, soon after he took his oath as Herbert Hoover's Vice President, he reacted indignantly when an old Senate colleague called him by that nickname. "Where do you get that 'Charlie' business?" he exploded. "I'm Vice President now, and I want you to address me as 'Mister Vice President,'" His former colleagues were surprised by the way he took on the Hoover hauteur.

Curtis was a widower when he became Vice President and he indicated that his sister, Mrs. Dolly Gann, was to be his "official hostess." Did this mean that she took the rank of her brother? Washington etiquette-mongers were all a-twitter over the prospect of a woman who was not the wife of a public official taking on the rank of one. Speaker Longworth didn't like the idea at all. He thought that putting the Vice President's sister ahead of the wives of foreign ambassadors was an act of discourtesy; he didn't think she should outrank the wives of American officials (including his wife Alice) either.

The matter came to a head when publisher Eugene Meyers and his wife planned a big party at their Washington residence and, though they had been serving drinks for years, decided to make the party dry out of deference to the Vice President. This exasperated Longworth; he could respect people who were dry from conviction, but, like Pennsylvania Senator Boies Penrose, he despised people who went dry for political reasons. Still, though looking forward to a bone-dry evening with melancholy, he told Alice to accept the invitation.

Then things went askew. A few days before the Meyers bash, Mrs. Meyer happened to run into Mrs. Longworth and told her, among other things, how she planned to seat her guests; her husband, she said, was going to take Mrs. Gann to the dinner table ahead of the wives of the other dignitaries, including ambassadors, there. Alice Longworth told her frankly that "the combination of a dry house and Mrs. Gann outranking the ambassadorial wives" would probably be too much for the Speaker.

Mrs. Longworth's instincts were right. When she told her husband about the seating arrangements, he promptly announced he was bowing out. He hadn't wanted to go to a "dry dinner" anyway; now he had the perfect excuse—the "slight" to foreign ladies—for getting out of the engagement. At lunch the next day he triumphantly told some of his colleagues how he had skillfully succeeded in getting out of doing what he hadn't wanted to do all along. Within hours newspaper reporters were besieging both the Meyerses and the Longworths. The story, as they wrote it, was that Alice Longworth had "taken a stand" against the pretensions of Charlie Curtis and Mrs. Gann.

In her memoirs Mrs. Longworth dismissed the episode as a tempest in a teapot. "Of course, obviously, there never was any row," she insisted; "any one who knows me was aware that rank and conventionality were things I always fled from and shirked. I could not very well tell the true story—that Nick had seized a straw to avoid a dry dinner, so all I could say was, 'I have really nothing to do in it.' It was fantastic, the interest that was taken in the so-called row. People took sides, not so much in Washington, where many knew the truth, but out in the country." Mrs. Longworth received many letters asking how she could be so "snobbish" as to "snub Mrs. Gann," while others urged her "stick to your guns." And many people, she recalled, "never believed that Charlie Curtis and Dolly Gann were just as good friends of mine as they had always been."[85]

Souvenir

Texas Congressman John Nance ("Cactus Jack") Garner, who became Speaker in 1930, was known for his stinginess and even joked about it himself. His friend Sam Rayburn once said that Garner had seventy-five cents out of every dollar he ever made. Once, New Hampshire Senator Frederick H. Brown talked him into a ten-dollar bet at a ball game and, to Garner's great distress, he lost. As he reluctantly handed a ten-dollar bill to Brown, the latter asked him to autograph it. "I want to give my grandson a souvenir," he explained. "Do you mean you are not going to spend it?" asked Garner. "No," said Brown. "I want to frame it." "If I gave you a check would you cash it?" asked Garner thoughtfully. "No," said Brown, "I would frame it." "Then," said Garner brightening up, "I will give you a check instead!"[86]

Who?

One day Speaker William B. Bankhead of Alabama was being introduced in a small town outside his state. The introducer rambled along for some twenty minutes and finally came toward the close of his introduction. "And who is the speaker of the occasion that I am about to introduce? One of the greatest lawyers in his state. And who is the speaker? A member of Congress with a long and honorable career. And who is the speaker of this occasion? One who has held all the posts of distinction in the body to which he belongs. And who is the speaker . . ." At this time an old countryman in the front row of the audience lost all patience, jumped to his feet, and shouted: "Well, I'll bite; who in heck is he?"[87]

Half and Half

One day Louisiana's flamboyant Senator Huey Long, who liked to needle Vice President John Nance Garner, jumped up for about the fiftieth time and said banteringly: "Mr. President, I rise to make a parliamentary inquiry. How should a Senator, who is half in favor of this bill and half against it, cast his vote?" "Get a saw and saw yourself in two!" glowered Garner. "That's what you ought to do anyway!"[88]

Whacker

Texas' Sam Rayburn, who became Speaker in 1940, was considered a "whacker." The way he used his gavel when presiding revealed his state of mind. A heavy thump meant anger; repeated hollow tappings indicated weary impatience; and an echoing blast meant finality. Most of Rayburn's gavels came to him as gifts, and they were all well constructed. "I broke the gavel once," Rayburn admitted. "A fellow kept talking after his time ran out. Wouldn't sit down. Kinda wish I'd hit him over the head."[89]

Legislative Elders

On occasion Speaker Rayburn regulated activity on the House floor without using the gavel. "Sam Rayburn used to be able to glare people down," recalled Thomas P. ("Tip") O'Neill of Massachusetts, who became Speaker himself in 1977.

Sometimes Rayburn "circulated." One day a bill came to the House that he wanted fully debated, and when West Virginia's Jennings Randolph started to make a motion to shut off debate and go directly to a vote, Rayburn quickly left the dais and headed for the Congressman's desk. As he approached, Randolph's voice got weaker and weaker, and when Rayburn reached his seat, he stopped talking entirely. Rayburn then put his hand on Randolph's shoulder, started talking quietly to him, and then, still talking, removed his hand, put it in his jacket pocket, and rocked back and forth for a moment or two. Then suddenly he turned and walked back to the rostrum. Randolph looked sheepish, as laughter swept the chamber, but then announced that he was withdrawing his motion, and added: "As a legislative son I am always willing to follow the advice of my legislative elders."[90]

Late

Speaker Rayburn emphasized brevity and forthrightness. Even when the President called him, he managed to finish the conversation in two or three minutes. Sometimes when making phone calls he didn't even bother to waste time introducing himself. Once, when a Congressman failed to show up for a meeting on time, he called the man's secretary and said, "Tell him he's late," and hung up.[91]

Trouble

On April 10, 1945, as the war in Europe was nearing its end, the Senate ended its debate on extending the Lend-Lease Act and then voted on an amendment offered by Ohio Republican Robert A. Taft prohibiting the use of Lend-Lease funds for postwar relief and rehabilitation. The outcome was a tie. "The vote is thirty-nine to thirty-nine," announced Vice President Harry Truman after the clerk handed him the tally. Then he broke the tie. "The chair," he said, "votes 'No.'"

Two days later, when the Senate got into a discussion of a treaty on water with Mexico, Wisconsin's Alexander Wiley got into a long and boring discourse on the subject. While he was rambling on, Truman took out his pen and began writing his mother and his sister back in Independence, Missouri. "I am trying to write you a letter today from the desk of the President of the Senate," he began, "while a windy Senator . . . is making a speech on a subject with which he is in no way familiar." Truman then explained what the issues were and went on to say: "I have to sit up here and make parliamentary rulings—some of which are common sense and some of which are not." Then, after talking briefly about the weather, he advised them: "Turn on your radio tomorrow night at 9:30 your time, and you'll hear Harry make a Jefferson Day address to the nation. I think I'll be on all the networks, so it ought not to be hard to get me. It will be followed by the President, whom I'll introduce."

About the time Truman finished his letter, Wiley ended his speech and Alben Barkley moved for a recess until noon the next day. By this time it was close to five, and Truman headed for the "Board of Education" hideaway in the Capitol, now the bailiwick of Speaker Sam Rayburn. When he arrived there Rayburn handed him a glass of bourbon and tap water and told him that Steve Early, the President's secretary, had called and wanted Truman to return his call as soon as possible. When Truman got on the line Early's voice was tense. "Please come right over," he told Truman, "and come in through the main Pennsylvania entrance." Truman hung up, told Rayburn and the others there that the White House wanted him, but that he would be back soon. "I did not know why I had been called," Truman wrote later; he thought FDR wanted to go over some matters with him before heading for Warm Springs.

When Truman got to the White House he was ushered to an elevator and taken to Mrs. Roosevelt's second-floor study. The moment he entered the room he realized something was wrong. Mrs. Roosevelt seemed calm enough, but Early looked upset, and the Roosevelt daughter, Anna, and her husband were standing there, looking under a strain too. "Harry," said Mrs. Roosevelt, putting her hand on his shoulder, "the President is dead." Truman was speechless for a moment, and then exclaimed: "Is there anything I can do for you?" He never forgot Mrs. Roosevelt's response. "Is there anything *we* can do for *you?*" she asked. "You are the one in trouble now."[92]

Hide the Pencils

Sam Rayburn warmly supported President Truman, but was bothered by the way the new President woke up early in the morning and wrote explosive letters. In one letter Truman said the Marine Corps had "a propaganda machine that is almost equal to Stalin's." Another time he said United Mine Workers head John L. Lewis was not worthy of being appointed "dog catcher." And to a music critic who said harsh things about his daughter Margaret's singing recital he wrote: "I never met you, but if I do you will need a new nose and plenty of beefsteak and perhaps a supporter below." When Speaker Rayburn heard about the President's latest blast, he cried: "My God! Why doesn't someone down there in the White House hide all the lead pencils from Harry so he can't find them?"[93]

Bald

Sam Rayburn was embarrassed about his shiny bald head, which Marquis Childs, one of his favorite newsmen, said resembled "a well-polished ostrich egg." When the Speaker was upset, his poker face stayed unchanged, but his head turned crimson. "When Speaker Sam's face gets red, beware," people on Capitol Hill warned; "if the red spreads to his bald head, start running!"

At the 1948 Democratic National Convention, someone released a bunch of pigeons in the auditorium to dramatize peace, and one of the birds landed on Rayburn's head, to his dismay, but to the amusement of the delegates. Rayburn disliked being photographed; he was convinced editors instructed the cameramen to focus on his head. "That's enough, boys!" he yelled to photographers as soon as they started clicking away. Sometimes he asked sarcastically: "Did you snap it when I was licking my lips?" He felt a bit better about it all, however, when a magazine writer reported that he had heard two newsboys in the Capitol discussing the Speaker's head. One of them asked if he knew why Rayburn was so bald and the second boy explained: "If you used your head as much as he does, you wouldn't have any hair either!"[94]

Speaker President

On Inauguration Day, January 20, 1953, President Truman, President-elect Dwight Eisenhower, Senator Styles Bridges (President *pro tem* of the Senate), and Speaker Joe Martin rode from the White House to the Capitol for the inauguration of the new President. While Truman, Bridges, and Martin took their places on the inaugural stand, Eisenhower became delayed inside the Capitol beyond the hour of noon, when Truman's term expired by law. After glancing at his watch, Truman turned to Speaker Martin, next in line of succession, and said: "Well, you're President now, Joe." A moment later, however, Ike appeared and saved the day.[95]

Rayburn's Methods

One of Sam Rayburn's friends in the House was Georgia's Eugene Cox, leader of the Southern conservatives, and sometimes Rayburn used his influence to keep Cox from issuing blasts against President Truman's liberal legislative proposals. "He was all right," Rayburn once said of Cox, "if I could keep my hand on his shoulder, but I couldn't keep my hand on his shoulder all the time." One day Cox took a seat in the front row of the House, obviously intending to ask recognition to make a violent speech against Truman. Rayburn motioned for him to come up to the Speaker's chair. "Gene," he whispered, "you look all swelled up like a tick with a speech against President Truman. Harry Truman is your friend and you are his friend. Now, don't do it!" Cox protested, but then left the House chamber without making his speech. Rayburn could have refused to recognize Cox when he rose to make the speech, but he preferred more friendly methods to restrain his friend.[96]

Hat Size

At a luncheon on January 6, 1950, to celebrate Sam Rayburn's sixty-eighth birthday, President Truman gave him a new hat and told the guests: "Sam is the only man I know who could stay in Washington over forty years and still wear the same hat size he wore when he came here."[97]

Poor Company

In April 1951, when Sam Rayburn defended President Truman's firing of General Douglas MacArthur for insubordination, he touched off a storm of criticism in his own Congressional district, for MacArthur was a popular war hero. One letter-writer said that Mrs. Truman was just as much a "traitor" as her husband was, and a Baptist minister addressed a letter to "Dishonorable Rayburn," and said that if the people of the district "ever elect you to office again, they will be blind, deaf, dumb and ignorant." In his reply Rayburn told the preacher: "Being a believer in God and His word and the teachings of His Son, which was, 'And on earth peace, good-will toward men,' I fear that your conduct will not be conducive to carrying out these things. In other words, I fear that God and His Son traveling with you would be in poor company."[98]

Follow Blindly

Once the wives of some Congressmen, looking for Sam Rayburn, burst by mistake into the men's room, to which he had repaired, and after the Congressional doorkeeper had tactfully escorted them out, Rayburn told him embarrassedly: "People do follow the public leaders blindly, don't they?"[99]

Arson

As chairman of the Rules Committee, Virginia's conservative Howard Smith could block legislation he didn't like and sometimes Rayburn bargained with him to get bills out of his committee. But when Smith violently opposed a measure he was in the habit of disappearing completely so the committee couldn't meet. On one occasion, when he excused his absence by saying that a barn had burned down on his Virginia farm, Rayburn exclaimed: "I knew Howard Smith would do most anything to block a civil rights bill, but I never suspected he would resort to arson!"[100]

Makes the Decisions

Once, at a meeting of the "Board of Education," Indiana's Charles Halleck, Republican floor leader, suggested adjourning the House for the year without acting on a half-dozen major bills. Missouri Democrat Richard Bolling, a member of the Rules Committee, argued heatedly with Halleck, insisting that the House had to act on the bills before adjournment. "Well," said Halleck, annoyed at having to argue with a man with less standing in the House than he had, "if this guy is going to make decisions around here, we're not going to get very far." There was an awkward silence, and then Rayburn said quietly: "I make the decisions around here." There was no adjournment.[101]

Best-Known Member

Whenever Rayburn heard about a somewhat shy Democratic freshman in the House, he went out of his way to make him feel at home. In 1959, a few days after Dan Inouye of Hawaii (a Japanese-American who had lost his right arm in combat during World War II) entered Congress, the phone rang and when he answered it, he heard the Speaker's voice. "Inn-oo-way or Inn-way or however you say it, this is Speaker Rayburn. I thought if you weren't too busy you might come around and see me." The Hawaiian Congressman hurried to Rayburn's office, where the Speaker welcomed him and then proposed a tour of the Capitol. As they walked through the House chamber, galleries, and lobby, Rayburn sketched the history of the place and then gave Inouye some pointers about life in Congress. After the tour, when they were back in his office again, he asked: "How does it feel to be a U.S. Congressman?" "I'm very proud and very happy," said Inouye, "and a little scared, Mr. Speaker." Rayburn nodded. "That's the way I felt," he said. "That's the way we all feel the first time, I guess. But there's no reason to be scared. If you're the right man you'll do well, and if you're the wrong man . . . well, being scared won't keep you from being found out." Leaning back in his chair, he went on: "I'll tell you a few things. The unwritten rules here are more important than the written ones. We don't sign contracts because a man's word is his bond. We are all different, representing a whole nation full of different people with different problems. . . . But we get along here by respecting the needs and integrity of every man in his place—each one, remember, is an elected representative of the people—and we ask the same of you. But he went on to encourage Inouye to think for himself, stand by his principles, and always do what he thought in his heart of hearts was right. Then he paused, looked out the window, and said: "I'm going to start right out calling you Dan, all right? Because I'm damned if I can pronounce that last name of yours. Now, Dan, I'm sure you know that I am the best-known member of the House of Representatives." "Yes, sir," said Inouye. "Well," Rayburn went on, "after me, do you know who the best-known member is?" "No," said Inouye. "You," said Rayburn. "Me?" cried Inouye, looking at Rayburn in astonishment. "Of course, you," repeated Rayburn. "But—why?" "Why?" cried Rayburn. "Well, just think about it, son. How many one-armed Japanese do you think we have in the Congress of the United States?"[102]

Couldn't Come

Speaker Rayburn may have been leery of photographers, but he got along fine with reporters. One day the teen-age daughter of a newsman he knew died suddenly. Early the following morning there was a rapping on the reporter's apartment door, and, to his surprise, when he opened it, there was Rayburn. "I just came by to see what I could do to help," said Rayburn. "I—I don't think there's anything you can do, Mr. Speaker," stuttered the newsman. "We're making all the arrangements." "Well," said Rayburn, "have you all had your coffee this morning?" "No," said the reporter, "we haven't had time." "Well," said Rayburn, "I can at least make the coffee this morning." So he went in and headed for the kitchen. While he was making coffee, the reporter remarked, "Mr. Speaker, I thought you were supposed to be having breakfast at the White House this morning." "Well, I was," admitted Rayburn. "But I called the President and told him I had a friend who was in trouble, and I couldn't come."[103]

The Bull

The wife of a Congressman once asked Speaker Sam Rayburn, as a long session of Congress dragged on, when he expected the House to adjourn. Rayburn told her about a farmer who was leading a restive bull along a country lane by a rope looped around the animal's neck. He met a neighbor who demanded, "Hey, where are you going with that bull?" "I don't know," said the farmer. "Ask the bull." Telling a friend about this later, the woman said: "I thought I *was* asking the bull."[104]

No Funny Stories

When Richard M. Nixon was Vice President, a group of friends who had served with him in the House decided to throw a party for him. So they called his secretary, Rosemary Woods, and said, "We would like some funny stories about Mr. Nixon." There was a pause at the other end of the line and then Ms. Woods said: "There *are* no funny stories about Mr. Nixon."[105]

Keeping the Store

One day, when President Kennedy was in Canada, Vice President Johnson in Southeast Asia, and Secretary of State Dean Rusk in Geneva, someone called the White House, and, failing to get in touch with any of them, cried: "Who's keeping the store?" "The same man who's always kept it—" cried the operator: "SAM RAYBURN!" JFK enjoyed telling Rayburn about the exchange.[106]

Rayburnisms

Only longtime members called Rayburn "Sam" or "Mr. Sam." Others addressed him as "Mr. Speaker," despite his informality and willingness to listen to them. He once explained his reluctance to use his status to dominate conversations. "It's better to be silent and pretend dumb," he said, "than to speak and remove all doubt." He was always frank and direct. "I always tell the truth the first time," he said, "and don't need a memory to remember it." Around Rayburn, "a lie never lives to be old," said one of his employees. Rayburn even disliked white lies. "There are no degrees of truthfulness," he said. "You are 100 percent, or you are not."

Even when irritated, Rayburn usually kept his temper. "The day of pounding the desk and giving people hell is gone," he said. "A man's got to be led by persuasion and kindness and the best reason—that's the only way he can lead people." But he could be blunt. Once he told a Congressman who was getting a reputation for meanness: "You remind me of a man I know in North Carolina. He ate some cabbages one day and found that it made him disagreeable. So he ate cabbage every day from then on."

When Rayburn gave his word he always kept it. "Sam stays hitched," said "Cactus Jack" Garner. One of Rayburn's most famous remarks was, "To get along, go along." But he never asked a member of the House to cast a vote which violated his conscience or hurt him politically. "And on any piece of legislation if you're convinced in your heart that something is right," he said, "do it, go after it, fight for it, even if you find yourself in a minority of one."

Rayburn came to be much quoted. Among the many "Rayburnisms" are the following:

Any fellow who will cheat for you will cheat against you.
If a man has good common sense, he has about all the sense there is.
The steam that blows a whistle will never turn a wheel.
When two men agree on everything, one of them is doing all the thinking.
Any man who will deceive the voters during a political campaign will deceive them after he is elected.
A man who becomes conceited and arrogant wasn't big enough for the job.
Damn the man who is always looking for credit. If a man does his job, and does it well, he will get more credit than he is really entitled to.
Any jackass can kick a barn down, but it takes a carpenter to build it.
There is a time to fish and a time to mend nets.
I have a greater trust in people who send their Congressmen postal cards and handwritten letters on tablet paper than those who send telegrams.
If there is anything I hate more than an old fogie, it's a young fogie.
Legislation should never be designed to punish anyone.[107]

Meritorious Spot

Soon after President Johnson initiated his Great Society programs, Vice President Hubert Humphrey spoke to the North Carolina Farmers Council in Raleigh. A member of the council said he was too old for Headstart and too young for Medicare and wondered what slot he fitted in the Great Society. "There's a meritorious spot for all good men like you in the Great Society," Humphrey assured him. "The Great Society is going to be right expensive. I'll appoint you a taxpayer of the Great Society."[108]

Konfused

During a Senate debate Idaho's Frank Church asked for Vice President Humphrey's ruling on a procedural point and the latter's response was so confusing that North Carolina's Sam Ervin, Jr., couldn't resist telling one of his little tales. "A young fellow, whom I shall call Frank, met an old friend, whom I shall call Hubert," said Ervin. "Hubert was wearing a beautiful sweater with the huge letter K emblazoned on it. Frank asked Hubert, 'What does the letter K mean?' Hubert replied, 'Confused.' Frank said, 'You don't spell confused with a K.' Hubert responded, 'If you are as confused as I am, you do!'"[109]

190 Million and One Bosses

Once, at a dinner party, actress Rosalind Russell remarked to Vice President Humphrey that the Presidency must be the most difficult office in the world. But Humphrey said the Vice Presidency was in some ways even harder. "The President has only 190 million bosses," he said. "The Vice-President has 190 million and one." Years later, reporter Nancy Dickerson asked Humphrey whether it had helped being Vice President when Lyndon Johnson was President because as Kennedy's Vice President LBJ had been 'through the torture of the position himself and understood what it was like. "There is *no* President who understands!" said Humphrey emphatically.[110]

Safe

Walter Mondale retained a sense of humor about his position as Vice President. He once told a story about a man who lived near Three Mile Island whom an expert had assured that the area was safe from radioactivity because the President had visited it. "What makes you think that proves it's safe?" the man had demanded. "Because," Mondale quoted the expert as saying, "if it wasn't safe, they would have sent the Vice President."[111]

IX

*   *   *   *   *   *   *   *

Congress and the President

* 🏳 *

In 1844, Chief Justice Roger Taney sent a message from Baltimore to Washington by means of the new Morse magnetic telegraph extending his compliments to President John Tyler and asking about his health. "The President returned his compliments immediately," observed one reporter, "stating that he enjoyed good health, and felt much better, since Congress had finally adjourned."[1]

Tyler wasn't the only President to feel bearish about the legislative branch of government. Even George Washington had his clashes. When he took a treaty to the Senate soon after becoming President, he was so upset to learn that the Solons wanted to advise as well as consent that he said he "would be damned if he ever went there again," and he never did.[2] Will Rogers once facetiously summed it all up: "Distrust of the Senate started with Washington, who wanted to have 'em courtmartialed. Jefferson proposed life imprisonment for 'em. Old Andy Jackson said, 'To hell with 'em' and got his wish. Lincoln said, 'The Lord must have hated 'em for he made so few of 'em.' Roosevelt whittled a big stick and beat on 'em for six years. Taft just laughed at 'em and grew fat. They drove Wilson to an early grave. Coolidge never let 'em know what he wanted, so they never knew how to vote against him."[3]

Friction was the rule from the outset. The Constitution-makers apparently wanted it that way; they placed conflict at the very heart of the American system of checks and balances. They gave Congress the initiative in legislation, but called on the President to send State of the Union messages and recommend measures to the lawmakers. They permitted the President to veto laws enacted by Congress, but allowed Congress to override his veto by a two-thirds majority. In foreign affairs, they empowered the President to conclude treaties with other nations, but only with the advice and consent of the Senate. They instructed the President, too, to seek Senate approval for appointments to the Federal courts and other high offices. The war-making power? They made the President Commander-in-Chief of the armed forces, but entrusted Congress with the power to declare war and make military appropriations for two-year periods. All in all, the framers of the Constitution succeeded admirably in constructing what historian Richard Hofstadter once called "a system of mutual frustrations."

Sometimes, though, one branch of government was more frustrated than the other. From the outset there was what political scientists called a "law of ebb and flow" at work.[4] In some periods power flowed into the hands of the Chief Executive; at other times it became concentrated in the nation's legislature. There were strong Presidents and weak Presidents; and there were assertive Congresses and compliant Congresses. In times of crisis, particularly during wartime, the Chief Executive tended to over-shadow Congress, though even then Congress usually continued to fight hard to maintain its prerogatives. Sometimes Congressmen accused Presidents of behaving like kings, czars, dictators, and despots, but on other occasions Presidents charged just as heatedly that Congress was trespassing on the Chief Magistrate's terrain and putting the American system of balanced powers in jeopardy.

The appearance of political parties in the 1790s added to the friction between Congress and the President, particularly whenever one party controlled the legislative branch and another the executive branch of government. In the beginning the Hamiltonian Federalists favored strong executive leadership while the Jeffersonian Republicans leaned toward legislative supremacy. Later on, the Jacksonian Democrats championed vigorous Presidents as "tribunes of the people," while the Whig party, which emerged in the 1830s in opposition to Andrew Jackson, insisted on Congressional dominance. For years the Republican party, which took shape in the 1850s, espoused the Whig view, although its first President, Abraham Lincoln, was, like Jackson, a strong President.

Henry Clay, the great Whig leader, was a zealous champion of legislative supremacy and led the first great Congressional assault on Presidential power. In a three-day speech in the Senate attacking Andrew Jackson, commencing on December 26, 1833, the eloquent Kentuckian, outraged by the President's financial policies, began ominously: "We are in the midst of a revolution hitherto bloodless, but rapidly tending toward a total change of the pure republican character of the government and to the concentration of all power in the hands of one man." He ended his blast just as ominously: "We behold the usual incidents of approaching tyranny. . . . People . . . no longer dare to speak in the fearless tones of manly freedom, but in the cautious whispers of trembling slaves. The premonitory symptoms of despotism are upon us, and if Congress do [*sic*] not apply an instantaneous and effective remedy, the fatal collapse will soon come on and we shall die, base, mean and abject slaves—the scorn and contempt of mankind—unpitied, unwept, unmourned." In between preface and peroration, Clay lambasted President Jackson for usurping authority, violating the Constitution, consulting only his own will in regard to the great public issues, and defying the national legislature. And at the end of his speech he persuaded the Senate to pass resolutions censuring Jackson— the only President ever to be so censured—for his arbitrary behavior.[5]

Jackson was furious at the Senate's action and he angrily hurled a "SOLEMN PROTEST" back at the Senators who supported the censure, defending himself as the "direct representative of the American people," and excoriating the condemnatory resolutions as flagrantly unconstitutional. Clay responded by making another fiery speech calling Jackson a "conqueror" and a "dictator," and then, backed by Daniel Webster and John C. Calhoun, sponsored new resolutions condemning the President's protest and refusing to enter it in the Senate's journal. Jackson did, of course, have friends in the Senate; and his most vocal champion, Missouri's Thomas Hart Benton, after repeated efforts, finally succeeded in mustering enough votes to expunge the censure from the Senate record just before Jackson left office. "The Senate," lamented Clay after Benton's victory, "is no longer a place for any decent man." Jackson, for his part, later said that his one regret in life was that he hadn't gotten around to hanging Clay and shooting Calhoun.[6]

After Jackson, Congress came into its own again, particularly when the Whigs were running things, but the Civil War tipped the balance of power back to the executive branch of government once more. After the firing on Fort Sumter in April 1961, Abraham Lincoln acted on his own: ordered a blockade of the South, enlarged the army and navy, called for volunteers, and authorized military commanders to suspend the writ of habeas corpus to deal with sedition. Congress endorsed most of the President's actions when it met in July, but also took measures of its own for expanding the armed forces and appropriating money to pay for the war. In December, moreover, the two houses voted to establish a Joint Committee on the Conduct of the War to keep tabs on Lincoln and his commanders. "I hold it to be our bounden duty," cried Maine's Republican Senator William Pitt Fessenden, "to keep an anxious watchful eye over all the executive agents who are carrying on the war at the direction of the people, whom we represent and whom we are bound to protect in relation to this matter."[7]

Lincoln more than held his own in clashes with Congress, but Andrew Johnson, his successor, failed miserably. After a brief honeymoon between the new President and Congress, the two became embroiled in a bitter dispute over Reconstruction policies in the South after the war that ended in Johnson's impeachment by the House in February 1868 and his acquittal by only one vote in the Senate three months later. After Johnson, Congress was in the saddle most of the time for the next few decades. "The executive department of a republic like ours should be subordinate to the legislative department," insisted Ohio's influential Republican Senator John Sherman. "The President should obey and enforce laws, leaving to the people the duty of correcting any errors committed by their representatives in Congress."[8] Sherman's was the prevailing Republican view during the Gilded Age, and until Woodrow Wilson most Presidents (Theodore Roosevelt was an exception) accepted it in the main. The Senate was particularly proud of itself during this period. "The most eminent Senators . . . ," observed Massachusetts Republican Senator George F. Hoar, "would have received as a personal affront a private message from the White House expressing a desire that they should adopt any course in the discharge of their legislative duties that they did not approve. If they visited the White House, it was to give, not receive advice."[9]

It was not possible, of course, for the energetic Theodore Roosevelt to accept a passive role for himself when he became President in 1901, but he worked hard to stay on good terms with Congress while he was in office and succeeded in achieving several legislative victories only by careful and continual consultation with Republican leaders in both houses. Like T.R., Woodrow Wilson had a legislative agenda of his own; and like his Republican predecessor he was willing to work closely with leaders of his party in both houses to ensure its victory. "The President," Wilson told an Ohio Congressman, "must be Prime Minister, as much concerned with the guidance of legislation as with just and orderly execution of the law."[10] Wilson did plenty of guiding; but with the entry of the United States into the First World War in 1917 he soon became the nation's supreme director as well as chief guide. As the nation mobilized for war there was a major shift in power to the executive branch of government going far beyond that achieved during the Civil War.

With the coming of peace, there was an inevitable reaction against the Presidential domination produced by the war. Congressional Republicans, who had won control of both houses in 1918, were particularly disgruntled. A President like Lincoln—or even T.R.—might have been able to deal successfully with a Congress eager to reassert itself after the war, but Wilson, like Johnson before him, was too proud and stubborn to try. The result was that in his clash with Senate Republicans, led by Massachusetts' supercilious Henry Cabot Lodge, over ratification of the Versailles Treaty (containing his beloved League of Nations), Wilson went down to inglorious defeat. With the election of Warren G. Harding in 1920, there was a return to the kind of legislative ascendancy favored by Republican conservatives ever since the Civil War.

The Great Depression opened a new era in the relations between Congress and the President. Even Herbert Hoover, a firm believer in "legislative independence," abandoned his hands-off policy toward the end of his administration; but he never went as far as Congressional leaders demanded in trying to cope with the economic crisis, and his relations with Congress after 1930 were extremely strained.[11] With Franklin D. Roosevelt, who took office in 1933, it was quite otherwise; his call for "action, and action now" to pull the nation out of the doldrums struck just the right chord, and for a time his relations with Congress were almost idyllic. "The President," FDR insisted, "is not merely an administrative office. That is the least of it. . . . It is pre-eminently a place of moral leadership."[12] It was a place of legislative leadership, too, for FDR. The Congress was eager to follow his lead when he called for a special session a few days after taking his oath of office.

From March 9 until June 16—one hundred frenetic days—the 73rd Congress enacted fifteen major pieces of legislation recommended by the Roosevelt administration covering just about every aspect of the American economy and laying the foundations for the development of the welfare state. Like T.R. and Wilson before him, FDR worked closely with Congressional leaders to win acceptance for his New Deal measures. He invited Congressional leaders of both parties to the White House to go over his proposals with them; he sent members of his administration to Capitol Hill to explain his recommendations before the appropriate committees and answer questions; and he spent many hours on the telephone discussing his proposals with individual members of both houses. He mustered the support of the public, too, for his New Deal policies, at press conferences and in his "fireside chats" with the American people over the radio. And, as a host of new Federal agencies sprang into existence to administer the new programs authorized by Congress, he dangled the lure of patronage before members of Congress who might be inclined to step out of line. "When the *Congressional Record* goes to President Roosevelt's desk in the morning," an old-timer told a freshman Congressman, "he will look over the roll call we are about to take and I warn you new Democrats to be careful where your names are found."[13]

The period of the Hundred Days was unprecedented in American history. Never before had there been such an outpouring of important legislation in such a short space of time; and never before such harmony between President and Congress. "The Roosevelt 'honeymoon' lasted till almost the very end of the Congressional session," observed the *Literary Digest* on June 17. "President and Congress displayed what seemed a marvelous exhibition of teamwork." Even arch-conservative Bertrand H. Snell of New York, the Minority Floor Leader, went along for a time with the New Deal President. "The house is burning down," he exclaimed, "and the President of the United States says this is the way to put out the fire!"[14]

But the lovefest came to an end and the "law of ebb and flow" resumed its natural course. By 1935, conservative Democrats in Congress, mainly from the South, were beginning to team up with Republican conservatives to block further New Deal reforms. Worse still for FDR: to the delight of conservatives in both parties, the U.S. Supreme Court began invalidating some of the New Deal's most ambitious measures. FDR complained that the Court was trying to take the country back to the "horse and buggy" age, and in February 1937 he finally came up with a plan for enlarging membership on the Court that would enable him to make appointments of his own choosing.[15] But when he outlined his plan to Democratic leaders at a White House meeting just before sending it to Congress, the reaction was decidedly lukewarm. Democratic Majority Leader Senator Joseph T. Robinson "flushed mahogany" while the President was speaking, and stared down at the table top, while House Speaker William B. Bankhead sat with a "pokerish expression" throughout. The others—Vice President John Nance Garner, House Majority Leader Sam Rayburn, and Hatton W. Sumners, chairman of the House Judiciary Committee—sat in silence as FDR read them his proposed legislation. "I loaded my automobile with Senators and Representatives," Garner said later, "and took them back to the Capitol. We were all so stunned we hardly spoke." En route, Hatton Sumners exclaimed: "Boys, here's where I cash in!" A little later, when Roosevelt, citing inefficiency and overwork on the Court, tossed his plan into the legislative hopper, he found to his chagrin that Congressional liberals as well as conservatives were offended by his disingenuous way of justifying reform.[16]

With Montana Senator Burton K. Wheeler, a devoted New Dealer, leading the opposition in the Senate, it was soon clear that FDR's Court plan was headed for rejection. Reluctant to abandon his plan, Roosevelt checked with Vice President Garner. "How did you find the Court situation, Jack?" he asked. "Do you want it with the bark on or off?" cried Garner. "The tough way," said FDR gamely. "All right," said Garner. "You are beat. You haven't got the votes." At this point Roosevelt shelved his plan. But the following year he decided to "purge" the party of anti-New Deal Democrats up for re-election and he made a trip through the South and the West, endorsing candidates friendly to the New Deal and speaking against the anti-New Dealers. Again he met defeat; his attempt to "purge" the party of conservatives was, as Postmaster James Farley put it, "a bust." In November, not only did all of the Senatorial conservatives he campaigned against win comfortable victories at the polls; the Republicans also increased their strength in both houses. Roosevelt, declared North Carolina's conservative Senator Joseph W. Bailey contentedly, "is at the end of his row and Congress is in control."[17]

But Congress did not long remain in control. The outbreak of World War II in 1939 opened another era, and, as during the Civil War and the First World War, mobilization of the nation's resources for war quickly redressed the balance of power in the Federal Government in favor of the President. Even before Pearl Harbor, the measures Congress voted in preparation for entry into the war—huge military appropriations, lend-lease aid to Britain and Russia, conscription, the arming of American merchant vessels—placed vast powers in the hands of the executive branch. And the Japanese attack on Pearl Harbor on December 7, 1941, unified the nation as never before and brought the President for a time overwhelming support from Congressional conservatives as well as liberals for his war measures. Even Clare E. Hoffman, ultra-conservative Congressman from Michigan, suspended his attacks on the President, at least for the moment. "Out of the sky came a vicious assault by a skillful and determined enemy," he announced, "and ere it ended a representative of the Democratic Party, who was President, became *our* President."[18]

By 1943, however, FDR's second honeymoon with Congress was over, and after that there were major clashes between the President and Congress over price controls and tax measures that left bad feelings on both sides. There were also scores of Congressional committees keeping a wary watch on the multitudinous wartime agencies established by the Roosevelt administration during the war. One of the anti-New Dealers' favorites: the Special Committee to Investigate Acts of Executive Agencies beyond the Scope of their Authority, headed by conservative House Democrat Howard W. Smith of Virginia. Still, the most important Congressional committee which the war produced—the Special Committee to Investigate the National Defense Program, established in 1941 and headed by Missouri Senator Harry Truman—worked harmoniously with the President throughout the war, and before it finished its work of uncovering fraud, waste, and inefficiency in war industries succeeded in saving the taxpayers billions of dollars; it saved countless lives, too, by its exposure of defective weapons being supplied to the armed forces. In the spring of 1944 a poll of Washington correspondents picked Senator Truman as the man next to Roosevelt who had contributed the most to the nation's war effort.

Long before the war ended, postwar planners were beginning to take a look at the Pentagon, that massive five-sided structure housing the defense establishment which had been authorized by Congress in 1941 and completed in 1943. What should be done with the building, they asked, when the war was over? Some people thought it would be a handy place for storing government documents; others suggested turning it into a barracks or a veterans' hospital. One Republican, gazing critically at the gray limestone colossus, said he "could see no peacetime future for the Pentagon except as the making of 'magnificent ruins.'"[19]

But the Pentagon was not destined for ruins; nor did it become a barracks or a veterans' hospital. Instead, when World War II ended and the Cold War commenced between the United States and the Soviet Union, the stupendous structure in Arlington, Virginia, continued to be the head-quarters of the American military establishment and steadily grew in power, prestige, and purpose during the postwar years. The executive branch of government as a whole also continued to be powerful after the war, to the dismay of some Congressmen. As crisis succeeded crisis in the postwar world, it came gradually to be the major decision-maker for the American people. With Presidents (Republican as well as Democratic) taking the lead, the United States busily established bases around the world to "contain" Communism, entered into military alliances with nations in Europe, Asia, and the Middle East, and sent billions in financial aid to anti-Communist governments around the world. It also fought two major wars, both undeclared: Korea and Vietnam.

The Cold War, in short, ensured Presidential primacy. There was plenty of grumbling in Congress to be sure, and efforts from time to time to rein in the Chief Executive, but from the 1950s to the 1980s America's role as world policeman made the President the center of power in the American system. In 1973, Congressman Carl Vinson of Georgia ruefully described the part that Congress had come to play in all this: "that of a somewhat querulous but essentially kindly uncle who complains while furiously puffing on his pipe, but who finally, as everyone expects, gives in and hands over the allowance, grants the permission, or raises his hand in blessing, and then returns to his rocking chair for another year of somnolence broken only by an occasional anxious glance down the avenue and a muttered doubt as to whether he has done the right thing."[20]

☆ ☆ ☆

Congressman Randolph and President Adams

In his first major speech in the House, Virginia's declamatory John Randolph took out after the army. He not only called large standing armies a menace to liberty; he also made fun of soldiers as parasites and free-loaders. "The military parade which meets the eye in almost every direction," he said, "excites the gall of our citizens; they feel a just indignation at the sight of loungers who live upon the public, who consume the fruits of their honest industry under the pretext of protecting them from a foreign yoke. They put no confidence, Sir, in the protection of a handful of ragamuffins; they know that, when danger comes, they must meet it and they only ask arms at your hands."

A night or two later, when Randolph was in a theater, two officers, offended by his cracks at the army, deliberately bumped into him as he sat down, made loud remarks about him during the performance, pushed and shoved him when he left the theater after the performance, and even tried to yank his collar off. In an extremely high and mighty dudgeon, Randolph wrote a letter to President Adams complaining about the officers' behavior. But Adams was a Federalist, so Randolph, a Jeffersonian Republican, omitted the customary deference—"To His Excellency" and "Your Most Humble and Obedient Servant"—which Adams expected, and simply addressed his letter "To the President of the United States," and signed it, "With Respect, Your Fellow-Citizen."

It was now Adams' turn to be offended. He assembled his Cabinet, announced that the dignity of his office had been injured, and, with the approval of his associates, sent Randolph's letter to Congress, together with a special message of his own, calling attention to the young Virginian's "matter and style." Congress leaped eagerly into the fray. The Federalist majority established a special committee to look into the matter, held an investigation, and recommended censure. But the Republicans vehemently defended Randolph, denounced Adams, and succeeded in defeating a resolution of censure. Finally, after hours of squabbling, the House ended by sending the President a polite response to his special message, and then dropped the subject.

The Randolph-Adams fracas, reported at length in the press, made the freshman Congressman famous. The Federalists castigated him for ridiculing the army, insulting the President, and trampling on the "ancient, respectable, and urbane usages" of America. But the Republicans hailed him as "a tribune of the people," who was the victim of an oppressive administration bent on gagging Congress the way it was gagging the press with its Alien and Sedition Acts. Randolph seems to have enjoyed the storm he had set in motion. He continued, indeed increased, his hyperbolic way of expressing himself on the issues before Congress.[21]

Unconstitutional

During the Senate debate on Jay's Treaty in 1795, Virginia's George Walton (one of the signers of the Declaration of Independence in 1776), a good Federalist, asked an anti-Federalist Senator who was cursing the treaty why he was so opposed to it. The latter insisted that the treaty was unconstitutional. "Well, my friend," said Walton, with some exasperation, "have you read it?" "No, sir," said the other Senator indignantly, "do you suppose I would read an unconstitutional document?"[22]

To the Victor

In January 1832, when President Jackson nominated his friend Martin Van Buren (who had just resigned as Secretary of State) to be minister to Britain, the latter's enemies in the Senate, fearing Jackson was building the New Yorker up to succeed him in the White House, denounced him as an unscrupulous wheeler-dealer and charged that he had introduced New York's unsavory political methods into national politics. One after another, they took to the floor to blister him: Henry Clay, Daniel Webster, and Robert Hayne (Vice President Calhoun's spokesman). But Van Buren's fellow New Yorker, William L. Marcy, came to his—and New York's—defense. "I know, sir," he said, "that it is the habit of some gentlemen to talk with censure or reproach of the politics of New York. Like other States, we have contests, and, as a necessary consequence, triumphs and defeats." But New York politicians, he went on, were not as fastidious as politicians in other states. "They boldly preach what they practice," he said. "When they are contending for victory they avow their intention of enjoying the fruits of it. If they are defeated, they expect to retire from office. If they are successful, they claim, as a matter of right, the advantages of success." Then he uttered the words that became famous: "They see nothing wrong in the rule, that to the victor belong the spoils of the enemy."

The vote on Van Buren's nomination was tied, 23 yeas, 23 nays, in the Senate. Then came the moment Vice President John C. Calhoun had been eagerly anticipating. Ambitious for the Presidency himself, and a bitter foe of both Jackson and Van Buren, he could hardly wait to act. "On the question of the nomination of Martin Van Buren," he announced triumphantly, "the Chair votes Nay!" Afterward, he told a friend in the Senate: "It will kill him, sir, kill him dead. He will never kick sir, never kick." But Senator Thomas Hart Benton, who overheard Calhoun's remark, thought differently. To Alabama Senator Gabriel Moore, who had voted against Van Buren, Benton declared: "You have broken a Minister and elected a Vice President." "How so?" asked Moore. "The people will see nothing in it but a combination of rivals against a competitor," explained Benton. "They will pull them all down and set Van Buren up." "Good God!" cried Moore. "Why didn't you tell me that before I voted, and I would have voted the other way."

Benton's prediction was correct. When Jackson sought a second term later that year, he picked Van Buren as his running mate. And in 1836, Vice President Van Buren ran on his own, with Jackson's hearty support, and became the eighth President.[23]

Knights of the Black Lines

Henry Clay loathed President Jackson, and Thomas Hart Benton adored him. When Jackson began withholding government funds from the Bank of the United States and placing them in state banks, Clay was so outraged that he proposed censuring him; and, after a three months' debate, succeeded in mustering enough votes in the Senate to pass a resolution reprimanding the President for having "assumed upon himself authority and power not conferred by the Constitution and laws, but in derogation of both." When the resolution passed in March 1834, Benton vowed he would see to it that the slur on Jackson was stricken from the record.

Benton's—and Jackson's—great day didn't come until almost three years later. On December 26, 1836, the third anniversary of the day Clay introduced his censure resolution in the Senate, Benton, for the fourth time, proposed a resolution on Jackson's behalf. He made it clear he wouldn't be satisfied with "rescinding" or "abrogating" the Clay resolution. The resolution must be "expunged," he insisted, and that meant having the Secretary of the Senate bring the manuscript *Journal* of the Senate's 1833–34 session into the Senate chamber and, in the presence of the Senators, actually cross out the offending passage.

Benton's resolution produced a lively debate when called up in January 1837. The Great Triumvirate—Clay, Webster, and Calhoun—opposed it to a man. Calhoun insisted "the measure proposed is a violation of the Constitution"; Clay inveighed against executive tyranny and efforts to "blot, deface and mutilate the records of the country"; and Webster declared that tampering with the *Journal* would be "a ruthless violation of a sacred instrument." But when Webster finished speaking, close to midnight, January 16, he knew Benton had the votes. "There was a pause, a dead silence, and an intense feeling," Benton remembered, when Webster resumed his seat, and then came calls for the question. To Benton's glee, his resolution passed by a vote of 23 to 19. "Nothing remains, sir, but to execute the order of the Senate," he exulted. "I move that it be done forthwith."

When the clerk of the Senate brought the *Journal* in and put it on the desk in front of the Senate chamber, three angry men—Clay, Calhoun, and Webster—stalked out in protest, followed by most of the other anti-expungers. There were hisses, groans, and catcalls in the gallery above Benton, too, and Alabama's William R. King, then in the chair, ordered the galleries cleared. "Let the ruffians who have made the distur-bance . . . be punished," cried Benton in a fury; "let them be appre-hended." Then, looking up, he added: "Here is one just above me, that may be easily identified—the bank ruffian!" King then revoked his order, the sergeant-at-arms arrested the ringleader of the protesters, who turned out to be a lawyer from Cleveland, and brought him to the bar of the Senate.

But Benton had calmed down by then, and he agreed to drop charges against the "bank ruffian."

The expunction ceremony now proceeded with due solemnity. The clerk opened the *Journal* to the page containing Clay's resolution of censure, drew an oblong square of heavy black lines around it, and then wrote vertically across it: "Expunged by order of the Senate, this 16th day of January 1837." Two nights later Benton and some of the other expungers—their critics called them "Knights of the Black Lines"—joined Jackson at the White House and presented him with the expunging pen.[24]

Webster's Impartiality

When Senator Webster argued a case before the Supreme Court in 1836, he began by noting the vast changes that had taken place on the Court since he first appeared as a counsel there. "No one of the judges who were here then, remains," he observed. Then he added: "It has been my duty [as a Senator] to pass upon the question of the confirmation of every member of the Bench; and I may say that I treated your Honors with entire impartiality, for I voted against every one of you!"[25]

Bishop

In February 1861, soon after Abraham Lincoln arrived in Washington for his inauguration, Massachusetts Senator Charles Sumner called on him at Willard's Hotel. Though he was impressed by the President-elect's "flashes of thought and bursts of illuminating expression which struck him as extraordinary," he was also disconcerted by Lincoln's informality and droll way of putting things. When Lincoln at one point suggested measuring backs to see who was taller, the fastidious Sumner was taken aback. "Sumner," Lincoln recalled, "declined to stand up with me, back to back, to see which was the taller man, and made a fine speech about this being the time for uniting our fronts against the enemy and not our backs. But I guess he was afraid to measure, though he is a good piece of a man. I have never had much to do with Bishops where I live, but, do you know, Sumner is my idea of a Bishop."[26]

Law of Nations

When the Civil War began, Pennsylvania Congressman Thaddeus Stevens took Lincoln to task for declaring a blockade of the seceded states, pointing out that inasmuch as a nation did not blockade its own ports, it was a tacit acknowledgment of the independence of the Southern states to blockade them. "Yes," said Lincoln thoughtfully, "that's a fact. I see the point now, but I don't know anything about the Law of Nations and I thought it was all right." The "Old Commoner," as Stevens was called, returned dryly that "as a lawyer, Mr. Lincoln, I should have supposed you would have seen the difficulty at once." "Well," drawled Lincoln, "I'm a good enough lawyer in a western law court, I suppose, but we don't practice the Law of Nations up there, and I supposed [Secretary of State William T.] Seward knew all about it, and I left it to him. But it is done now and can't be helped. So we must get along as best we can."[27]

Red Hot Stove

When Lincoln appointed Simon Cameron, Pennslyvania political boss, to head the War Department, Thaddeus Stevens was upset. He regarded Cameron as "the most consummate scoundrel in Pennsylvania," and went around to tell Lincoln so. "Why, Mr. Stevens," protested Lincoln, "you don't think that Cameron would steal?" "Well, Mr. President," said Stevens, "I don't think he would steal a red-hot stove."

Lincoln was so amused by Stevens' remark that he passed it on to his associates and eventually it reached Cameron, who angrily demanded a retraction. Stevens at once sought out Lincoln and asked him why he had repeated his comment. "I thought it was a good joke and I didn't think it would make him mad," said Lincoln defensively. "Well, he is very mad and made me promise to retract," said Stevens. "I will do so now. I believe I told you that I didn't think he would steal a red-hot stove. I now take that back!" Lincoln was again amused, but apparently kept Stevens' latest remark to himself.

Because of corruption in the awarding of army contracts, Cameron was eventually dropped from the Cabinet. But when Lincoln decided to send him off to Russia as ambassador, Stevens exclaimed: "Send word to the Czar to bring in his things of nights!"[28]

Call Again

Hordes of officer-seekers, including members of Congress trying to help out friends and relatives, descended on Lincoln after he became President, and since the demand for jobs far exceeded the supply, he had to develop pleasant ways of turning down their requests without turning them against him. At length he devised a disarming technique: he simply told them amusing stories and then ushered them out of his office without actually refusing their requests. One Congressman went to the White House four days in a row waiting for a chance to speak to the President. When he finally got to see him, he bluntly told him what he wanted. "Do you know," said Lincoln amiably, "I heard a good thing yesterday about the difference between the Amsterdam Dutchman and any other 'dam' Dutchman." The

Congressman listened impatiently as Lincoln went on to tell him more stories. "He told me three," fumed the Congressman afterward, "and I didn't listen to a word he said. I was mad enough to knock the old fellow down." About the time Lincoln launched into another tale, Secretary of State William Seward walked in and said he had to confer with the President in private. Lincoln then politely invited the Congressman to call again. "Bother his impudence," raged the Congressman later. "To keep me listening to his jokes for two hours, and then ask me to call again!"[29]

Episcopalian

One morning the usually even-tempered Senator William Fessenden of Maine, angry about some unjust distribution of patronage in his state, let loose a flood of profanity on Lincoln. Lincoln listened patiently until Fessenden wound down and then said gently: "You are an Episcopalian, aren't you, Senator?" "Yes, sir, I belong to that church," returned Fessenden. "I thought so," said Lincoln. "You Episcopalians all swear alike. Seward is an Episcopalian. But Stanton is a Presbyterian. You ought to hear him swear!"[30]

Crucified

Before appointing a commissioner to the Indians, it was reported, Lincoln called on Senators Ben Wade and Daniel Vorhees for advice and explained what kind of man he wanted for the post. "Gentlemen," he said, "for an Indian commissioner, I want a pure-minded, moral, Christian man— frugal and self-sacrificing." "I think," said Vorhees, "that you won't find him." "Why not?" asked Lincoln. "Because, Mr. President," said Vorhees, "he was crucified about 1800 years ago."[31]

Only Six Weeks

Senator Charles Sumner was disappointed because President Lincoln didn't move more rapidly toward an emancipationist policy after the Civil War began, but he never lost confidence in the man who had declared that "if slavery is not wrong, nothing is wrong." Lincoln himself reassured Sumner by telling him: "Mr. Sumner, you are only six weeks ahead of me."[32]

Somebody

One day Ohio's Ben Wade marched down to the White House, shook his finger at President Lincoln, and cried: "You have to fire General McClellan." "Well, whom shall I hire to replace him?" Lincoln wanted to know.

"Anybody," said Senator Wade firmly. "I cannot fight a war with anybody," said Lincoln; "I must have somebody."[33]

Them Three Fellers

One Sunday, during the gloomy period of 1862, Missouri Senator John B. Henderson called on the President and found him in a melancholy mood. "They are making every effort, Henderson," said Lincoln, "to induce me to issue a Proclamation of Emancipation. Sumner and Wilson and Stevens are constantly urging me, but I don't think it best now; do *you* think so, Henderson?" Henderson said he thought Lincoln was right; the time wasn't quite right for it yet, and the President should wait for a better time before issuing it. "Just what I think," sighed Lincoln, "but they are constantly coming and urging me, sometimes alone, sometimes in couples, and sometimes *all three together,* but constantly pressing me."

At this point Lincoln got up, walked across the room, and looked out of the window; sure enough, Senators Sumner and Wilson and Representative Stevens were approaching the Executive Mansion. Lincoln called Henderson to the window and pointed to the three approaching figures. "Henderson," he said, "did you ever attend an old field school?" When Henderson said he had, Lincoln went on: "So did I; what little education I ever got in early life was in that way. I attended an old field school in Indiana, where our only reading-book was the Bible. One day we were standing up reading the account of the three Hebrew children in the fiery furnace. A little tow-headed fellow who stood beside me had the verse with the unpronounceable names; he mangled up Shadrach and Meshach woefully, and finally went all to pieces on Abednego. Smarting under the blows which, in accordance with the old-time custom, promptly followed his delinquency, the little fellow sobbed aloud. The reading, however, went round, each boy in the class reading his verse in turn. The sobbing at length ceased, and the tow-headed boy gazed intently upon the verses ahead. Suddenly he gave a pitiful yell, at which the schoolmaster demanded, 'What is the matter with you now?' 'Look there,' said the boy, pointing to the next verse, 'there comes them same damn three fellers again!'"[34]

Feasting and Dancing

To show that the Federal Government was still a going concern and to boost Northern morale the Lincolns held a ball in the White House in 1862, but received a great deal of criticism from Unionists who regarded it as a wasteful frivolity in time of crisis. Over eighty notes of regret came to Mrs. Lincoln, who sent out the invitations, but Radical Republican Senator Ben Wade's reaction was the most censorious. He returned the invitation with the note: "Are the President and Mrs. Lincoln aware that there is a civil war? If they are not, Mr. and Mrs. Wade are, and for that reason decline to participate in feasting and dancing."[35]

Do as Romans Do

One day Lincoln was chatting with a minor official named John Eaton, with his leg draped over the arm of his chair, when suddenly the doorman let someone in. The end of a cane, with the handle at right angles to the stick, appeared in the doorway, and Lincoln knew at once who was entering: his dignified friend Senator Sumner. "As quick as thought," observed Eaton, "Mr. Lincoln had untangled himself and was upon his feet, returning with the utmost dignity the courteous bow with which Mr. Sumner greeted him." Lincoln discussed a consular appointment with Sumner for a few minutes and then the latter left with a pleasant good-bye. As soon as the door closed, Lincoln called out: "Come up, Eaton. When with the Romans, we must do as the Romans do!"[36]

Distance

One day Ohio Senator Ben Wade stormed over to the White House to demand the firing of General Grant and exploded when Lincoln resisted his demand. "You are the father of every military blunder that has been made during this war," he raged. "This government is on the road to hell, sir, by the reason of your obstinacy, and you are not a mile from there this minute!" "Senator," said Lincoln gently, "that is just about the distance from here to the Capitol, is it not?"[37]

Nevada

In 1864, when Lincoln decided to press for the adoption of a Constitutional amendment abolishing slavery, he wasn't sure enough states would ratify it, so he hoped to persuade Congress to create a new state out of the Nevada Territory which would support ratification. Unhappily for Lincoln, the legislation creating the state of Nevada ran into trouble and the passage of the bill was in doubt. But Lincoln learned that three Congressmen were willing to vote for the bill in return for some favors, and he at once authorized his Assistant Secretary of the Navy, Charles A. Dana, to negotiate with them for their votes. "What do they want?" Dana asked Lincoln. "I don't know," said Lincoln. "It makes no difference. We must carry this vote or be compelled to raise another million men and fight, no one knows how long. It is a question of three votes or new armies. . . . Whatever promises you make, I will perform." Dana thereupon met with the three Congressmen and promised them, "on the oath of the President," that they would get the patronage jobs they wanted. With their votes the statehood bill passed and Nevada entered the Union and voted to ratify the Thirteenth Amendment, which, with the necessary three-quarters of the states ratifying it, became part of the Constitution in 1865. But only two of the three Congressmen received the patronage jobs promised them. The third hadn't received his by the time of Lincoln's assassination. The new President, Andrew Johnson, refused to honor the pledge. "I have observed in the course of my experience," said Johnson, "that such bargains tend to immorality."[38]

Self-Made

Pennsylvania Congressman Thaddeus Stevens despised President Johnson because of his conservative Reconstruction policy. When a friend, defending the President, pointed out that Johnson was a self-made man, Stevens smirked: "I never thought of it that way, but it does relieve God Almighty of a heavy responsibility!"[39]

Hoax

In a speech in the White House on February 22, 1866, President Johnson lashed out against the Congressional Committee on Reconstruction and denounced Radical Republicans like Thaddeus Stevens and Charles Sumner as traitors to the Constitution as nefarious as Jefferson Davis and the other Confederate leaders had been. The following month, when Stevens got up in the House to discuss Reconstruction, his colleagues expected a counterblast. But to their astonishment, Stevens announced that he had no feelings of ill will toward the President, but, in fact, respected him for his "integrity, patriotism, courage, and good intentions."

At this point, Iowa's Hiram Price interrupted (perhaps by prearrangement) to ask whether the "Thad Stevens" the President mentioned bitterly in his speech was the same "Thad Stevens" now eulogizing the President. Stevens responded that he was surprised the "learned gentleman" from Iowa should refer to the White House speech as if it were a "fact." There never was such a speech, he declared; it was all a hoax. The Copperheads made it up; they had been persecuting Johnson ever since the day he was inaugurated as Lincoln's Vice President in March 1865 and they were still gunning for him. When Johnson took his oath as Vice President on March 4, 1865, Stevens recalled, he appeared to be tipsy; and the *New York World* (now a warm supporter of Johnson's Reconstruction policies) had denounced him as "an insolent and drunken brute" and lamented that there was "only one frail life between this clownish drunkard and the presidency." Stevens then called the 1865 *World* editorial a slander, charged that Johnson's enemies were still trying to discredit him by pretending he made another unseemly public appearance on February 22, and insisted that he, personally, was shocked by the latest "mendacious lie" they were circulating about him and said he hoped his "friendly relations" with the President would continue. Stevens' irony vastly amused the lawmakers.[40]

Back in the Senate

Andrew Johnson was the only President ever to serve in the Senate after leaving the White House. He first entered the Senate in 1857, resigned in 1862 to accept Lincoln's appointment as "War Governor" of Tennessee, became Vice President in March 1865, and the following month became President upon Lincoln's assassination. From almost the beginning he clashed violently with the Radical Republicans in Congress over Reconstruction policies, and in February 1868 the House impeached him and when the Senate tried him in May for "high crimes and misdemeanors" he escaped conviction by only one vote.

Soon after leaving the White House, Johnson campaigned for election to the Senate but was defeated in a close vote in the Tennessee legislature. In 1872 he met defeat again when he ran for election as Congressman-at-large. But in January 1875 the Tennessee legislature elected him to the Senate on the 55th ballot. "We shall not be sorry to see him again in public life," declared the *New York Times*. "Whatever his faults as President may have been, at any rate he went out of the White House as poor as he entered it and that is something to say in these times." The *New York Herald* thought it was fortunate that Johnson had "lived to see his vindication. . . . It is now generally conceded that the imaginary misdemeanors of 1868 . . . were in fact official merits." Before heading for Washington, Johnson told a crowd of his admirers: "I will go to the Senate with no personal hostility toward anyone, but with a large affection for, and a more increased devotion to, the ancient landmarks."[41]

Just before noon on March 6, 1875, Johnson appeared in the Senate chamber to take his oath of office along with two other Senators-elect. It was a snowy day, but people had crowded into the galleries to see the former President. George F. Edmunds of Vermont (who had voted for conviction in 1868) was speaking when Johnson walked in, but he stopped when he saw Johnson, sat down abruptly, and knocked over some books as he did so. Several other Senators who had also voted to convict looked the other way or pretended to be busy with papers at their desks. But the Vice President, Henry Wilson of Massachusetts, another former Johnson foe, stood up when Johnson entered the chamber and so did several other Senators. Oliver P. Morton felt particularly embarrassed; he had supported Johnson at first and then changed his mind and voted to convict. But Johnson offered his hand, and Morton gratefully grasped it. About this time the clerk began calling the roll. "Andrew Johnson," he called. "Present," responded Johnson. His Tennessee colleague, Henry Cooper, then escorted him to the Vice President's chair where Wilson administered the oath while standing. When Johnson shook hands with Wilson afterward there was a burst of applause on the Senate floor and in the galleries. "I miss my old friends," Johnson said, tears in his eyes, afterward, turning to Kentucky's Thomas McCreery. "All are gone, but yourself, Senator McCreery." Then he walked over to his desk, piled high with flowers, and a moment later a page handed him a bouquet. To avoid further demonstrations he retired to the cloakroom where he was quickly surrounded by Senators offering congratulations.[42]

After Johnson returned to his hotel, a *New York Tribune* reporter dropped by for an interview. "Will you not in your new position have an opportunity to pay off some old scores?" he asked. "I have no wrongs to redress but my country's," Johnson told him. When another visitor remarked that Johnson's lodgings were not as elegant as those he had once occupied farther up the avenue, Johnson smiled. "No," he said, "but they are more comfortable."[43]

Johnson made only one speech in the Senate. On March 22 he spoke at length in criticism of the reconstruction policies of the Grant administration, particularly in Louisiana. Two days later the Senate adjourned. By the time it met again in December Johnson was no more. He had died of a stroke in July at sixty-eight.

Grant and Sumner

President Grant loathed Senator Charles Sumner. "The reason Sumner doesn't believe in the Bible," he once said bitterly, "is because he didn't write it himself." He never forgave Sumner for thwarting his plans for annexing Santo Domingo, and he got even by persuading Senate Republican leaders to remove Sumner from his post as chairman of the Senate Foreign Relations Committee. One day Massachusetts Senator George F. Hoar was taking a walk with the President and they happened to pass Sumner's house. To Hoar's astonishment Grant stopped, shook his fist, and snarled: "The man who lives up there has abused me in a way I have never suffered from any other man living!"

Sumner reciprocated the President's disesteem. He continued denouncing him in Senate speeches, and at home he often walked his guests to the door expressing his disapproval of Grant so vehemently that they were afraid his voice could be heard all the way to the White House.[44]

His Fraudulency

The 1876 election ended inconclusively. The Democratic candidate, Samuel J. Tilden, won more popular votes than Rutherford B. Hayes, but the electoral count was in dispute, and it took an Electoral Commission, set up by Congress in December, to settle the contest after weeks of wrangling. Voting along party lines, the Commission (five Senators, five Representatives, and five Supreme Court justices) awarded all twenty of the disputed votes to Hayes, and on March 2, 1877, the President of the Senate announced that Hayes had been elected President by one vote. Not everyone was convinced. Many Democrats and even some Republicans questioned the fairness of the Commission's findings. Republican Senator Roscoe Conkling of New York (who liked Tilden and distrusted Hayes) privately referred to Hayes as "Ruther-fraud B. Hayes" and "His *Fraudulency*." He knew an enemy when he saw one; soon after the inauguration Hayes began his fight against the Conkling machine in New York.[45]

Great Man

Alabama Senator James L. Pugh waited a long time for President Grover Cleveland to act on his recommendations for some appointments in his state, but finally gave up, decided the President had rejected his slate, and began denouncing him in bitter terms. Cleveland was no Democrat, he said, but an enemy of the party, and his policies were wrecking it. "He is an ingrate," he once cried, banging his fist on the table and rattling the spoons and glasses. One day, when he was delivering a tirade against the President in the Senate, his good friend Missouri Senator George Vest entered the Chamber holding a newspaper and tried to interrupt the flow of invective. "Pugh," he said finally, when the Alabaman paused for breath, "I see here in the evening paper the announcement of some appointments down in Alabama. Did you have anything to do with recommending them?" Pugh took the paper, adjusted his glasses, read the list over, and then resumed his speech. "Well, gentlemen, as I was saying, Grover Cleveland is a great man and a great President; no criticism can harm him. He is a Democrat of the type of Andrew Jackson, and I stand by him!"[46]

Between Friends

When New York Congressman Timothy ("Tim") Campbell, a Tammany man, asked President Cleveland to sign a pension bill he was sponsoring, the President said it was unconstitutional. Campbell threw his arms around the President. "What's the Constitution between friends?" he cried.[47]

Horse Thieves

A prominent Senator from the West called on President Cleveland one day to urge him to make appointments faster; he wasn't satisfied, he said, with the speed at which the President was removing Republican officeholders. Cleveland reflected a moment; then he recalled that a year before he had appointed a man upon recommendation of the Senator who turned out to have been convicted of stealing horses. "You mean," said Cleveland, "you want me to appoint two horse thieves instead of one?"[48]

Foreigner

When President William McKinley decided to nominate Joseph H. Choate as ambassador to Britain and Horace Porter as ambassador to France, he thought he had better get in touch with Senator Tom Platt first, for he knew Choate and Porter had been fighting Platt in New York politics for years and he was afraid Platt might block confirmation of the two men in the Senate. "Platt," he said, in a conference with the New York boss in the White House, "two men in New York whom you do not like politically and who do not like you are candidates for important foreign posts. I would like to have your consent to their nomination." "Who are they?" asked Platt. "Choate and Porter," said McKinley. "Mr. President," said Platt at once, "nominate them quick, and the 'foreigner' you send them, the better!"[49]

The Brownsville Episode: Foraker vs. T.R.

Late one night in August 1906 some armed men went on a shooting spree in Brownsville, Texas, where a battalion of black soldiers was stationed, and ended by killing one man and wounding another. Some witnesses blamed the soldiers, but a series of investigations, military and civilian, failed to establish the identity of the rioters. In October, however, President Roosevelt sent the soldiers an ultimatum: either produce the guilty men or face discharge "without honor." When the soldiers protested their innocence, T.R. had them all cashiered from the army without any further hearings. In the Senate, though, Ohio's conservative Republican Senator, Joseph B. Foraker, persuaded the Senate Committee on Military Affairs to look into the matter and he was soon convinced that the President had acted unjustly.

While Foraker and T.R. were feuding, the two men appeared at a meeting of the Gridiron Club in Washington. In due course the toastmaster called on the President for a speech and T.R. spoke about thirty minutes, first, about railroad-rate regulation (over which he and Foraker were quarreling) and then about the Brownsville affair. Not only did Roosevelt defend his action in discharging the troops; he also announced that he would tolerate no interference from anybody in the discharge of his duties. As he talked, the room became tense; and when he sat down, the toastmaster arose and exclaimed: "Now is the time for bloody sarcasm. I introduce Senator Foraker."

Foraker was white with fury when he got up to address the crowd. In the strongest language possible, he justified his opposition to Roosevelt's railroad-rate bill, and then went on to defend the Brownsville troops and to denounce the President's conduct as illegal, unconstitutional, and unjustifiable. "This is the only place I am on the same plane with the President," he shouted. "If I go to the White House he has the drop on me. If I make a speech in the Senate he cannot answer it; but I wish it distinctly understood that I am free born, white, over thirty years of age, and the people of Ohio have honored me many times with high positions and sent me to the Senate twice. I did not come to the Senate to take orders from anybody, either at this end of the line or the other. Whenever I fall so low that I cannot express my opinion on a great question freely, and without reservation or mental evasion, I will resign and leave my place to some man who has the courage to discharge his duties."

Foraker spoke about twenty minutes and all the while he was talking the President gritted his teeth, clenched his fist, shook his head, and muttered: "This is not so; I am going to answer that; that is not true; I will not stand for it." Three or four times he even started to get up, but people sitting by him kept him from interrupting the Senator. The minute Foraker sat down, T.R. jumped up and belligerently defended the action he took against the Brownsville soldiers. "Some of those men were bloody butchers; they ought to be hung," he cried. "The only reason that I didn't have them hung was because I couldn't find which ones of them did the shooting. None of the battalion would testify against them, and I ordered the whole battalion discharged without honor. It is my business and the business of nobody else. It is not the business of Congress. It is not the business of the House. It is not the business of the Senate. All the talk on that subject is academic. If they pass a resolution to reinstate these men I will veto it; if they pass it over my veto, I will pay no attention to it. I welcome impeachment!"

When T.R. finished his tirade, the toastmaster caught sight of Speaker Joe Cannon and, hoping to relieve the tension, called on him to make a few remarks. "What in hell can I say about this mess?" Cannon muttered; but he put down his cigar, got up, decided to minimize the whole business, and started in. "People pay too much attention to individuals anyhow," he said. "If the earth were to yawn here and now and swallow this hotel, with the Vice President, members of the Cabinet, members of the Supreme Court, distinguished diplomats, Senators, and Representatives, railroad presidents from all parts of the country—well, tomorrow the newspapers would come out and say that a great calamity had befallen the nation, appropriate exercises would be held in many places and in the residential cities of all those so unfortunately lost; and then the ranks would again fill up, people everywhere would be chosen to take our places right off, the procession would move forward, and in two weeks, well, there wouldn't be anybody give a God-damn." Indiana Senator James Watson was amused by Cannon's line of reasoning, but T.R. wasn't. Cannon's remarks, Watson observed, "made Roosevelt madder . . . than anything Foraker had said about him, for that anyone should imply that he would be forgotten in two weeks, or that nobody would care about his departure, certainly did not set well with him."

When Cannon finished, the toastmaster, sensing the situation, decided to adjourn the meeting early; and as a result the guests received only part of their dinner that night. Missouri Congressman Champ Clark, who witnessed the Foraker-Roosevelt confrontation, thought it was the only case on record in which a President of the United States had a debate with another public figure in the presence of a large audience. This was years before TV debates between presidential candidates.[50]

Foraker seems to have had the better of the argument that night. Senate investigations, which he sponsored, uncovered evidence making it quite likely that some Brownsville people did the shooting themselves that night and then blamed it on the black soldiers, whose presence at Fort Brown, on the outskirts of the town, they deeply resented. Even Texas Senator Thomas Bailey thought Foraker was on the right track. "I think your husband is absolutely in the right," he told Julia Foraker; "I admire him. I'd like to stand by him. But, Mrs. Foraker, I am a Democrat from Texas." But despite Foraker's findings, T.R.'s order stood; and 167 soldiers were discharged from the service, including six Medal of Honor winners and thirteen men holding certificates of merit for bravery. Only a few of the troopers were reinstated after T.R. left office.

In his memoirs, published in 1916, Senator Foraker devoted a long chapter to the "Brownsville Affray," as he called it, and reiterated his conclusion that the Roosevelt administration had punished innocent men at Fort Brown without even giving them a chance to defend themselves in a fair trial. "Neither do I doubt," he added, "if the Government had spent the one-tenth part to discover the men who shot up Brownsville that it did spend to convict its innocent soldiers of a crime they never committed, the truth would have been easily and long ago established."

Sixty-six years after the shoot-up in Brownsville the black troopers did receive justice of a sort. On September 22, 1972, the Secretary of the Army directed that their discharges be changed from "without honor" to "honorable."[51]

Economics Lesson

Soon after John Nance Garner got to Washington he faced one of the duties a Congressman must perform for his district if he wants to stay in office. The War Department was planning to abandon several cavalry posts, and the one in Brownsville, Texas, in Garner's district, was on the list. At the advice of an older Congressman, Garner went to the office of Secretary of War William Howard Taft to discuss the matter. A clerk there took his name, told him to sit down, and—after a long wait—opened the door of Taft's office, and told him he could stay only a few minutes. When Garner entered the room Secretary Taft, busy at his desk, asked what he wanted and Garner stated his business. Without looking up, Taft said he would make a note of it, and the secretary quickly ushered Garner out by the side door.

Ten days passed and Garner had heard nothing. Meanwhile letters and telegrams poured into his office from his district asking him to keep the cavalry at Brownsville. At length he decided to go to Taft's office again. This time, however, he stood outside the little door through which callers were dismissed, waited until it opened to let a man out, grabbed the door, and walked in. Before the secretary could say anything, Garner went up to Taft's desk, said he thought he was entitled to the courtesy of an answer to his inquiry, and was so vehement about it that Taft looked up in astonishment and cried: "Young man, what's the matter? Have a seat." As Garner took his seat, Taft swung his chair around and asked what he could do. "It's about the cavalry," said Garner. "What cavalry?" asked Taft. "The troopers at Brownsville." "What about them?" "You are planning on moving them," said Garner, "and you can't move them. It's a matter of economics to us." "Economics," cried Taft, "what has the cavalry to do with economics?" "Mr. Secretary, it's this way," said Garner. "We raise a lot of hay in my district. We've got a lot of stores and we have the prettiest girls in the United States. The cavalry buys the hay for its horses, spends its pay in the stores, marries our girls, gets out of the army and helps us develop the country, and then more replacements come and do the same thing. It *is* economics. It *is* economics." Taft chuckled. "I won't move the cavalry without talking to you," he promised, and Garner left.

A few days later President Roosevelt sent word he wanted to see Garner and the latter went to the White House with some misgivings. But T.R. was friendly enough. "Young man," he said, "what is this I hear you have been telling my Secretary of War?" "Nothing, sir," said Garner, "but giving him a little lesson in economics." "Now look here," cried the President, "the next time you are giving any lessons in economics, you see me first. Why, don't you know the word about what you told of the attractions has got around and half the army is applying for transfer to Brownsville?" They both laughed, and T.R. went on: "I called you here to tell you that the cavalry will still patrol your border."

Taft never forgot the Texas Congressman. Years later, when he became Chief Justice of the Supreme Court, he ran into Garner at the Capitol and cried: "Well, John, how is the cavalry getting along?"[52]

Wind

Once, when visiting President William Howard Taft, New York Senator Chauncey Depew stepped up to the President, put his hand on Taft's big frontal development, and said: "What are you going to name it when it comes, Mr. President?" "Well," said Taft, "if it is a boy, I'll call it William; if it's a girl, I'll call it Theodora; but if it turns out to be just wind, I'll call it Chauncey."[53]

Half Your Votes

In his bid for re-election in 1912, William Howard Taft was clobbered; he captured only eight electoral votes, four from Utah and four from Vermont. A Republican leader who was conferring with Taft soon after the debacle happened to look out of the window and saw Utah's Senator Reed Smoot coming up the White House steps. "Look, Mr. President," he cried, "here comes that old Mormon from Utah with half your votes in his vest pocket!"[54]

Speech from the Throne

On April 6, 1913, the White House announced that Woodrow Wilson, in one of his first actions as President, would appear before Congress on the 9th to deliver a message calling for revision of the tariff. The announcement startled Washington. No President had delivered messages in person before Congress since John Adams. Thomas Jefferson had discontinued the practice when he became President because he thought it resembled "the speech from the throne" in Britain; and his decision had set a precedent lasting 113 years.

The introduction of a resolution in the Senate on April 7 providing for a joint session to hear the President touched off a lively debate. While Republicans like Henry Cabot Lodge (a good Hamiltonian) had no objection, many Democrats, particularly from the South, thought Wilson's action might jeopardize the principle of "separation of powers" and expressed great concern. "I for one very much regret the President's course . . . ," declared Mississippi Senator John Sharp Williams, even though he was friendly to the President. "I am sorry to see revived the old

Federalist custom of speeches from the throne. . . . I regret all this cheap and tawdry imitation of English royalty." Fearing trouble, Vice President Thomas Marshall refrained from submitting the usual request for unanimous consent to immediate consideration of the resolution; instead, he declared it a question of high privilege on which unanimous consent was not required.

When Wilson entered the House chamber on April 9, the atmosphere was "distinctly tense," one of his Cabinet members noticed, but when he stepped up to the rostrum, everyone rose and applauded. "I am very glad indeed to have this opportunity to address the two Houses directly," Wilson declared at the outset, "and to verify for myself the impression that the President of the United States is a person, not a mere department of Government hailing Congress from some isolated island of jealous power, sending messages, not speaking naturally with his own voice—that he is a human being trying to co-operate with other human beings in a common service." When he finished his ten-minute talk, there was a burst of applause and he drove back to the White House with his wife in a state of euphoria. When Mrs. Wilson remarked that it was the kind of thing Theodore Roosevelt would have liked to do, "if only he had thought of it," Wilson laughed. "Yes," he said, "I think I put one over on Teddy." His action set a new precedent.[55]

Keeping up with Him

One of President Wilson's most ardent supporters was a Mississippi Congressman named Percy Edwards Quin; he stuck with the President even when he seemed to vacillate. One day Wisconsin's Henry Allen Cooper arose to accuse the President of inconsistencies. " 'Stand by the President,' they tell us!" cried Cooper. "I am willing to stand by him if he'll stay in one place long enough!" Quin was instantly on his feet. "By George," he cried, without waiting to be recognized by the chair, "why don't you get yourself a pair of roller skates and keep up with him like I do?"[56]

Lodge and Wilson

One evening, during the fight between President Wilson and the Senate over the Versailles Treaty (with its League of Nations), Indiana's James E. Watson cornered Henry Cabot Lodge, leader of the group demanding important revisions in the treaty, and said: "Senator, suppose that the President accepts the Treaty with your reservations. Then we are in the League, and once in, our reservations become purely fiction." "But, my dear James," said Lodge with a confident smile, "you do not take into consideration the hatred that Woodrow Wilson has for me personally.

Never under any set of circumstances in this world could he be induced to accept a treaty with Lodge reservations appended to it." "But," replied Watson, "that seems to me to be rather a slender thread on which to hang so great a cause." "A slender thread!" he answered. "Why, it is as strong as any cable with its strands wired and twisted together."

A little later Wilson sent for Watson to discuss the situation in the Senate and after exchanging stories, Watson told him: "Mr. President, there is just one way by which you can take the United States into the League of Nations by the ratification of this Treaty." "What way is that?" asked Wilson. "Accept it with the Lodge reservations," said Watson. "Accept the Treaty with the *Lodge* reservations!" snorted Wilson, fire in his eyes. "Yes, with the Lodge reservations," repeated Watson, "the ones that have been adopted. That is the only way in which this country will ever ally itself with the League of Nations." "Never!" cried Wilson vehemently. "Never! I'll never consent to adopt any policy with which that impossible name is so prominently identified." After he left the President Watson recalled Lodge's statement that Wilson's hatred of him was as strong as "a cable with its strands coiled and twisted together," and realized that Wilson would never compromise to get his treaty. When the treaty went down to defeat, Watson talked it over with Senator Borah and they "agreed that the hatred of Wilson for Lodge and of Lodge for Wilson kept the United States out of the League of Nations."[57]

Prayers for Wilson

In the fall of 1919, after President Wilson suffered a stroke, Republican Senator Albert Fall of New Mexico, a strong opponent of Wilson's League of Nations, called on the semi-paralyzed President and remarked, just before leaving, "I shall pray for you, Mr. President." "Pray don't, Senator," Wilson is supposed to have exclaimed. But there's another version of the encounter between the two political foes. "Well, Mr. President," Senator Fall is reported to have said, "we have all been praying for you." "Which way, Senator?" was Wilson's ironic response.[58]

Breakfast with Coolidge

Soon after becoming President Calvin Coolidge instituted the practice of inviting party leaders from both Houses to the White House for breakfast. He always invited at least one Democrat; the rules for White House expenses specified that the President could charge the cost of breakfast to "official entertaining" only if members of both parties were present.

During the breakfasts Coolidge never discussed anything of importance;

in fact, he usually said little or nothing during the matutinal gatherings. He munched his ham and eggs in silence, after some comments on the weather, and his guests did the same. After a while it became difficult to round up Congressmen for the 8:00 a.m. feasts. Senator Key Pittman's wife once called to say that a wheel had come off their car down the road and the Senator couldn't make it. Senator Hiram Johnson begged off because his barn had burned down. Senator Frederick Hale pleaded that his servant forgot to wake him. Ike Hoover, chief usher at the time, was amused by the excuses that piled up: sick wives, bad colds, a touch of the gout. Members of Congress, it appeared, were not in the best of health, at least at breakfast time.[59]

Entitled

New Hampshire Senator George H. Moses is said to have stormed into the White House one day to complain to President Coolidge that a man whom the Republicans were thinking of running for the Senate was "an out-and-out S.O.B." "That could be," Coolidge is supposed to have said mildly, "but there's a lot of these in the country, and I think they are entitled to representation in the Senate."[60]

Which Place?

When Calvin Coolidge ran for re-election in 1924, Republican leaders decided to nominate William E. Borah as Vice President to balance the ticket and keep Republican voters from supporting Republican Senator Robert M. LaFollette who was running for President as a Progressive that year. President Coolidge sent for Borah and asked him whether he was willing to accept a place on the ticket. "Which place, Mr. Coolidge?" Borah is supposed to have asked. In the end the Republicans chose Charles C. Dawes, former Budget Director, for second place.[61]

Northampton Viewpoint

One morning Michigan Senator James Couzens, a progressive Republican, bounded into President Coolidge's office with the morning paper in his hand and sputtered: "Mr. President, the paper says you are opposed to a raise in salary for postal employees. Did you say that?" When Coolidge nodded in the affirmative, Couzens exclaimed: "Do you mean to tell me that you think a man can bring up a family on $1700 a year?" "They do in Northampton," drawled Coolidge. "My father-in-law died recently. Left a nice competence, although he never earned more than $1500 a year." "That's the trouble with you, Mr. President," snorted Couzens, banging his fist on the desk. "You have a Northampton viewpoint, instead of a national viewpoint!" Coolidge, thoroughly angry, made it clear the interview was over and Couzens left the White House just as angry as the President.[62]

Borah's Group

In the 1920s and 1930s it was said that there were four distinct political factions in Congress: Republicans, Democrats, Progressives, and the ruggedly independent Republican, William E. Borah of Idaho. One day, after Borah had talked himself hoarse urging President Hoover to name Benjamin N. Cardozo to the U.S. Supreme Court, the President asked: "If I name Justice Cardozo, will it be satisfactory to your group?" "Since there is only one member in my group, Mr. President," said Borah with a smile, "I can assure you that it will be satisfactory." Hoover made the appointment in 1930.[63]

Biting the Enemy

Virginia's Senator Carter Glass once protested to President Hoover's Secretary of the Navy Charles Francis Adams because a young Virginian was refused admittance to the Navy on the ground that two of his teeth had failed to mature. "Good Lord, Mr. Secretary," he cried, "do you train the Navy to bite the enemy?" "That's what we will have to do, Senator," retorted Adams, "if you keep cutting our appropriations!"[64]

Appointment

Texas Congressman Maury Maverick's feistiness, even when dealing with the President, became the talk of the town. Once, when Maverick tried without success to get an appointment with Stephen Early, FDR's secretary, he simply wrote a sharp letter to the President: "I am having difficulty in reaching Mr. Early. Will you be so kind as to help me in making an appointment with him?" The following day Early called Maverick.[65]

Fair Trade

In the spring of 1934, Senator "Cotton Ed" Smith of South Carolina pigeonholed the nomination of Rexford Tugwell as Undersecretary of Agriculture but indicated he might support Tugwell if President Roosevelt made a couple of appointments in his state that he wanted. FDR agreed to the deal. Later he told Tugwell: "You will never know any more about it, I hope; but today I traded you for a couple of murderers!"[66]

Right Direction

In 1934 conservative Virginia Senator Carter Glass rode with President Roosevelt to a dedication ceremony in Roanoke. Smiling broadly, FDR said, "Carter, for once I have you going along with me." "Yes, Franklin," Glass shot back, "for once you are going in the right direction!" They were headed south.[67]

Prima Donnas

While the fight was raging over FDR's plan to enlarge the Supreme Court, a White House aide told Burton Wheeler, Senate opposition leader, "The President says you and a lot of others on 'the Hill' are prima donnas." "Of course we're prima donnas," laughed Wheeler. "That's the reason we're here. He wants to be the only prima donna but we're going to show him there are three branches of government and he can't be the only one!"[68]

Better Listen

Sam Rayburn once visited FDR, whom he greatly admired, on House business, and mentioned that the mail from his district revealed that his constituents were overwhelmingly opposed to the Court-packing bill. "Looky here, Mr. President!" he said sharply, when the President seemed bored. "By God, I'm talking to you. You'd better listen." FDR at once gave Rayburn his undivided attention.[69]

Courageous Stand

When FDR sought legislation enlarging the U.S. Supreme Court so he could appoint justices sympathetic to the New Deal philosophy, he turned for help to Arizona Senator Henry F. Ashurst, chairman of the Senate Judiciary Committee and a loyal supporter of the administration. Ashurst helped shape the Court bill, shepherded it through his committee, and had it presented to the Senate. By this time, however, opposition to the "Court-packing" plan was so fierce, among liberals as well as conservatives, that Ashurst decided to abandon the bill. Not only that; he also helped lead the floor fight to defeat it. Just before the bill went down to defeat he received a telegram from one of his constituents saying: "I thank God for your courageous stand on that Supreme Court bill." Ashurst's prompt reply: "Which one?"[70]

Dear Alben

Majority leader Joseph Robinson of Arkansas was leading the fight in the Senate for FDR's Court plan and suddenly died of a heart attack. Opposition to the bill was fierce by that time; and, as acting Majority Leader, Kentucky's Alben Barkley felt obliged to call FDR's attention to the situation in the Senate. FDR replied in writing to Barkley's oral report in his famous "Dear Alben" letter, dated July 15, 1937, the day after Robinson's death. In it, FDR thanked Barkley for keeping him informed of the way things were going in the Senate, deplored the fact that there wasn't a period of mourning for Robinson instead of continued agitation by foes of the Court bill, and said he felt "compelled in the public interest, though against every inclination," to write Barkley as "the acting majority leader in the Senate" in order to spell out the details of the Court reform bill which the administration favored.

The release of the "Dear Alben" letter, as it was called, produced much talk. Anti-FDR Democrats in the Senate seized on it as proof that the President was interfering with the Senate's choice of a Majority Leader to succeed Robinson. Anti-FDR elements in the press also deduced that FDR regarded Barkley as "his" and was pushing him for Robinson's post. This meant that when the Senate came to vote on the matter, there was considerable tension between Barkley's supporters and those backing conservative Pat Harrison of Mississippi. The ballot was secret, and, as Barkley recalled, it was "a real horse race" to the last vote. Seventy-five Democrats voted, and, with only one ballot left in the hat, the score stood at 37 to 37. When the teller reached in and pulled out the last folded slip, "it looked as big as a bed quilt" to Barkley. The teller announced that the last vote was for Barkley, and Harrison moved to make Barkley's election unanimous.[71]

Purge

In the spring of 1938, FDR began toying with the idea of working against anti-New Deal Democrats in the Congressional elections that fall. "I don't think you ought to try to punish these men, Cap'n," Vice President Garner warned him. "On many details of party principles men disagree. Some branch off in one direction and some in another. Men who oppose you on one thing are for you on another and there is always a legislative program for which you have to find votes." But FDR rejected Garner's advice; he decided to go ahead with what came to be called his "purge." In a fireside chat in late June 1938 he denounced the "Copperheads" who were sabotaging New Deal programs in Congress and declared that the Congressional primaries and elections scheduled for the summer and fall represented a contest between liberals who saw that new conditions required new remedies, including government action, and conservatives who wanted to return to the kind of leadership the country had had in the 1920s. "As head of the Democratic Party . . . , charged with the responsibility of the definitely liberal declaration of principles set forth in the 1936 Democratic platform," he declared, "I feel that I have every right to speak in those few instances where there may be a clear issue between candidates for a Democratic nomination involving these principles, or involving a clear misuse of my own name." A few days later he started his trip through the South and the West in an effort to help his supporters in Congress and work against those whom he regarded as obstructionists.

FDR's strategy, as he traveled about the country, was to snub candidates whom he disapproved (like Senators Alva Adams and Pat McCarran) or attack them openly (like Senators Walter George and Millard Tydings) and make friendly remarks about their opponents. His most dramatic confrontation took place in Georgia, where Walter F. George, the number-one target of his anti-conservative campaign, faced a New Deal candidate in the state's Democratic primary. In the little town of Barnesville, where Roosevelt appeared on the same platform with Senator George and his challenger, Lawrence Camp, FDR compared the two candidates and then came out frankly for the latter. "I have no hesitation in saying," he announced, "that if I were able to vote in the September primaries in this state, I would most assuredly cast my vote for Lawrence Camp." Afterward, Senator George walked up to him, offered his hand, and said: "Mr. Roosevelt, I regret that you have taken this occasion to question my Democracy and to attack my record. I want you to know that I accept the challenge." "Let's always be friends," murmured FDR. In Maryland, his target, Millard Tydings, was less irenic. When FDR announced that the Maryland Senator had "betrayed the New Deal in the past and will again," the latter snorted that the President wanted a Senator with a "detachable head, which he must leave with his hat in the cloakroom before going on the floor of the Senate. He must cease to think and then do what he is told—nothing else."

FDR's intervention in the Congressional elections of 1938 turned out to be counter-productive. In November, not only did the Republicans increase their strength in the House from 88 to 170 and add eight seats in the Senate; the effort to "purge" anti-New Deal Democrats also failed almost completely. About the only clear-cut victory for FDR was the defeat in the New York primary of John O'Connor, Tammany Democrat who had given him much trouble as chairman of the House Rules Committee. The Senatorial conservatives he had worked against—Colorado's Alva Adams, Nevada's Pat McCarran, South Carolina's "Cotton Ed" Smith, Georgia's Walter George, and Maryland's Millard Tydings—all won comfortable victories at the polls despite FDR's opposition. The coalition of conservative Democrats and Republicans, which had been frustrating the President so much, emerged from the elections stronger than ever. After the elections, FDR tried to put on a brave front. "Will you not encounter coalition opposition?" a reporter asked him at a press conference. "No, I don't think so," said Roosevelt. "I do!" cried the reporter. When the new Congress assembled in January 1939, Republican Congressman Clifford R. Hope of Kansas noted that "the atmosphere here in Congress is certainly much different than it has been anytime since the present administration came into power."[72]

Enemy

After FDR's unsuccessful attempt to "purge" conservative Democrats during the 1938 Congressional elections, Senator Walter George, one of his major targets, is said to have remarked to South Carolina's conservative "Cotton Ed" Smith, another target: "Roosevelt is his own worst enemy." Snarled Smith: "Not so long as I am alive!"[73]

The Majority Leader and the President

Early in 1944 FDR recommended a tax bill that would raise $10,500,-000,000 in new revenue, and the House, balking at voting such "an astronomical figure," passed a bill which in its final form, after the Senate increased the amount, enlarged the national revenues by only about $2,300,000,000. In conferences at the White House in late February with Congressional leaders—Senate Majority Leader Alben W. Barkley, House Speaker Sam Rayburn, and House Majority Leader John McCormack—FDR made it clear he was going to veto the measure as hopelessly inadequate, even though it would be the first time in U.S. history that a President ever vetoed a general revenue bill. Barkley, Rayburn, and McCormack tried to dissuade the President; a veto would antagonize Congress, they warned, and it might mean the President would end up with no revenue at all. Why not let the bill become law without his signature? But FDR was adamant; he even read the rough draft of his veto message to them. "Well, Mr. President," sighed Barkley, "it is perfectly obvious that you are going to veto this bill and it is futile for me to argue with you any longer. I must say, however, that if you do so, and assign the reasons which you have given us here, I will be compelled to say something about it in the Senate." "Of course you have that right," murmured the President.

The veto message contained harsh words when it reached Capitol Hill in its final form. In it, the President seemed to go out of his way not only to criticize the tax measure, but also to question the motives of Congress in passing it. He had asked "for a loaf of bread with which to carry on the war," Roosevelt declared, "and had been handed a small piece of crust" containing "many extraneous and inedible" ingredients. "It is not a tax bill," he added, "but a tax relief bill, providing relief not for the needy, but for the greedy." Barkley, who had worked on the bill himself, was dismayed by the tone of the message; so were most of his colleagues in the Senate. And though Barkley had always loyally supported the President (anti-New Dealers called him a "Roosevelt stooge"), he realized that as Senate Majority Leader he had no alternative but to respond to the President's challenge. "Go to it," his wife told him. "I'm with you."

That night Barkley typed out some remarks to make in the Senate, but when he read them over the next morning they seemed so awkward and stilted that he threw them aside, started over again, and dictated a lengthy speech to his secretary that he felt came out much better. "Listen," he told her when he finished and she began typing up a nice copy, "type like the devil is after you! And just as fast as you get a sheet finished, send it over to me by page boy, because I'll be on my feet talking, and I may run out of speech!" The Senate floor and the galleries were crowded when he began reading his manuscript; and there were even tears in the eyes of some of his listeners as he got under way. Soon, though, be began to run out of pages to read, and he hastily arranged with Tennessee's Kenneth D. McKellar to stand at the cloakroom door, seize the pages of the manuscript as the page boys brought them from the secretary, and rush them over to him as he was speaking.

In his speech Barkley took up the President's points, one by one, and when he came to the charge that Congress had passed a relief bill "for the greedy," he said solemnly: "That statement is a calculated and deliberate assault upon the legislative integrity of every member of the Congress of the United States. The members of Congress may do as they please. But as for me, I do not propose to take this unjustifiable assault lying down. Mr. President, this is the first time during [my] long service, which I had thought was honorable, when I have been accused deliberately of voting for a bill that constituted a relief measure impoverishing the needy and enriching the greedy." Then, his voice close to breaking, Barkley went on to recall his years of service to the administration. "For twelve years," he said, "I have carried to the best of my ability the flag of Franklin D. Roosevelt. . . . I dare say that for the last seven years as Majority Leader, I have carried that flag over rougher territory than was ever traversed by any previous Majority Leader. Sometimes I have carried it with little help here on the Senate floor and more frequently with little help from the other end of Pennslyvania Avenue." Then, coming to the end of his speech, he announced that he was calling for a meeting of the Democratic majority at 10:30 the following morning at which he would resign his position. "Let me say . . . ," he added, "that if the Congress of the United States has any self-respect left, it will override the veto of the President and enact this tax bill into law, his objections to the contrary notwithstanding."

Barkley's speech touched off a wild demonstration. In the galleries people shouted and cheered, and on the Senate floor members of both parties crowded up to shake hands and congratulate the Majority Leader. Even Senator McKellar, who had clashed bitterly with him some months earlier, went around crying: "I forgive him! I forgive him everything he's ever done!" That night, when Barkley returned to his apartment he found the President's press secretary, Stephen J. Early, waiting for him with a letter from the President in which FDR insisted he hadn't intended to attack the integrity of members of Congress, wanted Barkley to change his mind about resigning, but hoped the Democrats would re-elect him at once if he did go through with it. A little later James F. Byrnes, former South Carolina Senator who was now one of FDR's top advisers, called to encourage a reconciliation between the two. "If men such as you and I desert the President," he exclaimed, "he is sunk."

But Barkley went ahead and resigned the following day, and, as everyone expected, the Democrats promptly and unanimously re-elected him Majority Leader. "Make way for liberty!" exulted Texas' Tom Connally, as he burst out of the Democratic conference room to notify Barkley of his colleagues' action. That afternoon the House of Representatives voted to override the President's veto by a vote of 299 to 95, and a little later the Senate followed suit, with 72 votes to 14. *Time,* which had been sniping at Congress ever since Pearl Harbor, was delighted by the legislators' emphatic rejection of FDR's tax proposals and their sudden assertion of independence. Barkley, the conservative newsweekly pronounced, was no longer FDR's "errand boy" and that was a good thing for the country: "When he went to the White House, he would present the Senate's views— that, at least, would be his opportunity." The liberal-minded *New Republic* had mixed feelings about what had happened. As to the revenue measure itself, the editors were convinced the President was "completely right" and Congress "completely wrong." But as to the clash between FDR and Barkley, the editors thought the President was criticizable. "It is quite true that the President in recent years has been regrettably remiss in keeping up his personal contacts with Congress," the editors conceded. "Neither he nor his immediate circle of advisers has ever paid enough attention to mollifying the feelings of the men on the Hill. . . . He has managed to give many legislators the impression that he considers them a necessary evil, to be bypassed if possible when they refuse to co-operate."

Barkley himself soon made his peace with President Roosevelt, writing to assure him of his continued loyalty and affection. But he added: "It seems to me there is something broader and more fundamental than any personal acquiescence as between you and me over matters of public policy and fundamental principles. In this great crisis of our nation's history we must all seek some common ground upon which we can meet and have confidence."[74]

Fooling Around

One night Kenneth McKellar, chairman of the Senate Appropriations Committee, couldn't sleep and began brooding about some of the matters before his committee. Suddenly he began wondering why the administration was asking the Senate to appropriate $2,000,000,000 "for something mysterious." The next day he called on Secretary of War Henry L. Stimson and told him he deserved to know something about the mysterious appropriation. Stimson admitted the Senator's request was reasonable, pondered for a moment, and then cried: "Can you keep a secret?" McKellar assured him he could. Then Stimson leaned forward and said solemnly: "We are about to split the atom!" McKellar was stupefied. "Here we are in the middle of a big war," he cried indignantly, "and you are fooling around trying to split an atom!" Months later, like everyone else, he learned about the atom bomb.[75]

Damn Lie

Shortly after Harry Truman became President upon Franklin Roosevelt's death in April 1945, his good friend Sam Rayburn said to him: "Harry, this will be the last time that I will address you in such an informal manner, calling you by your first name. From here on out, I will address you as 'Mr. President,' because that's the way I think our relationship ought to be. But I have just one other thing I want to say to you. While you are President of the United States, you are going to have a staff around you that is going to tell you day in and day out that you are the smartest man in the world, and that's going to have a real effect on you. But the truth is, Mr. President, you and I both know it's a damn lie."[76]

Congress and the General

On February 12, 1951, Republican Minority Leader Joe Martin gave a speech in Brooklyn in which he interjected himself into the dispute between President Truman and General Douglas MacArthur over how to wage the Korean war. MacArthur wanted to attack China, which had sent troops over the border to help the North Koreans; Truman, fearing a major war with China, favored the more limited objective of preserving South Korea's integrity. Martin sided with MacArthur. "What are we in Korea for—to win or to lose?" he cried. "If we are not in Korea to win, then this administration should be indicted for the murder of thousands of American boys."

After Congressional Democrats criticized Martin's speech, the Minority

Leader decided to get in touch with MacArthur. He sent him a letter, enclosing his Brooklyn speech, and a few days later, to his delight, received a reply in which MacArthur praised what he had said in Brooklyn and criticized the Truman administration's policy in Korea. Martin kept the letter to himself for a few days and then read it aloud on the floor of the House while discussing the war. On the night of April 10, a woman called him long-distance. "Isn't it terrible news about General MacArthur?" she cried. "What about MacArthur?" asked Martin. "Truman's fired him," she moaned. "I just heard it on the radio."

Truman's action produced a storm among conservative Republicans in Congress. Senator Joseph McCarthy charged that the President was drunk on "bourbon and Benedictine" when he fired the General, and added: "The son of a bitch should be impeached!" Indiana's William E. Jenner also favored impeachment. "This country," he announced," is in the hands of a secret inner coterie which is directed by agents of the Soviet Union." "The happiest group in the country will be the communists and their stooges . . . ," intoned California Senator Richard M. Nixon. "The President has given them what they have always wanted—MacArthur's scalp." Kenneth Wherry of Nebraska asked the American people to compare the "monumental record" of General MacArthur "with the record of his accusers—with the record of moral decay, greed, corruption, and confusion."

The moment Martin heard about the firing he got on the phone to invite MacArthur to address a joint session of Congress, and the General quickly accepted. The Democrats agreed to the invitation, but insisted it be billed as a "meeting," not a "session," to make it clear it was a voluntary meeting, not an official function of Congress. The Republicans agreed to this, but they rejected out of hand Illinois Democrat Adolph Sabath's proposal that the Rules Committee, which he headed, ask MacArthur "to explain and give his reasons for failure to comply with the orders of his superiors and in disregarding the instructions of the President, the Commander in Chief."

MacArthur returned to the United States for the first time in fourteen years, received a tremendous ovation wherever he went, and on April 19, made a moving address to Congress defending his policies. Soon afterward came a lengthy Congressional investigation of the administration's foreign policy, lasting from May 2 until June 22, during the course of which members of the Joint Chiefs of Staff as well as high administration officials explained and defended Truman's Korean war policy. By the time the investigation ended the excitement over MacArthur's firing had died down. The hearings made it clear that there was a lot to be said for the Truman approach, and that all-out war with China would be, as General Omar Bradley put it, "the wrong war, at the wrong time, and in the wrong place." It was also clear that, entirely apart from the Korean war, the principle of civilian supremacy, enshrined in the Constitution, gave President Truman, as Commander in Chief, no alternative but to fire a General who disobeyed his instructions.[77]

McCarthywasm

In the early 1950s Republican Senator Joseph R. McCarthy of Wisconsin kept Congress, the executive branch of government, and the nation as a whole in a state of perpetual agitation over charges that the Communists had infiltrated the Federal Government and were shaping the nation's domestic and foreign policies. His behavior became so reckless while Eisenhower was President that in December 1954 the Senate finally passed a resolution stating that his conduct was "contrary to Senatorial traditions" and "tended to bring the Senate into dishonor and disrepute, to obstruct the constitutional processes of the Senate, and to impair its dignity, and such conduct is hereby condemned." A day or so later, President Eisenhower greeted his Cabinet with a big smile. "Have you heard the latest?" he chortled. "McCarthyism is McCarthywasm!" He was right. McCarthy spent his remaining days in the Senate largely ignored by his colleagues.[78]

Pentagonish Extravagance

One day members of the Senate Appropriations Committee went to the Pentagon for lunch and for a conference with the Secretary of Defense. The Pentagon sent automobiles to pick up the Senators; and, as they rode into the basement of the building, they saw row after row of long, sleek, shiny black Cadillacs. "I had not supposed," said New Hampshire's Republican Senator Norris Cotton afterward, "there were so many swank automobiles in the world." The sight produced sharp criticism from members of the Appropriations Committee and much talk about Pentagonish extravagance.

The committee's next visit was quite different. This time the Pentagon sent a rickety old bus to pick up the Senators, and, as it rattled along toward the Potomac, the Senators couldn't help noticing a sign on the back of the driver's seat: "This bus cost $14,000 and can be quickly converted into an ambulance." And the bus delivered its passengers to the front door; there was no trip into the lower regions where they had seen all the luxury vehicles on their previous visit.[79]

Let You Win

Shortly after JFK became President, he sent for Senator Hubert Humphrey (who had lost to JFK in his campaign for the presidential nomination in the spring of 1960) to discuss his legislative agenda with him. After discussing some of the problems facing his administration, he suddenly smiled and said: "Hubert, if I'd known it was going to be like this, I would have let you win." "Well, Mr. President," said Humphrey with a big smile, "I knew it might be like this and that's why I *let* you win!"[80]

Explaining the Zinc Bill

In 1961, the story goes, when President Kennedy indicated he was going to veto a bill barring the importation of zinc, Oklahoma Senator Robert Kerr, strongly supported by zinc manufacturers in the western part of his state, called on the President to urge him not to veto the bill. Kennedy received him at the Oval Office with aides Mike Feldman and Ted Sorensen at his side and said, "Bob, I'm sorry, but it's a bad bill." "Mr. President, could I speak to you privately?" asked Kerr. "There are a few things you may not understand about the legislation." "Sure, Bob," said JFK, "but it's not going to change my mind. I've been briefed pretty thoroughly by Ted and Mike." When Sorensen and Feldman left, Kerr got down to business. "Mr. President," he said, "you are my leader and I will abide by your decision." "Bob, I appreciate that," said JFK. "But, Mr. President," Kerr went on, "people were pretty mad when Ike vetoed that same bill, and I will have to go back to Oklahoma and spend full-time defending your action." "I really appreciate that," nodded Kennedy. "But, Mr. President," said Kerr, "you understand that means that if I'm away in Oklahoma, your tax bill, which lies in the Finance Committee which I chair, will never come to the floor." "Bob," JFK is supposed to have exclaimed, "this is the first time anyone really explained the zinc bill to me—I'll sign it!"[81]

LBJ and Senator Byrd

One night in the spring of 1964 Senator Hubert Humphrey attended the annual Gridiron Dinner and left about the same time President Johnson did. When Johnson saw Humphrey he cried: "Hubert, get in the car. Let's go over to the White House for a nightcap." A moment later he spied Harry Byrd, the tough old conservative who was chairman of the Senate Finance Committee, and asked Humphrey to invite the Virginian to join them for a drink. "Tell him it's important," Johnson said. "I need to talk to him." He wanted to get Byrd to help him with a tax cut.

When the three of them got to the White House, Johnson asked Humphrey to get the drinks. "Just bring me a little scotch with some water," he said, "and just fix Harry up with about two fingers of bourbon," and he held up his massive hands to show what he meant. As they sipped their drinks, Johnson talked a bit about Congress and the Finance Committee and then got up rather suddenly and cried: "Harry, before you go home I think you ought to visit with your girl friend." He moved to the doorway of a nearby bedroom and shouted: "Lady Bird, your boy friend Harry is out here!" Mrs. Johnson had been asleep, but she soon appeared in her dressing gown, sat down by Byrd, and soon had him laughing. "Well, Lady Bird," said Johnson after a while, "we can't keep Harry up much longer. You better go back to bed now. He's had his chance to see you." As she left, LBJ told Byrd: "Harry, every time I can't find Lady Bird, I know she's either with you or Laurence Rockefeller or Hubert. That's why I don't dare leave town too much and leave her here."

By this time Byrd was in a good mood, and LBJ got to the point of it all. "Harry," he said, leaning over and peering into Byrd's eyes, "I know you're opposed to any tax reduction. But frankly I've just got to have that bill out of committee." Before Byrd could object, LBJ went on: "Now, whether we agree or not, and you and I may not feel too strongly about a tax reduction, I need your commitment that you'll get that bill out. Now, I know you can't vote for it and I don't expect you to. In fact, I would expect you to oppose it. But I don't want you to bottle it up. Will you give me your word that you'll just report the bill out as soon as possible." "Lyndon," Byrd said amiably, "if you want that bill out, I'll do nothing to stop it. If there're votes in the committee to report it out, I'll let it come out. You can be sure of that." At this, Johnson stood up and cried: "Harry, it's time to go to bed. I've kept you up late. Good night." And he asked Humphrey to escort Byrd to his car.

A few days later Byrd appeared on the Senate floor with the tax-reduction bill in hand, reported it out, and placed it on the calendar. And when it was called up for action he made a brief speech and then leaned over and whispered to Humphrey: "Now, you tell the President that I kept my word—that I've reported out the bill, that I've made my speech, and now I'm leaving." Humphrey called the President to tell him the news, and his guess was that LBJ placed a call to Byrd at once to thank him profusely, for it was part of "the Johnson treatment." Shortly after, the Senate passed the bill Johnson wanted.[82]

Hoping

President Johnson once called Ohio Congressman Wayne Hays at home around 2:00 a.m. to discuss some legislation. When he asked whether he was disturbing him, Hayes said: "Why no, Mr. President, I was just sitting here hoping you'd call."[83]

Lippmann Dam

Democratic Senator Frank Church of Idaho, an early critic of the Vietnam war, was surprised to learn from press reports the day after he had attended a White House reception that he had had an unpleasant exchange with President Johnson. When the subject of Vietnam came up, according to the news story, Church said, "As Walter Lippmann said," in a reference to the columnist's criticism of the war, and LBJ interrupted: "If you want any more dams for Idaho, why don't you go to Walter Lippmann?" Since no such conversation had taken place, Church took to the Senate floor to deny it. Afterwards, it occurred to him: "That's what the President would like to have said if he had thought of it. He didn't. But after I left, he probably told Press Secretary Bill Moyers to put it out."

A few days later, when Church was in the White House again, the President said: "Have you built any more dams in Idaho?" "Not yet, Mr. President," said Church stiffly, "but the first one to be finished will be named after Walter Lippmann." LBJ changed the subject.[84]

Friend of the President

While LBJ was President, Republican Senator Everett Dirksen was in a curious position; he was leader of the opposition party, but also a good friend of the President. Once he attended a Republican women's meeting dressed in formal dinner jacket, gave a speech severely denouncing LBJ's policies, and even criticizing his methods, and then stopped suddenly, looked at his watch, and cried: "I'll have to leave you girls or I'll be late for dinner at the White House." Then he left to see his friend.[85]

Representation

In 1970, when one Senator complained that Judge T. Harrold Carswell, President Nixon's nominee for the U.S. Supreme Court, was a mediocre judge, Nebraska Republican Roman Hruska exclaimed: "There are a lot of mediocre Americans! Don't *they* deserve some representation on the court?" But the Senate voted to reject the nomination.[86]

Obviously Guilty

Soon after his re-election in 1972, President Nixon began impounding funds voted by Congress in appropriation bills he had signed. As chairman of the Government Operations Committee, North Carolina Senator Sam Ervin took the position that under the Constitution the power of the purse belonged to Congress and that the President had no power to impound funds unless Congress authorized him to do so. When Ervin joined Edmund S. Muskie of Maine in sponsoring a bill to check presidential impoundments, Nixon sent Deputy Attorney-General Joseph T. Sneed to oppose the bill before the Senate committee considering the legislation.

Sneed contended the bill was unconstitutional because the Constitution states that the President "shall take care that the laws be faithfully executed" and that meant the President could impound congressionally appropriated funds. Ervin disagreed. "The word *execute*," he told Sneed," is used in different contexts to mean different things. For example, we say when it imposes the death penalty on a capital felon, the State has executed him. But the phrase you invoke . . . does not empower the President to inflict the death penalty on acts of Congress. It obligates him to carry out acts of Congress—including acts making appropriations—in accordance with the congressional intent." Ervin wound up his argument with a left-handed compliment. "You have striven manfully to confer on the President a nonexistent constitutional power," he told Sneed. "I pay you a compliment similar to one which a superior judge paid to me after he had submitted a criminal case defended by me to the jury. He said, 'You have made the best possible argument for an obviously guilty client.'"[87]

Hearsay

In February 1973, North Carolina's Sam J. Ervin, Jr., became chairman of a Senate committee investigating the burglary of Democratic headquarters in the Watergate Hotel on June 17, 1972, as well as other illegal activities undertaken during President Nixon's 1972 re-election campaign. The work of the Watergate Committee had scarcely begun when Senator Ervin began receiving telephone calls from all over the country giving him unsolicited advice about the Watergate affair.

Ervin's most unusual caller was a man in Kentucky who said he was a minister of the Gospel who was receiving daily communications from the Almighty about Watergate which he was instructed to report to the Senator. "Please ask the Good Lord to make his revelations about Watergate directly to me," Ervin implored, after several lengthy calls. "Inasmuch as the Good Lord has to look after this earth, all its inhabitants, and the entire universe, he couldn't possibly spend as much time talking about Watergate as you do."

The next time the Kentuckian called he had new instructions: the Almighty wanted him to be first witness before the Watergate committee. But Ervin told him that although the committee would be happy to welcome the Almighty as its lead-off witness, it couldn't permit the caller to be a stand-in for the Almighty, since he didn't know anything about Watergate except what the Almighty told him, and the people being investigated by the committee would object to his testimony as hearsay. The caller was disappointed; but a little later he called again. This time Mrs. Ervin answered the phone; and when the Kentuckian found himself talking to the Senator's wife he said the Almighty had authorized him to tell her what He had said about Watergate that day and that she should pass it on to her husband. Mrs. Ervin listened patiently until the man hung up and then announced briskly: "We'll get an unlisted telephone tomorrow."[88]

Lying

After President Nixon resigned in August 1974, a woman wrote Senator Sam Ervin, chairman of the Senate committee investigating the Watergate scandal, called him a "miserable wretch," charged that he had helped drive from office "the greatest President our nation ever had," and expressed the wish that the Senator was "feeling as bad as he deserved to feel." In response, Ervin wrote her that her letter indicated that he had a higher opinion of the former President than she had. When Nixon admitted, in substance, on the tapes of June 23, 1972, that he became engaged in the cover-up of the Watergate burglary six days after its commission, Ervin "believed he was telling the truth, and she evidently thought he was lying."[89]

Recess

In the winter of 1975, just before Christmas, Congress was about to pass a $28 billion tax cut which President Ford had proposed, and then go off on vacation without passing the related $28 billion budget cut he had also requested. Having been a Congressman himself, Ford got a sudden inspiration. He instructed the White House Congressional liaison office to ask the parliamentarian of Congress what the rules were for calling Congress back to Washington for a special session during the Christmas recess. "Now, make sure that you tell the parliamentarian that I want to keep this an absolute secret," he told his aides. "That will get the word around the Hill faster than Western Union!" It worked as Ford planned. The word about a possible Christmas recess spread quickly on Capitol Hill, and Congress quickly passed the compromise budget cut Ford wanted before voting to adjourn.[90]

X

* * * * * * * *

The Reagan Years
1981–89

* 🏴 *

Soon after the 1980 election Ronald Reagan paid a courtesy call on Thomas P. ("Tip") O'Neill, Speaker of the House since 1977, and listened quietly as O'Neill gave a little lecture on Congressional procedures and then went on to explain how, after years of eclipse by the executive branch of government, the legislative branch had finally regained its standing. But the Republican President-elect didn't seem much interested. "I could have been speaking Latin," mused O'Neill afterwards, "for all he seemed to care." When O'Neill finished, however, Reagan told him he expected to get along fine with Congress, even though the Democrats controlled the lower house, because he had been on good terms with the California legislature when he was governor, despite the fact that the state assembly was Democratic. "That was the minor league," O'Neill told him. "You're in the big league now."[1]

To O'Neill's astonishment—and to the surprise of the Democrats generally—Reagan began acting like a big leaguer once he entered the White House. He did not, to be sure, produce an outpouring of creative legislation the way Franklin Roosevelt did during his first Hundred Days in office, but he did succeed, in a few months, in getting from Congress just about everything he sought when he first became President: a big cut in government spending on social programs, a substantial reduction in taxes, especially in the higher brackets, and a massive increase in appropriations for the Pentagon. Reagan's aides skillfully organized the budget campaign: they imposed strict discipline on Republicans in Congress, courted conservative Democrats from the South and West, and planned the President's schedule carefully, especially his appearances on television. But Reagan himself plunged ahead with zest into the task of winning moderate Democrats to his side and was soon impressing his opponents in Congress with his talents as a Great Persuader. He was on the phone for hours, explaining, promising, joking, coaxing; he had numerous conferences with members of Congress in the Oval Office; he invited Congressmen to Camp David for hot dogs and sweet talk; he went on television, where he was a master with the TelePrompTer, to whip up public backing for his program; and he entertained more than two hundred business leaders at the White House, persuaded them to put pressure on their Congressmen to back the Reagan budget, and convinced them that they should encourage their employees to do the same. "There is no question," sighed O'Neill, "that this is the greatest lobbying in the history of this country."[2] A Chicago company, in an outburst of Reaganite enthusiasm, hired six singers, dressed in top hats and tuxedos, to make the rounds of Congressional offices in Washington to serenade the undecided with lines like these, sung to the tune of "The Yankee Doodle Boy":

> You'll have a job for every man
> So just say "Aye"
> Don't be a slob
> Some day you might have Reagan's job
> So please vote for Reagan's tax-cut plan.

Huffed a Los Angeles Democrat: "We are dealing with serious economic issues, and some of our loyal opposition seems to think it is time to send in the clowns."[3]

Speaker O'Neill, for one, found nothing amusing in what was happening. A good New Deal Democrat, he watched with dismay the jettisoning of social, health, and education programs he had long supported; he was angered, too, by what seemed to him a definite shift of the tax burden from the wealthy to the middle classes. "In 1981," he said later, "everything I fought for, everything I had believed in, was being cast aside." On the floor of the House and in newspaper and television interviews the harried Speaker criticized Reagan as "a rich man's President," and insisted that Reagan's program "made the rich richer and the poor poorer and it did nothing for the middle class." But the outburst of popular support for the President's program overwhelmed O'Neill (and the liberal Democrats generally) and prevented him from seizing the initiative. As torrents of pro-Reagan letters, cards, and telegrams poured into Washington, O'Neill ruefully told Reagan: "Mr. President, you're making my life miserable." "That's the best news I've heard today," laughed the President.[4]

At times pro-Reagan sentiment turned nasty. When O'Neill appeared in airport terminals during the budget battle, people began rushing up and yelling, "Leave the President alone, you fat bastard!" Sometimes there were even physical assaults, and for a while O'Neill sought police protection when he traveled around the country. In the House of Representatives, an ultra-conservative Congressman from Long Island announced that the Speaker was "big, fat, and out of control—like the federal government," and went on to organize a campaign to defeat him for re-election: "Repeal O'Neill!" The campaign to unseat the Speaker failed, but the animus continued. To O'Neill's chagrin, he even encountered hostility when he permitted the Boston Symphony Orchestra, in a fund-raising drive, to auction off a private lunch with the Speaker of the House. The Bostonian who won paid about $1500 for the privilege, but when he and his wife showed up for the meal he was not very friendly and his wife seemed nervous. "Not now, dear," she kept whispering to her husband. When they finished eating O'Neill exclaimed: "I'm delighted that you came here today. Tell me, how did you happen to bid on this lunch?" The man looked at his wife for a moment and then blurted out: "Because I wanted to tell you to your face that you're a son of a bitch for being so tough on the President."[5]

Tough or not, O'Neill was never able to organize effective opposition to the President's proposals. His liberal colleagues were impressed, not to say cowed, by Reagan's tremendous popularity, especially after the attempt on his life in March 1981, and they were fully alive to the dangers involved in trying to scuttle his program. "The attitude among Democrats here," observed Democratic Senate Whip Alan Cranston of California, "is that we can't be in the position of preventing him from trying what he was elected to do. We can't go along on every detail, but if we obstructed everything, it would be bad for the country, and bad for the Democrats. The voters would remove a lot more of us."[6] As it turned out, about all the Democrats managed to accomplish was to block the administration's proposals for making drastic reductions in Social Security benefits.

In the end, President Reagan's "velvet steamroller," as *Time* called it, pushed through the greatest increase in peacetime spending for defense in American history, as well as the greatest cutbacks in domestic programs and the largest tax cuts the country had ever seen.[7] "Well, Mr. President," cried Illinois' Dan Rostenkowski after the "Reagan Revolution" was assured, "you're tough. You beat us." Exclaimed House Majority Leader Jim Wright in a congratulatory telephone call: "We can see you're ready for the big time."[8] Still, the President's victory, though not exactly pyrrhic, bore strange fruits. What was called "Reaganomics"—cutting taxes to encourage investment in productive enterprises which would then generate more tax revenue—soon ran into trouble. Not only did the country experience a severe recession in 1981–82; the tax cuts and stepped-up defense spending also produced a succession of huge unbalanced budgets and a rapid ballooning of the national debt during the next eight years.

At the beginning of his Presidency, Reagan warned against unbalanced budgets, and, to dramatize his point, noted that the national debt, then approaching a trillion dollars, if stacked up in $1000 bills, would make a pile sixty-seven miles high. But the pile got steadily higher after 1981; by the time Reagan left office in 1989 it was close to two hundred miles high. Through it all, however, Reagan remained unruffled; and his high standing with the public continued undiminished. Though the Democrats held their majority in the House throughout the 1980s and won control of the Senate in 1986, Ronald Reagan, the Great Performer, as well as Great Communicator, especially on television, won his bid for a second term by a landslide. Electronics, if not Reaganomics, performed beautifully during the 1980s.

Despite his enormous popularity, President Reagan didn't always get his way. In 1987, to his dismay, the Senate rejected his nomination of Circuit Court Judge Robert H. Bork, a tried-and-true conservative, to the U.S. Supreme Court by the largest margin ever recorded for a vote against a Court nominee. The defeat was particularly humiliating because the President had announced that there was "no more important task" facing him than getting Bork confirmed, and his advisers had built up the nomination as the most important struggle of his last two years of office. In thirty hours of testimony, however, Bork came across as both arrogant and pedantic, and his record of consistent opposition to civil-rights legislation through the years and flat rejection of a "right to privacy" disturbed conservatives as well as liberals in both parties. In the end, even John Warner, Virginia Republican, who usually supported the President, voted against Bork. The President's statement that Bork was the victim of a "lynch mob" struck Warner as "unbecoming the office of the Presidency."[9]

Even more frustrating for Reagan than the Bork rejection was the refusal of Congress to give wholehearted support to his program for aiding the *contras,* anti-Communist rebels working to overthrow the Sandinista government in Nicaragua headed by Daniel Ortega, an avowed Marxist-Leninist. In opposing aid to the Nicaraguan guerrillas, Congress wasn't being merely perverse. The majority of Congressmen, like most Americans, feared another Vietnam; and although prodded by the administration, they did vote funds for the *contras* from time to time, they never did come through with the kind of all-out military assistance the President sought. In the fall of 1982, suspecting that the Central Intelligence Agency (CIA) was secretly helping the *contras* in their war against the Sandinista government, Massachusetts Democrat Edward F. Boland, chairman of the House Select Committee on Intelligence, proposed an amendment to the

Defense Appropriation Act prohibiting the use of funds "for the purpose of overthrowing the government of Nicaragua." The House passed the Boland Amendment by a unanimous vote and President Reagan signed it in December. But evidence that the CIA was still secretly working with the rebels led the House to adopt another amendment, proposed by Boland in 1983, placing a ceiling on funding for the *contras* and urging the President to seek a negotiated settlement of the conflict. "This secret war is bad U.S. policy—," Boland told the House, "because it does not work, because it is in fact counterproductive to U.S. interests, because it is illegal." But the CIA continued its covert activities anyway, even going so far as to mine Nicaraguan harbors at one point, and the House finally adopted another Boland Amendment in 1984 cutting off all aid to the *contras* during the 1985 fiscal year. "The secret war hasn't brought Central America closer to peace or Nicaragua closer to democracy," said Boland, in justifying the cutoff. "What it does is to provide the Sandinistas with the perfect excuse to foist unfair elections, a huge army, censorship and the draft on the Nicaraguan people."[10] The President and Congress were clearly on a collision course.

The collision came in 1986. That fall the so-called Iran-Contra scandal erupted. On November 3, a Lebanese newspaper carried an amazing news item reporting that the United States had secretly sold arms to Iran (which Reagan had blasted as "Murder, Inc.," for sponsoring terrorist activity) in the hope of securing the release of American hostages in Lebanon (despite the fact that the Reagan administration had repeatedly avowed its determination never to make deals with terrorists or sell arms to Iran). On November 23 came even more astonishing news: that the profits (about $20 million) derived from the sale of arms to Iran had not ended up in the U.S. Treasury, but had been "diverted" to the Nicaraguan *contras* in outright violation of the Boland Amendments. Reagan's response to the revelations was confused and contradictory, but he promptly appointed a special review board, headed by John Tower, former Republican Senator from Texas, to look into the matter. The response of Congress was to launch a joint Senate-House inquiry in May 1987 and hold ten weeks of public hearings (carried on television) to find out what had been going on.[11]

The Tower board report, released in February 1987, concluded that "the President's staff was doing what Congress forbade," and criticized the President for his lax "management style."[12] The majority report of the Congressional committee, signed by fifteen Democrats and three Republicans, filed in November, was much harsher. Not only did it blame the President for failing to live up to his Constitutional mandate to "take care that the laws be faithfully executed"; it also declared that he bore the "ultimate responsibility" for wrongdoing by his aides. "Fundamental processes of government were disregarded and the rule of law was subverted,"

312 · CONGRESSSIONAL ANECDOTES

according to the report. "If the President did not know what his national security advisers were doing, he should have." The report, among other things, charged that the President had approved selling arms to Iran and also instructed his National Security Council (NSC) staff to maintain the Nicaraguan rebels, "body and soul," during the period in which Congress had banned official U.S. military assistance; that he had refused to condemn NSC staff members (like Admiral John Poindexter, NSC director, and Marine Lt. Col. Oliver North, NSC staff assistant), for lying to Congress and shredding evidence about the Iran-Contra affair; that he made a number of false statements about the affair; and that, although there was no evidence that he knew about the diversion of funds to the *contras,* he "created or at least tolerated an environment where those who did know of the diversion believed with certainty that they were carrying out the President's policies."[13] A minority report, signed by eight Republicans, rejected the majority findings outright, vigorously defended the Reagan administration, and criticized Congress for intruding into the President's foreign-policy domain.[14]

Some observers compared the Iran-Contra affair to Watergate ("Contragate") and even talked of impeachable offenses, but the signers of the majority report refrained from going that far. In the Watergate crisis, they said, Richard Nixon had been defiant and uncooperative and had directed a coverup; during the Iran-Contra inquiry, by contrast, they noted, President Reagan had urged people on his staff to tell the truth, made thousands of pages of documents available to the investigating committees, waived all claims of executive privilege, permitted the investigators to examine portions of his personal diary, and, when the hearings ended, seemed willing to recognize the failures of his administration and take corrective action. Shortly after the reports appeared, the President inaugurated a series of negotiations with senior members of the House and Senate Intelligence Committees with the aim of establishing new guidelines for the implementation of covert action in the future. "While the President," he told them, "must retain the flexibility as Commander in Chief and Chief Executive to safeguard the nation and its citizens, maximum consultation and notification is and will be the firm policy of this Administration."[15] Even the President's severest critics on the Iran-Contra committee seemed mollified by his apparent eagerness to establish a healthier working relationship with Congress.

The Iran-Contra affair (which the *New Republic* dubbed "Iranamok") was the latest battle in a two-hundred-year war between Congress and the President over foreign policy. During the controversy some White House officials—Admiral Poindexter and Lt. Col. North, among others—claimed that the President had sole authority to make foreign policy and that Congress brought only trouble on the nation when it meddled in foreign affairs. But it would be difficult, as historian Theodore Draper pointed out in his study of the Iran-Contra scandal, to find support for this claim in the Constitution. The Constitution, he noted, "does *not* charge the President with 'making' foreign policy. It would be more nearly correct to say that the Constitution implicitly charges Congress with making, and the President with executing, foreign as well as domestic policy." But the words of the Constitution, he added (citing Constitutional expert Edward S. Corwin), are actually an invitation to a struggle between Congress and the President over the privilege of directing the nation's domestic and foreign policies.[16] And the struggle was unremitting; it began in 1789, when George Washington was President, and was still raging in 1989, when Ronald Reagan left the White House. The latest struggle was over his successor George Bush's nomination of former Texas Senator John Tower as Secretary of Defense.

On March 2, 1989, the day the Tower debate began, the House and the Senate gathered in joint session to celebrate the 200th anniversary of the convening of the First Congress. They heard music, poetry, and speeches about their past history and witnessed the unveiling of stamps and coins to commemorate the bicentennial. Like the First Congress, the 101st Congress lacked a quorum that morning; fewer than a quarter of the members showed up for the occasion, and Kansas Senator Robert Dole quipped that the session, in that respect, "truly represents the first absence of quorum." Sponsors of the event sent scores of Congressional staff members into the House chamber where the festivities were held in order to keep the place from looking empty.

The bicentennial speeches were, expectably, largely self-congratulatory. House Speaker Jim Wright recalled Sam Rayburn's famous remark—that he had served *with*, not *under*, eight Presidents—and also reminded the assembly that Congress-bashing was present from the beginning and should be taken in stride. Senate Majority Leader George Mitchell talked about Congressional relations with the President and about the crucial role Congress had played through the years in safeguarding the republican form of government. "I do not claim that Congress is the primary branch of government," he said, "but I do remind all that it is a co-equal branch of Government." He went on to point out that during the preceding two hundred years there had been many Presidents, but no kings, and that Congress was primarily responsible for that fact. For his part, historian David McCulloch deplored the lack of good histories of Congress and the neglect by historians and biographers of some of its most distinguished members. "Congress, for all its faults," he said, "has not been the unbroken parade of clowns and thieves and posturing windbags so often portrayed. . . . What should be spoken of more often and more widely understood, are the great victories that have been won here, the decisions of courage and vision achieved. . . ." And in a poem written for the bicentennial, Howard Nemerov, the Poet Laureate for the United States, put it this way:

> So it's a Republic, as Franklin said,
> If you can keep it; and we did
> thus far, and hope to keep our quarrel
> funny and just, though with this moral:
> Praise without end for the go-ahead zeal
> of whoever it was invented the wheel;
> But never a word for the poor soul's sake
> that thought ahead, and invented the brake.[17]

When the ceremonies ended, the Senators headed for their own chamber to consider the nomination of Tower. A few weeks later they turned him down; but then promptly approved President Bush's next nominee for the post: Pennsylvania Congressman Richard B. Cheney, the author, with his wife Lynne, of a book about Congress entitled *Kings of the Hill* (1983).

☆ ☆ ☆

Six O'Clock

When Ronald Reagan met with Speaker "Tip" O'Neill of Massachusetts shortly afer becoming President, the latter told him that although they belonged to different parties he looked forward to working with him. He went on to remind him that he was on good terms with the Republican leadership in the House and that despite their disagreements they were always friends after five o'clock and on weekends. After that, President Reagan often began telephone conversations with the Speaker by saying: "Hello, Tip, is it now six o'clock?"[18]

Government off the Back

One of South Carolina Senator Ernest F. Hollings' favorite stories was about the veteran who returned from Korea and went to college on the GI Bill; then he bought his house with an FHA loan; saw his kids born in a VA hospital; started a business with an SBA; got electricity from TVA and, then, water from a project funded by the EPA. His children participated in the school-lunch program and made it through college, with the help of government-guaranteed student loans. His parents retired to a farm on their Social Security checks, getting electricity from the REA and the soil tested by the USDA. When the father became ill, his life was saved with a drug developed through NIH and his family saved from financial ruin by Medicare. The veteran drove to work on the interstate, moored his boat in a channel dredged by army engineers, and, when floods hit, took Amtrak to Washington to apply for disaster relief. He also spent some of his time there enjoying the exhibits in the Smithsonian museums. Then one day he wrote his Congressman an angry letter complaining about high taxes and heavy government spending. The government, he said, echoing President Reagan, "should get off his back."[19]

Sleeping

California's Republican Senator S. I. Hayakawa had a tendency to doze off during Senate debates and it produced many quips. "Did you hear who Hayakawa is sleeping with these days?" ran one joke. "No, who?" "The entire U.S. Senate."

But when Ted Kennedy joked that his seat on the Senate floor was "next to Hayakawa's bed and pillow," the elderly Californian, angered by the remark, retorted: "We Japanese have been sleeping on the floor for a thousand years. Maybe Senator Kennedy should try it. I understand he does some of his best work in bed."[20]

Absentee

Phil Crane, Illinois Republican, famed for his absenteeism, once appeared at a late-night session of the Ways and Means Committee and so astonished his colleagues that they gave him a standing ovation. Commented Andy Jacobs, Indiana Democrat: Crane "probably gave the cab driver the wrong address."[21]

Not It

Once Senator Howard H. Baker, Jr., Republican of Tennessee, was walking from the Senate chamber back to his office, and an excited group of tourists stopped him and one of them said, "Say, I know who you are. Don't tell me. Let me remember. I'll get it in a minute." Baker waited for several seconds, and finally said: "Howard Baker." But the tourist shook his head. "No, that's not it." Baker enjoyed recounting the episode.[22]

Humpty Dumpty

On April 5, 1983, the Senate chaplain, the Rev. Richard C. Halverson, offered the following prayer: "Let us pray. Humpty Dumpty sat on a wall. Humpty Dumpty had a great fall. All the king's horses and all the king's men couldn't put Humpty Dumpty together again. Dear God, in mercy and grace, prevent the Senate from being like Humpty Dumpty. Keep it from being so fractured and fragmented that no one will be able to put it together again. . . ."[23]

Call the Whole Thing Off

In the fall of 1983, after President Reagan ordered the invasion of Grenada, there was much talk about whether the name of the island was pronounced Gre-na-da or Gre-nah-da. On October 26, Massachusetts Congressman James M. Shannon, a Democrat, rose in the House to remind his colleagues of a song composed by George Gershwin some forty years before: "you like po-ta-to and I like po-tah-to, You like to-ma-to, and I like to-mah-to, Po-ta-to, po-tah-to, To-ma-to, to-mah-to! Let's call the whole thing off!" Then he went on: "At about the same time that Mr. Gershwin was writing his tune, Reagan was starring in the kind of movies that recent incidents in Grenada cannot help but remind one of. Think about it for a moment—a small Caribbean island, a band of bearded local militia, a lot of beautiful and confused residents, and throw in a few angry tourists for comic relief. Unfortunately, this is not a grade B movie, it is not even a very good script—two American marines have already lost their lives. But if that is the way Mr. Reagan persists in looking at these issues, maybe he will listen to a little advice from Mr. Gershwin. If Gershwin were alive today, perhaps he would consider this rewrite: "You like po-ta-to, I like po-tah-to, You say Gre-na-da, I say Gre-nah-da, Let's call the whole thing off."[24]

A Dole on the Ticket

In 1984, when Kansas Senator Robert Dole attended the Republican convention in Dallas with his wife Elizabeth, the latter received considerable attention because of her fine work as Transportation Secretary in the Reagan administration. At one point a prominent columnist asked Senator Dole how he would feel about a Bush-Dole ticket in 1988. "I'm not sure," said Dole. "To tell you the truth, I don't believe I'd really be interested." "Good," said the columnist, "because I wasn't thinking of you."[25]

Cute

During the 1984 campaign columnist George Will wrote that Vice-Presidential candidate Geraldine Ferraro's husband hadn't paid his taxes, but when he learned he was in error, he sent Ferraro a dozen roses by way of apology, with a little note: "Has anyone told you you are cute when you're mad?" Ferraro called to thank him for the flowers and they chatted a bit. Finally she said: "Thank you for the roses, George, but there is something I think you should know." "What?" he asked. "Vice-Presidents aren't cute," she said, and hung up.[26]

Ticket

"Will the Senator yield for a question without losing his right to the floor?" asked Senator Pete V. Domenici, Republican, New Mexico. "Certainly," responded Alfonse M. D'Amato, Republican, New York, on October 16, 1986. "If the Senator is going to stay here and talk until Saturday night," said Domenici, "would he give me his ticket to the Mets game? He can stay here and I will go."[27]

Home Again

After the 1984 Democratic primary season, which began in New Hampshire, came to an end, South Carolina Senator Ernest F. Hollings, who had done poorly in the primaries, looked back on the experience with some wistfulness, and then thought of Thomas Wolfe's famous novel, *You Can't Go Home Again* (1936). "You know," he said, "Thomas Wolfe lied. You can go home again. In fact, in my case, the people of New Hampshire insisted on it."[28]

Sinned

At the 1985 Gridiron Club dinner in Washington Treasury Secretary James Baker told a story about a dream he had in which President Reagan, Republican Senate leader Robert Dole, and longtime Speaker of the House "Tip" O'Neill all died and went to heaven. They got to the pearly gates together, and stood there somewhat nervously, until a voice finally boomed out: "President Reagan, go into the room on the right." Reagan went in and found himself in a room with a mad dog. "President Reagan," the voice explained, "you have sinned and must spend all eternity in this room with this mad dog." Meanwhile Dole and O'Neill were still outside, waiting anxiously; and after a minute or two, the voice spoke again. "Mr. Dole," it said, "go into the room directly in front of you." Dole did so and found himself in a room with a gorilla. "Senator," said the voice, "you have sinned and you must spend all of eternity in this room with this gorilla." By this time O'Neill was getting very worried. But after a couple of minutes the voice spoke again, telling him to go into the room on the left. Somewhat apprehensively O'Neill did as instructed. To his amazement he found himself alone in a room with the sexy young actress Bo Derek. And the voice boomed out: "Bo Derek, you have sinned. . . ."[29]

Handicap

Once, introducing comedian Bob Hope at a banquet, President Reagan said: "You know, Bob Hope has two great loves. He loves to entertain the troops and he loves golf. Just the other day he asked me, 'What's your handicap?' And I said, 'Congress.'"[30]

Robert Redford Group

One day movie star Robert Redford went to Washington to lobby on behalf of one of his environmental concerns and arrived at the office of a senior member of what was then the Senate Interior Committee. As soon as the receptionist saw Redford, she left her desk in great excitement to tell her boss about the famous visitor. "Senator," she practically screamed, "Robert Redford is outside and would like to speak to you!" The Senator looked up from some papers with a puzzled look, repeated the name a few times, and then asked: "What group does this Redford represent?"[31]

Hell of a Place

Arizona Congressman Morris K. Udall liked to tell the story of the Congressman named Smedley who died and went to Heaven, but to his surprise was denied entry and sent to the other place. Weeks later another Congressman had the same experience, so he went up to Satan and asked: "Is Smedley here?" "Yes," replied Satan, "but he is damned disliked here." "Well, I can't understand that," said the second Congressman. "He was one of the most respected men in Washington. What happened?" "Oh, not too much," said Satan. "He just made a very bad impression when he arrived." "What do you mean?" "Well, when Smedley arrived," said Satan, "he said he owned this place, that his constituents had been giving it to him for twenty years."[32]

Special Access

Representative Ronald V. Dellums, a California Democrat, had long been bothered by the Pentagon's terms for secret programs, budgets, and operations. They were called "black programs" or "black budgets" and Pentagon people often talked of "operations in the black world." Dellums, who was black, said he had a hard time explaining to constituents who were unfamiliar with Pentagon jargon why he voted against this "black program" or that "black budget." So he set out to change the terminology and appeared to have succeeded, at least in part. At a meeting of the House Armed Services Committee's Research and Development Subcommittee, of which he was the new chairman, Dellums persuaded his colleagues to drop the word, "black," when applied to secret programs. The term would now be "special access programs" or "special access budgets." Whether the Pentagon would adopt the new term remained to be seen.[33]

Best Congress Money Can Buy

When Philip M. Stern's 1988 book, *The Best Congress Money Can Buy*, rolled off the presses, he tucked a crisp one-dollar bill into each of 519 copies and sent them off to all the members of the Senate and the House who he knew accepted campaign contributions from political-action committees (PACs). Reactions varied. House Democrat Frank J. Guarini of New Jersey sent the dollar back with a note saying, "I am precluded by House rules from accepting cash." Representative Helen Delich Bentley, Maryland Republican, also sent back the dollar and told Stern to pick up the book "at your convenience." Representative Don Sundquist, Republican of Tennessee, accepted the dollar as a contribution, but asked Stern to let him know his occupation and name of his employer so they could be reported to the Federal Election Commission. But Representative Eligio (Kika) de la Garza, Democrat of Texas, wrote to say that he would use the dollar "to light a candle in St. Peter's Church here in Washington with prayers for your continued success." Representative Jerry Lewis, Republican of California, returned the dollar, wrapped in toilet paper, and wrote: "Anyone who presumes that people who seek to serve in public affairs can have their principles purchased by one dollar or one thousand dollars should look in the mirror and carefully measure their own character." North Carolina Republican Senator Jesse Helms wrote Stern: "I don't resent your implication that I can be 'bought' because (1) I suspect both of us know it isn't so, and (2) I am willing to assume that you do have some exceptions in mind to what appears to be an indictment of everybody—and that I am one of the exceptions."[34]

Important Lesson

In June 1988, Claude Pepper, 87, Democratic Congressman from Florida, and Jimmy Hayes, 41, a freshman Louisiana Democrat, were chatting on a street corner near the Capitol when a Boy Scout troop walked by. The scout leader asked for directions to the "Jefferson Monument." Pepper told him to walk two blocks, turn left at the Library of Congress, walk a few yards, turn again, and "you'll be where you ought to be." Hayes knew the directions were wrong, but kept quiet. "I figured they'd find their way," he said later. But Pepper seemed to read his mind, for a moment or two later he put his hand on Hayes' shoulder and explained: "I know that the

Jefferson Memorial is in the opposite direction," he said. "But the young man asked me about the 'Jefferson Monument.' And I know that free speech is the monument to Thomas Jefferson. So I have directed these young people to the lawn in front of the Senate, where today a number of protesters have gathered. I want these people to see the only democracy on the face of the earth where those who wish to challenge and disagree with [their] government have the right to do so in its own front yard." He added: "That would be an extraordinarily important lesson for these young people. And it's not too damn bad a lesson for a freshman Congressman, either!"[35]

Bradley and the Butter

At a party for New Jersey Senator Bill Bradley in 1987, Tennessee Senator Albert Gore included a fanciful tale about the former basketball star in a speech he gave in his honor. Soon after Bradley entered the Senate, said Gore, he was invited to make a speech at a banquet and sat proudly at the head table waiting for his turn to speak. When the waiter came over at one point and put a pat of butter on his plate, Bradley stopped him. "Excuse me," he said, "can I have two pats of butter?" "Sorry," said the waiter, "one pat for a person." "I don't think you know who I am," said Bradley. "I'm BILL BRADLEY, the Rhodes Scholar, professional basketball player, world champion, United States Senator." "Well, maybe you don't know who I am," retorted the waiter. "Well, as a matter of fact, I don't," admitted Bradley. "Who are you?" "I'm the guy," said the waiter, "who's in charge of the *butter!*"[36]

Speaker Wright and the President

Texas Democrat Jim Wright's bold leadership as Speaker of the House irked members of the Reagan administration. "What Jim Wright is trying to do," grumbled one White House aide, "is put himself on an equal plane with the President. The Speaker is not a second President, although this one may think he is." But when President Reagan appeared on Capitol Hill one day to deliver an address to a joint session of Congress, Speaker Wright greeted him cordially at the entrance to the House Chamber and escorted him to the rostrum in front. Wright was an eloquent improviser himself, and the story (probably spurious) goes that he could not resist teasing the President about the carefully prepared speech he was about to give. En route to the front he is said to have whispered, "Mr. President, we're having trouble with the TelePrompTer. It looks as though you're going to have to wing it!" At this point the President looked so dismayed that Wright hastily admitted he was kidding; and the President then proceeded to put on his usual deft performance with the help of the TelePrompTer.[37]

100 Percent Increase

When Congress was discussing a proposed raise early in 1989, comedian Jay Leno told audiences: "They say if we give them a 50 percent pay increase they'll stop outside speaking engagements. Maybe if we give them 100 percent, they'll stop talking altogether." The joke ran on the nightly news.[38]

Two McCarthys

There was Joe McCarthy, Wisconsin Senator, famous Commie-chaser of the 1950s, and there was Eugene McCarthy, Minnesota Senator, famous anti-war leader of the 1960s, and the two had absolutely nothing in common but the last name. But one day, in the spring of 1989, the Minnesota McCarthy was crossing the street in New York City, and a man mistook him for some other political figure. When the Minnesotan said he was Senator McCarthy, the stranger apologized and then said thoughtfully: "But you're not as much against communism as you used to be!"[39]

Using the Gym

In the mid-1970s New York Congresswoman Bella Abzug succeeded in getting the Congressional swimming pool opened to women, but the workout facilities remained off-limits to them. There was, to be sure, a "ladies' health facility," as it was called, but, complained Colorado Democrat Pat Schroeder, it consisted of "10 hair dryers and a ping-pong table." In 1983, when Barbara Boxer, a California Democrat used to working out regularly, arrived in Washington, she went to work to get the lavish men's gym integrated and received the support of some of the Congressmen as well as of all her female colleagues. But "the initial reaction," sighed Marcia ("Marcy") Kaptur, Ohio Democrat helping out in the campaign, "was so disappointing. I mean," she added, almost in disbelief, "health is everybody's business." Finally, Boxer composed an amusing little song teasing her male colleagues, put it to the tune of "Has Anybody Seen My Gal?" and then sang it lustily at a Congressional leadership meeting: "We're not slim, we're not trim/Can't you make it hers or him/Can't everybody use your gym?" The song seems to have helped. Soon afterward, the "gym committee" voted to open the Congressional gym to the women in Congress.[40]

Understandable

After Gerry Studds, Massachusetts Democrat, was mugged by two Washington youths who were apparently unaware of the fact that he was a Congressman, he told friends: "I think if they had known I was a member of Congress, I could have understood it!"[41]

Wretched Excess

The rules of good behavior for politicians, according to political consultant Raymond Strother, used to be very simple. "If a politician stayed on his bar stool," said Strother, "he wasn't drunk. And if he didn't get caught, he wasn't cheating on his wife."

By 1989, however, the rules seem to have changed. One of President Bush's nominees for a position in the new administration announced he was giving up smoking; another told a Senate committee he would go on the wagon if confirmed. As Congressional committees dug into the personal habits of the President's appointees, consultant Strother said of Washington: "This may be America's squarest city now." Jim Buckley, communications director for the National Republican Congressional Committee, agreed. "I would venture to guess," he said, "that people will give a very wide berth to the bar at the Monocle on their way to the dinner table." He seemed to be right. The owner of the Monocle, located on Capitol Hill, reported that the lawmakers' habit of spending hours over whiskey and cigars was passé and that Chardonnay had replaced Scotch as the preferred drink.

In March 1989, Kansas' Robert Dole, Senate Republican leader, gave an up-to-date party in his office for departing staff members. "There are two punch bowls," he told the revelers. "For those of you who ever want to get confirmed, there is a nonalcoholic one right here. Those that don't care can step into the other room." But a Republican lobbyist who attended the party said he sampled both the spiked and the unspiked punch. "I was working both sides," he explained.

Some old-timers on Capitol Hill reminisced about the old days when "you sort of had to drink regularly to be an insider on Capitol Hill." John Sears, Republican political adviser, recalled the evening drinking sessions held by Sam Rayburn when he was Speaker of the House and Lyndon B. Johnson when he was Senate Majority Leader. And the Republican lobbyist who attended Dole's party recalled the era when guards were stationed at the doors of the Senate and House chambers so that committee chairmen would not "go out and get drunk" while their bills were on the floor. "I'd go into an office at 10:00 a.m., and a chairman would want to have a drink," he said. "And since I was a good lobbyist I had a drink." He remembered

Senators being carried off the Senate floor dead drunk thirty years before.

Allen Drury, author of *Advise and Consent,* best-selling novel about Washington politics, had mixed feelings about the new era. "It's not a disaster if somebody has to be reasonably sober when dealing with the public business," he said. "But the unfortunate trend now established is [that] one must tell all and promise all and be a good, good boy and promise to be a good, good boy forever after. It's not only ridiculous, it's humiliating and sad."

Georgia Congressman Ben Jones did not share Drury's concern. A freshman Democrat who had conquered cigarettes, alcohol, and a hard-living past, Jones doubted that Washington was in any danger of becoming over-Puritanic. "In many ways," he told Maureen Dowd, *New York Times* writer, "Washington will always be a town of wretched excess—certainly in terms of rhetorical hyperbole."[42]

Notes

Preface

1. Richard B. Cheney and Lynne V. Cheney, *Kings of the Hill: Power and Responsibility in the House of Representatives* (New York, 1983), xi.
2. George F. Hoar, *Autobiography of Seventy Years*, 2 vols. (New York, 1906), II, 22.
3. Champ Clark, *My Quarter Century of American Politics*, 2 vols. (New York, 1920), I, 220.
4. *As I Knew Them: Memoirs of James E. Watson* (Indianapolis, 1936), 37.
5. Robin Toner, "The House Democrat His Colleagues Lean On," *New York Times*, May 9, 1990, p. A-12.

I—At the Creation (1789–1791)

1. *The Records of the Federal Convention of 1787*, 4 vols. (ed. Max Farrand, New Haven, 1937), I, 66, 74, 92, 100, 101–2, 103.
2. Ibid., 254.
3. *The Journal of William Maclay, United States Senator from Pennsylvania, 1789–1791* (ed. Edgar S. Maclay, New York, 1890), 17–49; Rufus Griswold, *The Republican Court* (New York, 1854), 152–54; John Adams to William Tudor, May 3 and 9, 1789, quoted, Page Smith, *John Adams*, 2 vols. (Garden City, N.Y., 1962), II, 753–55.
4. "Titles for the President," May 11, 1789, *The Papers of James Madison* (Charlottesville, Va., 1979), XII, 155.
5. *Annals of Congress*, First Congress, 1789–91, I, 36.
6. *Writings of James Madison*, 9 vols. (ed. Gaillard Hunt, New York, 1900–1910), V, 373.
7. Fisher Ames to George Richards Minot, May 3, 1789, *Works of Fisher Ames*, 2 vols. (ed. Seth Ames, Boston, 1854), I, 35.
8. "The First Inaugural Address," April 30, 1789, *The Writings of George Washington*, 39 vols. (ed., John C. Fitzpatrick, Washington, 1931–44), XXX, 295.
9. Anson Phelps Stokes, *Church and State in the United States*, 3 vols. (New York, 1950), I, 339–50. See also William Lee Miller, "The Spirit of '89," *New Republic*, June 26, 1989, pp. 21–24.
10. Samuel S. Cox, *Why We Laugh* (New York, 1880), 115.
11. *Records of the Federal Convention*, III, 359.
12. *Journal of William Maclay*, 30.
13. Henry F. Reddall, *Wit and Humor of American Politics* (Philadelphia, 1903), 149.
14. *Journal of William Maclay*, 15, 69, 176–77, 206, 248, 255–56.
15. Alvin M. Josephy, *American Heritage History of Congress* (New York, 1975), 92; *Annals of Congress*, First Congress, II, 1843, 1848.
16. William Henry Smith, *Speakers of the House of Representatives of the United States* (Baltimore, 1928), 34.
17. Mrs. John A. Logan, *Thirty Years in Congress* (Hartford, Conn., 1901), 149.

II—Congress-Bashing

1. "Washington Notebook," *Fort Worth Star-Telegram*, Feb. 19, 1990, Sect. 1, p. 3.
2. Morris K. Udall, *Too Funny To Be President* (New York, 1988), 7.
3. H. L. Mencken, "Notes on Government," in *The Bathtub Hoax and Other Blasts and Bravos* (New York, 1958), 185; ibid., "The United States Senate," 174.
4. Ferdinand Lundberg, *Scoundrels All* (New York, 1968), 33; Udall, *Too Funny To Be President*, xiv, 138–39; Jonathan Yates, "'Reality' on Capitol Hill," *Newsweek*, Nov. 28, 1988, p. 12.
5. Rex Stout, *The Illustrious Dunderheads* (New York, 1942).
6. Raymond Clapper, May 16, 1942, in *Watching the World* (New York, 1944), 201–2.
7. Charles A. Beard, "In Defense of Congress," *American Mercury*, Nov. 1942, p. 531.
8. Jerry Voorhis, "Stop Kicking Congress Around!" *American Mercury*, June 1944, pp. 647–55.
9. "Congress," *Life*, Dec. 4, 1944, p. 24.
10. Bill Adler, ed., *The Washington Wits* (New York, 1967), 235–36.
11. Alvin Josephy, *The American Heritage History of Congress* (New York, 1975), 269.
12. Quoted in Marion Clark and Rudy Maxa, *Public Trust, Private Lust: Sex, Power and Corruption on Capitol Hill* (New York, 1977), 48.
13. "Fear and Trembling: The Keating Five Legacy," *Newsweek*, Dec. 25, 1989, p. 52.
14. Champ Clark, *My Quarter Century of American Politics*, 2 vols. (New York, 1920), I, 194–95.
15. Udall, *Too Funny To Be President*, 139.
16. Adler, *Washington Wits*, 256–57; Jim Wright, *You and Your Congressman* (New York, 1965), 186, has a somewhat shorter version, quoting Conte.
17. "'Nick' Feels Sorry for Congress—Awf'ly!" *Literary Digest*, Jan. 23, 1926, p. 46.
18. Ibid.
19. Ibid.
20. George D. Aiken, *Aiken: A Senate Diary, January 1972—January 1975* (Brattleboro, Vt., 1976), 266.
21. Wright, *You and Your Congressman*, 15.
22. Mickey Edwards, "What 'Permanent' Congress?" *New York Times*, Jan. 5, 1990, p. 23.
23. Edward C. Boykin, ed., *The Wit and Wisdom of Congress* (New York, 1961), 16–17; Melville D. Landon, *Eli Perkins: Thirty Years of Wit* (New York, 1891), 280–81, puts the story in the mouth of Senator Ben Wade and directs it against the Democrats.
24. Clark, *My Quarter Century of Politics*, I, 275; F. Hodge O'Neal and Annie Laurie O'Neal, *Humor: The Politician's Tool* (New York, 1964), 197–98; James A. Miller, *Running in Place: Inside the Senate* (New York, 1986), 96; Frank G. Carpenter, *Carp's Washington* (New York, 1960), 11.
25. Mark Twain, *The Adventures of Colonel Sellers* (ed. Charles Neider, Garden City, N.Y., 1965), 110–11. This book contains Twain's chapters from *The Gilded Age*.
26. Samuel W. McCall, *Thomas B. Reed* (Boston and New York, 1914), 252; Clark, *My Quarter Century of Politics*, I, 291.
27. Robert Rienow and Leona Train Rienow, *Of Snuff, Sin and the Senate* (Chicago, 1965), 109; Alexander Wiley, *Laughing with Congress* (New York, 1947), 80.
28. James Schermerhorn, *Schermerhorn's Stories* (New York, 1928), 90; Wiley, *Laughing with Congress*, 13.
29. Charles E. Schutz, *Political Humor: From Aristophanes to Sam Ervin* (Rutherford, N.J., 1977), 273–74; Henry F. Reddall, *The Wit and Humor of American Statesmen* (Philadelphia, 1903), 76–77.

30. Louis A. Coolidge and James B. Reynolds, *The Show at Washington* (Washington, 1894), 62–63.

31. Charles N. Lurie, *Make 'Em Laugh Again!* (New York, 1928), 226; "Country Sayin's of Sam Ervin," *Time*, April 16, 1973, p. 13; O'Neals, *Humor*, 198; Udall, *Too Funny to Be President*, 229.

32. Brooks Hays, *A Hotbed of Tranquillity* (New York, 1968), 10.

33. *Washington Merry-Go-Round* (New York, 1931), 228.

34. Wiley, *Laughing with Congress*, 56.

35. Ibid.

36. Louis Hurst, *The Sweetest Little Club in the World: The U.S. Senate* (Englewood Cliffs, N.J., 1980), 68.

37. Ibid., 38.

38. Wiley, *Laughing with Congress*, 223.

39. Boykin, *Wit and Wisdom of Congress*, 387–88.

40. July 2, 1942, *Congressional Record*, 77th Congress, 2nd Sess., 5950–51; Wiley *Laughing with Congress*, 3, 6–8.

41. Ibid., 12.

42. Ibid., 223–24.

43. Ibid., 64.

44. Norris Cotton, *In the Senate: Amidst the Conflict and Turmoil* (New York, 1978), 42–43.

45. Emanuel Celler, *You Never Leave Brooklyn* (New York, 1953), 262; Udall, *Too Funny To Be President*, 130, 209.

46. Alben W. Barkley, *That Reminds Me* (Garden City, N.Y., 1954), 210.

47. Ross K. Baker, *Friend and Foe in the U.S. Senate* (New York, 1980), 109–10.

48. Sam J. Ervin, Jr., *Humor of a Country Lawyer* (Chapel Hill, N.C., 1983), 122.

49. Wiley, *Laughing with Congress*, 14.

50. Ibid., 36; see *Respectfully Quoted: A Dictionary of Quotations Requested from the Congressional Research Service* (Washington, 1989), 9.

51. Neil MacNeil, *Forge of Democracy: The House of Representatives* (New York, 1961), 141; O'Neals, *Humor*, 104, 107; Udall, *Too Funny To Be President*, 179; Stephen M. Young, *Tales Out of Congress* (Philadelphia and New York, 1964), 90–95.

52. Adler, *Washington Wits*, 119.

53. Clark and Maxa, *Public Trust, Private Lust*, 246.

54. "Remembrances of a Good Friend," *Modern Maturity*, Oct.-Nov. 1989, p. 11.

55. Nancy Dickerson, *Among Those Present: A Reporter's View of Twenty-five Years in Washington* (New York, 1976), 237–38.

III—Manners and Morals

1. Henry G. Wheeler, *History of Congress: Biographical and Political*, 2 vols. (New York, 1848), I, 174.

2. L. A. Gobright, *Recollection of Men and Things at Washington* (Philadelphia, 1869), 73–75; Nathan Sargent, *Public Men and Events*, 2 vols. (Philadelphia, 1875), II, 287–88.

3. Benjamin Perley Poore, *Poore's Reminiscences of Sixty Years*, 2 vols. (New York, 1886), I, 300, 336–37.

4. Alexis de Tocqueville, *Democracy in America*, 2 vols. (New York, 1945), I, 211.

5. Ibid., 211–12.

6. Thomas Hart Benton, *Thirty Years' View*, 2 vols. (New York, 1854), I, 206.

7. *Perley's Reminiscences*, I, 144–45.

8. Don E. Fehrenbacher, *The South and Three Sectional Crises* (Baton Rouge, 1980), 62.

9. O. O. Stealey, *Twenty Years in the Press Gallery* (New York, 1906), 319.

10. Edmund Alton, *Among the Law-Makers* (New York, 1886), 223–24.

11. Mark Twain, *The Adventures of Colonel Sellers* (ed. Charles Neider, Garden City, N.Y., 1965), 186. This book is Mark Twain's share of *The Gilded Age.*

12. William A. Robinson, *Thomas B. Reed: Parliamentarian* (New York, 1930), 394.

13. Champ Clark, *My Quarter Century of American Politics*, 2 vols. (New York, 1920), II, 249.

14. Feb. 16, 1927, *Congressional Record*, 69th Congress, 2d Sess., 4012; Bill Hogan and Mike Hill, *Will the Gentleman Yield? The Congressional Record Humor Book* (Berkeley, Calif., 1987), 117–18.

15. Ebenezer Smith Thomas, *Sketches of My Life and Times*, 2 vols. (Hartford, Conn., 1840), II, 81–82.

16. Ibid.

17. Marion Clark and Rudy Maxa, *Public Trust, Private Lust* (New York, 1977), 214–15.

18. *Annals of Congress*, 5th Congress, 1797–1799, 3 vols. (Washington, 1851), I, 1034, 1040–41; James Morton Smith, *Freedom's Fetters: The Alien and Sedition Laws and American Civil Liberties* (Ithaca, N.Y., 1956), 223–24; Henry Adams, *The Life of Albert Gallatin* (Philadelphia, 1879), 192.

19. *Perley's Reminiscences*, I, 69.

20. William Cabell Bruce, *John Randolph of Roanoke, 1773–1833,* 2 vols. (New York and London, 1922), II, 263.

21. Freeman Hunt, *American Anecdotes*, 2 vols. (Boston, 1830), I, 51–52; Gerald W. Johnson, *Randolph of Roanoke: A Political Fantastic* (New York, 1929), 237.

22. Francis W. Beirne, *The War of 1812* (New York, 1949), 64.

23. Hugh A. Garland, *The Life of John Randolph of Roanoke,* 2 vols. (New York, 1890), II, 103.

24. Bruce, *Randolph*, II, 47.

25. Robert C. Winthrop, *A Memoir of Henry Clay*, 2 vols. (Boston, 1897), I, 5; *Perley's Reminiscences*, I, 62.

26. *A Compilation of the Messages and Papers of the Presidents*, 19 vols. (New York, 1897–1917), II, 490.

27. Thomas Hart Clay, *Henry Clay* (Philadelphia, 1910), 153–57; Benton, *Thirty Years' View*, I, 70–71; Powhatan Boudin, *Home Reminiscences of John Randolph of Roanoke* (Richmond, Va., 1877), 140–51.

28. Jack K. Williams, *Dueling in the Old South* (College Station, Texas, 1980), 8; *Perley's Reminiscences*, I, 75, 208, 439–42; Benton, *Thirty Years' View*, I, 148; II, 149–59; John F. Darby, *Personal Recollections of Many Prominent People* (St. Louis, 1880), 180–81; John W. Forney, *Anecdotes of Public Men*, 2 vols. (New York, 1873–81), II, 11, 302–3; Linus P. Brockett, *Men of Our Day* (Philadelphia, 1868), 245–46. See also Daniel F. Boorstin, *The Americans: The National Experience* (New York, 1965), 206–12.

29. Joseph C. Robert, *The Story of Tobacco in America* (New York, 1949), 102–3; Bulkley S. Griffin, ed., *Offbeat History* (Cleveland and New York, 1967), 62–65; Frances Trollope, *Domestic Manners of the Americans* (London, 1832), 183, 185; Charles Dickens, *American Notes and Pictures from Italy* (London, 1957), 112, 122. *American Notes* first appeared in 1842 in two volumes. See also Thomas, *Sketches of My Life and Times*, II, 178–79.

30. *Perley's Reminiscences*, I, 61.

31. *Wit and Humor of American Politics* (Philadelphia, 1903), 60, 64; *Perley's Reminiscences*, I, 288–89.

32. Chauncey M. Depew, *My Memories of Eighty Years* (New York, 1924), 328–29.

33. *Perley's Reminiscences*, I, 421.

34. Wheeler, *History of Congress*, I, 426–29.

35. Earl Schenck Miers, ed., *Lincoln Day by Day: A Chronology, 1809–1865*, 3 vols. (Washington, 1960), I: 314.

36. Melville D. Landon, *Kings of the Platform and Pulpit* (Chicago, 1891), 541–42.

37. Christian F. Eckloff, *Memoirs of a Senate Page* (New York, 1909), 42–43; William Carey Crane, *Life and Select Literary Remains of Sam Houston of Texas*, 2 vols. (Hallandale, Fla., 1884), I: 241; Virginia Clay-Compton, *A Belle of the Fifties* (New York, 1905), 99.

38. "The Crime against Kansas," *The Works of Charles Sumner*, 15 vols. (Boston, 1873–1883), IV: 137–256; Edward L. Pierce, *Memoir and Letters of Charles Sumner*, 4 vols. (Boston, 1877–1893), III: 441–524; *Poore's Reminiscences*, I: 462–63; David Donald, *Charles Sumner and the Coming of the Civil War* (New York, 1960), 278–327.

39. Stealey, *Twenty Years in the Press Gallery*, viii, 319; *Perley's Reminiscences*, I, 532–36; Gobright, *Recollection of Men and Things*, 176–79.

40. Edgcum Pinchon, *Dan Sickles* (Garden City, N.Y., 1945), 100, 112, 118; W. A. Swanberg, *Sickles the Incredible* (New York, 1956), 46, 54, 56, 64.

41. Thomas Frederick Wood, *Thaddeus Stevens* (Harrisburg, Pa., 1934), 561; Adlai E. Stevenson, *Something of Men I Have Known* (Chicago, 1909), 20.

42. Alton, *Among Law-Makers* 23–24.

43. Stealey, *Twenty Years in the Press Gallery*, 36.

44. Louis A. Coolidge and James B. Reynolds, *The Show at Washington* (Washington, 1894), 183.

45. Frank G. Carpenter, *Carp's Washington* (New York, 1960), 257–58.

46. Alexander Wiley, *Laughing with Congress* (New York, 1947), 21; Will M. Clemens, ed., *The Depew Story Book* (Chicago, 1898), 57–58.

47. Lambert St. Clair, *Juggling the Heavyweights* (Washington, 1919), 7.

48. *As I Knew Them: Memoirs of James E. Watson* (Indianapolis, 1936), 287.

49. Ibid., 288–89.

50. Walter Davenport, *Power and Glory: The Life of Boies Penrose* (New York, 1931), 104–5.

51. Ibid., 179–80.

52. Ibid., 185–86.

53. Joe Martin, *My First Fifty Years in Politics* (New York, 1960), 50–51.

54. George H. Haynes, *The Senate of the United States: Its History and Practice,* 2 vols. (New York, 1938), II, 945n.

55. William "Fishbait" Miller, *Fishbait: The Memoirs of the Congressional Doorkeeper* (Englewood Cliffs, N.J., 1977), 152–53; "Mirth Head-Lined," *Literary Digest*, June 6, 1936, p. 9; "Exit Madness," ibid., July 11, 1936, p. 7; "Seattle's Scuffler," *Time*, May 4, 1936, pp. 14–15; George Creel, "Loudest Radical," *Collier's*, May 30, 1936, p. 15.

56. Burton K. Wheeler, *Yankee from the West* (Garden City, N.Y., 1962), 280; Carleton Beals, *The Story of Huey Long* (Philadelphia, 1935), 228–31; T. Harry Williams, *Huey Long* (New York, 1970), 552–53.

57. Forrest Davis, *Huey Long: A Candid Biography* (New York, 1935), 158–59.

58. Alben W. Barkley, *That Reminds Me* (Garden City, N.Y., 1954), 160–61.

59. Miller, *Fishbait*, 370.

60. Martin, *First Fifty Years in Politics*, 62–63.

61. George Dixon, *Leaning on a Column* (Philadelphia, 1961), 39–40.

62. Forrest Davis, "Beauty and the East," *Saturday Evening Post*, July 17, 1943, p. 6; Duff Gilfond, "Gentlewomen of the House," *American Mercury*, Oct. 1929, p. 151; Wiley, *Laughing with Congress*, 152; Ida C. Clarke, *Uncle Sam Needs a Wife* (Philadelphia, 1925), 95; Irving N. Gertzog, *Congressional Women: Their Recruitment, Treatment, and Behavior* (New York, 1984), 58–63; Amy Porter, "Ladies of Congress," *Collier's*, Aug. 28, 1943, p. 22; *The Congressional Follies: Sense and Nonsense of the Seventy-second Congress of the United*

States of America (New York, 1932), 50–51; *Congressional Record*, 80th Congress, 1st. Sess., Jan. 27, 1947, p. 632.

63. Jane R. Barkley, *I Married the Veep* (New York, 1958), 205.

64. Robert Parker, *Capitol Hill in Black and White* (New York, 1986), 57–58.

65. *Adam by Adam: The Autobiography of Adam Clayton Powell* (New York, 1971), 72.

66. Ibid., 78–79.

67. Ibid., 217.

68. Hubert H. Humphrey, *The Education of a Public Man: My Life and Politics* (New York, 1976), 465.

69. Stephen M. Young, *Tales Out of Congress* (Philadelphia and New York, 1964), 111. Norris Cotton made the same point in *In the Senate: Amidst the Conflict and Turmoil* (New York, 1978), 41.

70. Graham, *Margaret Chase Smith*, 58, 65, 67.

71. F. Hodge O'Neal and Annie Laurie O'Neal, *Humor: The Politician's Tool* (New York, 1964), 209–10.

72. Neil MacNeil, *Forge of Democracy: The House of Representatives* (New York, 1961), 103.

73. Young, *Tales Out of Congress*, 66–67.

74. *Congressional Record*, 84th Congress, 2d Sess., June 18, 1956, p. 10457.

75. Jim Wright, *You and Your Congressman* (New York, 1965), 175–76.

76. James Abourezk, *Advise and Dissent: South Dakota and the U.S. Senate* (Chicago, 1989), 153.

77. Young, *Tales Out of Congress*, 64.

78. Cotton, *In the Senate*, 117.

79. Miller, *Fishbait*, 151.

80. Ibid., 253.

81. Alfred Steinberg, *Sam Johnson's Boy: A Close-up of the President from Texas* (New York, 1968), 417; Booth Mooney, *The Lyndon Johnson Story* (New York, 1956), 154.

82. Cotton, *In the Senate*, 152–53.

83. Ibid., 170; Neil MacNeil, *Dirksen: Portrait of a Public Man* (New York and Cleveland, 1970), 216.

84. Sam Shaffer, *On and Off the Floor: Thirty Years as a Correspondent on Capitol Hill* (New York, 1980), 202.

85. Abourezk, *Advise and Dissent*, 155.

IV—Oratory

1. Henry Hupfeld, *Wit and Wisdom* (Philadelphia, 1871), 933.

2. Benjamin Perley Poore, *Perley's Reminiscences of Sixty Years*, 2 vols. (New York, 1886), I, 65.

3. Alphonse B. Miller, *Thaddeus Stevens* (New York and London, 1939), 123.

4. Champ Clark, *My Quarter Century of American Politics*, 2 vols. (New York, 1920), I, 353–55; Festus P. Sumners, *William L. Wilson and Tariff Reform* (New Brunswick, N.J., 1953), 185.

5. Clark, *My Quarter Century of Politics*, II, 349.

6. See Dorothy Sarnoff and Gaylen Moore, *Never Be Nervous Again* (New York, 1988).

7. Harriot W. Warner, ed., *Autobiography of Charles Caldwell, M.D.* (Philadelphia, 1855), 114.

8. *The Writings of Thomas Jefferson*, 20 vols. (ed. Albert Ellery Bergh, Washington, 1904–05), IX, 329.

9. *Works of Fisher Ames*, 2 vols. (ed. Seth Ames, Boston, 1854), I, 192.

10. Winfred E. A. Bernhard, *Fisher Ames: Federalist and Statesman, 1758–1808* (Chapel Hill, 1965), 267.

11. April 26, 1796, *Annals of Congress*, 4th Congress, 1st Sess. (1795–96), V, 1239.

12. (Gilbert J. Clark), *Memoir, Autobiography and Correspondence of Jeremiah Mason* (Kansas City, Mo., 1917), 35.

13. "Fisher Ames," *Port Folio*, 3rd. Ser. 1, Vol. I (1813), 12; John H. Morison, *Life of the Hon. Jeremiah Smith* (Boston, 1845), 97.

14. *Annals of Congress*, 4th Congress, 1st Sess. (1795–96), V, 1263.

15. Bernhard, *Ames*, 272.

16. Morison, *Life of Jeremiah Smith*, 97.

17. Henry Adams, *The Life of Albert Gallatin* (Philadelphia, 1879), 155.

18. *Works of Ames*, I, 196.

19. James Parton, *The Life and Times of Aaron Burr* (New York, 1858), 374–79; Samuel H. Wendell and Meade Minnigerode, *Aaron Burr*, 2 vols. (New York, 1925), I, 320–24; William Plumer, Jr., *Life of William Plumer* (Boston, 1857), 331.

20. Sarah Harvey Porter, *The Life and Times of Anne Royall* (Washington, 1909), 83; Josiah Quincy, *Figures of the Past* (Boston, 1883), 212–13.

21. Hupfeld, *Wit and Wisdom*, 686–87; George W. Simpson, *Nuggets of Knowledge* (New York, 1928), 88–89.

22. Edward C. Boykin, *Congress and the Civil War* (New York, 1955), 59.

23. *Perley's Reminiscences*, I, 146; Charles Lanham, *The Private Life of Daniel Webster* (New York, 1852), 153; Peter Harvey, *Reminiscences and Anecdotes of Daniel Webster* (Boston, 1878), 362–63.

24. Rev. William Pinkney, *The Life of William Pinkney* (New York, 1853), 383–84.

25. Margaret Bayard Smith, *The First Forty Years of Washington Society* (ed. Gaillard Hunt, London, 1906), 309–10.

26. Boykin, *Congress and Civil War*, 68, 72.

27. Jan. 26, 27, 1830, *The Papers of Daniel Webster: Speeches and Formal Writings*, Vol. I, 1800–1833 (ed. Charles M. Wiltse, Hanover, N.H., 1986), 330, 348.

28. Harvey, *Reminiscences and Anecdotes of Webster*, 153.

29. S. P. Lyman, *The Public and Private Life of Daniel Webster*, 2 vols. (Philadelphia, 1852), I: 50–51, 67; Charles W. March, *Reminiscences of Congress* (New York, 1850), 151n.

30. Harvey, *Reminiscences and Anecdotes of Webster*, 269–71.

31. William Mathews, *Oratory and Orators* (Chicago, 1879), 311–12, 322, 326.

32. Nathan Sargent, *Public Men and Events*, 2 vols. (Philadelphia, 1875), II: 322–23.

33. Mathews, *Oratory and Orators*, 318–19.

34. Hupfeld, *Wit and Wisdom*, 777.

35. John Wentworth, *Congressional Reminiscences* (Fergus Historical Series, No. 24, Chicago, 1882), 13. See also Horace G. Rahskopf, "John Quincy Adams: Speaker and Rhetorician," in Lionel Crocker and Paul A. Carmack, eds., *Readings in Rhetoric* (Springfield, Ill., 1965), 463–75.

36. Clark, *My Quarter Century of Politics*, II, 206–7.

37. Ibid., II, 210.

38. Jan. 29, Feb. 5–6, 1850, *Congressional Globe*, 31st Congress, 1st Sess., Appendix, Vol. XXII, Pt. I, 115, 129; March 4, 1850, Ibid., 453; *Papers of Webster: Speeches and Formal Writings*, Vol. II, 1834–52 (Hanover, N.H., 1988), 516; S. P. Lyman, *Life and Memorials of Daniel Webster*, 2 vols. (New York, 1853), II, 157; *The Works of William H. Seward*, 3 vols. (ed. George E. Baker, New York, 1853), I, 74–75; to Peter Harvey, Oct. 2, 1850, *Writings and Speeches of Webster*, XVI, 568; Claude M. Fuess, *Daniel Webster*, 2 vols. (Boston, 1930), II, 241.

39. John F. Parker, *"If Elected, I Promise . . ."* (Garden City, N.Y., 1960), 249.

40. Varina Davis, *Jefferson Davis, Ex-President of the Confederate States: A Memoir by His Wife*, 2 vols. (New York, 1890), I, 686–99; Hudson Strode, *Jefferson Davis: American Patriot, 1808–1861* (New York, 1968), 176–77.

41. Robert S. Holzman, *Stormy Ben Butler* (New York, 1954), 180; Howard P. Nash, Jr., *Stormy Petrel: The Life and Times of Benjamin F. Butler, 1818–1893* (Cranbury, N.J., 1969), 261; Stanley F. Horn, *Invisible Empire: The Story of the Ku Klux Klan, 1866–1871* (Boston, 1939), 150–51.

42. George F. Hoar, *Autobiography of Seventy Years*, 2 vols. (New York, 1906), II, 178–79; Wirt Armistead Cate, *Lucius Q. Lamar: Secession and Reunion* (Chapel Hill, 1935), 5–6; *Congressional Record*, 43rd Congress, 1st Sess., April 27, 1874, pp. 3410–11.

43. Henry F. Reddall, *Wit and Humor of American Politics* (Philadelphia, 1903), 217–18.

44. Edmund Alton, *Among the Law-Makers* (New York, 1886), 256–57.

45. David S. Barry, *Forty Years in Washington* (Boston, 1886), 256–57.

46. Paul M. Zall, *Mark Twain Laughing: Humorous Anecdotes by and about Samuel L. Clemens* (Knoxville, Tenn., 1985), 143–44.

47. Parker, *If Elected*, 212; "Proctor Knott's Duluth Speech," Barry, *Forty Years in Washington*, 328–37.

48. Ibid., 49.

49. Belle Case LaFollette and Fola LaFollette, *Robert M. LaFollette*, 2 vols. (New York, 1953), I, 235.

50. F. Hodge O'Neal and Annie Laurie O'Neal, *Humor: The Politician's Tool* (New York, 1964), 103–4.

51. Clark, *Quarter Century of Politics*, II, 224–25.

52. Robert M. LaFollette, *LaFollette's Autobiography* (Madison, Wisc., 1913), 602–10; LaFollettes, *Robert LaFollette*, I, 398–406.

53. Wiley, *Laughing with Congress*, 49.

54. George E. Allen, *Presidents Who Have Known Me* (New York, 1950), 218.

55. James M. Cox, *Journey Through My Years* (New York, 1946), 102.

56. Chauncey M. Depew, *My Memories of Eighty Years* (New York, 1924), 342–43.

57. James C. Humes, *Speakers' Treasury of Anecdotes about the Famous* (New York, 1978), 55.

58. Wiley, *Laughing with Congress*, 53.

59. Marian C. McKenna, *Borah* (Ann Arbor, Mich., 1961), 87, 89; Claudius O. Johnson, *Borah of Idaho* (Seattle, 1936), 321–24; John F. Parker, *"If Elected, I Promise . . ."* (Garden City, N.Y., 1960), 115.

60. Stephen M. Young, *Tales Out of Congress* (Philadelphia and New York, 1964), 193; Carleton Beals, *The Story of Huey Long* (Philadelphia, 1935), 319, 322–23; Wiley, *Laughing with Congress*, 42; Allen, *Presidents Who Have Known Me*, 182.

61. Jane Barkley, *I Married the Veep* (New York, 1958), 271. 1954), 141.

62. Wiley, *Laughing with Congress*, 157.

63. A. Robert Smith, *The Tiger in the Senate: The Biography of Wayne Morse* (Garden City, N.Y., 1962), 21.

64. O'Neals, *Humor*, 155.

65. Joe Martin, *My First Fifty Years in Politics* (New York, 1960), 241–42.

66. Alfred Steinberg, *Sam Rayburn: A Biography* (New York, 1975), 188.

67. Bill Adler, ed., *The Washington Wits* (New York, 1967), 102–3.

68. Sam J. Ervin, Jr., *Humor of a Country Lawyer* (Chapel Hill, 1983), 141–42.

69. Young, *Tales Out of Congress*, 111. A somewhat different version appears in O'Neals, *Humor*, 91.

70. William "Fishbait" Miller, *Fishbait: The Memoirs of the Congressional Doorkeeper* (New York, 1977), 309–10.

71. Smith, *Tiger in Senate*, 285–86.

72. O'Neals, *Humor*, 143.

73. Morris K. Udall, *Too Funny To Be President* (New York, 1988), 159.

74. Miller, *Fishbait*, 324.

V—On the Campaign Trail

1. Sam Shaffer, *On and Off the Floor: Thirty Years as a Correspondent on Capitol Hill* (New York, 1980), 13–14.

2. John F. Parker, *"If Elected, I Promise . . ."* (Garden City, N.Y., 1960), 19.

3. Morris K. Udall, *Too Funny To Be President* (New York, 1988), 123.

4. Edward C. Boykin, ed., *The Wit and Wisdom of Congress* (New York, 1961), 8–9; F. Hodge O'Neal and Annie Laurie O'Neal, *Humor: The Politician's Tool* (New York, 1964), 89–90; Donald R. Matthews, *U.S. Senators and Their World* (Chapel Hill, 1960), 219; Alexander Wiley, *Laughing with Congress* (New York, 1947), 220–21; *Washington Post and Times-Herald*, May 1, 1956.

5. Epes Sargent, *The Life and Public Services of Henry Clay* (Auburn, N.Y., 1852), 69–70.

6. Neil MacNeil, *Forge of Democracy: The House of Representatives* (New York, 1961), 134–35; Charles E. Schutz, *Political Humor: From Aristophanes to Sam Ervin* (Rutherford, N.J., 1977), 202.

7. Keith W. Jennison, *The Humorous Mr. Lincoln* (New York, 1965), 41.

8. Champ Clark, *My Quarter Century of American Politics*, 2 vols. (New York, 1920), II, 187–88; *As I Knew Them: Memoirs of James E. Watson* (Indianapolis, 1936), 42.

9. Adlai E. Stevenson, *Something of Men I Have Known* (Chicago, 1909), 291–92.

10. John W. Forney, *Anecdotes of Public Men*, 2 vols. (New York, 1873–81), II, 179; Carl Sandburg, *Abraham Lincoln: The Prairie Years*, 2 vols. (New York, 1926), II, 126, 138.

11. Stevenson, *Something of Men I Have Known*, 238.

12. Allen Johnson, *Stephen A. Douglas: A Study in American Politics* (New York, 1908), 432–33; *Recollections of Thomas R. Marshall* (Indianapolis, 1925), 51–52.

13. Morris K. Udall, *Too Funny To Be President* (New York, 1988), 147. Texas Senator Tom Connally presented a different version of the story. See Wiley, *Laughing with Congress*, 132–33.

14. John F. Parker, *If Elected*, 39–40.

15. E. B. Callender, *Thaddeus Stevens: Commoner* (Boston, 1882), 153; George F. Hoar, *Autobiography of Seventy Years*, 2 vols. (New York, 1906), I, 268.

16. Stevenson, *Something of Men I Have Known*, 37–38.

17. Claude Gentry, *Private John Allen* (Decatur, Ga., 1951), 157–60; Edward C. Boykin, ed., *The Wit and Wisdom of Congress* (New York, 1961), 34–35; *As I Knew Them: Memoirs of James E. Watson*, 40–41; Clark, *My Quarter Century of Politics*, II, 198–99.

18. Henry F. Reddall, *Wit and Humor of American Politics* (Philadelphia, 1903), 154.

19. Gentry, *Private Allen*, 188.

20. Ibid., 123.

21. Walter Davenport, *Power and Glory: The Life of Boies Penrose* (New York, 1931), 76–78.

22. Stevenson, *Something of Men I Have Known*, 52–53.

23. Hoar, *Autobiography*, I, 227.

24. Stevenson, *Something of Men I Have Known*, 45.

25. Charles N. Lurie, *Make 'Em Laugh Again* (New York, 1928), 229; Boykin, *Wit and Wisdom of Congress*, 305.
26. Clark, *My Quarter Century of Politics*, I, 292.
27. Jacob M. Braude, *Braude's Treasury of Wit and Humor* (Englewood Cliffs, N.J., 1964), 7.
28. Boykin, *Wit and Wisdom of Congress*, 15; Udall, *Too Funny To Be President*, 210.
29. Clark, *My Quarter Century of Politics*, I, 223.
30. Watson, *As I Knew Them*, 25.
31. Wiley, *Laughing with Congress*, 23.
32. *Some After Dinner Speeches, with a Few Anecdotes of Famous Men* (Detroit, 1904), 195–96.
33. Clark, *My Quarter Century of Politics*, I, 431–32.
34. David S. Barry, *Forty Years in Washington* (Boston, 1924), 145.
35. Brooks Hays, *A Hotbed of Tranquillity* (New York, 1968), 55–56.
36. Davenport, *Power and Glory*, 96–97.
37. Ibid., 117, 179.
38. Watson, *As I Knew Them*, 77–78.
39. Ibid., 95–96.
40. *Wit and Humor of American Politics*, 150.
41. James M. Cox, *Journey Through My Years* (New York, 1946), 65.
42. Alben W. Barkley, *That Reminds Me* (Garden City, N.Y., 1954), 82.
43. Ibid., 19–20.
44. Wiley, *Laughing with Congress*, 16.
45. Neil MacNeil, *Forge of Democracy: The House of Representatives* (New York, 1963), 135.
46. Watson, *As I Knew Them*, 290–91.
47. Udall, *Too Funny To Be President*, 129.
48. Alfred Steinberg, *Sam Rayburn: A Biography* (New York, 1975), 27.
49. Lambert St. Clair, *Juggling the Heavyweights* (Washington, 1919), 50.
50. Barkley, *That Reminds Me*, 129–30.
51. O'Neals, *Humor*, 102–3.
52. Marquis James, *Mr. Garner of Texas* (Indianapolis, 1939), 83.
53. O'Neals, *Humor*, 95.
54. *The Autobiography of Sol Bloom* (New York, 1948), 211.
55. George Wharton Pepper, *In the Senate* (Philadelphia, 1930), 136.
56. Barkley, *That Reminds Me*, 74, 133.
57. "Ruths," *Time* (Nov. 12, 1928), pp. 11–12; "Mr. Hoover's Congress," *Literary Digest* (Nov. 24, 1928), pp. 10–11; Annabel Paxton, *Women in Congress* (Richmond, Va., 1945), 7.
58. Parker, *If Elected*, 58.
59. *Washington Merry-Go-Round* (New York, 1931), 219–20.
60. Sam J. Ervin, Jr., *Humor of a Country Lawyer* (Chapel Hill, 1983), 66–67.
61. Barkley, *That Reminds Me*, 271.
62. Schutz, *Political Humor*, 278; O'Neals, *Humor*, 140.
63. James, *Mr. Garner*, 130.
64. Burton K. Wheeler, *Yankee from the West* (Garden City, N.Y., 1962), 286.
65. Parker, *If Elected*, 43, 59–60.
66. Joe Martin, *My First Fifty Years in Politics* (New York, 1960), 156–57.
67. O'Neals, *Humor*, 100.
68. Hays, *Hotbed of Tranquillity*, 38.
69. Charles Edmundson, "How Kefauver Beat Crump," *Harper's Magazine*, Jan. 1949, pp. 78–84; Joseph Bruce Gorman, *Kefauver: A Political Biography* (New York, 1971), 46–53.
70. Miller, *Fishbait*, 76.

71. Alfred Steinberg, *Sam Johnson's Boy: A Close-up of the President from Texas* (New York, 1968), 272; Schutz, *Political Humor*, 268.

72. Shaffer, *On and Off the Floor*, 108; Claude D. Pepper, *Eyewitness to a Century* (New York, 1987), 203–4.

73. Frank Graham, Jr., *Margaret Chase Smith: Woman of Courage* (New York, 1964), 69–70.

74. William "Fishbait" Miller, *Fishbait: The Memoirs of the Congressional Doorkeeper* (Englewood Cliffs, N.J., 1977), 325–26.

75. Udall, *Too Funny To Be President*, 155.

76. Bill Adler, ed., *The Washington Wits* (New York, 1967), 51.

77. Stephen M. Young, *Tales Out of Congress* (Philadelphia and New York, 1964), 139.

78. Barkley, *That Reminds Me*, 107.

79. Steinberg, *Sam Johnson's Boy*, 436.

80. Ross K. Baker, *Friend and Foe in the U.S. Senate* (New York, 1980), 44.

81. O'Neals, *Humor*, 136.

82. Adler, *Washington Wits*, 247–48; Hays, *Hotbed of Tranquillity*, 37.

83. Ervin, *Humor of a Country Lawyer*, 181.

84. Edward Boyd, "Mr. Speaker: The Dynamo of Capitol Hill," *American Magazine*, April 1955, p. 101.

85. Ernest Gruening, *Many Battles: The Autobiography of Ernest Gruening* (New York, 1983), 404.

86. Fred R. Harris, *Potomac Fever* (New York, 1977), 95–96.

87. Bill Adler, ed., *The Johnson Humor* (New York, 1965), 37.

88. Udall, *Too Funny To Be President*, 238.

89. Hubert H. Humphrey, *The Education of a Public Man: My Life and Politics* (New York, 1976), 208, 472–73.

90. Nancy Dickerson, *Among Those Present: A Reporter's View of Twenty-five Years in Washington* (New York, 1976), 38.

91. Boykin, *Wit and Wisdom of Congress*, 10–11; Edward L. Schapsmeier and Frederick H. Schapsmeier, *Dirksen of Illinois: Senatorial Statesman* (Urbana, 1985), 130.

92. Eleanor Randolph, "The Best and the Worst of the U.S. Senate," *Washington Monthly*, Jan. 1982, p. 43; Fred Barnes, "The Zillionaire's Club," *New Republic*, Jan. 29, 1990, p. 25.

93. Barry M. Goldwater, *Goldwater* (New York, 1988), 207.

94. Udall, *Too Funny To Be President*, 216.

95. Miller, *Fishbait*, 280.

96. Christopher Matthews, *Hardball: How Politics Is Played—By One Who Knows the Game* (New York, 1988), 198.

97. Adler, *Washington Wits*, 11.

98. Udall, *Too Funny To Be President*, 218.

99. Ibid., 24–25.

100. Miller, *Fishbait*, 324.

101. Dickerson, *Among Those Present*, 152.

102. Udall, *Too Funny To Be President*, 219.

103. Miller, *Fishbait*, 324.

104. Harris, *Potomac Fever*, 203.

105. Miller, *Fishbait*, 323.

106. Randolph, "Best and Worst of the Senate," *Washington Monthly*, Jan. 1982, p. 35.

VI—Comedy

1. *Life and Speeches of Thomas Corwin* (ed. Josiah Morrow, Cincinnati, 1896), 90.
2. Calvin Colton, *The Life and Times of Henry Clay,* 2 vols. (New York, 1848), II, 416–17; Nathan Sargent, *Public Men and Events,* 2 vols. (Philadelphia, 1875), II, 15–16, tells it a little differently. So does Horace Greeley, *The Life and Public Services of Henry Clay* (New York, 1860), 88.
3. Neil MacNeil, *Dirksen: Portrait of a Public Man* (New York, 1970), 53.
4. *The "Man in the Street" Stories from the New York Times* (introd. by Chauncey M. Depew, New York, 1902), 126.
5. David S. Barry, *Forty Years in Washington* (New York, 1924), 147.
6. Sam J. Ervin, Jr., *Humor of a Country Lawyer* (Chapel Hill, 1983), 163.
7. Henry F. Reddall, *Wit and Humor of American Politics* (Philadelphia, 1903), 52.
8. Ibid., 144.
9. George Dixon, *Leaning on a Column* (Philadelphia, 1961), 55–56; MacNeil, *Dirksen,* 93n; "Phrasemaker," *Time,* Feb. 17, 1967, p. 24; Larry King, *Tell It to the King* (New York, 1988), 112; Alexander Wiley, *Laughing with Congress* (New York, 1947), 45–46.
10. Milton Lehman, "Salesman in the Senate," *Collier's,* Dec. 14, 1946, p. 56ff; Paul F. Healy, "Big Noise from Nebraska," *Saturday Evening Post,* Aug. 5, 1950, p. 22ff; Marvin E. Stromer, *The Making of a Political Leader: Kenneth S. Wherry and the United States Senate* (Lincoln, Neb., 1969), 150–51.
11. Morris K. Udall, *Too Funny To Be President* (New York, 1988), 169.
12. Melville D. Landon, *Eli Perkins: Thirty Years of Wit* (New York, 1891), 159; Leon Harris, *The Fine Art of Political Wit* (New York, 1965), 62.
13. Henry Hupfeld, *Wit and Wisdom* (Philadelphia, 1871), 778.
14. Richard Hauser, "The Lincoln Who Lives in Anecdote," *Reader's Digest,* Feb. 1959, p. 253.
15. Samuel S. Cox, *Why We Laugh* (New York, 1880), 189. See also W. H. Sparks, *The Memories of Fifty Years* (Philadelphia, 1870), 233.
16. Benjamin Perley Poore, *Perley's Reminiscences of Sixty Years,* 2 vols. (New York, 1886), I, 103–4.
17. Colton, *Life and Times of Clay,* I, 100–101.
18. Peter Harvey, *Reminiscences and Anecdotes of Daniel Webster* (Boston, 1878), 284–85.
19. Ibid., 292–93.
20. Wiley, *Laughing with Congress,* 21–22.
21. Edward C. Boykin, ed., *The Wit and Wisdom of Congress* (New York, 1961), 395–96.
22. Richard B. Cheney and Lynne V. Cheney, *Kings of the Hill: Power and Personality in the House of Representatives* (New York, 1983), 54.
23. Samuel S. Cox, *Three Decades of Federal Legislation, 1855–1885* (New York, 1885), 159–62; David Lindsey, *"Sunset" Cox: Irrepressible Democrat* (Detroit, 1959), 60–61.
24. James A. Woodburn, *The Life of Thaddeus Stevens* (Indianapolis, 1913), 594–95.
25. Ibid., 591.
26. George W. Julian, *Political Recollections* (Chicago, 1884), 313; *Reminiscences of Carl Schurz,* 3 vols. (New York, 1908), III, 215–16.
27. John W. Forney, *Anecdotes of Public Men,* 2 vols. (New York, 1873–81), I, 37.
28. Melville D. Landon, *Kings of the Platform and Pulpit* (Chicago, 1891), 559–60.
29. Samuel S. Cox, *Three Decades of Federal Legislation* (Providence, R.I., 1886), 425.
30. Neil MacNeil, *Forge of Democracy: The House of Representatives* (New York, 1963), 12; Melville E. Stone, *Fifty Years as a Journalist* (New York, 1921), 46.

31. John F. Parker, *"If Elected, I Promise . . ."* (Garden City, N.Y., 1960), 140.

32. *"Man in the Street" Stories*, 160.

33. George F. Hoar, *Autobiography of Seventy Years*, 2 vols. (New York, 1906), I, 278–79.

34. George E. Allen, *Presidents Who Have Known Me* (New York, 1950), 7–8, 28–29; Claude Gentry, *Private John Allen* (Decatur, Ga., 1951), 100, 108. Gentry says that Allen's feud was with James K. Vardaman.

35. Champ Clark, *My Quarter Century of American Politics*, 2 vols. (New York, 1920), II, 201.

36. Irvin S. Cobb, *A Laugh a Day Keeps the Doctor Away* (Garden City, N.Y., 1923), 144–45.

37. Adlai E. Stevenson, *Something of Men I Have Known* (Chicago, 1909), 271–72.

38. Jacob M. Braude, *Braude's Treasury of Wit and Humor* (Englewood Cliffs, N.J., 1964), 154.

39. Stevenson, *Something of Men I Have Known*, 269–70.

40. Ibid., 292.

41. F. J. Cahill, *Rare Bits of Humor* (New York, 1906), 9.

42. Werlich, *"Beast Butler,"* 140.

43. Frank G. Carpenter, *Carp's Washington* (New York, 1960), 21–22.

44. Clark, *Quarter Century of Politics*, II, 331–32; Stevenson, *Something of Men I Have Known*, 217, has a somewhat different version of the story.

45. Clark, *Quarter Century of Politics*, II, 79–80.

46. Ibid., II, 15.

47. Henry F. Reddall, *Wit and Humor of American Politics* (Philadelphia, 1903), 130–31.

48. *"Man in the Street" Stories*, 72.

49. Barry, *Forty Years in Washington*, 57–58.

50. Charles Lurie, comp., *Make 'Em Laugh Again* (New York, 1928), 226–27, 229.

51. Udall, *Too Funny To Be President*, 82; William "Fishbait" Miller, *Fishbait: The Memoirs of the Congressional Doorkeeper* (Englewood Cliffs, N.J., 1977), 263.

52. *Recollections of Thomas R. Marshall* (Indianapolis, 1925), 231–32.

53. Bill Severn, *Democracy's Messengers: The Capitol Pages* (New York, 1975), 103.

54. Joseph B. Foraker, *Notes of a Busy Life*, 2 vols. (Cincinnati, 1916), II, 64–65.

55. Wiley, *Laughing with Congress*, 46.

56. F. Hodge O'Neal and Annie Laurie O'Neal, *Humor: The Politician's Tool* (New York, 1964), 115.

57. Udall, *Too Funny To Be President*, 128–29; Bill Adler, ed., *The Washington Wits* (New York, 1967), 149. A similar exchange between President Grant and a Cabinet member visiting the West appears in Bill Hogan and Mike Hill, *Will the Gentleman Yield? The Congressional Record Humor Book* (Berkeley, 1987), 34. The story is also told of Ben Wade, crossing the plains on a train, in Clark, *Quarter Century of Politics*, II, 214.

58. Alben W. Barkley, *That Reminds Me* (Garden City, N.Y., 1954), 113–14.

59. Walter Davenport, *Power and Glory: The Life of Boies Penrose* (New York, 1931), 223.

60. Boyce House, *Laugh Parade of States* (San Antonio, 1948), 122.

61. Burton K. Wheeler, *Yankee from the West* (New York, 1962), 270.

62. Norris Cotton, *In the Senate: Amidst the Conflict and Turmoil* (New York, 1978), 7–8.

63. Claudius O. Johnson, *Borah of Idaho* (Seattle, 1936), 333.

64. Wheeler, *Yankee from the West*, 202.

65. Richard B. Henderson, *Maury Maverick: A Political Biography* (Austin, Texas, 1970), 71–72.

66. Udall, *Too Funny To Be President*, 200.

67. Stephen Shadegg, *Clare Boothe Luce* (New York, 1970), 176.

68. Ibid., 177.

69. Clifton Fadiman, ed., *The Little, Brown Book of Anecdotes* (New York, 1985), 370.

70. Ervin, *Humor of a Country Lawyer*, 140–41.

71. Barkley, *That Reminds Me*, 272.
72. Udall, *Too Funny To Be President*, 167.
73. Harry Fleischman, *Let's Be Human* (New York, 1960), 43–44.
74. Miller, *Fishbait*, 329–30.
75. James C. Humes, *Speakers' Treasury of Anecdotes about the Famous* (New York, 1978), 202.
76. Udall, *Too Funny To Be President*, 229.
77. O'Neals, *Humor*, 115.
78. Frank Madison, *A View from the Floor: The Journal of a U.S. Senate Page* (Englewood Cliffs, N.J., 1967), 120; Miller, *Fishbait*, 219–20; Severn, *Democracy's Messengers*, 60.
79. *Time*, May 17, 1954, p. 27; John G. Adams, *Without Precedent* (New York, 1983), 169.
80. Steve Allen, *Funny People* (New York, 1981), 2.
81. Ervin, *Humor of a Country Lawyer*, 158.
82. "Country Sayin's of Sam Ervin," *Time*, April 16, 1973, p. 13.
83. Ervin, *Humor of a Country Lawyer*, 182–83.
84. Ibid., 162.
85. Ibid., 161–62.
86. Wiley, *Laughing with Congress*, 46–47.
87. O'Neals, *Humor*, 197.
88. MacNeil, *Dirksen*, 157.
89. Cotton, *In the Senate*, 175.
90. MacNeil, *Dirksen*, 172; Louella Dirksen, *The Honorable Mr. Marigold: My Life with Everett Dirksen* (Garden City, N.Y., 1972), 278–79.
91. Ervin, *Humor of a Country Lawyer*, 181.
92. Ibid., 69–70.
93. Cotton, *In the Senate*, 177.
94. O'Neals, *Humor*, 380.
95. Barry M. Goldwater, *With No Apologies: The Personal and Political Memoirs of Barry M. Goldwater* (New York, 1979), 58.
96. O'Neals, *Humor*, 125.
97. Cotton, *In the Senate*, 175–76.
98. Udall, *Too Funny To Be President*, 180.
99. Ibid., 215.
100. O'Neals, *Humor*, 199–200.
101. Adler, *Washington Wits*, 266–67.
102. Bob and Elizabeth Dole, *The Doles: Unlimited Partners* (New York, 1988), 103.
103. 91st Congress, 1st Sess., April 22, 1969, pp. 9941–51.
104. Adler, *Washington Wits*, 234.
105. O'Neals, *Humor*, 204–5.
106. Carl Albert, *Little Giant* (Norman, Okla., 1990), 379.
107. Bella S. Abzug, *Bella! Ms Abzug Goes to Washington* (New York, 1972), 208.
108. Ervin, *Humor of a Country Lawyer*, 199.
109. James Haskins, *Barbara Jordan* (New York, 1977), 185.
110. Udall, *Too Funny To Be President*, 168.
111. Oct. 2, 1975, *Congressional Record*, 94th Congress, 1st Sess., 31449; Hogan and Hill, *Will the Gentleman Yield?*, 160.
112. Udall, *Too Funny To Be President*, 141.

VII—On the Floor

1. Alben W. Barkley, *That Reminds Me* (Garden City, N.Y., 1954), 209.
2. Henry G. Wheeler, *History of Congress*, 2 vols. (New York, 1848), I, 426.

3. Calvin Colton, *The Life and Times of Henry Clay*, 2 vols. (New York, 1846), I, 107.
4. Ibid., 116.
5. Melville D. Landon, *Eli Perkins: Thirty Years of Wit* (New York, 1891), 160–61. This exchange has been assigned to Mississippi Congressman John Allen and his opponent Zeke Chandler in 1900. See Claude Gentry, *Private John Allen* (Decatur, Ga., 1951), 165. It has also been assigned to Tom Reed in an exchange with a Georgia Congressman.
6. Champ Clark, *My Quarter Century of American Politics*, 2 vols. (New York, 1920), I, 287.
7. Ibid., II, 289; *Recollections of Thomas R. Marshall* (Indianapolis, 1925), 87.
8. Melville D. Landon, *Kings of the Platform and Pulpit* (Chicago, 1891), 562–63.
9. Clark, *Quarter Century of Politics*, II, 165, 289–90; *As I Knew Them: Memoirs of James E. Watson* (Indianapolis, 1936), 99.
10. Frank G. Carpenter, *Carp's Washington* (New York, 1960), 213.
11. Clark, *Quarter Century of Politics*, II, 309–10.
12. Ibid., II, 208–9.
13. Edward C. Boykin, ed., *The Wit and Wisdom of Congress* (New York, 1961), 156–57; Clark, *Quarter Century of Politics*, II, 291.
14. Alexander Wiley, *Laughing with Congress* (New York, 1947), 114.
15. Frank E. Smith, *Congressman from Mississippi* (New York, 1964), 146.
16. Clark, *Quarter Century of Politics*, II, 305.
17. George W. Julian, *Political Recollections* (Chicago, 1884), 90–92; Henry S. Foote, *A Casket of Reminiscences* (New York, 1874), 338–39; L. A. Gobright, *Recollection of Men and Things at Washington* (Philadelphia, 1869), 113–18; Nathan Sargent, *Public Men and Events*, 2 vols. (Philadelphia, 1875), II, 360–61. See *Congressional Record*, April 17, 1850, 31st Congress, 1st Sess., 762.
18. Clark, *Quarter Century of Politics*, II, 288.
19. Bertram M. Gross, *The Legislative Struggle* (New York, 1953), 366.
20. Bella S. Abzug, *Bella! Ms. Abzug Goes to Washington* (New York, 1972), 110.
21. John W. Forney, *Anecdotes of Public Men*, 2 vols. (New York, 1873), I, 202–3.
22. Adlai E. Stevenson, *Something of Men I Have Known* (Chicago, 1909), 391; William Cabell Bruce, *John Randolph of Roanoke, 1773–1833*, 2 vols. (New York and London, 1922), II, 201.
23. Tyler to Dr. Curtis, Feb. 5, 1820, in Lyon G. Tyler, *The Letters and Times of the Tylers*, 2 vols. (Richmond, Va., 1884), I, 316; Jefferson to Hugh Nelson, Feb. 7, 1820, *The Works of Thomas Jefferson*, 12 vols. (ed., Paul Leicester Ford, New York, 1905), XII, 157; Glyndon G. Van Deusen, *The Life of Henry Clay* (Boston, 1937), 142; Glover Moore, *The Missouri Compromise* (Lexington, Ky., 1953), 49.
24. William H. Sparks, *The Memoirs of Fifty Years* (Philadelphia, 1870), 237.
25. Benjamin Perley Poore, *Perley's Reminiscences of Sixty Years*, 2 vols. (New York, 1886), I, 69.
26. Boykin, *Wit and Wisdom of Congress*, 160–61.
27. Epes Sargent, *The Life and Public Services of Henry Clay* (Auburn, N.Y., 1852), 96.
28. Bruce, *Randolph*, II, 197, 200–223; Gerald W. Johnson, *Randolph of Roanoke: A Political Fantastic* (New York, 1929), 236; Boykin, *Wit and Wisdom of Congress*, 70.
29. *Perley's Reminiscences*, I, 145–46.
30. Ibid., I, 146.
31. Charles Lanham, *The Private Life of Daniel Webster* (New York, 1852), 142–43.
32. Samuel S. Cox, *Why We Laugh* (New York, 1880), 135–36; Thomas Hart Clay, *Henry Clay* (Philadelphia, 1910), 421–22.
33. Clark, *Quarter Century of Politics*, II, 308.
34. Nov. 7, 1830, *Memoirs of John Quincy Adams*, 12 vols. (Philadelphia, 1874–77), VIII, 247;

Josiah Quincy, *Memoir of the Life of John Quincy Adams* (Boston, 1858), 183; May 26, 1836, *Congressional Globe*, 24th Congress, 1st Sess. (1835–36), 406; Feb. 6–11, 1837, *Congressional Globe*, 24th Congress, 2d Sess. (1836–37), 162–75; Dec. 3, 1844, *Memoirs of Adams*, XII, 115–16.

35. Hugh McCulloch, *Men and Measures of Half a Century* (New York, 1889), 38.
36. Ibid., 50; Gobright, *Recollections of Men and Things,* 411. Italics added.
37. Sargent, *Public Men and Events*, II, 192–94; Stevenson, *Something of Men I Have Known*, 130, 134; Bulkley S. Griffin, *Offbeat History* (Cleveland and New York, 1967), 66–70.
38. Forney, *Anecdotes of Public Men*, I, 10–11.
39. Paul Findley, *A. Lincoln: The Crucible of Congress* (New York, 1879), 187.
40. Clay, *Henry Clay*, 359.
41. Clark, *Quarter Century of Politics*, II, 302.
42. Carl Sandburg, *Abraham Lincoln: The War Years*, 4 vols. (New York, 1939), I, 103–4.
43. Linus P. Brockett, *Men of Our Day, Or, Biographical Sketches* (St. Louis, 1868), 247–48.
44. Ibid., 439; Eli N. Evans, *Judah P. Benjamin: The Jewish Confederate* (New York, 1988), 97. There are at least four different versions of the episode, and the Benjamin statement has also been attributed to Benjamin Disraeli.
45. Henry B. Stanton, *Random Recollections* (New York, 1887), 204. Another version of the incident has Seward saying, "Come, Benjamin, give me a segar & I won't be mad with you." See Robert Douthat Meade, *Judah P. Benjamin: Confederate Statesman* (New York, 1943), 101.
46. Clark, *Quarter Century of Politics*, II, 213.
47. Patrick Mahony, *Barbed Wit and Malicious Humor* (Washington, 1956, 1983), 144.
48. Thomas Frederick Woodley, *Thaddeus Stevens* (Harrisburg, Pa., 1934), 305–6.
49. Julian, *Political Recollections*, 361; Samuel W. McCall, *Thaddeus Stevens* (New York, 1899), 314.
50. David S. Barry, *Forty Years in Washington* (Boston, 1924), 69–71; Alfred R. Conkling, *The Life and Letters of Roscoe Conkling* (New York, 1889), 261–65; Donald Barr Chidsey, *The Gentleman from New York: A Life of Roscoe Conkling* (New Haven, 1935), 80–91; Gail Hamilton, *Biography of James G. Blaine* (Norwich, Conn., 1985), 157–81; Julian, *Political Recollections*, 275–77; *Congressional Globe*, April 30, 1866, 39th Congress, 1st Sess., 2298–99.
51. Robert S. Holzman, *Stormy Ben Butler* (New York, 1954), 204–5; Robert Werlich, *"Beast" Butler: The Incredible Career of Major General Benjamin Franklin Butler* (Washington, 1962), 141; Richard S. West, *Lincoln's Scapegoat General: A Life of Benjamin F. Butler, 1818–1893* (Boston, 1965), 332.
52. Boykin, *Wit and Wisdom of Congress*, 159.
53. Melville S. Landon, *Eli Perkins: Thirty Years of Wit* (New York, 1891), 270–71.
54. John F. Parker, *"If Elected, I Promise . . ."* (Garden City, N.Y., 1960), 88.
55. Samuel S. Cox, *Why We Laugh* (New York, 1880), 190–91.
56. Boykin, *Wit and Wisdom of Congress*, 113.
57. *As I Knew Them: Memoirs of James E. Watson* (Indianapolis, 1936), 37–38.
58. Ida Tarbell, *The Tariff in Our Times* (New York, 1912), 66; David Lindsey, *"Sunset" Cox: Irrepressible Democrat* (Detroit, 1959), 114–15.
59. Boykin, *Wit and Wisdom of Congress*, 401.
60. Hoar, *Autobiography*, I, 237–38. Stevenson, *Something of Men I Have Known*, 34–36, tells a somewhat different story and attributes it to William S. Holman.
61. *Memoirs of William M. Stewart of Nevada* (New York, 1908), 205–6; Forney, *Anecdotes of Public Men*, I, 37; James Albert Woodburn, *The Life of Thaddeus Stevens* (Indianapolis, 1913), 592; Hoar, *Autobiography*, II, 23.

62. Claude Gentry, *Private John Allen* (Decatur, Ga., 1951), 162.

63. Clark, *Quarter Century of Politics*, II, 229.

64. Robert M. LaFollette, *LaFollette's Autobiography* (Madison, Wisc., 1911, 1913), 80–84.

65. Clark, *Quarter Century of Politics*, I, 282.

66. Barry, *Forty Years in Washington*, 226–27; Watson, *As I Knew Them*, 26.

67. O. O. Stealey, *Twenty Years in the Press Gallery* (New York, 1906), 253–54.

68. Clark, *Quarter Century of Politics*, II, 60–61.

69. Ibid., II, 61.

70. Samuel Leland Powers, *Portraits of a Half Century* (Boston, 1925), 236–37; Neil MacNeil, *Forge of Democracy: The House of Representatives* (New York, 1963), 295–96, 323.

71. James M. Cox, *Journey Through My Years* (New York, 1946), 107.

72. Clark, *Quarter Century of Politics*, II, 339.

73. *Recollections of Thomas R. Marshall* (Indianapolis, 1925), 312–13.

74. Robert Douglas Bowden, *Boies Penrose: Symbol of an Era* (New York, 1937), 232–33.

75. Hannah Josephson, *Jeannette Rankin: First Lady in Congress* (Indianapolis, 1974), ix, x, 56–57, 61, 73–77, 161–65; John F. Kennedy, "Three Women of Courage," *McCall's*, Jan. 1958, p. 55; Jim Wright, *You and Your Congressman* (New York, 1965), 86–90; *Washington Wife: Journal of Ellen Maury Slayden from 1897–1919* (New York, 1963), 301; Fiorello H. Laguardia, *The Making of an Insurgent: An Autobiography, 1882–1919* (Philadelphia and New York, 1948), 141.

76. Watson, *As I Knew Them*, 288.

77. Ibid., 187–88; George E. Allen, *Presidents Who Have Known Me* (New York, 1950), 238.

78. Cox, *Journey Through My Years*, 100.

79. Donald R. Matthews, "Folkways of the United States Senate," *American Political Science Review*, December 1959, p. 1066.

80. Fred R. Harris, *Potomac Fever* (New York, 1977), 81–82.

81. Ray Tucker, *Sons of the Wild Jackasses* (Boston, 1932), 211–15; Burton K. Wheeler, *Yankee from the West* (New York, 1962), 278–79.

82. Allen, *Presidents Who Have Known Me*, 51.

83. Joe Martin, *My First Fifty Years in Politics* (New York, 1960), 214–15.

84. *St. Louis Post-Dispatch*, Sept. 11, 1935; Alben W. Barkley, *That Reminds Me* (Garden City, N.Y., 1954), 161.

85. Richard B. Henderson, *Maury Maverick: A Political Biography* (Austin, Texas, 1970), 69–70.

86. Ibid., 109–10.

87. William "Fishbait" Miller, *Fishbait: The Memoirs of the Congressional Doorkeeper* (Englewood Cliffs, N.J., 1977), 162–63.

88. *The Autobiography of Sol Bloom* (New York, 1948), 243–44.

89. Miller, *Fishbait*, 68; Stephen Shadegg, *Clare Boothe Luce* (New York, 1970), 168–69.

90. George Dixon, *Leaning on a Column* (Philadelphia, 1961), 57–59.

91. F. Hodge O'Neal and Annie Laurie O'Neal, *Humor: The Politician's Tool* (New York, 1964), 209–10.

92. Alexander Wiley, *Laughing with Congress* (New York, 1947), 128.

93. Marvin E. Stromer, *The Making of a Political Leader: Kenneth S. Wherry and the United States Senate* (Lincoln, Neb., 1969), 18–19.

94. William S. White, *Citadel: The Story of the U.S. Senate* (New York, 1957), 190.

95. Wiley, *Laughing with Congress*, 58.

96. "A Woman's Conscience," *Time*, June 12, 1950, p. 17; Samuel Shaffer, *On and Off the Floor: Thirty Years As a Correspondent on Capitol Hill* (New York, 1980), 22–23; Frank Graham, Jr., *Margaret Chase Smith: Woman of Courage* (New York, 1964), 73–86.

97. Joe Martin, *My First Fifty Years in Politics* (New York, 1960), 216–20; Miller, *Fishbait*, 329; "Bloody Session," *Newsweek*, March 8, 1954, pp. 22–23; "Puerto Rico Is Not Free," *Time*, March 8, 1954, p. 19; O'Neals, *Humor*, 112–13. The O'Neals say the Congressman headed for Alabama was Frank Boykin, but Brooks Hays, *A Hotbed of Tranquillity* (New York, 1968), 87, says it was Clarence Brown, Ohio Republican.

98. Hubert H. Humphrey, *The Education of a Public Man: My Life and Politics* (Garden City, N.Y., 1976), 147–48.

99. Morris K. Udall, *Too Funny To Be President* (New York, 1988), 107.

100. Norris Cotton, *In the Senate: Amidst the Conflict and Turmoil* (New York, 1978), 41–42.

101. Frank E. Smith, *Congressman from Mississippi* (New York, 1964), 142.

102. Dec. 4, 1980, *Congressional Record*, 96th Congress, 2d Sess., 32339.

VIII—In the Chair

1. George H. Haynes, *The United States Senate*, 2 vols. (New York, 1938), I, 202.

2. Sol Barzman, *Madmen and Geniuses: The Vice-Presidents of the United States* (Chicago, 1974), 132.

3. Haynes, *Senate*, I, 204n.

4. Letter to wife, Dec. 19, 1793, *The Works of John Adams*, 10 vols. (Boston, 1856), I, 460.

5. April 25, 1789, *Journal of William Maclay, United States Senator from Pennsylvania, 1789–1791* (ed. Edgar S. Maclay, New York, 1890), 3.

6. Ibid.

7. *Works of Adams*, I, 468.

8. *Journal of Maclay*, 2, 55, 56, 78, 94, 155, 243.

9. July 14–16, 1789, in Page Smith, *John Adams*, 2 vols. (New York, 1962), II, 769.

10. Barzman, *Madmen and Geniuses*, 132.

11. Haynes, *Senate*, I, 211–12; Diane Dixon Healey, *America's Vice-Presidents* (New York, 1984), 151–52.

12. Healy, *America's Vice-Presidents*, 184.

13. Ibid., 191.

14. Carol Felsenthal, *Alice Roosevelt Longworth* (New York, 1988), 170.

15. Bascom N. Timmons, *Garner of Texas: A Personal History* (New York, 1948), 205.

16. Robert C. Winthrop, *A Memoir of Henry Clay*, 2 vols. (Boston, 1897), I, 6; Benjamin Perley Poore, *Perley's Reminiscences of Sixty Years*, 2 vols. (New York, 1886), I, 62.

17. Bernard Mayo, *Henry Clay: Spokesman of the New West* (Boston, 1937), 424.

18. M. P. Follett, *The Speaker of the House of Representatives* (New York, 1902), 81n.

19. *Columbian Centinel* (Boston), Nov. 9, 13, 16, 1811, quoted in Mayo, *Clay*, 403.

20. Edmund Quincy, *Life of Josiah Quincy* (New York, 1867), 255, 259.

21. M. P. Follett, *The Speaker of the House of Representatives* (New York, 1896), 296.

22. Ibid., 297.

23. Samuel W. McCall, *Thomas B. Reed* (Boston and New York, 1914), 238.

24. Joe Martin, *My Fifty Years in Politics* (New York, 1960), 180; Neil MacNeil, *Forge of Democracy: The House of Representatives* (New York, 1961), 67.

25. Marquis James, *Mr. Garner of Texas* (Indianapolis, 1939), 111.

26. Bascom N. Timmons, *Garner of Texas: A Personal History* (New York, 1948), 122; Alfred Steinberg, *Sam Rayburn: A Biography* (New York, 1975), 96.

27. Timmons, *Garner*, 123.

28. James, *Mr. Garner*, 112–13.

29. William "Fishbait" Miller, *Fishbait: The Memoirs of the Congressional Doorkeeper* (Englewood Cliffs, N.J., 1977), 55–56.

30. Ibid.

31. Samuel Arthur Bent, *Familiar Short Sayings of Great Men* (Boston, 1887), 150.

32. MacNeil, *Forge of Democracy*, 7n.

33. Thomas Hart Clay, *Henry Clay* (Philadelphia, 1910), 402.

34. Oliver Dyer, *Great Senators of the United States Forty Years Ago* (New York, 1889), 232.

35. Calvin Colton, *The Life and Times of Henry Clay*, 2 vols. (New York, 1846), I, 96.

36. Ibid., I, 97–98; Epes Sargent, *The Life and Public Services of Henry Clay* (Auburn, N.Y., 1852), 59.

37. Klyde Young and Lamar Middleton, *Heirs Apparent: The Vice-Presidents of the United States* (New York, 1948), 85.

38. *Perley's Reminiscences*, I, 64.

39. Henry B. Stanton, *Random Recollections* (New York, 1887), 205; Benton, *Thirty Years' View*, I, 420; March 7, 1834, *Congressional Debates*, 23rd Congress, 1st Sess., 829–32.

40. Robert Luce, *Legislative Assemblies* (Boston and New York, 1924), 634.

41. *Perley's Reminiscences*, II, 512.

42. John W. Forney, *Anecdotes of Public Men*, 2 vols. (New York, 1873), I, 9–10.

43. *Perley's Reminiscences*, I, 447–53; Boykin, *Congress and Civil War*, 239–40.

44. John Sherman, *Recollections of Forty Years*, 2 vols. (Chicago, 1895), I, 168–79; Boykin, *Congress and Civil War*, 244–61.

45. David S. Barry, *Forty Years in Washington* (Boston, 1924), 191–92; Leslie W. Dunlap, *Our Vice-Presidents and Second Ladies* (Metuchen, N.J., 1988), 88, 154.

46. Thomas Frederick Woodley, *Thaddeus Stevens* (Harrisburg, Pa., 1934), 17, 300; July 4, 1861, *Congressional Globe*, 37th Congress, 1st Sess., 4.

47. Melville D. Landon, *Kings of the Platform and Pulpit* (Chicago, 1891), 554.

48. George F. Hoar, *Autobiography of Seventy Years*, 2 vols. (New York, 1906), I, 201–2.

49. Adlai E. Stevenson, *Something of Men I Have Known* (Chicago, 1909), 31–32.

50. McCall, *Reed*, 162–71; William A. Robinson, *Thomas B. Reed: Parliamentarian* (New York, 1930), 175–234; Booth Mooney, *Mr. Speaker* (Chicago, 1964), 63–68; George B. Galloway, *History of the House of Representatives* (New York, 1961), 134–36; Champ Clark, *My Quarter Century of American Politics*, 2 vols. (New York, 1920), II, 62, 64.

51. Alexander Wiley, *Laughing with Congress* (New York, 1947), 120–21.

52. Morris K. Udall, *Too Funny To Be President* (New York, 1988), 142; Edward C. Boykin, ed., *The Wit and Wisdom of Congress* (New York, 1961), 165.

53. *"The Man in the Street" Stories from the New York Times* (New York, 1902), 151; Barry, *Forty Years in Washington*, 142; *As I Knew Them: Memoirs of James E. Watson* (Indianapolis, 1936), 30.

54. McCall, *Reed*, 127.

55. *"Man in the Street" Stories*, 152; Clark, *Quarter Century of Politics*, I, 290.

56. F. Hodge O'Neal and Annie Laurie O'Neal, *Humor: The Politician's Tool* (New York, 1964), 133.

57. Watson, *As I Knew Them*, 37; Clark, *Quarter Century of Politics*, II, 211–12.

58. Robinson, *Reed*, 237.

59. Ibid., 159.

60. Clark, *Quarter Century of Politics*, I, 291.

61. Robinson, *Reed*, 147, 251, 255, 270, 373, 380; Louis A. Coolidge, *The Show at Washington* (Washington, 1894), 74–75; DeAlva Stanwood Alexander, *History and Procedure of the House of Representatives* (Boston, 1916), 126, 128; Barry, *Forty Years in Washington*, 115, 142; Clark, *Quarter Century of Politics*, I, 286, 291; Watson, *As I Knew Them*, 35; McCall, *Reed*, 115, 246, 248.

62. Robinson, *Reed*, 356–57; Clark, *Quarter Century of Politics*, I, 291, 295; McCall, *Reed*, 247–48.

63. *Washington Post*, Dec. 21, 1902; Robinson, *Reed*, 130.

64. Healy, *America's Vice-Presidents*, 141; Haynes, *Senate*, I, 227n.

65. Archibald W. Butt, *Taft and Roosevelt: The Intimate Letters of Archie Butt*, 2 vols. (Garden City, N.Y., 1930), I, 341–42; Watson, *As I Knew Them*, 125.

66. Miller, *Fishbait*, 197–98.

67. Charles Willis Thompson, *Party Leaders of the Times* (New York, 1906), 180.

68. Jacob M. Braude, *Braude's Treasury of Wit and Humor* (Englewood Cliffs, N.J., 1964), 189–90.

69. Mooney, *Mr. Speaker*, 127.

70. Watson, *As I Knew Them*, 94.

71. Ibid., 96.

72. Wiley, *Laughing with Congress*, 49. The same story is told of Davy Crockett; Boyce House, *I Give You Texas* (San Antonio, 1943), 87.

73. Hubert Bruce Fuller, *The Speakers of the House* (Boston, 1909), 281; Mooney, *Mr. Speaker*, 101; J. Frederick Essary, *Covering Washington* (Boston, 1927), 204.

74. *The Autobiography of George W. Norris* (New York, 1945), 107–19; L. White Busbey, *Uncle Joe Cannon: The Story of a Pioneer American* (New York, 1927), 243–69; Richard Lowitt, *George W. Norris: The Making of a Progressive, 1861–1912* (Syracuse, N.Y., 1963), 166–88; Alfred Lief, *Democracy's Norris: The Biography of a Lonely Crusader* (New York, 1939), 85–107.

75. Barzman, *Madmen and Geniuses*, 195.

76. *Recollections of Thomas R. Marshall* (Indianapolis, 1925), 300–301.

77. Ibid., 230–31; Bascom N. Timmons, *Portrait of an American: Charles G. Dawes* (New York, 1953), 250.

78. Cheneys, *Kings of the Hill*, 144–45, 167.

79. Duff Gilfond, "Mr. Speaker," *American Mercury*, Aug. 1927, p. 457; Felsenthal, *Alice Longworth*, 96.

80. Gilfond, "Mr. Speaker," 454.

81. James Brough, *Princess Alice: A Biography of Alice Roosevelt Longworth* (Boston, 1975), 273.

82. Gilfond, "Mr. Speaker," 454.

83. Ibid.

84. Watson, *As I Knew Them*, 242–43; Timmons, *Portrait of an American*, 244–46.

85. Alben W. Barkley, *That Reminds Me* (Garden City, N.Y., 1954), 263; Alice Roosevelt Longworth, *Crowded Hours* (New York, 1933), 330–33; Howard Teichman, *Alice: The Life and Times of Alice Roosevelt Longworth* (Englewood Cliffs, N.J., 1977), 140–41; Bess Furman, *Washington By-Line: The Personal History of a Newspaperwoman* (New York, 1949), 64–69.

86. James, *Mr. Garner*, 87–88; Timmons, *Garner*, 188; Tom Connally, *My Name Is Tom Connally* (New York, 1954), 91.

87. Wiley, *Laughing with Congress*, 48.

88. Barkley, *That Reminds Me*, 159; T. Harry Williams, *Huey Long* (New York, 1970), 635.

89. Alfred Steinberg, *Sam Rayburn: A Biography* (New York, 1975), 189.

90. Ibid., 189–90.

91. Ibid., 177.

92. Harry S. Truman, *Memoirs*, Vol I, *Year of Decisions* (Garden City, N.Y., 1955), 4–5;

Bernard Asbell, *When F.D.R. Died* (New York, 1961), 62–67; Alfred Steinberg, *The Man from Missouri: The Life and Times of Harry S. Truman* (New York, 1962), 233–35.

93. Steinberg, *Rayburn*, 256–57.
94. Edward Boyd, "Mr. Speaker: The Dynamo of Capitol Hill," *American Magazine*, April 1955, p. 98.
95. Martin, *First Fifty Years*, 189.
96. MacNeil, *Forge of Democracy*, 77.
97. Steinberg, *Rayburn*, 258.
98. Ibid., 265–66.
99. Miller, *Fishbait*, 21.
100. Robert Bendiner, *Obstacle Course on Capitol Hill* (New York, 1964), 23.
101. MacNeil, *Forge of Democracy*, 90.
102. Daniel K. Inouye, *Journey to Washington* (Englewood Cliffs, N.J., 1968), 276–79.
103. Norris Cotton, *In the Senate: Amidst the Toil and Conflict* (New York, 1978), 175.
104. Mooney, *Mr. Speaker*, 129.
105. Gerald R. Ford, *Humor and the Presidency* (New York, 1987), 121.
106. Albright, *Washington Post*, June 11, 1961; Steinberg, *Rayburn*, 340.
107. Interview with Sam Rayburn, *U.S. News and World Report*, Oct. 13, 1950, pp. 28–31; *Time*, Oct. 13, 1961, pp. 26–27; MacNeil, *Forge of Democracy*, 75; Steinberg, *Rayburn*, 178–79, 349–51.
108. Ervin, *Humor of a Country Lawyer*, 70–71.
109. Ibid., 173–74.
110. Bill Adler, ed., *The Washington Wits* (New York, 1967), 40–41; Nancy Dickerson, *Among Those Present: A Reporter's View of Twenty-five Years in Washington* (New York, 1976), 230.
111. Louis Hurst, *The Sweetest Little Club in the World: The U.S. Senate* (Englewood Cliffs, N.J., 1980), 149.

IX—Congress and the President

1. L. A. Gobright, *Men and Things at Washington* (Philadelphia, 1869), 67.
2. *Journal of William Maclay* (ed. Edgar S. Maclay, New York, 1890), 128–32; *Memoirs of John Quincy Adams*, 12 vols. (Philadelphia, 1874–77), VI, 427.
3. Quoted, Norris Cotton, *In the Senate: Amidst the Conflict and Turmoil* (New York, 1978), 160.
4. George B. Galloway, *History of the House of Representatives* (New York, 1962), 261; Edward S. Corwin, *The President: Office and Powers* (New York, 1948), 333.
5. Carl Schurz, *Henry Clay*, 2 vols. (Boston and New York, 1887), II, 31–37; Thomas Hart Clay, *Henry Clay* (Philadelphia, 1910), 223–25; March 27, 1834, *Congressional Debates*, 23rd Congress, 1st Sess., 1172–77.
6. Schurz, *Clay*, II, 40–43; Clay, *Henry Clay*, 227–28, 238, 243; April 30, 1834, *Congressional Debates*, 23rd Congress, 1st Sess., 1564.
7. T. Harry Williams, *Lincoln and the Radicals* (Madison, Wisc., 1941), 63.
8. John Sherman, *Recollections of Forty Years in the House, Senate, and Cabinet*, 2 vols. (Chicago, 1895), I, 447.
9. George F. Hoar, *Autobiography of Seventy Years*, 2 vols. (New York, 1906), II, 46.
10. Wilfred E. Binkley, *The President and Congress* (New York, 1947), 206.
11. Herbert Hoover, *Challenge to Liberty* (New York, 1934), 125–26.
12. "Roosevelt on the Presidency," *New York Times*, Nov. 13, 1932, Sec. 8, p. 1.

13. E. Pendleton Herring, "American Government and Politics," *American Political Science Review*, Feb.-Dec. 1934, p. 71.

14. Ibid., 70.

15. May 31, 1935, *The Public Papers and Addresses of Franklin D. Roosevelt*, 13 vols. (New York, 1938–50), IV, 221.

16. Bascom N. Timmons, *Garner of Texas: A Personal History* (New York, 1948), 218; Harold L. Ickes, "My Twelve Years with F.D.R.," *Saturday Evening Post*, July 3, 1948, pp. 30–31; Joseph Alsop and Turner Catledge, *The 168 Days* (New York, 1938), 66–67.

17. Timmons, *Garner*, 222–23; James MacGregor Burns, *Roosevelt: The Lion and the Fox* (New York, 1956), 363; James T. Patterson, *Congressional Conservatism and the New Deal* (Lexington, Ky., 1967), 295.

18. Dec. 16, 1941, *Congressional Record*, 77th Congress, 1st Sess., 9856.

19. Richard E. Lauterbach, "The Pentagon Puzzle," *Life*, May 24, 1943, p. 13.

20. Arthur M. Schlesinger, Jr., *The Imperial Presidency* (Boston, 1973), 207.

21. William Cabell Bruce, *John Randolph of Roanoke, 1773–1833*, 2 vols. (New York and London, 1922), I, 157–65; Gerald W. Johnson, *Randolph of Roanoke: A Political Fantastic* (New York, 1929), 106–12.

22. Samuel S. Cox, *Why We Laugh* (New York, 1880), 307.

23. January 1832, Ivor Debenham Spencer, *The Victor and the Spoils: A Life of William L. Marcy* (Providence, R.I., 1959), 59–60; Edward C. Boykin, *Congress and the Civil War* (New York, 1955), 109–11; Thomas Hart Benton, *Thirty Years' View*, 2 vols. (New York, 1854–56), I, 215–19.

24. Benjamin Perley Poore, *Perley's Reminiscences of Sixty Years*, 2 vols. (New York, 1886), I, 141–42; Calvin Colton, *The Life and Times of Henry Clay*, 2 vols. (New York, 1846), II, 137; Henry A. Wise, *Seven Decades of the Union* (Philadelphia, 1872), 143–44; Benton, *Thirty Years' View*, I, 727–31.

25. George F. Hoar, *Autobiography of Seventy Years*, 2 vols. (New York, 1906), I, 141.

26. *Perley's Reminiscences*, II, 62–63; *The Diary of a Public Man* (New Brunswick, N.J., 1946), 63; *The Reminiscences of Carl Schurz*, 3 vols. (New York, 1907), II, 240–41.

27. Thomas Frederick Woodley, *Thaddeus Stevens* (Harrisburg, Pa., 1934), 578–79.

28. Samuel W. McCall, *Thaddeus Stevens* (Boston and New York, 1899), 311–12; Woodley, *Stevens*, 405; Albert Woodbury, *The Life of Thaddeus Stevens* (Indianapolis, 1913), 599–600.

29. *Perley's Reminiscences*, II, 144.

30. Carl Sandburg, *Abraham Lincoln: The War Years*, 4 vols. (New York, 1939), III, 369.

31. Melville D. Landon, *Eli Perkins: Thirty Years of Wit* (New York, 1891), 279.

32. *Reminiscences of Schurz*, II, 313.

33. Edward C. Boykin, ed., *The Wit and Wisdom of Congress* (New York, 1961), 216.

34. Adlai E. Stevenson, *Something of Men I Have Known* (Chicago, 1909), 352–53; A. K. McClure, ed., *Lincoln's Own Yarns and Stories* (Chicago and Philadelphia, n.d.), 314–15.

35. Allan Nevins, *Frémont: The West's Greatest Adventurer*, 2 vols. (New York, 1928), II, 631–32; Williams, *Lincoln and the Radicals*, 105.

36. Sandburg, *Lincoln: War Years*, II, 297.

37. Nathaniel Wright Stephenson, ed., *An Autobiography of Abraham Lincoln* (New York, 1926), 416–17.

38. Charles A. Dana, *Recollections of the Civil War* (New York, 1902), 175–78.

39. Woodley, *Stevens*, 557.

40. March 10, 1866, *Congressional Globe*, 39th Congress, 1st Sess., 1308–9; Alphonse B. Miller, *Thaddeus Stevens* (New Haven, 1939), 251–55.

41. March 5, 1875, *Congressional Record,* 44th Congress, 1st Sess., 1; James S. Jones, *Life of Andrew Johnson* (Greeneville, Tenn., 1901), 350–53; Robert W. Winston, *Andrew Johnson: Plebeian and Patriot* (New York, 1928), 503; Lloyd Paul Stryker, *Andrew Johnson: A Study in Courage* (New York, 1936), 808.

42. Lately Thomas, *The First President Johnson* (New York, 1968), 631–32; Winston, *Johnson,* 503–4.

43. Stryker, *Johnson,* 811.

44. Hoar, *Autobiography,* I, 210–11; Charles Schutz, *Political Humor: From Aristophanes to Sam Ervin* (Rutherford, N.J., 1977), 258; William B. Hesseltine, *Ulysses S. Grant: Politician* (New York, 1935), 237.

45. Donald Barr Chidsey, *The Gentleman from New York* (New Haven, 1935), 239.

46. David S. Barry, *Forty Years in Washington* (New York, 1924), 213–14.

47. O. O. Stealey, *Twenty Years in the Press Gallery* (New York, 1906), 56; Champ Clark, *My Quarter Century of American Politics,* 2 vols. (New York, 1920), I, 250.

48. John F. Parker, *"If Elected, I Promise . . ."* (Garden City, N.Y., 1960), 183.

49. Henry L. Stoddard, *As I Knew Them: Presidents and Politics from Grant to Coolidge* (New York, 1927), 257–58.

50. Clark, *Quarter Century of American Politics,* I, 444–49; Henry F. Pringle, *Theodore Roosevelt: A Biography* (New York, 1931), 458–64; Arthur W. Dunn, *Gridiron Nights* (New York, 1915), 185–88.

51. Joseph Benson Foraker, *Notes of a Busy Life,* 2 vols. (Cincinnati, 1916), II, 327; Julia F. Foraker, *I Would Live It Again* (New York, 1932), 269–98; John D. Weaver, *The Brownsville Raid* (New York, 1970), 138–44; Ann J. Lane, *The Brownsville Affair: National Crisis and Black Reaction* (Port Washington, N.Y., 1971), 145–61.

52. Timmons, *Garner of Texas,* 36–38.

53. *As I Knew Them: Memoirs of James E. Watson* (Indianapolis, 1936), 133, has Chauncey Depew make the remark. Alben W. Barkley, *That Reminds Me* (Garden City, N.Y., 1954), 94, names Minnesota Congressman Adam Bede.

54. Barkley, *That Reminds Me,* 91–92.

55. Ray Stannard Baker, *Woodrow Wilson: Life and Letters,* 8 vols. (Garden City, N.Y., 1927–39), IV, 104–5; David F. Houston, *Eight Years in Wilson's Cabinet,* 2 vols. (Garden City, N.Y., 1926), I, 52; *New York Times,* April 8, 9, 10, 1913, in Arthur Link, *Wilson: The New Freedom* (Princeton, 1956), 152–53.

56. Barkley, *That Reminds Me,* 112.

57. Watson, *As I Knew Them,* 200–202.

58. Stoddard, *As I Knew Them,* 544; Edith Bolling Wilson, *My Memoir* (Indianapolis, 1938), 299.

59. Irwin Hood (Ike) Hoover, *Forty-two Years in the White House* (Boston and New York, 1934), 126–28.

60. James C. Humes, *Speakers' Treasury of Anecdotes about the Famous* (New York, 1978), 178.

61. *Washington Merry-Go-Round* (New York, 1931), 214.

62. Ray Tucker, *Sons of the Wild Jackasses* (Boston, 1932), 225–26; Harry Barnard, *Independent Man: The Life of Senator James Couzens* (New York, 1958), 178.

63. Tucker, *Sons of Wild Jackasses,* 70.

64. Rixey Smith and Norman Beasley, *Carter Glass: A Biography* (New York, 1939), 238.

65. Richard B. Henderson, *Maury Maverick: A Political Biography* (Austin, Texas, 1970), 74.

66. James MacGregor Burns, *Roosevelt: The Lion and the Fox* (New York, 1956), 188.

67. Smith and Beasley, *Carter Glass,* 367.

68. Burton K. Wheeler, *Yankee from the West* (New York, 1962), 333.

69. Alfred Steinberg, *Sam Rayburn: A Biography* (New York, 1975), 145; Booth Mooney, *Mr. Speaker* (Chicago, 1964), 149.

70. Morris K. Udall, *Too Funny To Be President* (New York, 1988), 130.

71. Barkley, *That Reminds Me*, 155–56.

72. Timmons, *Garner of Texas*, 232; *Papers of Franklin Roosevelt*, VII, 391–400; Burns, *Roosevelt*, 3; Patterson, *Congressional Conservatism and the New Deal*, 280–81, 295, 305.

73. Hugh Gregory Gallagher, *FDR's Splendid Deception* (New York, 1985), 90.

74. Barkley, *That Reminds Me*, 171–80; *Papers of Franklin Roosevelt*, XIII, 13, 80–83; *Congressional Record*, 78th Congress, 2d Sess., Vol. 90, Feb. 23, 1944, pp. 1964–66; "The Man Who Started It," *Time*, March 6, 1944, p. 19; *New Republic*, March 6, 1944, p. 300; "The Barkley Incident," ibid., 20.

75. Barkley, *That Reminds Me*, 267.

76. Hubert H. Humphrey, *The Education of a Public Man: My Life and Politics* (Garden City, N.Y., 1976), 235.

77. Joe Martin, *My First Fifty Years in Politics* (New York, 1960), 202–11; Robert T. Donovan, *The Presidency of Harry Truman, 1949–1953: The Tumultuous Years* (New York, 1982), 358–59; Cabel Phillips, *The Truman Presidency* (New York, 1966), 345; Richard H. Rovere, *The General and the President* (New York, 1951), 176–85; Harry S. Truman, *Memoirs*, Vol. II, *Years of Trial and Hope* (Garden City, N.Y., 1956), 438.

78. John G. Adams, *Without Precedent* (New York, 1983), 249.

79. Cotton, *In the Senate*, 188.

80. Humphrey, *Education of a Public Man*, 249.

81. Humes, *Speakers' Treasury*, 98–99.

82. Humphrey, *Education of a Public Man*, 290–93.

83. Marion Clark and Rudy Maxa, *Public Trust, Private Lust* (New York, 1977), 63.

84. Sam Shaffer, *On and Off the Floor: Thirty Years as a Correspondent on Capitol Hill* (New York, 1980), 227.

85. Neil MacNeil, *Dirksen: Portrait of a Public Man* (New York, 1970), 280.

86. Udall, *Too Funny To Be President*, 168.

87. Sam J. Ervin, Jr., *Humor of a Country Lawyer*, 158–59.

88. Ibid., 187–88.

89. Ibid., 204.

90. Gerald R. Ford, *Humor and the President* (New York, 1987), 125.

X—The Reagan Years (1981–89)

1. Thomas P. O'Neill, *Man of the House: The Life and Political Memoirs of Speaker Tip O'Neill* (New York, 1987), 332; Lawrence Barrett, *Ronald Reagan in the White House* (New York, 1984), 32.

2. "Reagan's Big Win," *Time*, May 18, 1981, p. 15.

3. "Tracking the Great Persuader," *Time*, Aug. 10, 1981, p. 14.

4. O'Neill, *Man of the House*, 346–48; "Budget Counterpunch," *Time*, April 20, 1981, p. 16.

5. O'Neill, *Man of the House*, 351–53.

6. "Challenge to Change," *Time*, March 2, 1981, p. 14.

7. "Reagan's Big Win," *Time*, May 18, 1981, p. 14.

8. "Yeas 238—Nays 195," *Time*, Aug. 10, 1981, p. 13.

9. Elizabeth Drew, "Letter from Washington," *New Yorker*, Nov. 2, 1987, p. 159.

10. "Edward F. Boland," *Current Biography: Yearbook 1987* (New York, 1987), 59; see Jane Mayer and Doyle McManus, *Landslide: The Unmaking of the President, 1984–1988* (Boston, 1988), 80–81, 156, 251, 254.

11. See William S. Cohen and George J. Mitchell, *Men of Zeal: A Candid Inside Story of the Iran-Contra Hearings* (New York, 1988).

12. Steven V. Roberts, "Tower Panel Portrays the President as Remote and Confused Man," *New York Times,* Feb. 27, 1987, pp. A1, A12; Mayer and McManus, *Landslide,* 381–83.

13. "Iran-Contra Report Says President Bears 'Ultimate Responsibility' for Wrongdoing," *New York Times,* Nov. 19, 1987, pp. A1, A13; Cohen and Mitchell, *Men of Zeal,* 275–77.

14. Cohen and Mitchell, *Men of Zeal,* 278.

15. Ibid., 279–80.

16. Theodore Draper, "An Autopsy," *New York Review of Books,* quoted in Cohen and Mitchell, *Men of Zeal,* 293.

17. Robin Toner, "Senators Mark Congress' Rich Past Before Facing the Painful Present," *New York Times,* March 3, 1989, p. 10; Don Phillips, "Congress Wishes Itself a Happy Birthday," *Washington Post,* March 3, 1989, p. A14.

18. O'Neill, *Man of the House,* 333.

19. Jonathan Yates, "'Reality' on Capitol Hill," *Newsweek,* Nov. 28, 1988, p. 12.

20. Eleanor Randolph, "The Best and the Worst of the U.S. Senate," *Washington Monthly,* Jan. 1982, p. 38.

21. Jack Anderson, "Rating the Congressmen," *Edmond Evening Sun* (Oklahoma), Sept. 9, 1981, Section A, p. 9.

22. Bill Hogan and Mike Hill, *Will the Gentleman Yield? The Congressional Record Humor Book* (Berkeley, Ca., 1987), 220–21.

23. 98th Congress, 1st Sess., April 5, 1983, p. S4105.

24. Hogan and Hill, *Will the Gentleman Yield?,* 107–8.

25. Bob and Elizabeth Dole, *The Doles: Unlimited Partners* (New York, 1988), 240–41.

26. Geraldine A. Ferraro, *Ferraro: My Story* (New York, 1985), 181–82.

27. Hogan and Hill, *Will the Gentleman Yield?,* 116.

28. Morris K. Udall, *Too Funny To Be President* (New York, 1988), 229.

29. Gerald R. Ford, *Humor and the Presidency* (New York, 1987), 133.

30. Ibid., 36.

31. Ross K. Baker, *Friend and Foe in the U.S. Senate* (New York, 1980), 104–5.

32. Udall, *Too Funny To Be President,* 145–46.

33. "A Revision in Jargon," *New York Times,* Feb. 28, 1989, p. 12.

34. "Dollars for Congress," *New York Times,* June 7, 1988, p. 10.

35. "Monumental Direction," *New York Times,* June 13, 1988, p. B6.

36. Christopher Matthews, *Hardball: How Politics is Played—By One Who Knows the Game* (New York, 1988), 226.

37. Steven V. Roberts, "The Foreign Policy Tussle," *New York Times Magazine,* Jan. 24, 1988, p. 26.

38. Peter Tauber, "Jay Leno," *New York Times Magazine,* Feb. 26, 1989, p. 26.

39. "Washington Notebook," *Fort Worth Star-Telegram,* Nov. 29, 1989, sect. I, p. 3.

40. Lois Romano, "Jack and Jill Went Up the Hill," *Washington Post National Weekly Edition,* March 19–25, 1990, p. 10.

41. "Perspectives," *Newsweek,* June 25, 1990, p. 15.

42. Maureen Dowd, "The Old Vices Are Out and New Morality Is In," *New York Times,* March 3, 1989, p. 12; "Holier Than Anyone," *Newsweek,* March 13, 1989, p. 22.

Index